THE 36-HOUR DAY

Nancy L. Mace, M.A., is a consultant to the Office of Technology Assessment, U.S. Congress, and to the Alzheimer's Association. She was formerly an assistant in psychiatry and coordinator of the T. Rowe and Eleanor Price Teaching Service of the Department of Psychiatry and Behavioral Sciences of the Johns Hopkins University School of Medicine.

Peter V. Rabins, M.D., M.P.H., is associate professor of psychiatry, director of the psychogeriatric unit, and director of the T. Rowe and Eleanor Price Teaching Service of the Department of Psychiatry and Behaviorial Sciences of the Johns Hopkins University School of Medicine.

THE 36-HOUR DAY

A Family Guide to Caring for
Persons with Alzheimer's Disease,
Related Dementing Illnesses,
and Memory Loss in Later Life

REVISED EDITION

NANCY L. MACE, M.A.
PETER V. RABINS, M.D., M.P.H.

THE JOHNS HOPKINS UNIVERSITY PRESS
Baltimore

This book is dedicated to everyone
who gives a "36-hour day" to the care
of a person with a dementing illness.

Copyright © 1981, 1991 The Johns Hopkins University Press
All rights reserved
Printed in the United States of America on acid-free paper

03 02 01 00 99 98 97 96 95   14 13 12 11

The Johns Hopkins University Press
2715 North Charles Street
Baltimore, Maryland 21218-4319

Words from "Joy Is Like the Rain" by Sister Miriam Therese Winter
© 1965 by Medical Mission Sisters, Philadelphia, Pa.
Reprinted by permission from Vanguard Music Corp.,
1595 Broadway, New York, N.Y. 10019
Further reproduction prohibited.

Library of Congress Cataloging-in-Publication Data

Mace, Nancy L.
The 36-hour day : a family guide to caring for persons with
Alzheimer's disease, related dementing illnesses, and memory loss in
later life / Nancy L. Mace, Peter V. Rabins.—Rev. ed.
                    p.   cm.
Includes bibliographical references and index.
ISBN 0-8018-4033-3.—ISBN 0-8018-4034-1 (pbk.)
1. Alzheimer's disease—Patients—Home care. Senile dementia–
–Patients—Home care. I. Rabins, Peter V. II. Title. III. Title:
Thirty six hour day.
RC523.M33   1991
616.8'31—dc20   90-49523 CIP

A catalog record for this book is available from the British Library.

Contents

Foreword

I am glad to be able to introduce *The 36-Hour Day* for a second edition. We in the Department of Psychiatry at Johns Hopkins thought at the time of the publication of the first edition that the book might prove helpful to readers and so express a major purpose of our department in caring for patients and teaching about dementia. The book's success has been astounding and pleasing. Its wide distribution indicates a great need for information by the caregivers of these patients. But as well as providing such information in a fashion that acknowledges the abiding wish of people to be close to their loved ones—and to devote "36-hour days" to the goal— the book has spoken to both the hearts and the minds of families facing this condition. We have all been gratified by the many reports of the guidance families have found in this book.

This effort began as an enterprise in transmitting some helpful facts to the families of patients in our Alzheimer's clinic. At first it took the form of a few mimeographed pages. The remarkable call for these brief notes prompted our authors to produce this book with the help of the Johns Hopkins University Press. This second edition is now the outcome of our communicating with readers of the first edition and is updated with information derived from new clinical knowledge. These new sources make this edition, I believe, even more helpful. It brings out evidence of experience, both ours as professionals and those of the other practitioners here—the families of patients campaigning against the deprivations of dementia. We are all veterans now in this campaign, and this book is an even better help to new recruits on the 36-hour day service. We all look forward, and with good reason, to an end to this war in the form of a cure for Alzheimer's disease. There are plenty of reasons to be hopeful about that outcome within the next decade. Until that time comes, though, this book should continue to prove helpful and supportive to the families who use it.

Paul R. McHugh, M.D.
Director, Department of Psychiatry and Behavioral Sciences
Johns Hopkins University School of Medicine

Preface

Since the publication of *The 36-Hour Day* in 1981, approximately half a million copies have been sold in ten languages worldwide. The magnitude of this number conveys the extent of the tragedy of the dementing illnesses, yet those who buy books are only a fraction of the millions of families throughout the world who are coping with dementing illnesses.

Caregivers the world over face the same problems, the same need for assistance, and the same desire to care for their family member as long as possible. The vignettes that have had meaning for American and English readers are understood by readers in Spanish, Italian, German, Dutch, Swedish, Danish, Norwegian, Hebrew, and Japanese. That the experiences and feelings ring true in so many diverse cultures is another indication of the universal tragedy of the dementias.

The 36-Hour Day was originally written for family caregivers. However, professionals and paraprofessional caregivers have told us that it has been helpful to them as well. They tell us that the problems of behavior and the ill person's needs for care are similar whether the caregiver is a family member, a day care or home care provider, or a nursing home staff member. This edition, like the first, is written for families; we have avoided professional jargon and focused on care from the family's perspective. At the same time, we recognize that the material will be useful for professionals, paraprofessionals, and students. We hope that this revised edition, even more than the first, will meet their needs and that the absence of jargon will make it accessible to people from different disciplines.

You will find large sections of new material; you will also find many short changes reflecting new knowledge about caregiving.

Chapter 3 includes a new section on why people with dementia act the way they do, guidance for coping with angry overreactions, and a discussion of why symptoms seem to fluctuate from day to day. Many people with dementia are living alone; new material has been added in Chapter 4 for families who suspect that someone living alone is becoming confused.

Chapter 5 contains a new section listing "gadgets" families can purchase which may make caregiving easier. There is new information on how to modify the home environment to help people with dementia function as well as possible. Families told us that they needed more information about the late stages of the illness. Chapter 5 addresses eating problems, weight loss, tube feeding, and patients who are chair- or bedbound. Chapter 6 discusses the painful decisions about when to use or not use aggressive, life-prolonging medical interventions and the pros and cons of caring at home for a person who is in the final stages of the illness. A new section gives information about how to help the person through an acute hospitalization.

Much is new in Chapter 7, not because behavior problems have changed but because so many families have shared with us successful behavior-management skills. We are, in turn, sharing these with you.

Chapter 8 discusses the reasons why people with dementia sometimes remember feelings longer than they remember facts. It also discusses coping with the seeming "boredom" the person with dementia may show and whether or not to tell the person about his or her dementing illness.

Chapter 10 has been entirely rewritten. In 1981 there were few resources such as day care and home care to give families a much-needed break from the demands of caregiving. As this book goes to press there are many more such resources—although not enough. The new Chapter 10 describes these and offers suggestions on how to select and use them, how to encourage the confused person to participate in them, and what to look for in good-quality programs.

Not everyone who provides care lives at home with the confused person. Some are worried family members who live out of town. Others work part time or full time and struggle with multiple demands on their time. Chapter 11 includes new material that addresses these concerns. Illness and death can strike any family, and Chapter 11 discusses how to tell the confused person bad news.

Many family caregivers have told us about the effects of the dementing illness on their lives. We have added their insights in Chapter 12.

Since the first edition of this book was written, the Alzheimer's Association, which supports research, education, advocacy, and family support, has grown from a few volunteers to an effective national network with more than 1,000 support groups. In 1981 Alzheimer's disease was called the "hidden epidemic." Today, due in large part to the efforts of the Alzheimer's Association, it is no longer hidden, but is widely recognized as a serious medical concern. The association offers resources to help carers. Chapter 13, in a new description of the voluntary sector, reflects this growth.

In 1987 Congress passed extensive legislation on nursing home reform. Other state and federal legislative action has been taken on financial and legal issues, Medicaid, and Social Security disability rights. Chapter 15 includes new sections on these financial and legal matters. Although we do not yet know completely how the nursing home reform will be implemented by the states, Chapter 16 has been rewritten to help you understand this new law. As awareness of the special needs of people with dementia has spread, nursing homes and board-and-care homes have set up units that care for only people with dementia. Chapter 16 gives information about selecting such a program.

AIDS, the acquired immune-deficiency syndrome, often causes a dementia in its victims. This dementia and the special concerns of families of people with Alzheimer's disease and related disorders who share services with an AIDS victim are discussed in Chapter 17.

In 1981 the federal budget for research on dementia was $16.7 million; in 1990 it was $148 million. This means that research is expanding rapidly, and a completely revised Chapter 18 describes this new research.

Appendix 1 is entirely new. At the time of the first edition, almost nothing had been written on dementia and we scraped together what was available. Now a complete listing of books and articles for either the layperson or the professional would fill another book. In response to this, we have selected some of the important books and articles and provided guidelines to help you find technical or scientific literature of interest.

Appendixes 2, 3, and 4 have been substantially updated. Appendix 5 summarizes the rights granted by the federal nursing home reform law of 1987.

Despite all these additions, this book is not markedly longer than the first edition. It is still intended to be a handbook, small and easy to use. You may want to read only those sections that you need at a given time, rather than tackle the entire book at once.

In sum, we are excited about this new edition of *The 36-Hour Day*. It contains a substantial amount of new material and the contents, old and new, have been tested many times by families and professionals. Finally, it reflects our own growing knowledge of the dementing illnesses and our new skills in caring for patients and their families.

Acknowledgments

So many people have given of their time, experience, and wisdom that it is not possible to name them all. We wish to thank all those known and anonymous who have contributed ideas and information.

The influence of the teachers and colleagues who shaped our ideas in the first edition remains. Paul R. McHugh, M.D., Director of the Department of Psychiatry and Behavioral Sciences at the Johns Hopkins University School of Medicine, who encouraged us to write the first edition, continues to be a dynamic influence in our approach to these issues.

In the nine years following the publication of the first edition of *The 36-Hour Day*, hundreds of family caregivers and professionals have shared their ideas and solutions to problems. We have used many of these ideas in the revised edition. Many people have mentioned areas that needed further elaboration in the revised edition. A few people who suffer from a dementing illness have read and shared their comments. Our friends and colleagues, translators of foreign editions, physicians, dentists, and others have answered our questions and offered suggestions. Over time we have considered this information and tested it against the experience of caregivers and professionals. This process of learning, growth, testing, and reshaping created the revised edition. It would be impossible to list every name and would violate the privacy of many. Nevertheless, we are indebted to the generosity of this worldwide community.

The Alzheimer's Association has distributed countless copies of the first edition and its board members and staff have contributed to the revised edition. Kathryn Ling, Tom Kirk, Joan Dashiell, and Nancy Lombardo, Ph.D., made generous contributions of time to this edition.

David Chavkin reviewed the accuracy of sections on nursing home reform legislation, Medicare, and Medicaid. Staff members at the National Senior Law Center also advised us on legal issues. The staff of the National Citizens Coalition for Nursing Home Reform, particularly Barbara Frank, Ruth Nee, M.S.W., Sarah Burger, M.S.W., and Elma Holder, M.S.P.H., reviewed the sections on nursing homes and nursing home law. Gene Vandekieft assisted us in understanding insurance issues. Katie Maslow,

M.S.W., of the Office of Technology Assessment, U.S. Congress, and Lisa Gwyther, M.S.W., of Duke University, long supporters of the first edition, shared expertise in many areas. Jean Marks, M.S.W., and her staff in the New York City chapter of the Alzheimer's Association shared their experiences of confused people living alone and of minority families. Ray Rasco also shared his knowledge of confused people who live alone. The Internal Revenue Service Information Department and John Kenneally provided information about tax law. Thomas Milleson, D.D.S., and Richard Dixon, D.D.S., gave us guidance in dental care. Carter Williams, M.S.W., and Mildred Simmons helped us understand the role of physical restraints. Mary Barringer, R.N., and Jean Marks helped us with incontinent care. Thomas Price, M.D., gave us information about multi-infarct dementia. Glenn Kirkland, M.S., reviewed the entire manuscript and gave us extensive valuable comment; he also researched the "gadgets" that might be useful to families.

A good editor is vital to a good book, and *The 36-Hour Day* has had the good fortune to have two good editors dedicated to its success. Anders Richter, editor to the first edition, facilitated many of the foreign language editions. It was he who initiated the writing of the revised edition. Wendy Harris has carried on the tradition of energy, skill, and dedication in the editorial management of *The 36-Hour Day*. We are indebted to both of these fine editors.

Preface to the First Edition

Although this book was written for the families of people with dementing illnesses, we recognize that other people, including those suffering from these conditions, may read this book. We welcome this. We hope that the use of such words as *patient* and *brain-injured person* will not discourage those who have these illnesses. These words were chosen because we want to emphasize that the people who suffer from these conditions are ill, not "just old." We hope the tone of the book conveys that we think of you as individuals and people and never as objects.

This book is not intended to provide medical or legal advice. The services of a competent professional should be obtained when legal, medical, or other specific advice is needed.

At present, not all professionals are knowledgeable about dementia. We frequently refer to trained personnel who can help you, but we recognize that you may have difficulty finding the help you need. You, the caregiver, will need to utilize both professional resources and your own good judgment. This book cannot address the particulars of your situation, but is intended only as a general guide.

In addition, we recognize that often resources such as day care, in-home care, or evaluation programs are not available or their availability may change, and that many such resources are dependent on federal funds and therefore on federal policy.

We use examples of family situations to illustrate our discussion. These examples are not descriptions of real families or patients. They are based upon experiences, feelings, and solutions that families and patients have discussed with us. Names and other identifying information have been changed.

Both men and women suffer from these diseases. To simplify reading, we will use the masculine pronouns *he* and *his* and the feminine pronouns *she* and *hers* in alternate chapters.

1

DEMENTIA

For two or three years Mary had known that her memory was slipping. First she had trouble remembering the names of her friends' children, and one year she completely forgot the strawberry preserves she had put up. She compensated by writing things down. After all, she told herself, she was getting older. But then she would find herself groping for a word she had always known, and she worried that she was getting senile.

Recently, when she was talking with a group of friends, Mary would realize that she had forgotten more than just an occasional name—she lost the thread of the conversation altogether. She compensated for this too: she always made an appropriate answer, even if she secretly felt confused. No one noticed, except perhaps her daughter-in-law, who said to her best friend, "I think Mother is slipping." It worried Mary— sometimes depressed her—but she always denied that anything was wrong. There was no one to whom she could say, "I am losing my mind. It is literally slipping away as I watch." Besides, she didn't want to think about it, didn't want to think about getting old, and, most important, she didn't want to be treated as if she were senile. She was still enjoying life and able to manage.

Then in the winter Mary got sick. At first she thought it was only a cold. She saw a doctor, who gave her some pills, and asked her what she expected at her age, which annoyed her. She rapidly got much worse. She went to bed, afraid, weak, and very, very tired. Mary's daughter-in-law got a telephone call from Mary's neighbor. Together they found the old woman semiconscious, feverish, and mumbling incoherently.

During the first few days in the hospital Mary had only an intermittent, foggy notion of what was happening. The doctors told her family that she had pneumonia, and that her kidneys were working poorly. All the resources of a modern hospital were mobilized to fight the infection.

Mary was in a strange place, and nothing was familiar. People, all strangers, came and went. They told her where she was, but she forgot. In strange surroundings she could no longer compensate for her forgetfulness, and the delirium caused by the acute illness aggravated her confusion. She thought her husband came to see her: a handsome young man in his war uniform. Then when her son came, she was surprised that they would come together. Her son kept saying, "But Mom, Dad has been dead for twenty years." But she knew he wasn't, because he had just been there. Then when she complained to her daughter-in-law that she never came, she thought the woman lied when she said, "But Mother, I was just here this morning." In truth, she could not remember the morning.

People came and poked and pushed, and shoved things in and out and over her. They gave her needles and they wanted her to blow into their bottles. She did not understand and they could not explain that blowing in the bottles forced her to breathe deeply to strengthen her lungs and improve her circulation. The bottles became part of her nightmare. She could not remember where she was. When she had to go to the bathroom, they put rails on her bed and refused to let her go, so that she cried and wet herself.

Gradually, Mary got better. The infection cleared and the dizziness passed. Only during the acute phase of her illness did she imagine things, but after the fever and infection had passed, the confusion and forgetfulness seemed more severe than before. Although the illness had probably not affected the gradual course of her memory loss, it had weakened her considerably and taken her out of the familiar setting in which she had been able to function. Most significantly, the illness had focused attention on the seriousness of her situation. Now her family realized she could no longer live alone.

The people around Mary talked and talked. No doubt they explained their plans, but she forgot. When she was finally released from the hospital, they took her to her daughter-in-law's house. They were happy about something that day, and led her into a room. Here at last were some of her things, but not all. She thought perhaps the rest of her things had been stolen while she was sick. They kept saying they had told her where her things were, but she couldn't remember what they said.

This is where they said she lived now, in her daughter-in-law's house—except that long ago she had made up her mind that she would never live with her children. She wanted to live at home. At home she could find things. At home she could manage—she believed—as she always had. At home, perhaps, she could discover what had become of a lifetime of possessions. This was not her home: her independence was gone, her things were gone, and Mary felt an enormous sense of loss. Mary could not remember her son's loving explanation—that she couldn't manage alone and that bringing her to live in his home was the best arrangement he could work out for her.

Often, Mary was afraid, a nameless, shapeless fear. Her impaired mind could not put a name or an explanation to her fear. People came, memories came, and then they slipped away. She could not tell what was reality and what was memory of people past. The bathroom was not where it was yesterday. Dressing became an insurmountable ordeal. Her hands forgot how to button buttons. Sashes hung inexplicably about her, and she could not think how to manage them or why they hung there.

Mary gradually lost the ability to make sense out of what her eyes and ears told her. Noises and confusion made her feel panicky. She couldn't understand, they couldn't explain, and often panic overwhelmed her. She worried about her things: a chair, and the china that had belonged to her mother. They said they had told her over and over, but she could not remember where her things had gone. Perhaps someone had stolen them. She had lost so much. What things she still had, she hid, but then she forgot where she hid them.

"I cannot get her to take a bath," her daughter-in-law said in despair. "She smells." "How can I send her to the adult day care center if she won't take a bath?" For Mary the bath became an experience of terror. The tub was a mystery. From day to day she could not remember how to manage the water: sometimes it all ran away, sometimes it kept rising and rising, so that she could not stop it. The bath involved remembering so many things. It meant remembering how to undress, how to find the bathroom, how to wash. Mary's fingers had forgotten how to unzip zippers; her feet had forgotten how to step into the tub. There were so many things for an injured mind to think about that panic overwhelmed her.

How do any of us react to trouble? We might try to get away from the situation for a while, and think it out. One person may go out for a beer; another may weed the garden or go for a walk. Sometimes we react with anger. We fight back against those who cause, or at least participate in, our situation. Or we become discouraged for a while, until nature heals us or the trouble goes away.

Mary's old ways of coping with trouble remained. Often when she felt nervous, she thought of going for a walk. She would pause on the porch, look out, drift out, and walk away—away from the trouble. Yet the trouble remained and now it was worse, for Mary would be lost, nothing would be familiar: the house had disappeared, the street was not the one she knew—or was it one from her childhood, or where they lived when the boys were growing up? The terror would wash over her, clutching at her heart. Mary would walk faster.

Sometimes Mary would react with anger. It was an anger she herself did not understand. But her things were gone, her life seemed gone. The closets of her mind sprang open and fell shut, or vanished altogether. Who would not be angry? Someone had taken her things, the treasures of a lifetime. Was it her daughter-in-law, or her own mother-in-law, or a sister resented in childhood? She accused her daughter-in-law but quickly forgot the suspicion. Her daughter-in-law, coping with an overwhelming situation, was unable to forget.

Many of us remember the day we began high school. We lay awake the night before, afraid of getting lost and not finding the classrooms the next day in a strange building. Every day was like that for Mary. Her family began sending her to an adult day care center. Every day a busdriver came to pick her up, and every day her daughter-in-law came to get her, but from day to day Mary could not remember that she would be taken home. The rooms were not dependable. Sometimes Mary could not find them. Sometimes she went in the men's bathroom. Sometimes she did not know whether they would come to get her in the evening.

Many of Mary's social skills remained, so she was able to chat and laugh with the other people in the day care center. As Mary relaxed in the center she enjoyed the time she spent there with other people, although she could never remember what she did there well enough to tell her daughter-in-law.

Mary loved music; music seemed to be imbedded in a part of her mind that she retained long after much else was lost. She loved to sing old, familiar songs. She loved to sing at the day care center. Even though her daughter-in-law could not sing well, Mary did not remember that, and the two women discovered that they enjoyed singing together.

The time finally came when the physical and emotional burden of caring for Mary became too much for her family and she went to live in a nursing home. After the initial days of confusion and panic passed, Mary felt secure in her small, sunny bedroom. She could not remember the schedule for the day but the reliability of the routine comforted her.

Some days it seemed as if she were still at the day care center, sometimes she was not sure. She was glad the toilet was close by where she could see it and did not have to remember where it was.

Mary was glad when her family came to visit. Sometimes she remembered their names, more often she did not. She never remembered that they had come last week, so she regularly scolded them for abandoning her. They could never think of much to say but they put their arms around her frail body, held her hand, and sat silently or sang old songs. She was glad when they didn't try to remind her of what she had just said or that they had come last week, or ask her if she remembered this person or that one. She liked it best when they just held her and loved her.

Someone in your family has been diagnosed as having a dementia. This could be Alzheimer's disease, multi-infarct dementia, or one of several other diseases. Perhaps you are not sure yet which condition it is. Whatever the name of the disease, a person close to you has lost some of his intellectual ability—the ability to think and remember. He may become increasingly forgetful. His personality may appear to change, or he may become depressed, moody, or withdrawn.

Many, although not all, of the disorders that cause these symptoms in adults are chronic and irreversible. When a diagnosis of an irreversible dementia is made, the patient and his family face the task of learning to live with this illness. Whether you decide to care for the person at home or to have him cared for in a nursing home, you will find yourself facing new problems and coping with your feelings about having someone close to you develop an incapacitating illness.

This book is designed to help you with that adjustment and with the tasks of day-to-day management of a chronically ill family member. We have found that there are questions many families ask. This material can help you begin to find answers, but it is not a substitute for the help of your doctor and other professionals.

WHAT IS DEMENTIA?

You may have discovered that many names have been given to the symptoms of memory loss and loss of thinking and reasoning capacity in adults. This is the result of different descriptions and definitions in older medical books. Commonly used terms include "organic brain syndrome," "senility," "hardening of the arteries," or "chronic brain syndrome." Your doctor may say "Alzheimer's disease," "multi-infarct disease," "senile dementia," or "presenile dementia." In this book we will refer to these conditions as *dementia*.

Doctors use the word *dementia* in a specific way. It means a loss or impairment of mental powers. It comes from two Latin words, which mean *away* and *mind*. Dementia does not mean crazy. It has been chosen by the medical profession as the least offensive and most accurate term to describe this group of illnesses. *Dementia* describes a group of symptoms and is not the name of a disease or diseases that cause the symptoms.

There are two major conditions that result in the symptoms of mental confusion, memory loss, disorientation, intellectual impairment, or similar problems. These two conditions may look similar to the casual observer and can be confused. (They will be discussed in more detail in Chapter 17.) The first condition, delirium, comprises a group of symptoms in which the person is less alert than normal. He is often drowsy but may fluctuate between drowsiness and restlessness. Like the demented person, he is also confused, disoriented, or forgetful. These conditions have also been called "acute brain syndromes" or "reversible brain syndromes." Delirium can be caused by illnesses such as pneumonia or kidney infection, by malnutrition, or by reactions to medications.

With the second condition, dementia, there is impaired intellectual functioning in a person who is clearly awake. The symptoms of dementia can be caused by many different diseases. Some of these diseases are treatable, others are not. Thyroid disease, for example, may cause a dementia that can be reversed with correction of a thyroid abnormality. In Chapter 17, we have summarized some of the diseases that can cause dementia.

Alzheimer's disease appears to be the most frequent cause of irreversible dementia in adults. The intellectual impairment progresses gradually from forgetfulness to total disability. Structural changes in the brain are visible in autopsies of people who suffered from Alzheimer's disease. The cause of the illness is not known, and at present physicians know of no way to stop or cure it. However, much can be done to diminish the patient's behavioral and emotional symptoms and to give the family a sense of control of the situation.

Multi-infarct dementia is believed to be the second most common cause of irreversible dementia. This is a series of strokes within the brain. Sometimes strokes may be so tiny that neither you nor the afflicted person is aware of any change, but all together they can destroy enough bits of brain tissue to affect memory and other intellectual functions. This condition used to be called "hardening of the arteries," but autopsy studies have shown that it is stroke damage rather than inadequate circulation that causes the problem. In some cases, treatment can reduce the possibility of further damage.

Alzheimer's disease and multi-infarct dementia sometimes occur together. The diagnosis and characteristics of these diseases are discussed in detail in Chapter 17.

People who have dementing illness may also have other illnesses, and their dementia may make them more vulnerable to other health problems. Other illnesses or reactions to medications often cause delirium in people with dementing illnesses. The delirium can make the person's mental functions and behavior worse. It is vital, for his general health and to make his care easier, to detect and treat other illnesses promptly. It is important to have a doctor who is able to spend time with you and the patient to do this.

Depression is common in older people, and can be the cause of memory loss, confusion, or other changes in mental function. Dementia caused by depression is reversible. The depressed person's memory frequently gets better when the depression is treated. Although depression can also occur in a person with an irreversible dementia, depression should always be treated.

Several other uncommon conditions cause dementia. These will be discussed in Chapter 17.

The dementing diseases know no social or racial lines: the rich and the poor, the wise and the simple alike become victims. There is no reason to be ashamed or embarrassed because a family member has a dementing illness. Many brilliant and famous people have suffered from dementing illnesses. Although dementias associated with the final stage of syphilis were common in the past, this is very rare today.

Severe memory loss is *never* a normal part of growing older. According to the best studies available, 5 percent of older people suffer from a severe intellectual impairment and a similar number may suffer from milder impairments. The diseases become more prevalent in people who survive into their 80s and 90s, but about 80 percent of those who live into very old age never experience a significant memory loss or other symptoms of dementia. A slight forgetfulness is common as we age but usually is not enough to interfere with our lives. Most of us know elderly people who are active and in full command of their intellect in their 70s, 80s, or 90s. Margaret Mead, Pablo Picasso, Arturo Toscanini, and Duke Ellington all were still active in their careers when they died: all were past 75; Picasso was 91.

As more people in our population live into later life, it becomes crucial that we learn more about dementia. It has been estimated that 2–4 million people in the United States have some degree of intellectual impairment. A study estimated that Alzheimer's disease alone cost the United States $30 billion in 1983.

THE PERSON WITH A DEMENTING ILLNESS

The person suffering from a dementing illness has difficulty remembering things, although he may be skillful at concealing this. His ability to understand, reason, and use good judgment may be impaired. The onset and the course of the condition depend upon which disease caused the condition and upon other factors, some of which are unknown to researchers. Sometimes the onset of the trouble is sudden: looking back, you may say, "After a certain time, Dad was never himself." Sometimes the onset is gradual: family members may not notice at first that something is wrong. Sometimes the afflicted person himself may be the first to notice something wrong. The person with a mild dementia is often able to describe his problem clearly: "Things just go out of my mind." "I start to explain and then I just can't find the words."

People respond to their problems in different ways. Some people become skillful at concealing the difficulty. Some keep lists to jog their memory. Some vehemently deny that anything is wrong or blame their problems on others. Some people become depressed or irritable when they realize that their memory is failing. Others remain outwardly cheerful. Usually, the person with a mild to moderate dementia is able to continue to do most of the things he has always done. Like a person with any other disease, he is able to participate in his treatment, in family decisions, and in planning for the future.

Early memory problems are sometimes mistaken for stress, depression, or even mental illness. This misdiagnosis creates an added burden for the person and the family.

A wife recalls the onset of her husband's dementing illness, not in terms of his forgetfulness but in terms of his mood and attitude: "I didn't know anything was wrong. I didn't want to see it. Charles was quieter than usual; he seemed depressed, but he blamed it on people at work. Then his boss told him he was being transferred—a demotion, really—to a smaller branch office. They didn't tell me anything. They suggested we take a vacation. So we did. We went to Scotland. But Charles didn't get any better. He was depressed and irritable. After he took the new job, he couldn't handle that either; he blamed it on the younger men. He was so irritable, I wondered what was wrong between us after so many years. We went to a marriage counselor and that only made things worse. I knew he was forgetful but I thought that it was caused by stress."

Her husband said at the time, "I knew something was wrong. I could feel myself getting uptight over little things. People thought I knew things about the plant that I—I couldn't remember. The counselor said it was stress. I thought it was something else, something terrible. I was scared."

Some people experience changes in personality. Many of the qualities that a person has always had may remain: he may always have been sweet and lovable and may remain so, or he may always have been a difficult person to live with and may become more so. Other people may change dramatically, from amiable to demanding or from energetic to apathetic. They may become passive, dependent, and listless, or they may become restless, easily upset, and irritable. Sometimes they become demanding, fearful, or depressed.

A daughter says, "Mother was always the cheerful, outgoing person in the family. I guess we knew she was getting forgetful but the worst thing is that she doesn't want to do anything anymore. She doesn't do her hair, she doesn't keep the house neat, she absolutely won't go out."

Often little things enormously upset people with memory problems. Tasks that were previously simple may now be too difficult for a person, and he may react to this by becoming upset, angry, or depressed.

From another family: "The worst thing about Dad is his temper. He used to be easygoing. Now he is always hollering over the least little thing. Last night he told our ten-year-old that Alaska is not a state. He was hollering and yelling and stalked out of the room. Then when I asked him to take a bath we had a real fight. He insisted he had already taken a bath."

It is important for those around him to remember that many of the person's behaviors are beyond his control: for example, he may not be able to keep his anger in check or to stop pacing the floor. The changes that occur are not the result of an unpleasant personality grown old; they are the result of damage to the brain and are usually beyond the control of the patient.

In those illnesses in which the dementia is progressive, the person's memory will gradually become worse, and his troubles cannot be concealed. He may become unable to recall what day it is or where he is. He may be unable to do simple tasks such as dressing, and may not be able to put words together coherently. As the dementia progresses, it becomes clear that the damage to the brain affects many functions, including memory, motor functions (coordination, writing, walking), and speaking. The person may have difficulty finding the right name for familiar things and he may become clumsy or walk with a shuffle. The sick person's abilities may fluctuate from day to day or even from hour to hour. This makes it harder for families to know what to expect.

Some people with dementing illnesses have hallucinations (hearing, seeing, or smelling things that are not real). This experience is real to the person experiencing it and can be frightening to family members. Some people become suspicious of others; they may hide things or accuse people of stealing from them. Often they simply mislay things and forget where they put them, and in their confusion think someone has stolen them.

A son recalls: "Mom is so paranoid. She hides her purse. She hides her money, she hides her jewelry. Then she accuses my wife of stealing it. Now she is accusing us of stealing the silverware. The hard part is that she doesn't seem sick. It's hard to believe she isn't doing this deliberately."

In the final stages of a progressive dementing illness, so much of the brain has been affected that the person is often confined to bed, unable to control urination and unable to express himself. In the last stages of the illness the patient may require skilled nursing care.

It is important to remember that not all these symptoms will occur in the same person. Your family member may never experience some of these symptoms or may experience others we have not mentioned. The course of the disease and the prognosis vary with the specific disorder and with the individual person.

WHERE DO YOU GO FROM HERE?

You know or suspect that someone close to you has a dementing illness. Where do you go from here? You will need to take stock of your current situation and then identify what needs to be done to help the impaired person and to make the burdens on yourself bearable. There are many questions you must ask. This book will get you started with the answers.

The first thing you need to know is the cause of the disease and its prognosis. Each disease that causes dementia is different. You may have been given different diagnoses and different explanations of the disease, or you may not know what is wrong with the person. You may have been told that the person has Alzheimer's disease when the person has not had a thorough diagnostic examination. However, you must have a diagnosis and some information about the course of the disease before you or the doctor can respond appropriately to day-to-day problems or plan for the future. It is usually better to know what to expect. Your understanding of the illness can help to dispel fears and worries, and it will help you plan how you can best help the person with a dementing disease.

You need a physician who is willing and able to devote the time and interest required to care for the patient. Chapter 2 describes how a diagnostic evaluation is done and how to find a physician who will care for the ill person.

Even when the disease itself cannot be stopped, *much can be done to improve the quality of life for the afflicted person and for the family.* Chapters 3 through 9 list many of the problems that families face in caring for a person with a dementing illness and offer suggestions for managing them.

Dementing illnesses vary with the specific disease and with the individual who is afflicted. You may never face many of the problems discussed in this chapter. You may find it most helpful to skip through these chapters to those sections that apply to you.

The key to coping is common sense and ingenuity. Sometimes a family is too close to the problem to see clearly a way of managing. At other times there is no one more ingenious at solving a difficult problem than the family members themselves. Many of the ideas offered here were developed by family members who have called or written to share them with others. These ideas will get you started.

At some point you may find that you will need additional help in caring for an impaired person. Chapter 10 discusses the kinds of help that may be available and how to locate them.

You and the impaired person are part of a family that needs to work together to cope with this illness. Chapter 11 discusses families and the problems that can arise in families. Chapter 12 discusses your feelings and the effects this illness may have on you. Caring for yourself is important for both you and the confused person who is dependent on you, and is discussed in Chapter 13.

Chapter 14 is written for young people who know someone with a dementing illness. Perhaps, as a parent, you will want to read this section also and plan a time to discuss it with your son or daughter. The entire book is written in such a way that a young person will be able to understand any other sections he may want to read.

Chapter 15 discusses legal and financial matters. Although it may be painful to plan ahead, it is most important to do so. Perhaps now is the time to get started with things you may have been avoiding.

A time may come when the impaired person cannot live alone. Chapter 16 discusses nursing homes and other living arrangements. There is a shortage of good nursing home beds in many states and nursing home care can impoverish a family. For both these reasons, we urge you to read Chapter 16, on nursing home care, and to plan ahead, even if you do not plan to use a nursing home.

Chapter 17 discusses the diseases that cause dementia and explains how they differ from other brain disorders. However, it is written to give you a general understanding of terms and conditions, not as a tool for diagnosis.

Chapter 18 briefly reviews the research into Alzheimer's disease and multi-infarct dementia. The reading list in Appendix 1 refers you to other, more detailed information.

You may want to use this handbook to inform others about the diseases that cause dementia. The dementing illnesses affect large numbers of people, but their effects on families and their potential management are sometimes poorly understood by professionals and by the general community. Education does not always have to come from the professional person. You, the family, can effectively inform others. Share what you know about dementia with your physician, nursing home staff, and others. The grassroots education of people by people is helping to bring dementia out of the closet. This has already led to effective advocacy, to research into possible causes and cures, and to better-informed professionals. Use what you know and use this handbook. You will increase the understanding of those around you, and you will reach families who have been struggling in isolation.

Caring for a person with a dementing illness is not easy. We hope the information in this book will help you, but we know that simple solutions are not yet at hand.

This book often focuses on problems. However, it is important to remember that confused people and their families do still experience joy and happiness. Since dementing illnesses develop slowly, they often leave intact the impaired person's ability to enjoy life and to enjoy other people. When things go badly, remind yourself that, no matter how bad the person's memory is or how strange his behavior, he is still a unique and special human being. We can continue to love a person even after he has changed drastically, and even when we are deeply troubled by his present state.

2

GETTING MEDICAL HELP
FOR THE IMPAIRED PERSON

THIS BOOK IS WRITTEN for you, the family. It is based on the assumption that you and the sick person are receiving professional medical care. The family and the medical professionals are partners in the care of the impaired person. Neither should be providing care alone. This book is not meant to be a substitute for professional skills. Many professionals are knowledgeable about the dementing illnesses, but misconceptions about dementia still exist. Not all physicians or other professionals have the time, interest, or skills to diagnose or care for a person with a dementing illness.

What should you expect from your physician and other professionals? The first thing is an accurate diagnosis. Once a diagnosis has been made, you will need the ongoing help of a physician and perhaps other professionals to manage the dementing illness, to treat concurrent illnesses, and to help you find the resources you need. This chapter is written as a guide to help you find the best possible medical care in your community.

In the course of a dementing illness, you may need the special skills of a physician, neuropsychologist, social worker, nurse, or recreational, occupational, or physical therapist. Each is a highly trained professional whose skills complement those of the others. They can work together first to evaluate the impaired person and then to help you with ongoing care.

THE EVALUATION OF THE PERSON WITH A
SUSPECTED DEMENTIA

When a person suffers from difficulty in thinking, remembering, or learning or shows changes in personality, it is important that a thorough evaluation be made. A complete evaluation tells you and the doctors several things:

1. the exact nature of the person's illness,
2. whether or not the condition can be reversed or treated,
3. the nature and extent of the disability,
4. the areas in which the person can still function successfully,
5. whether the person has other health problems that need treatment and that might be making her mental problems worse,
6. the social and psychological needs and resources of the sick person and the family or caregiver, and
7. the changes you can expect in the future.

Procedures vary depending on the physician or hospital. However, a good evaluation includes a medical and neurological examination, an evaluation of the person's social support system, and an evaluation of her remaining abilities.

The evaluation may begin with a careful examination by a physician. The doctor will take a *detailed history* from someone who knows the person well and from the sick person if possible. This may reveal how the person has changed, what symptoms the person has had, and information about other medical conditions. The doctor will also give the person a *physical examination*, which may reveal other health problems. A *neurological examination* (asking the person to balance with her eyes closed, tapping her ankles or knees with a rubber hammer, and other tests) may reveal changes in the functioning of the nerve cells of the brain or spine.

The doctor will do a *mental status examination*, in which he asks the person questions about the current time, date, and place. Other questions test her ability to remember, to concentrate, to do abstract reasoning, to do simple calculations, and to copy simple designs. Each of these reveals problems of function in different parts of the brain. When he does this test, he will take into consideration the person's education and the fact that the person may be nervous.

The doctor will order *laboratory tests*, including a number of blood tests. The *CBC* (complete blood count) detects anemia and evidence of infection, either of which can cause or complicate a dementing illness. *Blood chemistry tests* check for liver and kidney problems, diabetes, and a number of other conditions. *Vitamin B_{12} and folate level tests* check for vitamin deficiencies, which might cause dementia. *Thyroid studies* evaluate the function of the thyroid gland. Thyroid problems are among the more common reversible causes of dementia. The *VDRL test* can indicate a syphilis infection (syphilis was a common cause of dementia before the discovery of penicillin), but a positive VDRL test does not necessarily indicate that the person has ever had syphilis. The blood tests usually involve inserting one needle, which is no more unpleasant than a pin prick.

The *lumbar puncture* (LP), or spinal tap, is done to rule out infection in the central nervous system (for example, tuberculosis) and it may reveal other abnormalities. It is usually done after a local anesthetic has been injected into the back and has few complications. It may not be done if there is no reason to suspect these conditions.

The *EEG* (electroencephalogram) records the electrical activity present in the brain. It is done by attaching little wires to the head with a pastelike material. It is painless but may confuse the forgetful person. It aids in the diagnosis of delirium and can offer evidence of abnormal brain functioning, but occasionally is normal in a person with dementia.

The *CT* (computerized tomography) *scan* is a sophisticated x-ray that produces a picture of the brain. (Ordinary skull x-rays show primarily the bones and do not show the brain itself.) Changes compatible with Alzheimer's disease may be visible on a CT scan, but this diagnosis should not be made on the basis of a CT scan alone. The CT scan can find evidence of stroke, multi-infarct dementia, tumors, changes in the flow of the fluid that surrounds the brain, and collections of blood which can put pressure on the brain.

The CT scan involves lying on a table and placing one's head in an object that looks like a very large hair dryer. It is painless but may confuse an already impaired person. If so, a mild sedative can be prescribed to help the person relax. The CT scan has replaced the *pneumoencephalogram* (PEG), in which air is injected by means of a needle into the sac surrounding the spine. The PEG was an uncomfortable test and sometimes made patients temporarily worse.

For some procedures, such as the lumbar puncture and dye injections for the CT scan, you will be asked to sign an informed consent form. This lists all the possible side effects of the procedure. Reading this can make the procedure seem alarming and dangerous, but in fact, these are safe procedures. If you have any concerns about possible side effects, ask a doctor to explain them to you.

A new diagnostic tool, MRI or NMR (magnetic resonance imaging or nuclear magnetic resonance scanner), provides the physician with a picture similar to that of a CT scan but it uses magnetic energy rather than x-rays to produce an image. At present MRI is not being used to evaluate all patients with dementia but only those who are very young or whose condition raises certain diagnostic questions (such as whether they have had a small stroke). CT is more widely available, is less expensive, and often provides more straightforward information.

The history, physical and neurological exams, and laboratory tests will identify or rule out known causes of dementia. Other evaluations in addition to the medical assessment are done to understand the person's abilities and help you to plan for the future.

A *psychiatric and psychosocial evaluation* is based on interviews with the person and her family. This provides the basis for the development of a specific plan for the care of the individual. It may be done by the doctor, nurse, or social worker who works with the physician. It includes helping the family evaluate their own emotional, physical, and financial resources, the home in which the person lives, the available community resources, and the patient's ability to accept or participate in plans.

It is important that the physician determine whether the patient is depressed. Depression can cause symptoms similar to dementia and it can make an existing dementia worse. Whenever there is a question about depression, a psychiatrist experienced in geriatrics should see the patient. Depression is quite common and usually responds well to treatment.

An *occupational therapy evaluation* helps to determine how much the person is able to do for herself and what can be done to help her compensate for her limitations. It is done by an occupational, rehabilitation, or physical therapist. These therapists are important members of the health care team. Their skills are sometimes overlooked because in the past they were consulted only in cases where there was the potential for physical rehabilitation. However, they are able to identify the things that the person can still do, and to devise ways to help the person remain as independent as possible. Part of this assessment is an *ADL* (activities of daily living) evaluation. The person is observed in a controlled situation to see if she can manage money, fix a simple meal, dress herself, and perform other routine tasks. If she can do part of these tasks, this is noted. These therapists are familiar with a variety of appliances that can help some people.

Neuropsychological testing (also called cortical function testing or psychometric testing) may be done to determine in which areas of mental function the person is impaired and in which she is still independent. This testing takes several hours. The tests evaluate such things as memory, reasoning, coordination, writing, and the ability to express oneself and understand instructions. The testing psychologist will be experienced in making people feel relaxed and will take into consideration differences in education and interests.

The final part of the evaluation is your *discussion with the doctor* and perhaps with other members of the evaluating team. The doctor will explain the findings to you and to the patient if she is able to understand at least part of what is happening.

At this time the doctor should give you a specific diagnosis (he may explain that he cannot be certain) and a general idea of the person's prognosis (again, he may not be able to tell you exactly what to expect). The findings of other tests, such as the ADL evaluation, the psychological tests, and the social history, will also be explained to you. You should be able to ask questions and come away with an understanding of the findings of the evaluation. The doctor may make recommendations such as the use of medications or community support services or he may refer you to someone who can advise you about community services. You, he, and the afflicted person may identify specific problems and set up a plan to cope with them.

A complete evaluation may take more than one day. You may want to arrange to spread the evaluation over more than one day so that the patient will not get too tired. It usually takes several days for the laboratories to report their findings to the doctor and for him to put all these data together into a report.

Evaluations may be done either with the patient admitted to the hospital or on an outpatient basis. Several factors, including your insurance coverage, the general health of the patient, and your convenience, affect the decision to do an inpatient or outpatient evaluation.

Sometimes family members and occasionally professionals advise against "putting a confused person through the 'ordeal' of an evaluation." We feel that every person with problems in memory and thinking should be fully evaluated. An evaluation is not an unpleasant ordeal. Staff accustomed to working with people with dementia are usually gentle and kind. It is important that they make the person as comfortable as possible so that they will be able to measure her best performance.

As we have said, there are many reasons why a person might develop the symptoms of dementia. Some of these are treatable. If a treatable problem is not found because an evaluation is not done, the afflicted person and her family may suffer unnecessarily for years. Certain diseases can be treated if they are found promptly, but can cause irreversible damage if they are neglected.

Even if it is found that a person has an irreversible dementia, the evaluation will give you information about how best to care for the impaired person and how best to manage her symptoms. It gives you a basis upon which to plan for the future and, finally, it is important that you know that you have done all that you can for her.

FINDING SOMEONE TO DO AN EVALUATION

In most areas, a family can locate someone to do a thorough evaluation of a person with a suspected dementia. Your family physician may do the evaluation or may refer you to a specialist who can do an evaluation. Your local hospital may give you the names of physicians who are interested in evaluating people with dementing illnesses. Teaching hospitals or medical schools in your area may know of people with a special interest in this field. The NIA Alzheimer's Disease Centers (see Appendix 2) may accept the patient or give you a referral. The local Alzheimer's Association (see Appendix 2) may be able to give you the names of physicians in your area. "Memory disorder clinics" have opened in some areas. If you hear of one, you may want to ask your physician about its reputation.

Before you schedule an evaluation, you can ask the evaluating physician what procedures he uses and why. If you feel from this preliminary conversation that he is not really interested in dementia, you may want to seek someone else.

How do you decide whether an accurate diagnosis has been made for someone in your family? In the final analysis, you must settle on a doctor whom you trust and who you feel has done all he can, and then rely on his judgment. This is much easier when you understand something about the terminology, the diagnostic procedures, and what is known about the dementias. If you have been given differing diagnoses, discuss this frankly with the doctor. It is important that you feel certain that an accurate diagnosis has been made. Occasionally a physician will make a diagnosis of Alzheimer's disease without doing a complete evaluation. It is not possible to make an accurate diagnosis without a complete assessment and tests that rule out other conditions. If this happens to you, we suggest you consider getting a second opinion.

You may hear about people with similar symptoms who are "miraculously" cured, or you may hear statements like "senility can be cured." Considerable confusion has arisen because some of the causes of dementia are reversible and because dementia and delirium (see Chapter 17) are sometimes confused. There are some unscrupulous individuals who offer bogus "cures" for these tragic illnesses. An accurate diagnosis and a doctor you trust can assure you that all that can be done is being done. You can also keep informed about the progress of legitimate research through the Alzheimer's Disease and Related Disorders Association and from the major research institutes.

THE MEDICAL TREATMENT AND MANAGEMENT OF DEMENTIA

Dementing illnesses are diseases that require continuing medical attention. The availability of professional services varies. You, the caretaker, will provide much of the coordination of care. However, there are times when you will need the help of professionals.

The Physician

You will need a physician who will prescribe and adjust medications, answer your questions, and treat other, concurrent illnesses. The physician who provides continuing care will not necessarily be the specialist who provided the initial evaluation of the person. He may be your family doctor, part of a geriatric team, or someone with a special interest in geriatric medicine. This doctor does not have to be a specialist, although he should be able to work with a neurologist or psychiatrist if necessary. The doctor you select for continuing care must:

1. be willing and able to spend the necessary time with you and the sick person,
2. be knowledgeable about dementing illnesses and the special susceptibility of demented patients to other diseases, medications, and delirium,
3. be easily accessible,
4. if possible, be able to make referrals to physical therapists, social workers, and other professionals.

Not all doctors meet these criteria. Some doctors have large practices and do not have the time to focus on your problems. It is impossible for any one person to keep up with all the advances in medicine, so some doctors may not be skilled in the specialized care of a person with dementia. Finally, some doctors are uncomfortable caring for people with chronic, incurable diseases. However, no physician should give you a diagnosis without following through with referrals to professionals who can give you the help and follow-up you need. You may have to talk with more than one doctor before you find the one who is right for you. Discuss your needs and expectations honestly with him, and talk over how you can best work with him. Doctors have been trained to keep the patient's problems confidential. Because of this, some doctors are reluctant to talk to other members of the family or will talk to only the patient's spouse. There may be good reasons why you need to know about the patient. Physicians who work with many families of dementia patients find that conferring with the whole family is important. Discuss this problem frankly with the doctor and ask him to be as open as he can be with the whole family.

The Nurse

In addition to the knowledge and experience of a physician you may need the skills of a registered nurse who can work with the physician. The nurse may be the person whom you can reach most easily and who can coordinate the work that you, the doctor, and others do to provide the best possible care. She may be the person who understands the difficulties of caring for a person at home. She can observe the person for changes in her health status which need to be reported to the doctor and she can give you support and counsel. After talking with you, the nurse can identify and help solve many of the problems you face. She can teach you how to provide a practical care for the person (coping with catastrophic reactions, giving baths, helping with eating problems, managing a wheelchair). She can teach you how and when to give medicine and how to know whether it is working correctly. A nurse may be available to come to your home to assess the patient and offer suggestions for simplifying the person's environment and minimizing the effort you need to expend.

A licensed vocational (practical) nurse may also be helpful to you.

Your physician should be able to refer you to a nurse, or you can locate this help by calling your health department or a home health agency such as the Visiting Nurse Association.

Medicare or health insurance may pay for nursing services if they are ordered by a physician (see p. 175).

In some areas an occupational therapist or physical therapist may be available to help.

The Social Worker

Social workers have a unique combination of skills: they know the resources and services in your community and they are skilled in assessing your situation and needs and matching these with available services. Some people think of social workers as "just for the poor." This is not true. They are professionals whose skills in helping you find resources can be invaluable. They can also provide practical counseling and help you and your family think through plans. They can help families work out disagreements over care.

Your physician may be able to refer you to a social worker, or, if the sick person is hospitalized, the hospital social worker may be able to help you. The local office on aging may have a social worker on the staff who will help anyone over sixty.

Most communities have family service agencies staffed by social workers. To locate local social service agencies, look in the telephone book yellow pages under "social services organizations" or under the listings for your state and local governments. You can write to the national office of Family Service America (see Appendix 2). They accredit private agencies and can provide you with the names of your nearest agencies.

Social workers work in a variety of settings, including public social service agencies, some nursing homes, senior citizen centers, public housing projects, and local offices of the state department of health. Sometimes these agencies have special units that serve the elderly. There are social workers in private practice in some communities. Some social workers will arrange supportive services for a relative who lives out of town. Social workers are professionally trained. In many states they must also be licensed or accredited. You should know the qualifications and training of the person you select.

Fees for social services vary, depending on the agency, the services you need, and whether or not you are using other services of that agency (such as a hospital). Some agencies charge according to your ability to pay.

It is important to select a social worker who understands the dementing illnesses.

3

CHARACTERISTIC PROBLEMS
OF DEMENTIA

IN CHAPTERS 3 through 9 we will discuss many of the problems that families may encounter in caring for a person with a dementing illness. Although as yet nothing can be done to cure some dementing illnesses, it is important to remember that *much can be done to make life easier for you and the person with a dementing illness.* The suggestions we offer come from our clinical experience and from the experiences that family members have shared with us.

Each individual and each family is different. You may never experience many of these problems. The problems you will face are influenced by the nature of the specific disease, by your personality, by the sick person's personality, and, often, by other factors, such as where you live. We do not want you to read through this section as if it were a list of what lies ahead of you. It is a comprehensive list of problem areas for you to use as a reference when a specific problem arises.

THE BRAIN, BEHAVIOR, AND PERSONALITY:
WHY PEOPLE WITH DEMENTIA
DO THE THINGS THEY DO

The very nature of brain injuries can make them difficult to live with. The brain is a vast, complex, mysterious organ. It is the source of our thoughts, our emotions, and our personality. Injury to the brain can cause changes in emotions, personality, and the ability to reason. Most dementing illnesses do their damage gradually, so the effects are not seen suddenly, as are the effects of a major stroke or head injury. Consequently, the behavior of a person with a dementing illness often seems puzzling in contrast to behaviors due to other illnesses. It is not always evident that many of the visible symptoms (changes in personality, for example) are the result of a disease, because the sick person often looks well.

You may wonder which behaviors are caused by the disease and which are deliberate or willful, or family members may disagree about this. In the following chapters we will discuss some of the behavior problems you may face and suggest ways you can respond. Understanding that the damage to the brain causes these behaviors will help you cope with them.

The brain is an incredibly complex organ composed of billions of microscopic neurons, or brain cells. All the tasks of the brain—thinking, talking, dreaming, walking, listening to music, and hundreds of others—are carried out when these cells communicate with one another. This communication is accomplished by a chemical, manufactured inside the cell, that jumps the tiny gap from one cell to the neighboring cell. Because it is known that some of these chemicals are in short supply in the brains of people with Alzheimer's disease, scientists are studying the chemicals in an effort to alleviate the symptoms of Alzheimer's disease.

Different parts of the brain carry out different tasks. When a person has a stroke and cannot speak, we know that the stroke occurred in the speech center of the brain and destroyed cells that are necessary for the person to talk. A stroke often causes extensive damage, but to only a few areas of the brain. In dementia, damage is done in many areas and affects many aspects of mental function. While a stroke does all its damage at once, Alzheimer's disease gradually does more and more damage. This means that different cognitive abilities are damaged *unevenly* and the person will be able to do some things but not others. For example, he may be able to remember things from long ago but not from yesterday.

Our brains do thousands of tasks and we are usually not aware of most of them. We assume that other people's brains, like ours, are working as they should—but with a person who has a dementia we cannot make this assumption. When the person does something odd or inexplicable, it is usually because some part of the brain has failed to do its job. In addition to controlling memory and language, the brain enables us to move our various body parts, filters out the things we don't want to pay attention to, gives feedback on the things we do, enables us to recognize familiar objects, and coordinates all the activities it is carrying out. *When brain damage is uneven, the person may do things that don't make sense to us.*

John Barstow can remember he was angry with his wife, but he cannot remember her explanation of why she did what she did. In fact, he may not even remember what she did that made him angry.

Researchers think that our brain stores and processes memories of emotions differently from memories of fact. It is possible for the dementia to damage one without damaging the other as much. Old social skills and the ability to make customary social remarks are often retained longer than insight and judgment. Thus a person may sound fine to the doctor but in fact be unable to responsibly care for himself.

It may be that damaged nerve cells, like a loose light bulb, connect sometimes and fail other times. This may be why a person can do something one day and not another. Even when we do something that seems simple, the brain must carry out many tasks. *If the dementia prevents the brain from performing any one of the steps in a task, the task will not get done.*

"I asked my sister to make us both a cup of tea, but she ignored me. Then half an hour later, she went to the kitchen and made herself a cup of tea."

Obviously this sister was still able to do this task but probably was not able to understand or act on language even though she heard the request.

Behavior problems are caused by the damage to the brain and are not something the person can control or prevent. Behavior that upsets you is almost never deliberate and almost never intended to "get your goat." Because the brain itself is damaged, the person has a severely limited ability to learn things or understand explanations. It is futile to expect the person to remember or learn and frustrating to both of you to try to teach him. The person does not want to act like this and *is trying as hard as he can.*

Mrs. Robinson helped out in her older daughter's kitchen, but when she visited her younger daughter she only sat and criticized. The younger daughter felt that Mrs. Robinson had always preferred the older sister and that her refusal to help was a less than subtle reminder of her preference. In fact, the mother had been familiar with the older sister's kitchen before she became forgetful, but could no longer learn new information, even things as simple as where the dishes were kept in her younger daughter's unfamiliar kitchen.

A person's feelings also affect his behavior. The person with dementia probably feels lost, worried, anxious, vulnerable, and helpless much of the time. He may also be aware that he fails at tasks and feel that he is making a fool of himself. Imagine what it must feel like to want to say something nice to your caregiver but all that comes out are curse words. Think how frightening it must be if a familiar home and familiar people now seem strange and unfamiliar. If we can find ways to make a person with dementia feel more secure and comfortable, behavior problems may decline.

Other things also affect behavior. When a person is not feeling well, he will be less able to think. In Chapter 6 we discuss how *illness, pain, and medication* can make a person's thinking—and behavior—worse.

When you speak to a person, he must hear you: the first step in the processes of communication is *sensory input*. The ability to immediately repeat what is heard may be retained but the next step, to store what was said, at least temporarily, is often lost in people with dementia. If the person cannot temporarily store what you said, he cannot respond. Often a person can store only part of what was said and will act on only that part. If you say, "The grandchildren are coming to dinner, so you must have a bath," he may retain only "have a bath" and act accordingly. If he retains nothing of what you said, he may be angry when you lead him to the bathroom. As well as retaining what was heard, the person must comprehend what the words mean and evaluate what was said. Many things may go wrong in this process and may result in a reply that seems inappropriate to you. The person will act on what he *thinks* he heard. But he can act on only what his ears heard, his brain registered, his mental dictionary understood, and his mind processed. If his brain scrambles the message, he will respond in a way that is appropriate to what he understood, and if, in his confusion, he thinks that you are a stranger or that he is a young man and you are his mother, his response will be based on the faulty understanding of the situation. A person who was usually placid may respond calmly, a person who was usually irritable may respond with anger, but whatever the response, it will be appropriate to the message *received*, not necessarily the message you gave.

The final step in communication is the person's answer. Things can go wrong here, too. What comes out may not be what the confused person intended. This too can sound like an intentional evasion, insult, or foolish answer.

There is much that we do not know about this process. Neuropsychologists study the mind and try to understand these complex cognitive processes. Often a neuropsychologist can figure out why a particular person acts as he does, and sometimes can devise a way around the disability. Although there is still an enormous amount to learn about how this process works, when people with a dementing illness say or do things that don't make sense or that seem nasty or deliberate, it is almost certainly the brain damage at work. *The person you are caring for is also often miserable and is doing the best he can.* In the rest of this book we will show you many ways you can help.

You may not be able to figure out what the person understood or intended.

Because the brain is so complex, even the best experts are often at a loss. In addition, most families do not have access to a neuropsychologist. Do the best you can, regard problems as the brain damage at work, not as something you did or something the confused person intended. Affection, reassurance, and calm are best, even when things make no sense.

CAREGIVING: SOME GENERAL SUGGESTIONS

Be informed. The more you know about the nature of dementing illnesses, the more effective you will be in devising strategies to manage behavior problems.

Share your concerns with the patient. When a person is only mildly to moderately impaired, he can take part in managing his problem. You may be able to share with each other your grief and worries. Together you may be able to devise memory aids that will help him remain independent. Mildly impaired people may benefit from counseling that can help them accept and adjust to their limitations.

Try to solve your most frustrating problems one at a time. Families tell us that the day-to-day problems often seem to be the most insurmountable. Getting mother to take her bath or getting supper prepared, eaten, and cleaned up can become daily ordeals. *If you are at the end of your rope, single out one thing that you can change to make life easier, and work on that.* Sometimes changing small things makes a big difference.

Get enough rest. One of the dilemmas families often face is that the caregiver may not get enough rest or may not have the opportunity to get away from his caregiving responsibilities. This can make the caregiver less patient and less able to tolerate irritating behaviors. If things are getting out of hand, ask yourself if this is happening to you. If so, you may want to focus on finding ways to get more rest or more frequent breaks from your caregiving responsibilities. We recognize that this is difficult to arrange. We will discuss this in Chapter 10.

Use your common sense and imagination; they are your best tools. Adaptation is the key to success. If a thing cannot be done one way, ask yourself if it must be done at all. For example, if a person can eat successfully with his fingers but cannot use a fork and spoon appropriately, don't fight the problem; serve as many finger foods as possible. Accept changes. If the person insists on sleeping with his hat on, this is not harmful; go along with it.

Maintain a sense of humor; it will get you through many crises. The sick person is still a person. He needs and enjoys a good laugh too. Sharing your experiences with other families will help you. Surprisingly, these groups of families often find their shared experiences funny as well as sad.

Try to establish an environment that allows as much freedom as possible but also offers the structure that confused people need. Establish a regular, predictable, simple routine for meals, medication, exercising, bedtime, and other activities. Do things the same way and at the same time each day. If you establish regular routines, the person may gradually learn what to expect. Change routines only when they aren't working. Keep the person's surroundings reliable and simple. Leave furniture in the same place. Put away clutter.

Remember to talk *to* the confused person. Speak calmly and gently. Make a point of telling him what you are doing and why. Let him have a part in deciding things as much as possible. Avoid talking *about* him in front of him, and remind others to avoid this also.

Have an ID necklace or bracelet made for the confused person. Include on it the nature of his disease (e.g., "memory impaired") and your telephone number. This is one of the single most important things you can do. Many confused people get lost or wander away at one time or another and an ID can save you hours of frantic worry.

Keep the impaired person active but not upset. Families often ask if retraining, reality orientation, or keeping active will slow down or stop the course of the disease. Likewise, they may ask if being idle hastens the course of the disease. Some people with dementing illnesses become depressed, listless, or apathetic. Families often wonder whether encouraging such a person to do things will help him to function better.

The relationship of activity to the course of dementing illnesses is not clear. Research continues in this area. Activity helps to maintain physical well-being and may help to prevent other illnesses and infections. Being active helps the ill person to continue to feel that he is involved in the family and that his life has meaning.

It is clear that people with dementing illnesses cannot learn as well as before because brain tissue has been damaged or destroyed. It would be unrealistic to expect them to learn new skills. However, some individuals can learn simple tasks or facts if they are repeated often enough. Some impaired people who feel lost in a new place eventually "learn" their way around.

At the same time, too much stimulation, activity, or pressure to learn may upset the confused person, may upset you, and may accomplish nothing. The key to this is balance:

1. Accept that lost skills are gone for good (the woman who has lost the ability to cook will not learn to fix a meal), *but* know that

repeatedly and gently giving information that is within the person's abilities will help him function more comfortably (the person going into a strange day care setting will benefit from frequent reminders of where he is).

2. Know that even small amounts of excitement—visitors, laughter, changes—can upset the confused person, *but* plan interesting, stimulating things within his capabilities—a walk, visiting one old friend.

3. Look for ways to simplify activities so that a person can continue to be involved within the limits of his abilities (the woman who can no longer fix a whole meal may still be able to peel the potatoes).

4. Look for things the person is still able to do and focus on them. A person's intellectual abilities are not all lost at once. Both of you will benefit from carefully assessing what he can still do and making the best use of those abilities. For example,

Mrs. Baldwin often cannot remember the words for things she wants to say but she can make her meaning clear with gestures. Her daughter helps her by saying, "point to what you want."

5. Consider having a trained person come into the home to visit the confused person or trying a group program such as day care for people with dementia. (See Chapter 20.) Day care often offers the right level of stimulation for some confused people and gives you time off as well.

MEMORY PROBLEMS

People with dementing illnesses forget things quickly. For the person with a memory impairment, life may be like constantly coming into the middle of a movie: one has no idea what happened just before what is happening now. People with dementing illnesses may say they will call a friend and forget to do so, may start to prepare a meal and forget to turn the stove off, may forget what time it is or where they are. This forgetfulness of recent events can seem puzzling when the person seems to be able to remember clearly events long past. There are some specific suggestions for memory aids throughout this book. You may think of others that will help you.

Forgetful people may remember events long past more clearly than recent events or they may remember some things and not others. This has to do with the way the brain stores and receives information; *it is not something the person does deliberately.* The success of memory aids depends on the severity of the dementia. A mildly demented person may devise reminders for himself, while a severely impaired person will only become more frustrated by his inability to use the aid. People who are able to read may be able to do chores if you write out instructions. Writing down names and often-used phone numbers also helps. If you are going out, write down where you are going. If you will be gone at mealtime, leave a written reminder to eat.

Have clocks and calendars in view to help the confused person remember what time it is. Mark off the days as they pass. It is often helpful to put a simple list of the day's activities where the person can easily see it. A regular daily routine is much less confusing than frequent changes.

Leave familiar objects (pictures, magazines, television, radio) in their usual places where the person can see them easily. A tidy, uncluttered house will be less confusing to an impaired person and misplaced items will be easier to find. Some families have found that putting labels on things helps. Labeling drawers "Mary's socks," "Mary's nightgowns" may help.

Remember, however, that with progressive dementing illnesses the person will eventually be unable to read or will not be able to make sense out of what he reads. He may be able to read the words but unable to act on them. Some families then use pictures instead of written messages. For example, it may help to put a picture of a toilet on the bathroom door if the person is in an unfamiliar place or has trouble remembering where the bathroom is.

People are often more confused at night and may get lost going to the bathroom. Strips of reflector tape on the wall from the bedroom to the bathroom help. Night lights will help him see where he is.

Pictures of family members and close friends may help the more confused person remind himself of who these people are. If you are visiting someone in a nursing home, you might try taking along a family picture album. Looking at the pictures may stir bits of pleasant memory in the confused mind.

OVERREACTING OR CATASTROPHIC REACTIONS

Even though Miss Ramirez had told her sister over and over that today was the day to visit the doctor, her sister would not get into the car until she was dragged in, screaming, by two neighbors. All the way to the doctor's office she shouted for help and when she got there she tried to run away.

Mr. Lewis suddenly burst into tears as he tried to tie his shoelaces. He threw the shoes in the wastebasket and locked himself, sobbing, in the bathroom.

Mrs. Coleman described several incidents similar to this one, in which her husband had mislaid his glasses.
　　"You threw out my glasses," he told her.
　　"I didn't touch your glasses," she answered.
　　"That's what you always say," he responded. "How do you explain that they are gone?"
　　"You do this to me every time you lose your glasses."
　　"I did not lose them. You threw them out."
　　Reflecting back, Mrs. Coleman knew that her husband had changed. In the past he would have merely asked her if she knew where his glasses were instead of accusing her and starting an argument.

People with brain diseases often become excessively upset and may experience rapidly changing moods. Strange situations, confusion, groups of people, noises, being asked several questions at once, or being asked to do a task that is difficult for them can precipitate these reactions. The person may weep, blush, or become agitated, angry, or stubborn. He may strike out at those trying to help him. He may cover his distress by denying what he is doing or by accusing other people of things.

When a situation overwhelms the limited thinking capacity of a brain-injured person, he may overreact. Normal people sometimes do this when they are bombarded with more things at one time than they can manage. Impaired people have the same reaction to simpler, everyday experiences. For example,

Every evening, Mrs. Hamilton gets upset and refuses to take a bath. When her daughter insists, she argues and shouts. This makes the rest of the family tense. The whole routine is dreaded by everyone.

Taking a bath actually means that Mrs. Hamilton must think about several things at once; undressing, unbuttoning, finding the bathroom, turning on faucets, and climbing in the tub. At the same time, she feels insecure without clothes on and she feels she has lost her privacy and independence. This is overwhelming for a person who cannot remember doing the thing before, who can't remember how to do all these tasks, and whose mind cannot process all these activities at once. One way to react to this is to refuse to take a bath.

We use the term *catastrophic reaction* to describe this behavior. (The word *catastrophic* is used in a special sense; it does not mean that these situations are necessarily very dramatic or violent.) *Often a catastrophic reaction does not look like behavior caused by a brain illness. The behavior may look as if the person is merely being obstinate, critical, or overemotional.* It may seem inappropriate to get so upset over such a little thing.

Catastrophic reactions are upsetting and exhausting for you and for the confused person. They are especially upsetting when it seems as if the person you are trying to help is being stubborn or critical. The person may get so upset that he refuses necessary care. Learning how to avoid or lessen catastrophic reactions is a major key to easier management of them.

Sometimes catastrophic reactions and forgetfulness are the first behaviors family members see when they begin to realize that something is wrong. The mildly impaired person may benefit by being reassured that his panic is not unusual and that you understand his fear.

The things that can help prevent or reduce catastrophic reactions depend on you, on the impaired individual, and on the extent of his limitations. You will gradually learn how to avoid or limit these reactions. *First, you must fully accept that these behaviors are not just stubbornness or nastiness but a response that the person with a dementing illness cannot help.* The person is not just denying reality or trying to manipulate you. Though it seems strange, you may have more control over the person's reaction than he does.

The best way to manage catastrophic reactions is to stop them before they happen. The things that trigger these outbursts vary from one person to another and from one time to another, but as you learn what upsets your family member, you will be able to reduce the number and frequency of outbursts. Some of the common causes of catastrophic reactions are:

- needing to think about several things at once (for example, all the tasks involved in taking a bath);
- trying to do something that the person can no longer manage;
- being cared for by someone who is rushed or upset;
- not wanting to appear inadequate or unable to do things (for example, if the doctor asks a lot of questions that the person cannot answer);
- being hurried (when he thinks and moves more slowly now);
- not understanding what he was asked to do;
- not understanding what he saw or heard;
- being tired (none of us is at our best when we are tired);
- not feeling well;
- not being able to make himself understood (see also the next section);
- feeling frustrated;
- being treated like a child.

Anything that helps remind the confused person about what is going on, such as following familiar routines, leaving things in familiar places, and written instructions (for people who can manage them), can help to reduce catastrophic reactions. Because catastrophic reactions are precipitated by having to think of several things at once, simplify what the confused person has to think about. Take things one step at a time, and give instructions or information step by step. For example, when you help a person bathe, tell the person one thing at a time. Say, "I'm going to unbutton your shirt" and then reassure him, "It's all right." Say, "Now I'm going to slip your shirt off. That's fine. You're a big help. Now take a step up into the tub. I will hold your arm."

Give the confused person time to respond. He may react slowly and become upset if you rush him. Wait for him. If a person is having frequent catastrophic reactions, try to reduce the confusion around him. This might mean having fewer people in the room, having less noise, turning off the television, or reducing the clutter in the room. The key is to simplify, to reduce the number of signals the impaired, disoriented brain must sort out.

Find things the impaired person can realistically do. If strange places upset him, you may not want to take him on a trip. If he gets tired or upset quickly, plan shorter visits with friends.

Plan demanding tasks for the person's best time of day. Avoid asking him to do things when he is tired. Know what his limits are and try not to push him beyond them.

You can avert some catastrophic reactions by simplifying the task facing the impaired person. Mr. Lewis's family recognized that tying shoelaces had become too difficult for him but that he needed to remain as independent as possible. Buying him slip-on shoes solved the problem. Mrs. Coleman's husband often lost things because he forgot where he put them. She found it helpful to ignore his accusations and help him find his glasses. Knowing that accusing her was his way of reacting to his forgetfulness made it easier for her to accept the insult.

Simplify tasks for him. Do the parts he finds difficult yourself. Families often worry that they are doing too much for a person and might make him more dependent. A good rule of thumb is to let a person do for himself until he shows the *first signs* of frustration, then assist him *before* he becomes more upset. Urging him on will usually only upset him more.

If a person seems more irritable than usual, check carefully for signs of illness or pain. *Even minor illness or discomfort can make the person's thinking worse.* Have the person's medications been changed in the past three weeks? Reactions to medication sometimes cause these outbursts.

Reconsider your approach. Are you unintentionally rushing him? Did you misunderstand him? Did you ignore his protests? Are your behavior and voice communicating your own frustration to him? Although it is easy to treat a person who is so dependent like a child, this may make him angry and precipitate an outburst.

When the person does become upset or resistant, remain calm and remove him from the situation in a quiet, unhurried way. Often the emotional storm will be over as quickly as it began and the confused person will be relieved that the upset is over. His short memory may work to your advantage: he may quickly forget the trouble.

As a person with cognitive impairment becomes upset, his ability to think and reason temporarily declines even more. It is useless to argue with him, explain things to him, or even get him to complete a task when he is in the grip of a catastrophic reaction. Arguing, explaining, or restraining him may make things worse. Help him calm down and relax so that he can think as well as possible. Take him away from what upset him, if possible.

You may lose your temper with a person who is having catastrophic reactions or is unable to do what seems like a simple task. This usually will make the person's behavior worse. Occasionally losing your temper is not a calamity; take a deep breath and try to approach the problem calmly. The person will probably forget your anger much more quickly than you will.

Try not to express your frustration or anger to the confused person. Your frustration will further upset him when he cannot understand your reaction. Speak calmly. Take things one step at a time. Move slowly and quietly. Remember that the person is *not* being obstinate or doing this intentionally.

Gently holding a person's hand or patting him may help calm him. Some people respond to being slowly rocked. Try putting your arms around him and rocking back and forth. Some people will be soothed by this but others may feel that your arms are restraining them and will become more upset. Physically restraining a person often adds to his panic. Restrain a person only if it is absolutely essential and if nothing else works.

If catastrophic reactions are happening often, keeping a log may help you identify their cause. After the outburst is over, write down what happened, when it happened, who was around, and what happened just before the outburst. Look for a pattern: are there events, times, or people that might be triggering upsets? If so, can you avoid them?

These overreactions are distressing to the confused person as well as to you. After he has calmed down, reassure him. Tell him that you recognize his distress and that you still care for him.

If you find that catastrophic reactions are occurring frequently and that you are responding with anger and frustration, this is a warning that you are overtired. You are caught in a vicious circle that is bad for both you and the impaired person. It is essential that you have time away from the person. Read Chapter 10, "Getting Outside Help," and make the effort to get some time off for yourself even if you feel too tired and overwhelmed to do so.

You may feel that none of these suggestions will work, that you are caught in an endless battle. The suggestions we offer may not work, but if you are feeling that nothing will help you, this may be an indication of your own depression. See p. 210. In fact, some things can be found that will reduce catastrophic reactions in most people with dementia.

COMBATIVENESS

Mrs. Frank was having her hair done. The beautician was working on the back of her head and Mrs. Frank kept trying to turn around. When this happened the beautician would turn Mrs. Frank's head back. Then Mrs. Frank began batting at the beautician's hands. She looked as if she were about to cry. Finally, Mrs. Frank turned around in the chair and hit the beautician.

Mr. Williams stood close to a group of nurses who were talking. He bounced up and down on his toes. The nurses ignored him even though he bounced faster and faster. When he began to shout, one of the nurses took his arm to lead him away. He pulled away from her but she held on. When she did not let go, he struck her.

When a person with dementia hits (or bites, pinches, or kicks) another, it is upsetting for everyone. Sometimes this happens frequently and the caregiver or nursing home may feel they cannot continue to provide care.

Combativeness is almost always an extreme catastrophic reaction. It often can be prevented by being alert to the person's signals that his stress level is rising. Perhaps if the beautician had talked to Mrs. Frank about what she was doing and showed her in a mirror how her hair was coming, Mrs. Frank would have understood what was going on and been less upset. Turning and batting at the hairdresser were warnings that she was becoming distressed.

Perhaps Mr. Williams wanted to join the conversation. If the nurses kept a log of his outbursts, they might observe that bouncing on his toes was a sign of his rising agitation. If the nurses had included him in their conversation or suggested something else he might enjoy doing, he might not have gotten upset. Physically holding or pulling someone is often perceived by the person as an attack and leads to an angry response.

When a person becomes agitated, immediately stop whatever is upsetting him and let him relax. Do not continue to push him. Reread the material on catastrophic reactions in this section and in other books (see Appendix 1). Look for ideas for preventing outbursts or stopping them when they first begin. Sometimes small amounts of medication help people who are upset much of the time; however, medication is not a substitute for changing the things going on around the person or how caregivers respond to him.

PROBLEMS WITH SPEECH AND COMMUNICATION

You may have problems understanding or communicating verbally with the impaired person. There are two kinds of problems of communication: the problems a person with a dementing illness has in expressing himself to others, and the problems he has in understanding what people say to him.

Problems the Impaired Person Has in Making Himself Understood

The nature of communication problems and whether or not they will get worse depend on the specific disease. Do not assume that things will get worse.

Some people have only occasional difficulty finding words. They may have trouble remembering the names of familiar objects or people. They may substitute a word that sounds similar, such as saying "tee" for "tie" or "wrong" for "ring." They may substitute a word with a related meaning, such as saying "wedding" for "ring" or "music thing" for "piano." They may describe the object they cannot name, such as "it's a thing that goes around" for "ring" or "it's to dress up" for "necktie." Such problems usually do not interfere with your ability to understand what the person means.

Some people have difficulty communicating their thoughts.

Mr. Zuckerman was trying to say that he had never had a neurological examination before. He said, "I really have not, not really, ever have been done, I have never . . ."

In some language problems the person cannot communicate the whole thought but he can express a few of the words in the thought.

Mr. Mason wanted to say that he was worried about missing his ride home. He could say only, "Bus, home."

Sometimes people are able to ramble on quite fluently, and it seems as if they are talking a lot. They will often string together commonly used phrases, so what they say at first seems to make sense, but upon reflection the listener may not be sure he understood the thought being expressed.

Mrs. Simmons said, "If I tell you something, I might stop in the middle and . . . I'll be real sure about what I've done, . . . said, . . . sometimes I stop right in the middle and I can't get on with . . . from . . . that. In past records . . . I can be so much more sure of the . . . After I get my bearing again I can just go on as if nothing happened. We thought it was high time to start remembering. I just love to . . . have to . . . talk."

In these examples, it is possible to understand what the person is saying if we know the context.

When the limitations in ability to communicate frustrate the confused person and frustrate you, they can lead to a series of catastrophic reactions. For example, the impaired person may burst into tears or stamp out of the room when no one understands him.

Sometimes a person is able to conceal language problems. When a doctor asks a person if he knows the word for a wristwatch (a common question used to evaluate language problems), the patient may say, "Of course I do. Why do you ask?" or "I don't want to talk about it. Why are you bothering me?" when he cannot think of the word.

Some people begin to use curse words, even if they have never used such language before. This disturbing behavior appears to be a strange quirk of diseases that take away important language skills. It is commonly seen after a stroke to the language area of the brain. It must be like opening a "mental dictionary" to say something and having only curse words come out. One person who was asked why he cursed the day care staff said, "These are the only words I have." This behavior is rarely deliberate and sometimes upsets the person as much as it does you.

In severe language problems, the person may remember only a few key words, such as "No," which he may use whether or not he means it. Eventually the person may be unable to speak. He may repeat a phrase, cry out intermittently, or mumble unintelligible phrases. In some language problems there seems to be no meaning in the jumbled words the person produces. Family members and caregivers often grieve when this happens and they can no longer communicate verbally with a loved one. We sense that language is the most human of mental skills. In some families the person continues to be a friend and companion—although a forgetful one— for a long time, but when he is unable to communicate anymore, the family feels they have lost that companionship. You may worry that the person will be sick or in pain and unable to tell you.

How you help the impaired person communicate depends on the kind of difficulty he is having. If he has been diagnosed as having had a stroke that interferes with language function, he should be seen by a stroke rehabilitation team as soon as he has recovered from the acute phase of his illness. Much can be done to rehabilitate stroke victims.

If the person is having difficulty finding the right word, it is usually less frustrating for him to have you supply the word for him than it is to let him search and struggle for the word. When he uses the wrong word and you know what he means, it may be helpful to supply the correct word. However, if doing so upsets him, it may be best to ignore it. When you don't know what he means, ask him to describe it or point to it. For example, the nurse did not know what Mrs. Kealey meant when she said, "I like your wrong." If the nurse had said, "What?" Mrs. Kealey might have become frustrated in trying to express herself. Instead, the nurse asked, "Describe a wrong." Mrs. Kealey said, "It's a thing that goes around." "Point to it," said the nurse. Mrs. Kealey did and the nurse responded, "Oh, yes, my ring." If the person gets lost in the middle of what he is saying, repeat his last few words—this may help get him started again.

When a person is having trouble expressing an idea, you may be able to guess what he is trying to say. *Ask* him if you are guessing correctly. You might guess wrong, and if you act on an erroneous guess you will add to the confused person's frustration. Say, "Are you worried about catching the bus home?" or "Are you saying you have never had an examination like this before?"

People with dementia communicate better when they are relaxed. Try to appear relaxed yourself (even if you have to pretend) and create a calm environment. Never rush the person who is trying to make himself understood.

When you cannot communicate in other ways, you can often guess what a person is trying to tell you. Remember that his feeling is usually accurate, although it may be exaggerated or not appropriate to the actual situation, but his explanation of why he feels a certain way may be confused. If Mr. Mason says, "Bus, home," and you say, "You aren't going on the bus," you will not have responded to his feelings. If you correctly guess that he is worried about going home, you can reassure him by saying, "Your daughter is coming for you at 3:00."

If a person can still say a few words, or shake or nod his head, you will need to ask him simplified questions about his needs. Say "Do you hurt?" or "Does this hurt?" Point to a body part rather than name it.

When a person cannot communicate, you must establish a regular routine of checking his comfort. Make sure that clothing is comfortable, that the room is warm, that there are no rashes or sores on his skin, that he is taken to the toilet on a regular schedule, and that he is not hungry or sleepy.

When a person repeats the same thing over and over, try distracting him. Change the subject, ask him to sing a familiar song, or talk about the feelings behind the statement. For example, if the person is searching for his mother, try saying, "You must miss your mother" or "Tell me what your mother was like."

Problems the Impaired Person Has in Understanding Others

Often people with brain impairments have difficulty comprehending or understanding what you and others tell them. This is a problem that families sometimes misinterpret as uncooperative behavior. For example, you may say, "Mother, I am going to the grocery store. I will be back in half an hour. Do you understand?" Your mother may say, "Oh yes, I understand," when in fact she does not understand at all and will get upset as soon as you are out of sight.

People with dementing illnesses also quickly forget what they did understand. When you give them a careful explanation, they may forget the first part of the explanation before you get to the rest of it.

People with dementia can have trouble understanding written information even when they can still read the letters or words. For example, to determine exactly what a person can still comprehend, we may hand him a newspaper and have him read the headline, which he may be able to do correctly. Then when we hand him the written instructions "Close your eyes," he does not close his eyes although he correctly reads the words aloud. This indicates that he cannot understand what he is repeating.

Jan told her mother that lunch was in the refrigerator. She left a note on the refrigerator door to remind her mother. Her mother could read the note but not understand what it said, so she didn't eat her lunch. Instead she complained that she was hungry.

This can be infuriating until you consider that reading and understanding are two different skills, one of which may be lost without the loss of the other. It is not safe to assume that a person can understand and act upon messages he can hear or read. You will need to observe him to know whether he *does* act upon them. If he does not act on instructions, assume he has a problem in understanding language.

The person who can understand what he is told in person may not be able to comprehend what he is told over the telephone. When a person with a dementing illness does not understand what you told him, the problem is not inattentiveness or willfulness, but an inability of the malfunctioning brain to make sense out of the words it hears.

There are several ways to improve your verbal communication with a person who has a dementing illness.

1. Make sure he does hear you. Hearing acuity declines in later life and many older people have a hearing deficit.
2. Lower the tone (pitch) of your voice. A raised pitch is a nonverbal signal that one is upset. A lower pitch also is easier for a hearing-impaired person to hear.
3. Eliminate distracting noises or activities. Both because of the possible hearing deficit and because of the impaired person's inability to sort things out, he may be unable to understand you when there are other noises or distractions around him.
4. Use short words and short, simple sentences. Avoid complex sentences. Instead of saying, "I think I'll take the car to the garage tonight instead of in the morning because in the morning I will get caught in traffic," just say, "I'm going to take the car to the garage now."
5. Ask only *one* simple question at a time. If you repeat the question, repeat it exactly. Avoid questions like "Do you want an apple or pie for dessert or do you want to have dessert later?" Complex choices may overload the person's decision-making ability.
6. Ask the person to do one task at a time, not several. He may not be able to remember several tasks or may be unable to make sense out of your message. Most of the things we ask a person to do—take a bath, get ready for bed, put on a coat so we can go to the store—involve several tasks. The impaired person may not be able to sort out these tasks. We help him by breaking down each project into individual steps and asking the person to do one step at a time.
7. Speak slowly, and wait for the person to respond. The impaired person's response may be much slower than what seems natural to us. Wait.

You can improve communication with the person and your understanding of his needs without the usual forms of conversation. People communicate through both what they say and the way they move their faces, eyes, hands, and bodies. Everyone uses this nonverbal system of communication without thinking about it. For example, we say, "he looks mad," "you can tell by the way they look at each other that they are in love," "you can tell by the way he walks who's boss," "I know you aren't listening to me," etc. These are all things we are communicating without words. Brain-impaired people can remain sensitive to these nonverbal messages when they cannot understand language well, and they often remain able to express themselves nonverbally.

For example, if you are tired, you may send nonverbal messages that upset the impaired person. Then he may get agitated, which will upset you. Your hands, face, and eyes will reveal your distress, which further agitates the confused person. If you are unaware of the significance of body language, you may wonder what happened to get him upset. In fact, we all do this all the time. For example, "No, I am not upset," you tell a spouse. "But I know you are," he replies. He can tell by the set of your shoulders that you are upset.

If you are living with a person suffering from dementia, you have already learned to identify many of the nonverbal clues that he sends to make his needs known. Here are some additional ways to communicate nonverbally:

1. Remain pleasant, calm, and supportive. (Even if you feel upset, your body language will help to keep the confused person calm.)
2. Smile, take the person's hand, put an arm around his waist, or in some other physical way express affection.
3. Look directly at him. *Look* to see if the person is paying attention to you. If he uses body language to signal that he is not paying attention, try again in a few minutes.
4. Use other signals besides words: point, touch, hand the person things. Demonstrate an action or describe it with your hands (for example, brushing teeth). Sometimes if you get him started he will be able to continue the task.
5. Avoid assuming complex reasons for the person's behavior. Because the person's brain can no longer process information properly, he experiences the world around and within differently from the way you see things. Since nonverbal communication depends on a whole different set of skills from verbal communication, you may be better able to understand him by considering what it *feels* like he is saying rather than what you *think* he is saying, either through actions or words.

Even when a person is severely confused and unable to communicate, he or she still needs and enjoys affection. Holding hands, hugging, or just sitting companionably together is an important way to continue to communicate. The physical care that you give a severely impaired person communicates to him your concern and that he is protected.

LOSS OF COORDINATION

Because dementing illnesses affect many parts of the brain, the person with a dementia may lose the ability to make his hands and fingers do certain familiar tasks. He may understand what he wants to do, and although his hands and fingers are not stiff or weak, the message just does not get through from the mind to the fingers. Doctors use the word *apraxia* to describe this. An early sign of apraxia is a change in a person's handwriting. Another, later indication is a change in the way a person walks. Apraxias may progress gradually or change abruptly, depending on the disease. For example, at first a person may seem only slightly unsteady when walking, but he may gradually change to a slow, shuffling gait.

It can be difficult for a person not trained to evaluate dementing illness to separate problems of memory (can the person remember what he is supposed to do?) from problems of apraxia (can the person not make his muscles do what they are supposed to do?). Both problems occur when the brain is damaged by disease. It is not always necessary to distinguish between them in order to help the person manage as independently as possible.

When apraxia begins to affect walking, the person may be slightly unsteady. You must watch for this and provide either a handrail or someone to hold on to when the person is using stairs and stepping up onto or down off of a curb.

Losses of coordination and manual skills may lead to problems in daily living such as bathing, managing buttons or zippers, dressing, pouring a glass of water, and eating. Dialing a telephone requires good coordination, and a person who does not appear to have any motor impairment may in fact be unable to dial a telephone to call for help. A pushbutton telephone may help, but it may also be difficult for the confused person to learn the new skill of using a touch-tone phone.

Some of the things a person has difficulty with may have to be given up. Others can be modified so that the impaired person can remain partially independent. When you modify a task, the key is to simplify, rather than change, the task. Because of his intellectual impairment, the person with a dementing illness may be unable to learn a new, simpler task. Consider the nature of each task. Ask yourself if it can be done in a simpler way. For example, shoes that slip on are easier than shoes with laces. Soup is easier to drink out of a mug than to spoon from a bowl. Finger foods are more easily managed than things that must be cut with knife and fork. Can the person do part of the task if you do the difficult part? You may already have discovered that the person can dress himself if you help with buttons or snaps.

A person may feel tense, embarrassed, or worried about his clumsiness. He may try to conceal his increasing disability by refusing to participate in activities. For example,

Mrs. Fisher had always enjoyed knitting. When she abruptly gave up this hobby her daughter could not understand what had happened. Mrs. Fisher said only that she no longer liked to knit. In fact, her increasing apraxia was making knitting impossible, and she was ashamed of her awkwardness.

A relaxed atmosphere often helps make the person's clumsiness less apparent. It is not unusual for a person to have more difficulty with a task when he is feeling tense.

Sometimes a person can do something one time and not another time. This may be a characteristic of the brain impairment, not laziness. Being hurried, being watched, being upset, or being tired can affect an impaired person's ability to do things—just as it does to a normal person. Having a brain disease makes these natural fluctuations more dramatic. Sometimes people can do one task with no problem, such as zipping up trousers, and be unable to do another similar task, such as zipping up a jacket. It may seem that the person is being difficult, but the reason may actually be that one task is impossible because it is different in some way.

Sometimes a person can do a task if you break it down into a series of smaller tasks and take one step at a time. For example, brushing your teeth involves picking up the toothbrush, putting the toothpaste on it, putting the toothbrush in your mouth, brushing, rinsing, etc. Gently remind the person of each step. It may help to demonstrate. You may have to repeat each step several times. Sometimes it helps to put a familiar tool, such as a spoon or comb, into the person's hand and gently start his arm moving in the right direction. Beginning the motion seems to help the brain remember the task.

An occupational therapist is trained to assess what motor skills the person has retained and how he may make the best use of them. If you can obtain an occupational therapy evaluation, this information can help you give the confused person the help he needs without taking away his independence.

In the later stages of some of the dementing diseases, extensive loss of muscle control occurs and the person may bump into things and fall down. This will be discussed in Chapter 5.

People with dementing illnesses may have other diseases that also interfere with their ability to do daily tasks. Part of the problem may be in the muscles or joints and another part of the problem in the impaired brain. Such complicating conditions include tremors (shaking), muscle weakness, joint or bone diseases such as arthritis, or stiffness caused by medications.

There are many techniques and devices to help people with physical limitations remain independent. When you consider such techniques or devices, remember that most of them require the ability to learn to do something a new way or to learn to use a new gadget. People with dementing illnesses may not be able to learn the new skills needed.

Some people have tremors. These are shaking movements of the hands or body. These can make many activities difficult for a person, but an occupational therapist or physical therapist may be able to show you how to minimize the effects of tremors.

Some people with neurological conditions, especially Parkinson's disease, have difficulty starting a movement or may get "stuck" in the middle of a movement. This can be frustrating for both of you. If this is a problem, here are some helpful hints:

1. If the person becomes "glued to the floor" while walking, tell him to walk toward a goal or to look at a spot on the floor a few feet in front of him. This may help him get going again.
2. It may be easier to get out of a chair that has armrests. Also, try raising the sitting person's center of gravity by raising the chair seat two to four inches. A firm seat is needed. Use a firm pillow or a higher chair such as a dining room chair or a director's chair. Avoid low chairs with soft cushions. Instruct the person to move forward to the edge of the chair and spread his feet about one foot apart to give a wider base to stand on. Ask the person to put his hands on the armrests and then to rock back and forth to gain momentum. On the count of 3, have him get up quickly. Have him take time to get his balance before he begins to walk.
3. Sitting down in a chair may be easier to do when the person puts his hands on the armrests, bends forward as far as possible, and sits down slowly.

Muscle weakness or stiffness may occur when a person does not move around much. Exercise is important for memory-impaired people.

Occasionally a person who is taking one of the major tranquilizers or neuroleptic drugs will get stiff and rigid or may become restless. These may be side effects of the medication. They can be very uncomfortable. Notify your doctor. He can change the dosage or give another medication to overcome this effect.

LOSS OF SENSE OF TIME

The uncanny ability normal individuals have for judging the passage of time is one of the first losses of a dementia patient. He may repeatedly ask you what time it is, feel that you have left him for hours when you are out of sight for a few minutes, or want to leave a place as soon as he has arrived. It is not hard to understand this behavior when you consider that in order to know how much time has passed, one must be able to remember what one has done in the immediate past. The person who forgets quickly has no way to measure the passage of time.

In addition to this defect of memory, it appears that dementing diseases can affect the internal clock that keeps us on a reasonably regular schedule of sleeping, waking, and eating. It will be helpful to you to recognize that this behavior is not deliberate (although it can be irritating). It is the result of the loss of brain function.

The ability to read a clock may be lost early in the course of the disease. Even when a person can look at the clock and say, "It is 3:15," he may be unable to make sense out of this information.

Not being able to keep track of time can worry the forgetful person. Many of us, throughout our lives, are dependent upon a regular time schedule. Not knowing the time can make a person worry that he will be late, be forgotten, miss the bus, overstay his welcome, miss lunch, or miss his ride home. The confused person may not know just what he is worried about, but a general feeling of anxiety may make him ask you what time it is. And, of course, as soon as you answer him, he will forget the whole conversation and ask again.

Sometimes a person feels that you have deserted him when you have been gone only briefly. This is because he has no sense of how long ago you left. Setting a timer or an old-fashioned hourglass or writing a note— "I am in the backyard gardening and will be in at 3 P.M."—might help the person wait more patiently for your return. Be sure to select a cue (timer, note) that he can still comprehend. Perhaps you can think of other ways to reduce this behavior. For example,

> *When Mr. and Mrs. Jenkins went to dinner at their son's house, Mr. Jenkins would almost immediately put his hat and coat on and insist that it was time to go home. When he could be persuaded to stay for the meal, he insisted on leaving immediately afterward. His son thought he was just being rude.*

Things went more smoothly when the family understood that this was because the unfamiliar house, the added confusion, and Mr. Jenkins's lost sense of time upset him. The family thought back over Mr. Jenkins's life and hit upon an old social habit that helped them. In earlier years, he had enjoyed watching the football game after Sunday dinner. Now his son turned on the TV as soon as Mr. Jenkins finished eating. Since this was an old habit, Mr. Jenkins would stay for about an hour, giving his wife time to visit, before he got restless for home.

SYMPTOMS THAT ARE BETTER SOMETIMES AND WORSE AT OTHER TIMES

Families often observe that the person can do something one time but not another time.

"In the morning my mother does not need as much help as she does in the evening."

"My wife can use the bathroom alone at home, but she insists she needs help at our daughter's house."

"My husband does not get as angry and upset at day care as he does at home. Is this because he is angry with me?"

"Bill said a whole sentence yesterday, but today I can't understand a thing he says. Was he trying harder yesterday?"

Fluctuations in ability are common in people who suffer from dementia. Well people also have fluctuations in ability, but they are less noticeable. People with dementia have good days and bad days; some are better in the morning, when they are rested; some have more problems in less familiar settings; some do better when they feel more relaxed. Some fluctuations have no explanation. Whatever the likely reason, such fluctuations are normal and do not signal a change in the course of the disease.

People with dementia are more vulnerable than others to minor changes in health. (See Chapter 6.) An abrupt change in the ability to do something or in overall level of function may indicate a medication reaction or a new illness. If you suspect this kind of change, it is important to contact the person's physician.

The brain damage itself accounts for some changes in ability. It is possible that damaged nerve cells that fail most of the time do work occasionally. It is also possible that less damaged or undamaged areas can intermittently take over and temporarily "fix" a defective system.

All of these causes for variation in ability are beyond the person's deliberate control. People with dementia are usually trying as hard as they can. You can help them the most by learning which things in their environment bring out their best and which things cause more disability.

4

PROBLEMS IN INDEPENDENT LIVING

AS A PERSON BEGINS to develop a dementing illness, she may begin to have difficulty managing independently. You may suspect that she is mismanaging her money, worry that she should not be driving, or wonder if she should be living alone. People with dementing illnesses often appear to be managing well, and they may insist that they are fine and that you are interfering. It can be difficult to know when you should take over and how much you should take over. It can also be painful to take away these outward symbols of a person's independence, especially if the confused person adamantly refuses to move, to stop driving, or to relinquish her financial responsibilities.

Part of the reason that making these changes is so difficult is because they symbolize giving up independence and responsibility, and therefore all of the family members may have strong feelings about them. (We will discuss these role changes in Chapter 11.) Making necessary changes will be easier when you understand the feelings involved.

The first step in deciding whether the time has come to make changes in a person's independence is to get an evaluation. This will tell you what the person is still able to do and what she is no longer able to do. It can also give you the authority to insist upon necessary changes. When a professional evaluation is not available, you and your family must analyze each task as thoroughly and objectively as possible, and decide whether the person can still do specific tasks *completely*, *safely*, and *without becoming upset*.

A dementing illness brings about many kinds of losses. It means losing control over one's daily activities, losing independence, losing skills, and losing the ability to do those things that make one feel useful or important. A dementing illness limits the possibilities the future can hold. While others can look forward to things getting better, the ill person must gradually realize that her future is limited. Perhaps the most terrible loss of all is the loss of memory. Losing one's memories means losing one's day-to-day connections with others and with one's past. The far past may seem like the present. Without a memory of today or an understanding that the past is past, the future ceases to have meaning.

As losses accumulate in anyone's life, it is natural for him or her to cling even more tightly to the things that remain. Understandably, a confused person might respond to such changes with resistance, denial, or anger. The confused person's need for familiar surroundings and the determination of most people not to be a burden on anyone make it understandable that the disabled person will not want to give up these things. To accept that, she would have to face the extent and finality of her illness, which she may not be able to do.

In addition, the person may be unable to make complete sense out of what is going on. Even early in the disease the person may completely forget recent events. If she has no recollection of leaving the stove on or of having an auto accident, she may reasonably insist that she can take care of herself or that she is still a good driver. She is not "denying" the reality of her situation; she cannot remember the mistakes that are evidence of her impairment. If she is not able to assess her own limitations, it may seem to her as if things are being unfairly taken away from her and that her family is "taking over." By recognizing how she may feel, you may be able to find ways to help her make the necessary changes and still feel that she is in control of her life.

WHEN A PERSON MUST GIVE UP A JOB

The time when the person must give up a job depends on the kind of job she has and whether she must drive as part of her job. Sometimes an employer will tell you or the impaired person that she must retire. Some employers will be willing to maintain a person in a job that is not too demanding. Sometimes the family must make this decision. You may realize that this time has come.

If the person must give up her job, there are two areas that you must consider: the emotional and psychological adjustments involved in such a major change, and the financial changes that will be involved. A person's job is a key part of her sense of who she is. It helps her to feel that she is a valued member of society. The impaired person may resist giving up her job or may insist that nothing is wrong. Her adjustment to retirement may be a painful and distressing time. If these things happen, a counselor or social worker can be invaluable in helping you.

It is important that you consider the financial future of the impaired person. (This will be discussed in Chapter 15.) Retirement can create special problems. Individuals who are forced to retire early because of a dementing illness should be entitled to the same retirement and disability benefits as a person with any other disabling *disease*. In some cases, benefits have been denied on the erroneous grounds that "senility" is not a disease and the impaired person has been forced to resign or take an early retirement. This can substantially reduce her income. If this happens, you may want to obtain legal counsel.

Federal law (the Social Security Disability Act) provides assistance to people who become disabled. The disabled person must have worked 20 out of the past 40 calendar quarters and she must no longer be able to do gainful work because of a medically determinable physical or mental illness that will result in death or that has lasted for at least 12 months. People with dementia are sometimes inappropriately denied benefits. The Alzheimer's Association has prepared a disability log, which will help you gather the information necessary to demonstrate that the person is disabled.

Many people are denied disability on their initial application and give up. Persistence through the appeals process often results in reversal of the initial decision. (See Chapter 15.)

WHEN A PERSON CAN NO LONGER MANAGE MONEY

The impaired person may be unable to balance her checkbook, she may be unable to make change, or she may become irresponsible with her money. Occasionally, when a person can no longer manage her money, she may accuse others of stealing from her.

Said Mr. Fried, "My wife has kept the books for the family business for years. I knew something was wrong when my accountant came to me and told me the books were a terrible mess."

Mr. Rogers said, "My wife was giving money to the neighbors, hiding it in the waste basket, and losing her purse. So I took her purse—and her money—away from her. Then she was always saying I stole her money."

Since money often represents independence, sometimes people are unwilling to give up control of their finances.

You may be able to take over the household accounts by simply correcting the person's efforts. If you have to take the person's checkbook away against her wishes it may help to write down a memo such as "my son John now takes care of my checkbook" and put this note where the confused person can refer to it to refresh her memory.

It can be upsetting when a person accuses others of stealing, but this is easier to understand when you think about human nature. We have been taught all our lives to be careful with money, and when money disappears most of us wonder if it was stolen. As a person's brain becomes less able to remember what is really happening, it is not surprising that she becomes anxious and suspicious that her money is being stolen. Avoid getting into arguments about it, since they may upset her more.

Some families find that giving the forgetful person a small amount of spending money (perhaps small change or one-dollar bills) helps. If it is lost or given away, it is only a minimal amount. People often need to know that they have a little bit of cash on hand, and this is a way around conflicts about money. One peculiarity of the dementing diseases is that they can cause a person to lose the ability to make change before she loses the knowledge that she needs money.

Mrs. Hutchinson had always been fiercely independent about her money, so Mr. Hutchinson gave her a purse with some change in it. He put her name and address in it in case she lost her purse. She insisted on paying her hairdresser by check long after she could not responsibly manage a checkbook. So Mr. Hutchinson gave her some checks stamped VOID by the bank. Each week she gives one to the hairdresser. Mr. Hutchinson privately arranged with the hairdresser that these would be accepted and that he would pay the bills.

This may seem extreme. It may also seem unfair to dupe the confused person this way. In reality, this allows a sick woman to continue to feel independent and it allows her tired and burdened husband to manage the finances and keep the peace.

Money matters can cause serious problems, especially when the person is also suspicious or when other members of the family disagree. (It may be helpful here to read Chapters 8 and 11.) Your ingenuity can be a great help to you in making money matters less distressing.

WHEN A PERSON CAN NO LONGER DRIVE SAFELY

The time may come when you realize that your parent or spouse can no longer drive safely. While some people will recognize their limits, others may be unwilling to give up driving. As a group, people with dementia who continue to drive are more likely to have accidents.

For most experienced drivers, driving is a skill so well learned that it is partly "automatic." A person can go back and forth to work every day with her mind on other things—perhaps dictating or listening to music. It does not take much concentration to drive, but if the traffic pattern should suddenly change, she can rely on the mind to focus on the road immediately and respond swiftly to a crisis. Because driving is a well-learned skill, a confused person can still *appear* to be driving well when she is not really a safe driver. Driving requires a highly complex interaction of eyes, brain, and muscle, and the ability to solve complicated problems quickly. A person who is still apparently driving safely may have lost the ability to respond appropriately to an unexpected problem on the road. She may be relying entirely on the habits of driving and may be unable to change quickly from a habitual response to a new response when the situation demands it.

Often people make the decision themselves to stop driving when they feel that they "aren't as sharp as they used to be." But if they do not, you have a responsibility to them and to others to assess carefully whether or not the person's driving is dangerous, and to intervene when it is. This may be one of the first situations in which you take a decision out of the hands of the impaired person. You may feel hesitant to do this, but you will probably be relieved once you have stopped a forgetful person from driving. To decide whether the time has come, look at the skills that a person needs to drive safely and evaluate whether the confused person still has these skills—both in the car and in other situations.

1. *Good vision*: A person must have good vision, or vision corrected with glasses, and be able to see clearly, both in front and out of the corners of her eyes (peripheral vision) so that she sees things coming toward her from the sides.
2. *Good hearing*: A person must be able to hear well or have her hearing corrected with a hearing aid, so that she is alert to the sounds of approaching cars, horns, and so forth.
3. *Quick reaction time*: A driver must be able to react quickly—to turn, to brake, and to avoid accidents. Older people's reaction time, when it is formally tested, is slightly slower than that of young people, but in well older people it is usually not slow enough to interfere with driving. However, if you see that a person seems slowed down or reacts slowly or inappropriately to sudden changes around the house, this should alert you to the possibility of the same limitations when she is driving.
4. *Ability to make decisions*: A driver must be able to make *appropriate* decisions rapidly and *calmly*. The ability to make a correct decision

when a child darts in front of the car, a horn honks, and a truck is approaching all at once necessitates being able to solve complicated, unfamiliar problems quickly and without panicking. People with a dementing illness often rely on habitual responses that may not be the correct responses in a driving situation. Some people also get confused and upset when several things happen at once. You will see these problems, if they are occurring, around the house as well as in the car.

5. *Good coordination*: Eyes, hands, and feet must all still work together well to handle a car safely. If a person is getting clumsy, or if her way of walking has changed, it should alert you that she may also have trouble getting her foot on the brake.

6. *Alertness to what is going on around her*: A driver must be alert to all that is going on without becoming upset or confused. If a person is "missing things" that happen around her, she may no longer be a safe driver.

Sometimes driving behaviors alert you to problems. Forgetful people may get lost on routes that would not have confused them previously. Being lost can distract the driver and further interfere with her ability to react quickly. Sometimes driving too slowly is a clue that the driver is uncertain of her skills—but this does not mean that every cautious driver is an impaired driver.

Confused people may become angry or aggressive when they drive or they may inappropriately believe that other drivers are "out to get them." This is dangerous. Occasionally a person with a dementing illness is also drinking too much. Even small amounts of alcohol impair the driving ability of people with a brain injury. This is a dangerous combination, and you must intervene.

If you are concerned about a person's driving ability, you might first approach the problem by discussing it frankly with her. Even though a person is cognitively impaired she is still able to participate in decisions that involve her. How you initiate such a discussion may affect her response. People with brain impairments are sometimes less able to tolerate criticism than when they were well, so you will want to use tact in such a discussion. If you say, "Your driving is terrible, you are getting lost, and you're just not safe," a person may feel she has to defend herself and may argue with you. Instead, by gently saying, "You are getting absent-minded about stoplights," you may be able to give a person an "easy way out." Giving up driving can mean admitting one's increasing limitations. Look for ways to help the person save face and maintain her self-image at the same time you react to the need for safety. Try offering alternatives: "I'll drive today and you can look at the scenery." As a last resort some families have sold the car and told the impaired person that it could not be repaired.

Sometimes a person will absolutely refuse to give up driving, despite your tact. It may help to enlist the support of the doctor or a family lawyer. Some physicians will write an order on a prescription pad that says, "Do not drive." Families report that having the physician be the "bad guy" takes great pressure off the caregiver. Some states require that physicians report drivers with dementia; other states are frustratingly lax. Often a person will cooperate with the instructions of an authority when she may regard your advice as nagging. As a last resort, you may have to take away the car keys. If you cannot do this, you can make it impossible to start a car by removing the distributor cap or the wire to the distributor. This is small and easy to replace when you want to drive. A gas station attendant can show you how to do this.

States vary in their policies regarding a driver's license. In some states the Department of Motor Vehicles will issue any nondriver an identification card that can be used to cash checks, etc. They may also investigate and sometimes suspend a license if they receive a written opinion from a physician that the person's health makes her an unsafe driver. Some states issue limited licenses that allow a person to drive only under certain circumstances, such as only in daylight. Call the state police or the Department of Motor Vehicles to find out the policy in your area. If a person has been told by a physician not to drive, the caregiver may be found to have been negligent if the person has an accident. If someone is injured in the accident, this could bankrupt the family. One wife who did not drive sold the car and put the money in a cookie jar. Every week she added the amount they used to spend on gas, maintenance, and car insurance. She said it was easier to spend money on taxis knowing they used to spend it on the car.

WHEN A PERSON CAN NO LONGER LIVE ALONE

When a person has lived alone but can no longer do so, the move to live with someone else can be difficult for everyone. Some people welcome the sense of security that living with others provides. Others vigorously resist giving up their independence.

Often patients go through a series of stages from complete independence to living with someone. When a gradual transition from independence is possible, it may be easier for the person to adjust and it may postpone the time when she must live with someone. For example, at first the help of the neighbors or a Meals-on-Wheels program may be adequate; later, a family member or a paid helper may spend part of the day with the confused person. A few people may need someone to come in only to give medications or help with a meal, not constant supervision.

When You Suspect That Someone Living Alone Is Getting Confused

You need to be alert to the possibility that the person's ability to function alone may change suddenly: some minor stress or even a mild cold can make her worse. Or, you may not notice the gradual, insidious decline until something happens. Families often wait too long before taking action.

When things do go wrong, the person may react by trying to "cover up." Some confused people do not realize they have problems; others may blame the family or withdraw. Close family members may also deny that there are problems. Therefore, it can be difficult to know for sure what is going on. Here are some questions to consider when deciding whether a person who is living alone is in need of help:

Changes in Personality or Habits

Is she uncharacteristically apathetic, negative, pessimistic, suspicious, or unusually fearful of crime?

Does she insist that everything is fine, or not admit that there are any problems when you know there have been problems?

Is the person able to manage her own personal care and grooming? Some forgetful people wear dirty clothes, forget (or refuse) to bathe or brush their teeth, or in other ways neglect themselves.

Has she become isolated? Does she say she is going out when she does not?

Telephone Calls

Have her conversations become increasingly vague? (Details require more memory.)

Do conversations ramble, or does she seem to forget what she was saying? Does she repeat herself?

Does she become "edgy" when talking on the telephone, more than she used to? Is she less tolerant of frustration?

Are you getting fewer phone calls from her, too many calls, or calls late at night?

Does she repeat the same story at each conversation as if it were new?

Letters

Has she stopped writing letters or notes, or are her letters uncharacteristically rambling? Has her handwriting changed?

Meals and Medications

Is the person eating her meals and taking her medications correctly? A forgetful person may not eat, or may eat only sweets even when you have provided a hot meal. The person may take too much medicine or forget her medicine. This can make her mental impairment worse and can jeopardize her physical health. If the person is safe in other ways, she may be able to live alone if someone else helps daily with food and medicine, but it has been our experience that people who forget to eat properly are experiencing sufficient cognitive impairment that they probably cannot safely live alone.

Is the person forgetting to turn off the stove or burning the food? People who appear to be managing well often forget to turn off the stove. Has she stopped cooking? Are pots burned? Is the person using candles or matches? It can be hard to believe that a person is really a danger to herself when she looks so well, but fire is a real and serious hazard. Cases of severe or even fatal accidental burns are not uncommon. If you suspect that the person is forgetting to turn off the stove, you must intervene.

Other Problems

Is the person wandering away from home? She could get lost or be robbed or assaulted. Is she wandering around outside at night? Such behavior is dangerous. Have her friends or neighbors called you with concerns about her behavior or safety? Has she failed to keep appointments or not come to family events? Has she given you confusing reports of a mishap, such as a car accident? Did she retire from work early or abruptly?

Is the person keeping the house tidy, reasonably clean, and free of hazards? Forgetful people may spill water in the kitchen or bathroom and forget to clean it up. A person can slip and fall on a wet floor. Sometimes people forget to wash the dishes or forget to flush the toilet or in other ways create unsanitary conditions. If the house is badly cluttered, they can trip and fall. A confused person may pile up newspapers and rags, which become a fire hazard. Does the house smell of urine? This is a signal that the person is unable to manage alone or is ill.

Is the person keeping herself warm? A forgetful person may keep her house too cold or dress improperly. Her body temperature can drop dangerously if she does not keep herself warm. In hot weather the confused person may dress too warmly or may be afraid to open the house for adequate ventilation. This can lead to heat stroke.

Is the person acting in response to "paranoid" ideas or unrealistic suspiciousness? Such behavior can get her in trouble in the community. Sometimes people call the police because of their fears and make their neighbors angry. Sometimes, too, confused elderly people become the targets of malicious teenagers. Such problems may occur in suburban neighborhoods as well as in the inner city.

Is the person showing good judgment? Some confused people show poor judgment about whom they let in the house and can be robbed by the people they invite in, or they may give away money or do other inappropriate things.

Who is paying the bills? Often the first indication family members have that something is wrong is when the heat or water is shut off because the bill has not been paid or because the person will not let the meter reader in. The person may stop balancing her checkbook or her spending habits may change.

Such clues indicate that *something* may be wrong—but not necessarily that the person has a dementing illness. Once you are aware that there may be a problem, it is essential to get a complete assessment for the person. These changes can indicate many other treatable conditions.

What You Can Do

Contact the Alzheimer's Association chapter in your community. Most chapters have had experience helping families who live at a distance and can give you valuable information. Talk to neighbors and other family members to get as complete a story as possible. If the person lives in a city, talk to a close friend of the person, an apartment house neighbor, or a doorman. If she lives in a rural area, talk to the mail carrier, bank manager, clergyman, or neighbor. They may be aware of problems. Give these people your telephone number and ask them to alert you if there are problems.

Visit in person to assess the situation and to arrange for a diagnosis. Talk to the Alzheimer's Association and the office on aging in your relative's town. They will be able to tell you about local resources.

Sometimes a person can continue to live independently for a while if you can arrange for supervision. Perhaps her physician can give you an idea of how able the person is to continue functioning alone. In major cities there are social workers who will, for a fee, function as a stand-in relative, taking a person for appointments, helping with the checkbook, and keeping an eye on things. You should check the credentials of any person who offers to provide these services. Ask for references. Contact the references and ask about honesty, reliability, length of time they have known the person, and what the person did for them. Ask if any state agency regulates this service and check to see if any complaints have been registered against the person. Tell the person you are concerned about the confused person and will be checking frequently.

Moving to a New Residence

If you believe that the person can no longer live alone, you must make other arrangements for her. You might consider full-time help or you may arrange for the person to move into someone else's home, a nursing home, or a sheltered housing setting. (These facilities will be described in detail in Chapter 16.)

> *Mr. Sawyer reports, "Mother simply cannot live alone anymore. We hired a housekeeper and Mother fired her—and when I called the agency, they said they could not send anyone else. So we talked with Mother, told her we wanted her to come live with us. But she absolutely refused. She says nothing is wrong with her, that I am trying to steal her money. She won't admit she isn't eating. She says she changed her clothes and we know she hasn't. I don't know what to do."*

If a confused person refuses to give up her independence and move into a safer setting, understanding something of what she may be thinking and feeling may help make the move easier. A move from independent living to living with someone else may mean giving up one's independence and admitting one's impairment. Moving means more losses. It means giving up a familiar place and often many familiar possessions. That place and those possessions are the tangible symbols of one's past and reminders when one's memories fail.

The confused person is dependent upon a familiar setting to provide her with cues that enable her to function independently. Learning one's way around in a new place is difficult or impossible. She feels dependent upon familiar surroundings to survive. The person with a dementing illness may forget the plans that have been discussed or may be unable to understand them. You may reassure your mother that she is coming to live in your house—which is very familiar to her—but all her damaged mind may perceive is that a lot of things are going to be lost.

As you make plans for this person to live with someone, there are several things to consider.

1. *Take into careful consideration the changes that this move will mean in your life, and plan, before the move, for financial resources and emotional outlets and supports for yourself.* If the impaired person is to move in with

you, what effect will this have on her income? States may consider room and board as income and reduce Public Assistance benefits to people living with someone. You will also want to review such things as whether you can claim the person as your dependent on your income tax.

If the person is coming to live with you, how does the rest of the family feel about this? If there are children or teenagers in the family, will their activities upset the confused person or will the "odd" behavior of the confused person upset them? How does your spouse feel about this? Is your marriage already under stress? Having a person with dementia in the home creates burdens and stresses under the best of circumstances. If the ill person and her spouse are both moving in, you must also consider how the spouse will interact in the household. All of the people affected need to be involved in the decision and need the opportunity to express their concerns.

Assuming the care of a forgetful person may mean changes in other things: leisure time (you may not be able to go out because there is no one to sit with Mother), peace (you may not be able to read the newspaper or talk to your wife because Mother is pacing the floor), money (you may have increased medical bills, or bills for remodeling the bedroom), rest (the confused person may wake at night), visitors (people may stop visiting if the person's behavior is embarrassing). These are the things that make life tolerable and that help to reduce your stress. It is important to plan ways for you and your family to relax and get away from the problems of caring for a sick person. Remember also that other problems are not going to go away. You may still worry about your children, come home exhausted from your job, have the car break down, etc.

Is the person you are bringing into your home someone you can live with? If you never could get along with your mother and if her illness has made her behavior worse instead of better, having her move in with you may be disastrous. If you have had a long-standing poor relationship with the person who is now sick, that poor relationship is a reality that can make things more difficult for you.

2. *Involve the person as much as possible in plans for the move, even if she refuses to move.* The patient is still a person, and her participation in plans and decisions that involve her is important, unless she is too severely impaired to comprehend what is happening. Confused people who have been hoodwinked into a move may become even more angry and suspicious and their adjustment to the new setting may be extremely difficult. Certainly the extent and nature of the impaired person's participation depend on the extent of her illness and her attitude toward the move.

Keep in mind that there is a key difference between making the decision, which you may have to do, and participating in the planning, which the confused person can be encouraged to do. Perhaps Mr. Sawyer's story will continue like this:

> *"After we talked it over with Mother she still absolutely refused to consider a move. So I went ahead with the arrangements. I told Mother gently that she had to move because she was getting forgetful.*
>
> *"I knew too many decisions at once would upset her, so we would just ask her a few things at a time: 'Mother, would you like to take all your pictures with you?' 'Mother, let's take your own bed and your lovely bedspread for your new bedroom.'*
>
> *"Of course, we made a lot of decisions without her—about the stove and the washer, and the junk in the attic. And of course she kept saying she wasn't going and that I was robbing her. Still, I think some of it sank in, that she was 'helping' us get ready to move. Sometimes she would pick up a vase and say, 'I want Carol to have this.' We tried to comply with her wishes. Then after the move, we could honestly tell her that the vase was not stolen: she had given it to Carol."*

When a person is too impaired to understand what is happening around her it may be better to make the move without the added stress of trying to involve her in it.

3. *Be prepared for a period of adjustment.* Changes are frequently upsetting to people with dementing illnesses. No matter how carefully and lovingly you plan the move, this is a major change, and the person may be upset for a while. It is easy to understand that it takes time to get over the losses a move involves. A forgetful person also needs extra time to learn her way around in a new place.

When people with dementia move before their illness becomes severe, they are often better able to adjust to their new environment. They have greater ability to adapt and learn new things. Waiting until someone is "too far gone to object" may mean that she will not be able to learn her way around or recognize that she is in a new setting.

Reassure yourself that after an adjustment period the person usually will settle into her new surroundings. Signs on doors may help her find her way around an unfamiliar home. An additional sedative for a brief time may help her sleep at night. Try to postpone other activities or changes until after everyone has adjusted to the move.

Occasionally an impaired person never really adjusts to moving. Don't blame yourself. You did the best you could and acted for her well-being. You may have to accept her inability to adjust as being the result of her illness.

5

PROBLEMS ARISING
IN DAILY CARE

HAZARDS TO WATCH FOR

A PERSON WITH A DEMENTING ILLNESS is less able to take responsibility for his own safety. He is no longer able to evaluate consequences the way the rest of us do, and, because he forgets so quickly, accidents can easily happen. He may attempt to do familiar tasks without realizing that he can no longer manage them. For example, the disease may affect those portions of the brain which remember how to do simple things, such as buttoning buttons or slicing meat. This inability to do manual tasks is often unrecognized and causes accidents. Since the person also cannot learn, you will have to take special precautions to guard against accidents. Because a person seems to be managing well, you may not realize that he has lost the judgment he needs to avoid accidents. Families may need to take responsibility for the safety of even a mildly impaired person.

Accidents are most likely to occur when you are cross or tired, when everyone is hurrying, when there is an argument, or when someone in the household is sick. At these times you are less alert to the possibility of an accident and the impaired person may misunderstand or overreact to even the slightest mishap with a catastrophic reaction.

Do what you can to reduce confusion or tension when it arises. This is difficult when you are struggling with the care of a person with a dementing illness. If you are rushing with him to keep an appointment or finish a job, *stop,* even if it means being late or not getting something done. Catch your breath, rest a minute, and let the confused person calm down.

Be aware that mishaps can be warning signs of impending accidents: you banged your shin on the edge of the bed, or dropped and broke a cup, and the impaired person is getting upset. This is the time to create a change of pace before a serious accident occurs. Alert others in the household to the relationship between increased tension and increased accidents. At such times, everyone can keep a closer eye on the impaired person.

Be sure you know the limits of the impaired person's abilities. Do not take his word that he can heat up his supper or get into the tub alone. An occupational therapist can give you an excellent picture of what the person can do safely. If you do not have this resource, observe the person closely as he does various tasks.

Have an emergency plan ready in case something does happen. Whom will you call if someone is hurt? How will you get the upset person out in case of a fire? Remember that he may misinterpret what is happening and resist your efforts to help him.

Change the environment to make it safer. This is one of the most important ways to avoid accidents. Hospitals and other institutions have safety experts who regularly inspect for hazards. You can and should do the same thing. Go thoughtfully through your home, yard, neighborhood, and car, looking for things a person with a dementing illness could possibly misuse or misinterpret that might cause an accident.

In the House

A neat house is safer than a cluttered one. There are fewer things to trip over or knock over, and hazards are more easily seen. Knickknacks or clutter may distract or confuse an impaired person.

Remove things that cause problems. If a person tries to use the iron and leaves it on, causing a fire hazard, put it away where he cannot find it. Whenever possible take the easiest path to safety without conflict. Does the impaired person have access to power tools, lawn mower, knives, hair dryer, sewing machine, or car keys when he can no longer safely use them? You must put these in a locked closet.

Are all medications kept out of reach of a person who may forget that he has already taken them? Buy a metal file box and equip it with an inexpensive lock to keep medications safely away from the forgetful person and visiting grandchildren.

Are things stored on the stairs? Clutter is always dangerous, particularly when a person is confused, clumsy, or misinterprets what he sees. Are extension cords stretched across the floor where a person might trip on them?

Lower the temperature on your water heater so that water is not hot enough to scald the person who accidentally turns it on. People with dementing illnesses can lose the ability to realize that hot water is too hot and they can burn themselves badly. If hot water pipes are exposed, cover them with insulation.

If the confused person readjusts the furnace or water heater, you may need to lock the basement door.

If you have stairs, install gates at the top. The confused person can easily get "turned around" and fall down the steps, especially at night. Check the handrails; be sure they are sturdy. Handrails should be anchored into the stud and not into drywall or plaster. They will not hold a person's weight if they are not securely fastened. Install handrails if there are none. As the person becomes unsteady on his feet, he will need them. Put away rugs that slip. If stairs are carpeted, check to see that the carpet is securely tacked down.

Remove furniture with sharp corners or sharp finials. Put away or block off large areas of breakable glass; a person can fall against a glass china cabinet and be badly cut. Put away rocking chairs that tip over easily. Put away coffee tables and fragile antiques.

Use stable chairs that are easy to get out of (see p. 91). Check to see if fingers or toes could get caught in parts of recliners. Furniture upholstery should be easy to clean; you may have to wipe up spills. Fabric, draperies, and cushions should be flame resistant.

A confused person can easily lean too far out of a window or over a balcony rail and fall—a particular danger in high-rise buildings. Install security locks on windows and balcony doors. There are inexpensive devices that enable you to lock a window in an open position so that a person cannot get out but fresh air can get in, or open the window a little at the top and a little at the bottom and secure it.

Block off hot radiators by putting a sturdy chair in front of them. You may want to put a gate around a floor furnace.

Can the person lock himself in a room so that you cannot get in? Remove the lock, take the tumblers out, and replace the knob, or tape the latch open.

Never keep insecticides, gasoline, paint, solvents, cleaning supplies, etc., in other than their original, clearly labeled containers. Store them safely out of reach of the confused person. Childproof (and patient-proof) cabinet latches are available at hardware stores. Mildly confused people may try to use such materials inappropriately.

Impaired people forget what can be eaten and what cannot; they may drink solvents by mistake. These people may also eat other inappropriate items. Put small things such as pins and buttons out of reach. Give away poisonous houseplants. Some people will eat chips of loose paint from walls or furniture. Watch for any behavior that involves putting things in the mouth.

Most accidents happen in the kitchen and the bathroom. Confused people often try to turn on the stove but forget they have done so, or try to cook but put empty pans on a hot burner. *This is a serious fire hazard.* You must watch for this and intervene immediately. People left alone at home or those who get up at night are especially at risk.

You may be able to take the knobs off the stove so that the disabled person cannot operate it. If you have an electric stove, you can have a switch installed behind it so that when the switch is off the burners will not operate. You can remove the fuse or circuit breaker when you are not using the stove.

If you have a gas stove, ask the gas company to assist you in making the stove safe. Depending on the stove and your house, there are several things you can do. You may have to be quite persistent and talk to several people before you reach a company official who is helpful and understanding.

Confused people often spill water on the kitchen or bathroom floor and forget to wipe it up. It is easy to slip and fall on a wet spot, so watch for this and keep the floor dry. Perhaps you will want to give up waxing the floor, also. Waxing is work for you and makes the floor slippery.

Handrails and grab bars should be installed in the bathroom (see p. 82). They are available from medical supply houses. Put a skid-resistant mat or decals on the floor of the tub or shower. It is sometimes helpful to replace the bathmat with bathroom carpeting. This is easily cleaned, doesn't slip, and soaks up puddles.

If you live in an apartment or condominium, let the doorman know that this member of your family is forgetful and may have trouble finding his apartment. Some doormen will call you if the person tends to wander away.

Outdoors

Both adults and children can easily put a hand through the glass in a storm door. Storm doors should be covered with a protective grillwork. Sliding glass patio doors should be well marked with stick-on decals.

Check to see if a confused person might fall off a porch or deck. If there are steps, paint them bright, contrasting colors, attach outdoor no-skid tape to the edges, and install a banister.

Check for uneven ground, cracked pavement, holes in the lawn, fallen branches, thorny bushes, or molehills that the person can trip over.

Take down the clothesline so the person will not run into it.

If you have an outdoor grill, never leave it unattended while the coals are hot. Make sure the coals are out and cold. If you have a gas barbecue, be sure the confused person cannot operate it.

Lock up garden tools.

Check yard furniture to be sure it is stable, will not tip or collapse, and has no splinters or chipped paint.

Fence in or dispose of poisonous flowers.

Outdoor swimming pools are very dangerous. Be sure that yours or your neighbor's pool is securely fenced and locked so that the person cannot get to it. You may have to explain carefully the nature of the person's disability to the owner of the pool, making certain that the confused person is not ever assumed to be competent around a pool. Even if he has always been a good swimmer, a confused person may lose his judgment or his ability to handle himself in the water.

In the Car

Problems with driving are discussed in Chapter 4. Never leave a confused person alone in a car. He may wander away, fiddle with the ignition, release the handbrake, be harassed by strangers, or run the battery down with the lights. Automatic windows are dangerous for confused people and for children, who may close the window on their head or arm.

Occasionally a confused person will open the car door and attempt to get out while the car is moving. Locking the doors may help. If this continues to be a problem, you may need a third person to drive while you keep the impaired person calm.

Smoking

If the person smokes, the time will come when he lays down lighted cigarettes and forgets them. *This is a serious hazard.* If it occurs, you must intervene. Try to discourage smoking. Many families have taken cigarettes completely away from a patient. Things may be difficult for a few days or weeks, but much easier in the long run. However, some people forget they ever smoked, and do not complain when you take their cigarettes away. Other families allow the impaired person to smoke only under their supervision. All smoking materials and kitchen or fireplace matches must be kept out of reach of the forgetful person. (The person who has cigarettes but not matches may use the stove to light his cigarette and may leave the stove on.)

Hunting

The use of firearms requires complex mental skills that are usually lost early in dementia. Guns must be put in a safe place. If necessary, ask your doctor or clergyman to explain to the confused person's hunting buddies that hunting is now too dangerous for him. Ask the local police or sheriff's department if they can help dispose of a gun or rifle if you do not know how to do so.

Highways and Parking Lots

Highways are dangerous. If you think the confused person may be walking along a highway, notify the police immediately. They do not mind being alerted unnecessarily. This is much better than not alerting them and having a tragedy occur.

People driving in parking lots often assume that pedestrians will get out of their way. People with dementia may not anticipate cars coming or may move slowly. Be especially alert to entrances into enclosed garages. These often put the pedestrian directly into the path of cars.

NUTRITION AND MEALTIMES

Good nutrition is important to both you and the chronically ill person. If you are not eating well, you will be more tense and more easily upset. It is not known to what extent a proper diet affects the progress of dementing diseases, but we do know that forgetful people often fail to eat properly and can suffer nutritional deficiencies.

A balanced daily diet, as recommended by the Council on Foods and Nutrition of the American Medical Association, includes: two or more glasses of milk (or servings of cheese, ice cream, or cottage cheese); two or more servings of meat, fish, poultry, eggs, cheese, or dried beans, peas, or nuts; four or more servings of vegetables and fruits, including dark green or yellow vegetables, citrus fruit, or tomatoes; and four or more servings of enriched or whole-grain breads and cereals. Both you and the person with a dementing illness need this balanced diet to avoid other illnesses and to cope with the stress of a chronic illness. If your doctor has recommended a special diet for managing other diseases, like diabetes or heart disease, it is important that you know from him what foods you should eat in order to maintain a balanced diet. He can refer you to a nutritionist or a nurse who can help you manage a special diet.

There is no known link between nutrition and Alzheimer's disease and there are no special diets that have proven to help memory problems.

Meal Preparation

When you must prepare meals in addition to all your other responsibilities you may find yourself taking short cuts such as fixing just a cup of coffee and toast for yourself and the confused person. If preparing meals is a job you had to take on for the first time when your spouse became ill, you may not know how to serve good nutritious meals quickly and easily and you may not want to learn to cook. There are several alternatives. We suggest you plan a variety of ways to get good meals with a minimum of effort.

There are Eating Together programs for people over sixty and Meals-on-Wheels programs in most areas. Both services provide one hot, nutritious meal a day. You can find out what meal services are available through a social worker or by calling the local office on aging. Meals-on-Wheels programs bring a meal to your home. Eating Together programs, funded under the Older Americans Act, provide lunch and often a recreation program in the company of other retired people at a community center. Transportation is often provided.

Many restaurants will prepare carry-out meals if requested. This helps when a person can no longer eat in public.

There are numerous inexpensive cookbooks on the market that explain the basic steps in easy meal preparation. Some are written for the man who is "bacheloring." Some are in large print. An experienced homemaker can show you how to prepare quick, easy meals. The home economist in your county extension office or a public health nurse can give you good, easy recipes for two. She also has helpful information on budgeting, shopping, meal planning, and nutrition, and she can help you understand and plan menus for special diets.

Some frozen dinners provide well-balanced meals, but these are often expensive. Many, however, are low in vitamins and high in salt, and lack the fiber older people need to prevent constipation.

Problem Eating Behaviors

Forgetful people who are still eating some meals alone may forget to eat, even if you leave food in plain sight. They may hide food, throw food away, or eat it after it has spoiled. These are signals that the person can no longer manage alone and that you must make new arrangements. You may manage for a time by phoning at noon to remind him to eat lunch now, but this is a short-term solution. Confused people who live alone are frequently malnourished. Even when they appear overweight, they may not be getting the proper foods. A poor diet can worsen their confusion.

Many of the problems that arise at mealtime involve catastrophic reactions. Make mealtime as regular a routine as possible, with as little confusion as you can arrange. This will help prevent catastrophic reactions. Fussy or messy eaters do better when things are calm.

Check that dentures are tight fitting if the person uses them to eat. If they are loose, it may be safer to leave them out until they can be adjusted.

Check the temperature of foods, especially food heated in a microwave oven. Confused people often lack the judgment to avoid burning themselves.

People with dementing illnesses may develop rigid likes and dislikes and refuse to eat certain foods. Such people may be more willing to eat familiar foods, prepared in familiar ways. If the person never liked a particular food, he will not like it now. New foods may confuse him. If the person insists on eating only one or two things and if all efforts at persuasion or disguising foods fail, you will need to ask the doctor about vitamins and diet supplements.

Mealtimes

Seat the person in a comfortable position, as close to a normal eating position as possible. Be sure that possible distractions (such as a television or needing to use the toilet) are taken care of. Some people do better with someone else at the table. Others are distracted by this.

The dining area should be well lit so that the person can easily see his food. Use a plate that contrasts with the placemat and with the food. (For example, it is easier to see a white plate if it is on a bright blue placemat.) Avoid glass if he has difficulty seeing it. Avoid dishes with patterns if the person is confused by this. If the person is confused by condiments (salt, pepper, sugar, etc.) on the table, remove them. If he is confused by several utensils, put out only one. Some people do better in a dining room or kitchen where there are many subtle cues like food smells that remind them to eat. Let the person feed himself as much as possible.

Some people are unable to decide among the foods on their plate. If so, limit the number of foods you put in front of the confused person at one time. For example, serve only his salad, then only his meat. Having to make choices is often what leads to playing with food. Don't put salt, ketchup, etc., where he can reach it if he mixes it inappropriately into his food; season his food for him. Be sure that food is cut into pieces that are small and tender enough to be eaten safely; people with dementing illnesses may forget to chew or fail to cut up meats properly, because the hands and brain no longer work together.

Messiness

As the person develops problems with coordination, he may become messy and begin to use his fingers instead of silverware. It is almost always easier to adjust to this than to fight it. Use a plastic tablecloth or placemats. Serve meals in a room in which the floor can be easily cleaned. Don't scold when he uses his fingers. Eating with his fingers will postpone the time when he needs more help from you. Serve things that are easy to pick up in bite-sized pieces.

If the person continues to use a fork or spoon, he will be more successful eating from a dish with sides. You can purchase a scoop plate or plate guard (which attaches to a plate) from a medical supply store. Use fairly heavy dishes (they slip less).

Dycem® (available from medical supply houses) placed under a plate will keep the plate from slipping. Plates with suction cups are also available. A damp cloth under a plate may keep the plate from slipping. Utensils with large (thick) handles are easier for people with arthritis or coordination problems to use. You can purchase these or build up your own handles with foam rubber. (Do this to your own pens and notice how much less tiring writing is.)

Some patients will wear a smock over their clothing. Others will be confused or offended by it. If you try this, use a smock or large apron rather than a bib. You can purchase the large smocks beauticians use at variety stores. Turn the bottom up into a large pocket to catch spilled food.

Some people lose the ability to judge how much liquid will fill a glass and overfill glasses. They will need your help. If a person dribbles or spills when drinking from a cup, try a convalescent feeding cup, which has a plastic cover with a spout. Similar spillproof cups are sold for children. To prevent spilling, don't fill glasses or cups full.

Hoarding Food

Some people save food and hide it in their room. This is a problem if it attracts insects or mice. Some people will give this up if they are frequently reassured that they can have a snack at any time. Leave a cookie jar where they can find it and remind them where it is. Some families give the person a container with a tightly fitting lid to keep snacks in. You may need to remind him to keep the snacks in the container. Others persuade the person to "trade" their old, spoiled food for fresh food.

If the person has a complicating illness, such as diabetes, which requires a special diet, it may be necessary to put foods he should not eat where he cannot get them and allow him only those foods he should have. Remember, he may lack the judgment to decide responsibly between his craving and his well-being. Since a proper diet is important to his health, you may have to be responsible for preventing him from getting foods he should not have, even if he vigorously objects. A locksmith can put a lock on the refrigerator door if necessary. Childproof locks will secure cabinets. But before you invest in locks, ask yourself whether you need to keep all those sweets in the house anyway.

Nibbling

Sometimes a person seems to forget that he ate and will ask for food again right after a meal. Sometimes people seem to want to eat all the time. Try setting out a tray of small, nutritious "nibbles" such as small crackers or cheese cubes. Sometimes people will take one at a time and be satisfied. If weight gain is a problem, put out carrots or celery.

Eating Things He Should Not Eat

People with dementing illnesses may be unable to recognize that some things are not good to eat. You may need to put out of sight foods like salt, vinegar, oil, or Worcestershire sauce, large amounts of which can make a person sick. Some people will eat nonfood items like soap, soil in planters, or sponges. This probably results from damage to perception and memory. If this occurs you will need to keep these objects out of sight. Many patients do not develop this problem, so we do not recommend removing these objects unless a problem does occur.

Fluids

Be sure that the person gets enough fluid each day. Even mildly impaired people may forget to drink, and inadequate fluid intake can lead to other physical problems. (See p. 99.)

Always check the temperature of hot drinks. The person may lose the ability to judge temperature and can burn himself.

Puréed Diet

If the person is on a puréed diet, use a babyfood grinder. You can purée normally prepared foods in it. This saves time and money. Home-cooked foods will be more appealing to the person than babyfoods.

Drooling or Respiratory Problems

If the person drools or has respiratory problems, milk or citrus juice may produce more mucus and make the problem worse. Check with your doctor to determine the cause of the problem. Then offer fruit nectar or cranberry juice instead of orange juice or milk.

Spoonfeeding

If you spoonfeed a person, put only a small amount of food on the spoon at a time; wait until the person swallows before giving him the next bite. You may have to tell him to swallow.

Not Swallowing

Sometimes a person will carry food around in his mouth but not swallow it. This is due to forgetting how to chew or swallow. This is an apraxia (see p. 41) and is best handled by giving the person soft foods that do not require much chewing, such as chopped meat, Jell-o, and thick liquids.

If the person does not swallow pills, crush the pill and mix it with food.

Weight Loss

People with dementia lose weight for all the same reasons that any other person does. Therefore, if he loses weight, the first step is to consult the person's physician. Weight loss often indicates a treatable problem or a disease unrelated to the dementia. Do not assume that it signals a decline. It is important that the physician search carefully for any contributory illness. Is the person constipated? Has the person had a new small stroke? Is the person depressed? Depression can account for weight loss even in a person who has a dementia. Poorly fitting dentures or sore teeth or gums often contribute to weight loss. Some clinicians think that some weight loss is a part of the disease process itself. Other clinicians disagree. Certainly all other possible causes should be considered.

When a person is still eating and yet losing weight, he may be pacing, agitated, or so active that he is burning up more calories than he is taking in. Offer nutritious, substantial snacks between meals and before bedtime. Some clinicians think that several small meals and several snacks help prevent this kind of weight loss.

Sometimes all that is needed to get a person to eat better is a calm, supportive environment. You may have to experiment before you find the arrangement that best encourages the person to eat. Be sure the food tastes good. Offer the person his favorite foods. Offer only one thing at a time and do not rush the person. People with dementia often eat slowly. Frequently offer snacks. Gently remind him to eat.

Eating problems often arise in nursing homes. Most people eat better in a small group or at a table with one other person in a quiet room. Perhaps the nursing home will set aside space to serve a few confused people on the unit instead of in a large, noisy dining room. Sometimes nursing home staff members are too rushed to coax a person to eat; a familiar family member may have better success. Homemade goodies may be more appealing than institutional food. We have had one patient respond by having her back gently stroked while she was being fed. One patient responded to a low dose of medication given one hour before meals.

You may give a person who is not eating well a liquid high-calorie diet supplement like Ensure, Mariteme, or Sustacal. You can purchase these by the case from most pharmacies. They contain vitamins, minerals, and proteins the person needs. They come in different flavors; the person may like some better than others. Offer this as the beverage with a meal or as a "milk shake" between meals. Consult your physician about using them.

Choking

Sometimes people with coordination problems begin to have trouble swallowing. If the person has difficulty changing his facial expression, he may also have trouble chewing or swallowing. When this occurs, it is important to guard against choking. Do not give the person foods that he may forget to chew thoroughly, such as small hard candy, nuts, carrots, chewing gum, or popcorn. Soft, thick foods are less likely to cause choking. Easy to handle foods include chopped meat, soft-boiled eggs, canned fruit, and frozen yogurt. Foods can be ground in a blender. Seasoning will make them more appealing.

If the person has trouble swallowing, be sure he is sitting up straight with his head slightly forward—never tilted back when he eats. He should be sitting in the same position in which a well person would sit at a table. He should remain sitting for fifteen minutes after he eats.

Do not feed a person who is agitated or sleepy.

Foods like cereal with milk may cause choking. The two textures—solid and liquid—make it hard for him to know whether to chew or swallow.

Some fluids are easier to swallow than others. If a person tends to choke on fluids like water, try a thicker liquid. A nurse can help you cope with this problem.

First Aid for Choking

A nurse or the Red Cross can teach you a simple technique that can save the life of a choking person. It takes only a few minutes to learn this simple skill. Everyone should know how to do it.

If the person can talk, cough, or breathe, *do not interfere*. If the person cannot talk, cough, or breathe (and he may point to his throat or turn bluish), *you must help him*. If he is in a chair or standing, stand behind him, then reach around him and lock or overlap your two hands in the middle of his abdomen (belly) below the ribs. Pull hard and quickly back and up (toward you). If he is lying down, turn him so he is face up, put your two hands in the middle of his belly, and push. This will force air up through the throat and cause the food to fly out like a cork out of a bottle.

(You can practice where to put your hands, but you should not push hard on a breathing person.)

When to Consider Tube Feeding

People with dementia stop eating for many reasons. They may have difficulty swallowing due to an apraxia, to ulcers in the esophagus, esophageal obstruction (narrowing), or overmedication. They may dislike the food being offered, not recognize it as food, lose the sense of feeling hungry or thirsty, or be sitting in an uncomfortable position. People with dementia may stop eating when they are experiencing a concurrent illness; they *may* resume eating when they recover. Even severely impaired people may suffer from a depression that causes them to stop eating. However, some people reach a point in their illness when they are no longer able to eat or swallow. Good care, even in the last stage, requires that a physician carefully review the person's medical status. Then, if weight loss cannot be stopped, you and the doctors are left with an ethical dilemma. Should you allow the insertion of a nasogastric (NG) tube (a tube that goes through the nose into the stomach) to feed the patient, or should you allow the insertion of a feeding tube directly into the stomach (a gastrostomy)? Or should you allow the patient to die? Only you can make this decision.

It is helpful if you can talk about this issue before it arises. We discuss these ethical dilemmas on page 112. Here we will discuss the options you have for sustaining life.

Many physicians believe that a gastrostomy tube (a tube placed through the abdominal wall directly into the stomach) is more comfortable for the patient than the more familiar nasogastric tube (a tube that goes through the nose, down the esophagus, and into the stomach). Patients are less likely to pull gastrostomy tubes out and these tubes need to be changed less often. New surgical procedures make inserting them safe and easy. However, these tubes do require a surgical opening through the abdomen and this may present a slightly higher risk to the patient. If the person has dementia, someone will be required to sign a consent form for this procedure. Nasogastric tubes are now quite thin and less uncomfortable than they once were. New machines are available which can continuously feed a person through this tube. They too carry some risks. The tube may become dislodged or cause irritation and bleeding in the nose, throat, or esophagus.

People with dementia often try and sometimes succeed in pulling out nasogastric tubes. We do not know whether this means they find the tube uncomfortable or whether they think that it does not belong there. Or it may happen because they are restless. People who pull out their tubes may have their hands restrained, further adding to their discomfort.

It is important to discuss all aspects of the decision to place a feeding tube with a physician who knows the patient well. A visiting nurse can show you how to manage either kind of tube at home.

We know very little about the experience of a person with dementia who is not tube fed. We do not have enough information to balance the discomfort of a tube against the discomfort of not using tube feedings. While some think that a person this seriously ill is comfortable without nourishment and water, others disagree. If kidneys or other organs stop functioning, the person may be more uncomfortable when food and water are forced. Also, knowledge gained from people dying from other causes may not apply to people with dementia. In the end you and your family must make the decision you feel most comfortable with. If the person had previously written or stated his preference, this may help guide your decision, but ultimately it is the family member or guardian who makes the decision.

EXERCISE

Remaining physically fit is an important part of good health. We do not know the precise role that exercise plays in good health, but we do know that it is important for both you and the confused person to get enough exercise. Perhaps exercise will refresh you after the daily burdens of caring for a chronically ill person. We do not know the relationship between tension and exercise, but many people who lead intense, demanding lives are convinced that physical exercise enables them to handle pressure more effectively.

Dementia is not caused by inadequate circulation. Therefore, improving circulation with exercise does not prevent or reverse memory disorders, but it does have other useful effects.

Some practitioners have observed that people with dementing illnesses who exercise regularly seem to be calmer and do less agitated pacing. Some have observed that motor skills seem to be retained longer if they are used regularly. Exercise is a good way to keep an impaired person involved in activities, since it may be easier for him to use his body than to think and remember. Perhaps of most importance to you is the fact that sufficient exercise seems to help confused people sleep at night, and it helps to keep their bowel movements regular.

You may have to exercise with the impaired person. The kind of exercise you do depends on what you and the impaired person enjoy. There is no point to adding an odious exercise program to your life. Consider what the person did before he got sick and find ways to modify that activity so that it can continue. Sometimes an exercise project can also be a time for you and the impaired person to share closeness and affection without having to talk.

How much exercise can an older person safely do? If you or the impaired person has high blood pressure or a heart condition, check with the doctor before you do anything. If both of you can do normal walking around the house, climb steps, and shop for groceries, you can do a moderate exercise program. Always start a new activity gradually and build up slowly. If an exercise causes either of you stiffness, pain, or swelling, do less of it or change to a gentler activity. Check the person's feet for blisters or bruises if you begin walking.

Walking is excellent exercise. Try to take the person outside for a short walk in all but the worst weather. The movement and the fresh air may help him sleep better. If the weather is too rainy or cold, drive to a shopping mall. Make a game of "window shopping." Be sure both of you have comfortable, low-heeled shoes, and soft, absorbent cotton socks. You may gradually build up the distance you walk, but avoid steep hills. It may be easier for a forgetful person to walk the same route each day. Point out scenery, people, smells, etc., as you walk.

Dancing is good exercise. If the person enjoyed dancing before he became ill, encourage some sort of movements to music.

If the person played golf or tennis, he may be able to enjoy hitting the ball around long after he becomes unable to play a real game.

Confused people often enjoy doing calisthenics as part of a group, for example, in a day care setting. If you are doing exercises in a group or at home, try having him imitate what you are doing. If he has trouble with specific movements, try gently helping him move.

If the person is able to keep his balance, standing exercises are better than those done sitting in a chair. However, if balance is a problem, do the same exercises from a chair.

Even people who are confined to bed can exercise. However, exercises for seriously chronically ill patients must be planned by a physical therapist so they do not aggravate other conditions and are not dangerous to a person who has poor coordination or poor balance.

Exercise should be done at the same time each day, in a quiet, orderly way, so it does not create confusion that would add to the person's agitation. Follow the same sequence of exercises, starting from the head and working your way down toward the feet. Make the exercises fun and encourage the person to remember them. If the person has a catastrophic reaction, stop and try again later.

When a person has been sick or inactive, he may become weak and tire more easily. He may get stiff joints. Regular, gentle exercise can help keep his joints and his muscles in healthy condition. When stiffness or weakness is caused by other diseases, such as arthritis, or by injury, a physical or occupational therapist can plan an exercise program that may help prevent further stiffness or weakness.

If the person has any other health problems or if you are planning a vigorous exercise program, discuss this with your physician before you begin. You should notify your doctor of any new physical problems and of marked changes in existing ones.

RECREATION

Recreation, having fun, and enjoying life are important for everyone. A dementing illness does not mean an end to enjoying life. It may mean that you will need to make a special effort to find things that give pleasure to the impaired person.

As the person's illness progresses, it may become more difficult to find things he can still enjoy. In reality, you may already be doing as much as you can and adding an "activity" program may further exhaust you and add to the stress in the household. Instead, look for things you can still do that both of you will enjoy. Perhaps something as simple as taking a walk or playing with the dog will be relaxing for both of you.

Consider an adult day care program or an in-home visitor program. The sheltered social setting of adult day care may provide just the right balance of stimulation and security. If they are able to adjust to the new setting, people with dementia enjoy the camaraderie with other people who are also confused. Some in-home visitor programs offer occupational or recreational therapy services for the ill person. These professionals can help you plan exercises or activities the person will enjoy. Both visiting at home and day care offer social activities and opportunities for success and fun. If at all possible, involve the person in such a program.

People with dementia often lose the ability to entertain themselves. For some, idleness leads to pacing or other repetitive behaviors. The person may resist your suggestions of things to do. Frequently, this is because he does not understand what you are suggesting. Try beginning an activity and then inviting him to join you. Select simple, adult activities rather than childish games. Select an activity that will be fun rather than one that is supposed to be "therapeutic." Look for things that the person will enjoy and that he will succeed at (like sanding wood, playing with a child, cranking an ice cream maker).

The amount of activity a person can tolerate varies widely. Plan activity when the person is rested; help whenever the person becomes anxious or irritable, and break the activity down into simple steps.

Previously enjoyed activities may remain important and enjoyable even for seriously impaired people. However, the things the person used to enjoy, such as hobbies, guests, concerts, or going out to dinner, can become too complicated to be fun for someone who is easily confused. These must be replaced by simpler joys, although it can be hard for family members to understand that simple things can now give just as much pleasure.

Music is a delightful resource for many confused people. Sometimes a severely impaired person seems to retain a capacity to enjoy old, familiar songs. Some people will sing only when someone sits close by and encourages them. Others may be able to use a simple tape deck or radio with large knobs. Very impaired people are sometimes still able to play the piano or sing if they learned this skill earlier.

Some memory-impaired people enjoy television. Others get upset when they cannot understand the story anymore. The quick shifts from one scene to another precipitate catastrophic reactions in some people.

Most confused people enjoy seeing old friends, although sometimes visitors upset them. If this happens, try having only one or two people visit at a time, instead of a group. It is often the confusion of several people at once that is upsetting. Ask visitors to stay for shorter periods, and explain to them the reason for the person's forgetfulness and other behaviors.

Some families enjoy going out to dinner, and many people with dementing illnesses retain their social graces well. Others embarrass the family by their messy eating. It is helpful to order for the confused person and select simple foods that can be eaten neatly. Remove unnecessary glasses and silverware. Some families have found that it helps to explain to the waitress discreetly that the person is confused and cannot order for himself.

Consider the hobbies and interests the person had before he became ill, and look for ways he can still enjoy these. Often, for example, people who liked to read continue to enjoy leafing through magazines after they can no longer make sense of the text. Sometimes a person puts away a hobby or interest and refuses to pick it up again. This often happens with something a person had done well and can no longer do as effectively. It can seem degrading to encourage a person to do a simplified version of a once fine skill unless he particularly enjoys it. It may be better to find new kinds of recreation.

Everyone enjoys experiencing things through his senses. You probably enjoy watching a brilliant sunset, smelling a flower, or tasting your favorite food. People with dementia are often more isolated and may not be able to seek out experiences to stimulate their senses. Try pointing out a pretty picture, a bird singing, a familiar smell or taste. Remember the sense of touch. The person may enjoy stroking a furry animal, touching a smooth piece of wood, or putting his hand under running water. Some individuals enjoy a patchwork apron or lap robe made of different textured fabrics: fur, corduroy, satin, vinyl. Like you, the person will enjoy certain sensations more and others less.

Many families have found that confused people enjoy a ride in the car.

If the person has always enjoyed animals, he may respond with delight to pets. Some cats and dogs seem to have an instinctive way with brain-impaired people.

Some individuals enjoy a stuffed animal or doll. A stuffed toy can be either childish and demeaning or comforting; much depends on the attitude of the people around the confused person.

As the dementing illness continues and the person develops trouble with coordination and language, it is easy to forget his need to experience pleasant things and to enjoy himself.

Never overlook the importance of hand holding, touching, hugging, and loving. Often when there is no other way we can find to communicate with a person, he will respond to touching. Touch is an important part of human communication. A backrub or foot or hand massage can be calming. You may enjoy just sitting and holding hands. It's a good way to share some time when talking has become difficult or impossible.

Meaningful Activity

Much of what a well person does during the day has a purpose that gives meaning and importance to life. We work to make money, to serve others, to feel important. We may knit a sweater for a grandchild or bake a cake for a friend. We wash our hair and clothes so we will look nice and be clean. Such purposeful activities are important to us—they make us feel useful and needed.

When the person with a dementing illness is unable to continue his usual activities, you need to help him find things to do that are meaningful and still within his abilities. Such tasks should be meaningful and satisfying to him—whether they seem so to you or not. For example, folding and refolding towels might have meaning for some people but not for others. Seeing themselves as "volunteers" rather than "patients" is important to some people. This provides both a sense of worth and the benefit of participation. The person may be able to spade a garden for you and for the neighbors or may be able to peel the vegetables or set the table when no longer able to prepare a complete meal. Confused people can wind a ball of yarn, dust, or stack magazines while you do the housework. Encourage the person to do as much as he can for himself, although you can simplify the tasks for him.

PERSONAL HYGIENE

The amount of help a person with a dementing illness needs in personal care varies with the extent of his brain damage. The person with Alzheimer's disease will be able to care for himself in the early stages of the disease, but may gradually begin to neglect himself and will eventually need total help.

Problems often arise over getting a person to change his clothes or take a bath. "I already changed," the person may tell you, or he may turn the tables and make it sound as if you are wrong to suggest such a thing.

A daughter says, "I can't get her to change clothes. She has had the same clothes on for a week. She sleeps in them. When I tell her to change, she says she already did or she yells at me, 'Who do you think you are, telling me when to change my clothes?'"

A husband relates, "She screams for help the whole time I am bathing her. She'll open the windows and yell, 'Help, I'm being robbed.'"

A person with a dementing illness may become depressed or apathetic and lose any desire to clean up. He may be losing the ability to remember how much time has passed: it doesn't *seem* like a week since he changed clothes. To have someone telling him he needs to change his clothes may embarrass him. (If someone came up to you and told you that you should change your clothes, you might well become indignant.)

Dressing and bathing are personal activities. We each have our own individual ways of doing things. Some of us take showers, some take tub baths, some of us bathe in the morning, some bathe at night. Some of us change clothes twice a day, some every other day, but each of us is quite set in our way of doing things. Sometimes when a family member begins to help the demented person, he inadvertently overlooks these established habits. The change in routine can be upsetting to the confused person. A generation ago, people often did not wash and change as frequently as we do today. Once a week may have been the way the person did things in his childhood.

We begin to bathe and dress ourselves as small children. It is a basic indication of our independence. Moreover, bathing and dressing are private activities. Many people have never completely bathed and dressed in front of anyone else. Having other people's hands and eyes on our naked, aging, not-so-beautiful body is an acutely uncomfortable experience. When we offer to help with something a person has always done for himself— something everybody does for himself and does in private—it is a strong statement that this person is not able to do for himself any longer, that he has, in fact, become like a child who must be told when to dress and must have help.

Changing clothes and bathing involve making many decisions. A man must select among many socks, shirts, and ties for an outfit that goes together. When he begins to realize he can't do this, when looking at a drawer full of blue, green, and black socks becomes overwhelmingly confusing, it can be easier just not to change.

Such factors as these often precipitate catastrophic reactions involving bathing and dressing. Still, you are faced with the problem of keeping this person clean. Begin by trying to understand the person's feelings and his need for privacy and independence. Know that his behavior is a product of his brain impairment, and is not deliberately offensive. Look for ways to simplify the number of decisions involved in bathing and dressing without taking away his independence.

Bathing

When a person refuses to take a bath, part of the problem may be that the business of bathing has become too confusing and complicated. Try to follow as many of the person's old routines as possible while you encourage him to bathe, and at the same time simplify the job for him. If a man has always shaved first, then showered, then eaten breakfast, he is most likely to cooperate with your request if you time it for before breakfast. Then lay out his clothes and towels and start the water.

Be calm and gentle when you help with a bath. Avoid getting into discussions about whether a bath is needed. Instead, tell the person *one step at a time* what to do in preparation for the bath.

> *Avoid:* *"Dad, I want you to take a bath right after breakfast." ("Right, after breakfast" means he has to remember something.)*
>
> *Avoid:* *"I don't need a bath." "Oh yes you do. You haven't had a bath in a week." (You would not like him saying that to you, especially if you couldn't remember when you last had a bath.)*
>
> *Try:* *"Dad, your bath water is ready." "I don't need a bath." "Here is your towel. Now, unbutton your shirt." (His mind may focus on the buttons instead of on the argument. You can gently help him if you see him having difficulty.) "Now stand up. Undo your pants, Dad." "I don't need a bath." "Now step into the tub."*

One daughter drew her father's bath, got everything ready, and then, when he wandered down the hall, said, "Oh, look at this lovely bath water. As long as it is here, why not take a bath? It would be terrible to waste it." Her father, who had always pinched pennies, yielded. One wife told her husband, "As soon as your bath is over, you and I will eat those good cookies Janie brought."

Some families have found that the confused person will let an aide in uniform or another family member bathe him. Think over the person's life-long bath habits: did he bathe or shower? In the morning or at night?

If all else fails, give partial baths or sponge baths. Watch the person's skin for rashes or red areas.

The bath should be a regular routine, done the same way at the same time. The person will come to expect this and may put up less resistance. If bathing continues to be difficult, it is not necessary for the person to bathe every day. Always check the temperature of the bath or shower water, even if the person has been successfully doing this for himself. The ability to gauge safe temperatures can be lost quite suddenly. Avoid using bubble bath or bath oils that can make the tub slippery. These can also contribute to vaginal infections in women.

It can be difficult to get a person in and out of a tub, especially if he is clumsy or heavy. An unsteady person can slip and fall while stepping over the side. An unsteady person may also fall while standing in the shower. There are several appliances that you can rent or purchase that make bathing much safer and easier (see p. 82). Many families have told us that a bath seat and a hand-held hose greatly reduce the bathtime crisis. You have control of the water (and the mess). The seat is safer and the controlled flow of water is less upsetting to the confused person.

Never leave the person alone in the tub. Use only two or three inches of water. This helps the person feel more secure, and is safer in case he slips. Put a rubber mat or no-skid decals on the bottom of the tub. People can often continue to wash themselves if you gently remind them one step at a time of each area to wash.

Sometimes it is embarrassing for a family member to see that the genital area is thoroughly washed, but rashes can develop, so see that this is done. Be sure that you or the confused person has washed in folds of flesh and under breasts.

Use a bathmat that will not slip for the person to step out onto and be sure there are no puddles on the floor. It may be helpful to replace bathmats with bathroom carpeting that does not slip, soaks up puddles, and is washable. If the person still dries himself, check to see that he doesn't forget some areas. If you dry the person, be sure he is completely dry. Use body powder, baby powder, or cornstarch under women's breasts and in creases and folds of skin. Cornstarch is an inexpensive, odorless, and nonallergenic substitute for talcum powder. Baking soda is an effective substitute if the person resists using a deodorant.

While the person is undressed, check for red areas of skin, rashes, or sores. If any red areas or sores appear, ask your physician to help you manage them. Pressure sores or decubitus ulcers develop quickly on people who sit or lie down much of the time. Use body lotion on dry skin. There are unscented lotions for men.

Dressing

If all of the person's socks will go with all of his slacks, he doesn't have to decide which is right to wear with what.

Hang ties, scarves, or accessories on the hanger with the shirt or dress they go with. Eliminate belts, scarves, sweaters, ties, and other accessories that are likely to be put on wrong.

Lay out a clean outfit for the confused person. Laying out clothes in the order in which he puts them on may also help.

Put away out-of-season or rarely worn clothes so they do not add to the decisions the person must make. If the person refuses to change clothes, avoid getting in an argument. Make the suggestion again later.

As the disease progresses, it becomes difficult for a person to get clothes on right side out and in the right sequence. Buttons, zippers, shoelaces, and belt buckles become impossible to manage. If the person can no longer manage buttons, replace them with Velcro tape, which you can purchase in a fabric store. People can often manage this after their fingers can no longer cope with buttons. One wife, sensitive to her husband's need to continue to dress himself independently, bought him clothes that were reversible. She bought attractive t-shirts, which don't look bad if they are worn backward and which don't have buttons, pants with elastic waistbands, and tube socks. (Tube socks don't have heels, so it takes less skill to put them on.) Slip-on shoes are easier than shoes with laces or ties.

Women can look pretty in reversible, slip-on blouses and reversible, wrap-around or elastic-waistband skirts or slacks. Loose-fitting clothing is easier to manage.

Select clothing that is washable and that doesn't need ironing; there is no reason to add to your work load.

Sometimes "busy" patterns confuse and distract the impaired person. Select colors with considerable contrast; these are easier for the older person to distinguish.

Women's underwear is difficult for a confused person to manage, and a mystery to many husbands. Buy soft, loose-fitting panties. It won't matter if they are on backward or wrong side out. Skip the slip; it is not necessary. If you must put a bra on a woman, ask her to lean forward to settle her breasts in the cups. Pantyhose are difficult to put on, and knee socks or garter belts are bad for people with poor circulation. Short cotton socks may be best to wear at home.

Grooming

Have the person's hair cut in an attractive, short style that is easy to wash and care for. Avoid a style that requires setting. People who have always gone to the beauty shop or barber shop may still enjoy doing so. If this is too upsetting an experience, it may be possible to arrange for a beautician or barber to come to your home.

It may be safer (and easier on your back) to wash hair in the kitchen sink rather than the tub unless you have a sprayer attached to the bathtub. Invest in a hose attachment for the sink. Be sure you rinse hair well. It should squeak when rubbed through your fingers.

You will need to trim fingernails and toenails or check to see that he can still do this. Toenails can curl back against the toes and be quite painful.

Encourage the person to get dressed and to look nice. Moping around in a bathrobe will not help his morale. If a woman has always worn makeup, it may be good for her to continue to wear simple makeup. It is not difficult for a husband to put powder and lipstick on his wife. Use pastel colors and a light touch on an older woman. Skip the eye makeup.

When the bath and dressing are finished, encourage the person to look in the mirror and see how nice he looks (even if you are exhausted and exasperated). Get the rest of the family to compliment him also. Praise and encouragement are important in helping him continue to feel good about himself even when a task he has always been able to do, such as dressing, has become too much for him.

Oral Hygiene

With all the other chores of caring for a chronically ill person it is easy to forget what we can't see, but good oral hygiene is important for the person's comfort and for his health. A person who appears to be able to care for himself in other ways may, in fact, be forgetting to care for his teeth or dentures.

Dentures are particularly troublesome. If they don't fit just right or if a person is not applying the denture adhesive properly, they interfere with chewing. The natural response is to stop eating those things one can't chew. This can lead to inadequate nutrition or constipation. Dentures should be in place when a person is eating. If they don't fit properly or are uncomfortable, insist that the dentist fix them. If a person forgets to take his dentures out and clean them, or if he refuses to let you do it, he can develop painful sores on his gums which also interfere with a proper diet.

Since you want the person to be as independent as possible, you can assume the responsibility of remembering, but let the person do as much of the actual care as possible. One reason people stop caring for their teeth or dentures is that these are actually complicated tasks with many steps and they get confused about what to do next. You can help by breaking down the job into simple steps and reminding the person one step at a time. If you take over the care of the person's dentures, you must remove them daily, clean them, and check the gums for irritation. The dentist can show you how to do this. If the person has his own teeth, you may have to brush them for him and check the mouth for sores.

Some dentists recommend foam applicators instead of brushes for cleaning teeth. You can clean the teeth more gently with these. If the person will not unclench his teeth, try to clean the outside of the teeth.

Make oral care a part of a regular, expected routine and do it calmly; you will get less resistance. Select a time of day when the person is most cooperative. If the person does get upset, stop, and try again later. Someone else may be better able to get the person's cooperation.

Healthy teeth or properly fitting dentures are critically important. People with dementing illnesses tend not to chew well and to choke easily. Dental problems make this worse. Even mild nutritional problems caused by sore teeth can increase the person's confusion or cause constipation. Sores in the mouth can lead to other problems and can increase the person's impairment. (See p. 103.)

Bathroom Supplies

Medical supply houses carry a variety of bathroom aids which make the bathroom safer and easier for the impaired person.

Raised toilet seats make it easier for an impaired person to get off and on the seat and easier to transfer a person from a wheelchair to the toilet. The seat should fasten securely to the toilet so it does not slip when the person sits on it. Padded (soft) toilet seats are more comfortable for the person who must sit for some time. This is especially important for the person who develops pressure sores easily.

You can rent portable commodes that can be placed near a person's bed or on the ground floor, so that the person does not have to climb stairs. Urinals and bedpans are available to meet a variety of needs. Discuss your specific problem with the supply house so that they can help you select the appliance that is best for you.

Grab bars are important. There are bars that help a person lift himself off and on the toilet and bars that he can grasp as he gets in and out of the bathtub. You can rent or buy bars that mount into your wall (the rental agency may install them for you) or that are free standing or clamp onto the tub. These latter are helpful if you are renting and cannot attach things to the walls.

Towel racks and the bar on the soap dish in many homes and apartments are glued to the wall or fastened only into the wallboard. They may come loose if a person grabs them for balance or to lift himself up. Ask someone knowledgeable about carpentry to be sure they are anchored into the stud in the wall or are designed for the purpose. A seat for the shower or tub can be purchased or rented. This often makes a person feel more secure and raises him up so that you can reach him without so much bending and stretching. Hose attachments are helpful for rinsing the person thoroughly and they make washing hair much easier.

Grab bars, bath seats, and hoses are sold and rented by medical supply houses, large drug stores, and some department stores. They come in a variety of designs to fit different bathrooms and to meet different needs. Medicare, Medicaid, or major medical insurance may pay part or all of the rental cost of equipment ordered by a physician.

INCONTINENCE (WETTING OR SOILING)

People with dementing illnesses may begin to wet themselves or have their bowel movements in their clothing. This is called, respectively, urinary incontinence and bowel or fecal incontinence. The two are really separate problems, and one often occurs without the other. There are many causes of incontinence, so it is important to begin by assessing the problem.

Urinating and moving one's bowels are natural human functions. However, ever since childhood we have been taught that these are private activities. Many of us have also been taught that they are nasty, dirty, or socially unacceptable. In addition, we associate caring for our own bodily functions in private with independence and personal dignity. When another person has to help us, it is distressing for both the helper and the disabled person. Often, too, people find urine or bowel movements disgusting and may gag or vomit when cleaning up. It is important for both family members and professional caregivers to be aware of their own strong feelings in these areas.

Urinary Incontinence

Urinary incontinence has many causes, some of which respond well to treatment. Ask yourself the following questions.

If the person is a woman, is she "leaking" rather than completely emptying her bladder, especially when she laughs, coughs, lifts something, or makes some other sudden exertion? Do accidents happen only at certain times of day, such as at night? (It is helpful to keep a diary for several days of the times accidents occur, the times the person successfully uses the toilet, and the times the person eats or drinks.) How often does the person urinate? Is the urination painful? Did the incontinence begin suddenly? Has the person's confusion suddenly gotten worse? Does the incontinence occur occasionally or intermittently? Is the person living in a new place? Is the person urinating in improper places, such as in closets or in flower pots? (This is different from the person who wets himself and his clothing wherever he happens to be.) Do accidents happen when the person cannot get to the bathroom on time? Are they happening on the way to the bathroom?

Whenever incontinence begins, it is important to check with the doctor. You can help him diagnose the problems by having the answers to these questions. If the person has a fever, report this to the doctor at once. Do not let a physician dismiss incontinence without carefully exploring all treatable causes.

Incontinence may be brought on by either chronic or acute bladder infections, uncontrolled diabetes, a fecal impaction, an enlarged prostate, dehydration, medications, or many other medical problems. (See Chapter 6, "Medical Problems.") "Leaking" can be caused by weakening muscles and other conditions that are potentially treatable.

"Common sense" might suggest that giving less fluid would reduce incontinence, but this can be dangerous, because it can lead to dehydration. A first step in addressing incontinence is to be sure that the person is getting enough fluid to adequately stimulate the bladder to work. Both too little and too much fluid can be bad. If you are uncertain how much fluid the person should get, ask your doctor or nurse. A doctor or nurse can also determine if the person is dehydrated.

If the problem is that the person moves slowly or uses a walker or is clumsy and cannot get to the bathroom in time, you can bring the toilet closer to the person. For example, if a person must go upstairs to the toilet, renting a commode for the ground floor may solve the problem. You can improvise a portable urinal that will help when you travel. You can also simplify clothing so the awkward person can manipulate it faster. Try Velcro tape instead of zippers or buttons. Can the person easily get up out of his chair? If he is sunk in a deep chair, he may not be able to get up in time.

Sometimes people cannot find the bathroom. This often happens in a new setting. A clear sign or a brightly painted door may help. People who urinate in waste baskets, closets, and flower pots may be unable to locate the bathroom or unable to remember the appropriate place. Some families find that putting a lid on the waste basket, locking closet doors, and taking the person to the bathroom on a regular schedule help. Remember that older people may have been taught as children to urinate outdoors or in a can by the bed. If so, it may be easier to supply them with a can than to clean up the waste basket.

Purchase washable chair cushion covers. Slide them on over a large garbage bag to waterproof cushions. If you have a favorite chair or rug that you are afraid will be damaged, take the easy way out and put it where the person will not use it.

Sometimes people need help and are either unable to ask for it or embarrassed to ask for it. People may have always used children's words such as *pee, piss, tinkle*, or *take a leak*, or even obscure euphemisms such as *go for a walk*. The person with language problems may say "I want tea" or "take a peek." If the caregiver (particularly someone unfamiliar with the patient) does not understand what the person is asking for, accidents can result. Learn what the person means and be sure that sitters or other caregivers know also.

If the person is incontinent at night, limit the amount of fluid he drinks after supper unless there is some medical reason why he needs extra fluid. (The rest of the day, be sure he is getting plenty of fluids.) Get him up once at night. It may be helpful to get a bedside commode he can use easily, especially if he has trouble moving around. Night lights in the bathroom and bedroom greatly help, too.

Falls often occur on the way to the bathroom at night. Make sure there are adequate lights and no throw rugs, that the person can get out of bed, and that he has slippers that are not slick-soled or floppy.

A diary will provide you with the information you need to prevent many accidents. If you know when the person usually urinates (immediately upon awakening, about 10 A.M., an hour after he has his juice), you can take him to the toilet just before an accident would occur. This is, in fact, training yourself to the confused person's natural schedule. Many families find that they can tell when the patient needs to go to the bathroom. He may get restless or pick at his clothes. If the person does not give you clues, routinely take him to the toilet every two to three hours. A regular schedule will avoid most accidents, reduce skin irritations, and make life easier for both of you. While it may be embarrassing to ask the person to go to the bathroom, this routine will save the person the humiliation of wetting himself.

Certain nonverbal signals that tell us it is time or not time to urinate may influence some impaired people. Taking down one's underpants or opening one's fly, or sitting down on a toilet seat is a clue to "go." Dry clothes and being in bed or in public are signals to "not go." (Some people are unable to urinate when there are "no go" clues, such as in the presence of another person or into a bedpan.) Taking down panties when undressing a woman may cause her to urinate. You may be able to use such nonverbal clues to help a person go at the right time.

One man urinated every morning as soon as he put his feet on the floor. If this is what is happening, you may be able to be prepared and catch the urine in a urinal. There are urinals for women as well as men, but they may be hard to find. Use a plastic bowl for a standing woman. People may also be inhibited and unable to go when you are in the bathroom with them or if you ask them to use a commode in a room that is not a bathroom. It is often this involuntary "no go" response that leads families to say, "He wouldn't go when I took him and then he wet his pants. I think he is only being difficult."

Sometimes, if a person has trouble urinating, it may help to give him a glass of water with a straw and ask him to blow bubbles. This seems to help the urine start.

Sometimes a person asks to go to the bathroom every few minutes. If this is a problem, it is helpful to have a urologist see the person to determine whether there is a medical reason why the person feels he needs to urinate frequently. A urinary tract infection or certain medications can give a person this feeling or can prevent his completely emptying his bladder. (If his bladder is not completely empty, he will soon feel the need to urinate again.) If you have ruled out medical reasons and are sure the person is emptying his bladder when he urinates, take him to the toilet every two to three hours and try to distract him in the interim period.

Some doctors and nurses may still dismiss incontinence as inevitable. It is true that some people with dementia will eventually lose independent control of their functions, but many do not, and many causes of incontinence can be controlled. Even when the person has lost independent function, there is much you can do to make your work load easier and to reduce embarrassment for him. If you are having problems, ask for a referral to a nurse or physician with experience managing incontinence in dementia patients.

Bowel Incontinence

Bowel incontinence, like urinary incontinence, should be discussed with a doctor. Abrupt onset or temporary incontinence may be the result of an infection, diarrhea, constipation, or a fecal impaction. (See Chapter 6, "Medical Problems.")

Be sure that the bathroom is comfortable and that the person can sit without discomfort or instability long enough to move his bowels. His feet should rest on the floor and he should have something to hold on to. A bar, made from a broom handle and crossing in front of the person between two professionally installed supports, will give him something to hold and will encourage a restless person to stay put. Try giving him something to do or letting him listen to music.

Learn when the person usually moves his bowels and take him to the toilet at that time.

Avoid reprimanding the person who has accidents.

Consult your physician if the person may be constipated or have an impaction. Also see page 100.

Cleaning Up

A person who remains in soiled or wet clothing can quickly develop skin irritations and sores. It is important to watch for these. Keeping the skin clean and dry is really the best protection against skin problems. The skin must be washed after each accident. Powder will keep the skin dry. Using a catheter as a continuing way to manage urinary incontinence should be avoided if possible.

The personal care of an incontinent person can seem degrading for him and unpleasant or disgusting to you. Therefore, some families have made a deliberate effort to use the clean-up time as a time to express affection. This can help to make a necessary task less unpleasant.

There is wearing apparel available for incontinent people. Should you use them? Professionals disagree over the use of incontinence wear. Some think that "diapers" are demoralizing and encourage infantile behavior. Some find that scheduled toileting is easier than managing incontinence wear. The answer lies in your own feelings about this and in the confused person's response. Incontinence clothing may make things easier for you and more comfortable for the confused person. However, nursing homes should not routinely use diapers as a cost savings without weighing the impact of this on the individual. We believe a toileting schedule is ideal when it works, but we recognize that some people resist it and others are incontinent even when a scheduled is tried. The doctor or nurse will help you decide what is right for you.

Disposable adult diapers and plastic outer pants are sold in drug stores and can be ordered through catalog stores. Some are more comfortable and stay on better if regular underpants are worn over them. Because of the negative feeling about the word *diaper*, these products are advertised as "adult briefs." Some are made so that one size fits all; for others, size is by hip or waist measurement. The type of filler used determines how much urine the brief will absorb. Products with a "gelling property," or super-absorbent polymers, usually hold much more than fiber-filled materials.

There are both disposable and washable garments. Some washable garments are not lined with soft materials, so the protective layer comes in contact with the skin and is uncomfortable. Many families find disposable liners are better because they hold larger volumes of urine. Liners with "gel" hold more urine with less bulk than fiber-filled materials.

Several products consist of an outer, washable pant that holds a disposable pad. The ideal is a soft, cool material in which the absorbent pad tends to draw urine away from the crotch so that the person's skin feels dry. It is helpful if the garment is designed so that the pad can be changed without lowering the garment and so that the garment can be lowered for toileting.

The leg of the pant should fit snugly, to prevent leakage, but should not bind. Adult briefs may leak around the legs of a thin person. Families have found that using a toddler-size diaper plus the absorbent section of an adult brief helps. Using a safety pin to attach the brief to the undershirt of a bedfast person will help contain a bowel movement. Some briefs have greater absorbency in the front, while others are more absorbent toward the back. Experiment to find the one that works best for you.

Garments that don't fit or that are too saturated may leak. Don't expect the garment to hold more than one urination. Pads may say how much fluid they will hold. A full bladder may empty eight to ten ounces (one cup) of urine.

In large cities, there are adult diaper services that save you the burden of washing these garments.

Disposable pads are made to protect bedding, and you can also buy rubberized flannel baby sheets. These are much less unpleasant than the older rubber sheets you may remember from your childhood.

Use a draw sheet on the bed. This is a regular sheet folded in half lengthwise and tucked in across the bed. It holds a plastic pad in place between it and the bottom sheet. Should the patient have an accident, you have only the draw sheet and the pad to change. Absorbent bed pads used in combination with a draw sheet and rubber pad will help keep the bed dry. Look for pads with a polymer (gelling) effect and an embossed back to keep them from slipping. Follow the manufacturer's washing and drying instructions.

It is not a good idea to use plastic pants, plastic bags, or rubber sheets that are not shielded by a layer of cloth next to the skin. They cause moisture to stay in contact with the skin and lead to irritation and rawness.

PROBLEMS WITH WALKING AND
BALANCE; FALLING

As the person's illness progresses, he may become stiff or awkward and
have difficulty getting out of a chair or out of bed. He may develop a
stooped or leaning posture or a shuffling walk. He will need close supervision when he is at risk of falling.

*A family member writes, "His steps are very slow now. As he walks,
he often raises his feet high, for he has little sense of space. He clutches
door frames or chairs. Sometimes he just grasps at the air. His gaze is
unfocused, like that of a blind man. He stops in front of mirrors, and
he talks and laughs with the images there."*

*A wife says, "He sometimes falls down. He trips over his own feet or
just crumples up. But when I try to lift him—and he is a big man—he
yells and struggles against me."*

Any of these symptoms *may* be caused by medications. Discuss with
the doctor any change in walking, posture, stiffness, repetitive motions,
or falling. He needs to be sure that there is not a treatable cause for them,
such as medications, a delirium, or a small stroke. These same symptoms
will occur when the dementing process has damaged the areas of the brain
which control muscle movements. But do not assume this is the cause until
the doctor has eliminated other causes.

Watch for the time when the person can no longer safely negotiate stairs,
or trips, or has other difficulties walking. If a person is unsteady on his feet,
have him take your arm, if he will, rather than your grasping his. Hold your
arm close to your body. This maximizes your ability to keep your balance.
Or you may steady him by walking behind him and holding his belt.

Put away scatter rugs, which may slide when the person steps on them.
Install hand rails, especially in the bathroom. Pad the steps with rug
samples. Staple or tack down rug edges. Round off shelf corners or pad
them with foam rubber scraps. Be sure that chairs or other furniture that
the person tends to lean on are sturdy; put unstable or antique furniture
away. Simplify traffic patterns. Get things out of the way in areas where
the person usually walks. Stair rails in many homes are inadequately
anchored, and will come loose if a person leans on them heavily. Have
someone knowledgeable about carpentry check this out for you.

Some people fall when they first get out of bed. Have the person sit on the
edge of the bed for a few minutes before walking. Many slippers and shoes
have slick soles that can cause falls. Some people will stumble more in crepe-

soled shoes. Others benefit from the grip crepe gives. Some people can learn to use canes or walkers. Others cannot learn this new skill. If the person cannot learn to use an appliance properly, it is safer for them not to use it.

When you help a person, it is important that you not hurt yourself or throw yourself off balance. A physical therapist can show you ways to assist a person without strain. Avoid leaning forward or bending over when you lift. If you must bend to lift something, bend at the knees, not at the waist. Take your time; accidents happen when you rush yourself or the confused person. If you lift a person, lift from under his arms in the armpit. Avoid pulling him up out of bed by the arms. Avoid trying to put an awkward or heavy person into the back seat of a two-door car.

When a person falls:

1. Remain calm.
2. Check to see if he is visibly injured or in pain.
3. Avoid precipitating a catastrophic reaction.
4. Watch the person for signs of pain, swelling, bruises, agitation, or increased distress; call the doctor if any of these symptoms appears or if you think there is any chance that he hit his head or otherwise hurt himself.

Instead of trying to get her husband up, one wife trained herself to sit down on the floor with him. (Obviously this took an effort to calm her own distress.) She would pat him and chat with him gently until he calmed down. When he was relaxed she was able to encourage him to get himself up one step at a time rather than having to lift him.

Becoming Chairbound or Bedbound

As the disease progresses, many people gradually lose the ability to walk. This begins with occasional stumbling and falling, progresses to taking smaller and smaller steps, and develops, usually after years, into the person's being unable to stand. Eventually the person may not be able to straighten his legs to the floor when held upright by others. This is sometimes called an apraxia of gait. (See pages 41–43.)

In contrast to this gradual progression, an abrupt loss of the ability to stand or walk or the sudden onset of falling means that the person has another illness or a medication reaction. This should be investigated promptly by a physician.

The gradual loss of the ability to walk or stand is the result of progressive brain damage; the person has forgotten how to walk. Keeping people as active as possible helps to maintain their muscle strength and general health, but there is no evidence that exercise or activity can postpone or prevent the loss of the ability to walk.

Even though a person cannot walk, he may be able to sit up. Sitting in a chair much of the day enables him to continue to be a part of family or institutional life. If the person has a tendency to fall forward or out of the chair, you can prop him with pillows or use a waist restraint. You can purchase a waist restraint made for support or you can make one. It is a padded belt several inches wide, which can be adjusted so that it will not be tight. It should be easy to unfasten from the back in an emergency.

An alternative is a lounge chair or a Gerichair (you can rent or purchase these from medical supply houses). When a lounge chair is kept in the reclined position, it protects the person from falling forward. You may prop him with pillows so that he is comfortable. You may want to move the person from chair to chair to bed so that his position changes. Use pieces of "egg crate" foam (available from a medical supply house) to cushion him.

Some people eventually become unable to sit. They usually have con-tractures—stiffened tendons that do not allow their joints to fully open or extend. Contractures may be postponed or reduced by keeping people physically active and with physical therapy, but they can occur late in Alzheimer's disease or following a stroke, even when the person's joints are moved and exercised by others.

When patients are no longer able to move voluntarily and are confined to bed, they require almost constant physical attention. They are at high risk of developing bedsores or pressure sores (see p. 98) and getting food, saliva, and other substances into their lungs because they cannot swallow or are lying down.

Bedbound patients should be carefully moved from one side to the other every two hours. Your doctor may recommend more frequent turning. Care must be taken to avoid putting undue pressure or weight on any one part of the body, because these patients tend to have brittle bones and fragile skin. Satin or silk sheets and pajamas can make it easier to move someone who cannot move independently. When the person is lying on his side, he should be propped up with a pillow. A pillow or pad is sometimes necessary between the knees to prevent sores from forming. Skin must be kept clean and dry.

Moving a totally bedbound person requires skill and training. Visiting nurses and physical therapists can be helpful in teaching you how to move and turn the person.

Wheelchairs

If the time comes when the person needs a wheelchair, your doctor or a visiting nurse can give you guidance in selecting and using one. Your library will have several books with information about maneuvering wheelchairs. Wheelchairs can be uncomfortable for people who sit in them for long periods. The seats of many chairs are hard and can cause pressure sores. Chairs that do not support the patient's body correctly can cause muscle and nerve damage as well. Sometimes patients slump in the chair or are left sitting with an arm hanging so that fingers go numb. There are different kinds of wheelchairs. A qualified person should help you select a chair that is comfortable and supports the patient. You will also need a chair that meets your needs in weight (Can you lift it?), portability (Will you need to take it in the car?), and width (Will it go through your doorways?). Ask a physical therapist or nurse to show you how to help the patient in and out of the chair and how to support the person correctly.

CHANGES YOU CAN MAKE AT HOME

There are many changes you can make at home which might make life easier for you and for the confused patient (see Appendix 3). While they may help, gadgets are not the total solution. When you consider changes, ask yourself whether you can live with them comfortably. Also, remember that people who have dementing illnesses may not be able to learn even simple new things and sometimes cannot adjust to minor changes. You might purchase a new telephone that is easy for you to operate, only to find that the person cannot learn to use it; or you might rearrange the furniture and then realize this upsets the person more.

Some of the products we will mention here are sold for other purposes. It takes a bit of imagination to apply them to the care of people with dementia. It is important to remember that no single suggestion will work in all situations. However, most of these are helpful and low in cost.

Products that promote safety.
    These include no-skid mats (for bathtub, under rugs, and elsewhere), grab rails (for bath, hall, bedroom), a temperature control on the water heater, fire and smoke alarms, and shower seats. We have discussed these elsewhere in the book. Look for them in hardware stores, electronics stores, or medical supply houses.

    Long-reach lighters work like cigarette lighters but have a long nozzle. They make lighting a gas stove safer and make it unnecessary to have matches lying around. Some people with dementia will be unable to learn to operate them—which is another safety advantage. Sound-activated switches can turn on a light when you or the patient gets up at night. Timers can be put on an electric stove so that it will operate only between certain hours and will shut off automatically.

Gadgets that make life easier for older people.
    These include recliners, special cushions for thin people or those with

sensitive skin, all sorts of lights (to make vision easier, some clip onto a cabinet to increase light in bath or bedroom), heating pads, magnifying glasses for people with vision problems, amplifiers and lights that alert people with hearing problems to sounds such as the telephone or doorbell. Catalogs advertised in magazines that cater to older people carry many such products.

Tools that help people with arthritis.

Many devices are available to enlarge the size of handles on dinnerware, pens and pencils, and any other item that must be grasped. There are also long reaching devices for getting things off the floor or down from a high shelf. There are several devices for opening jars. These are usually advertised in magazines aimed at an older audience.

Devices that allow you to record telephone calls.

In combination with a tape recorder, a "record adapter" or "record control" will turn on the tape recorder when the telephone is picked up and turn it off when the phone is hung up. These will allow you to monitor calls the confused person is getting or making. There are also telephones that have large numbers for people with coordination or vision problems and telephones that are voice activated for people who cannot pick up the receiver. People with dementia may not be able to learn to use these. Adapters are sold in electronics stores. Special telephones are sold through the catalogs mentioned above.

Devices that alert you that the person is up at night or is going out the door.

There are many inexpensive ways to be warned that the person is opening a door or moving about. A handyman can install them. (Expensive "wandering devices" are seldom needed.) Most of these are sold as burglar alarm devices in electronics stores and from catalogs. (These stores often know of someone who can install them.)

These devices can be sensitive to motion or sound (when the person approaches or is moving around); to pressure (a pressure pad beside the bed will warn you that the person is up; one by the door will alert you that he may be going out); an open or closed circuit (a pair of small magnetic switches on the door or window will activate a buzzer); a switch recessed into the door will also activate a buzzer when the door is opened; or light (a person passing through the light beam will trigger a buzzer).

Gadgets that turn on the lights.

These devices can be wired to turn on lights outside (to ward off burglars) or inside (a light going on in the bathroom may help the person find his way without your having to get up).

Gadgets that provide sound for you or him.

A headset will allow you to listen to music while the person listens to television (or vice versa). A clock radio will play soothing music at bedtime and then turn itself off. Some gadgets play "white noise," soothing background sounds that help some people fall asleep. Test them before purchasing.

Gadgets for security.

You might consider some of these same low-cost devices for security. Lighting stores and electronics stores carry small switches that will turn on your house lights from outside as you approach.

Gadgets that monitor sounds.

Originally designed for parents of small babies, these systems enable you to hear what is going on while you are in another room or in the yard. You place a small transmitter in the ill person's pocket and carry a small receiver with you which picks up the sounds of whatever the person is doing.

Home videos.

Home video use is limited only by one's imagination. Some people with dementia enjoy watching films (especially from their own era); nursing homes use videos for staff training; staff members sometimes videotape each other interacting with patients, and then study the film for ways to improve care; home movies can be converted to videotape so that family members can reminisce together. You can tape yourself giving a message to the person, for example, "John, this is Mary, your wife. I have gone to work. Mrs. Lambe will be with you until I come home at six. She will fix your lunch and then you will go for a walk. I want you to stay with her. I love you. See you at 6:00."

Should Environments Be Cluttered or Bare?

How cluttered should the environment be? People with dementia often have difficulty focusing on one thing in a cluttered room. Order, routine, and simplicity are helpful to the person who has trouble concentrating or thinking. However, some environments are so barren that they add to sensory deprivation and disorientation. Some people urge families to put away many things; others say that patients need stimulation. Some people argue that pictures on the wall or wallpaper cause hallucinations or disorientation. How do you know what is right? The answer depends on the individual person and the kind of clutter or interest the room offers.

Observe your patient: Does he tend to grab at everything in the bathroom? Does he put his hands into serving dishes or play with the condiments in the center of the table? Does he seem unable to decide what food to eat first or what piece of tableware to pick up? If you observe these things, try simplifying. Remove unnecessary things from the bathroom; leave serving dishes in the kitchen or put only one item of food on his plate at a time. An occasional person will talk to the pictures on the wall or try to pick the flowers off the wallpaper. However, most people will not do this. One woman in a nursing home was proud of the wallpaper "her husband put up." If a picture or mirror is distressing the person, remove it; but there is no reason to remove it if she just talks to it and is not distressed by it.

In general, people, animals, noise, lights, and action in a room are more distracting than the decor. If the person is restless, irritable, or having difficulty attending to you, consider reducing these distractions, but be sure that plenty of meaningful, focused, one-to-one interactions are provided in their place.

Things a person has to choose between (like several bottles of shampoo in the shower or several kinds of food on a plate) cause more problems than things that are "just there," like several cushions on the sofa. If the person stacks the pillows or carries them around, there is no need to put them away. Remove things only if they are causing a problem.

In contrast to family homes, nursing homes may not offer enough stimulation, interest, or environmental cues. Whatever the setting, observe the person's response to it. People who pace, fiddle, or repeat the same thing over and over may stop if they are helped to do an activity they can focus on.

There are many ways we can help a confused person function by changing the physical environment. We can also use the environment to keep the person away from certain areas. For example, as we age, we need more light to see; therefore, be sure that there is enough light. People with dementia are doubly handicapped because they may not think to turn on a lamp or go over to the window for light. Colors with considerable contrast are easier to see than pastels or colors similar in intensity. To the person with some visual impairment, it may be impossible to see light-colored food on a white plate. If the bathroom rug is deep blue, the person may have more success targeting the white toilet than if the rug is also white.

Just as color can be used to help people notice things, it can be used to hide things. Paint a door (frame, baseboard, and all) to match the adjoining walls if you want the person to ignore it. A curtain over a door also helps.

Hearing aids magnify background noise, and people with dementia often cannot learn to compensate for this. Eliminate background noise wherever possible, unless the person is enjoying it and focused on it.

6

MEDICAL PROBLEMS

PEOPLE WITH DEMENTING ILLNESSES can also suffer from other diseases ranging from relatively minor problems, like the flu, to serious illnesses. They may not be able to tell you they are in pain (even if they are able to speak well) or they may neglect their bodies. Cuts, bruises, or even broken bones can go unnoticed. People who sit or lie for long periods of time may develop pressure sores. Their physical health may gradually decline. *Correction of even minor physical problems can greatly help people who suffer from dementing illnesses.*

You may have experienced a feeling of mental "dullness" when you were sick. This phenomenon can be worse in people with dementing illnesses, who seem to be especially vulnerable to additional troubles. A delirium can be brought about by other conditions (flu, a minor cold, pneumonia, heart trouble, reactions to medications, and many other things) and it may look like a sudden worsening of the dementia. However, the delirium (and the symptoms) usually goes away when the condition is treated. You should check routinely for signs of illness or injury and call them to the attention of your doctor.

People who cannot express themselves well may not be able to answer yes or no when you ask them specific questions such as, "Does your head hurt?" Even people who still express themselves well may fail to recognize or may be unable to report pain.

All indications of pain or illness must be taken seriously. It is important to find a physician who is gentle, who understands the patient's condition, and who will take care of general medical problems. Do not let a doctor dismiss a patient because she is "senile" or "old." Insist that her infection be treated and her pains diagnosed and relieved. Because of the person's vulnerability to delirium, it is wise to check with the doctor about even minor conditions, such as a cold.

Signals of illness include:

- abrupt worsening of behavior (such as refusal to do things she was previously willing to do),
- fever (a temperature over 100° F). When taking a temperature, use the new liquid-crystal thermometers that are placed against the skin or thermometers with a plastic-coated "probe." These are available in drug stores. Confused people may bite a glass thermometer. Older people may not have a significant fever even when they are seriously ill. Lack of a fever does not mean that the person is well.
- flushing or paleness,
- a rapid pulse (over 100), not obviously associated with exercise. Normal for most people is between 60 and 100 beats per minute. Have a nurse show you how to find a pulse in the wrist. Count for 20 seconds and multiply by 3. It is helpful to know what a normal pulse is for the individual.
- vomiting or diarrhea,
- changes in the skin (it may lose its elasticity or look dry or pale),
- dry, pale gums or sores in the mouth,
- thirst or refusal of fluids or foods,
- a change in personality, increased irritability, or increased lassitude or drowsiness,
- headache,
- moaning or shouting,
- sudden onset of convulsions, hallucinations, or falls,
- becoming incontinent,
- swelling of any part of the body (check especially hands and feet),
- coughing, sneezing, signs of respiratory congestion, or difficulty breathing.

Ask yourself the following questions: Has the person had even a minor fall? Has she moved her bowels in the last seventy-two hours? Has she had a recent change (within the past month) in medication? Is she suddenly not moving an arm or leg? Is she wincing in pain? Does she have other health problems, such as heart disease, arthritis, or a cold?

If a person begins to lose weight, this may indicate the presence of a serious disease. It is important that your doctor determine the cause of any weight loss. A person who has lost 10 percent of her weight needs to be seen by a physician as soon as possible.

PAIN

Families ask if people suffer pain as part of a dementing illness. As far as is known, Alzheimer's disease does not cause pain and multi-infarct dementia causes pain only very rarely. People with dementing illnesses do suffer pain from other causes, such as stomach and abdominal cramps, constipation, hidden sprains or broken bones, sitting too long in one position, flu, arthritis, pressure sores, bruises, cuts, sores or rashes resulting from poor hygiene, sore teeth or gums, clothes or shoes that rub or are too tight, and open pins.

Indications of pain include a sudden worsening of behavior, moaning or shouting, refusal to do certain things, and increased restlessness. All signals of pain must be taken seriously. If the person cannot tell you where or whether she is in pain, a physician may have to search for a specific site and cause of the pain.

FALLS AND INJURIES

People with dementing illnesses may become clumsy; they can fall out of bed, bump into things, trip, or cut themselves. It is easy to overlook serious injuries for several reasons: (1) older people are more vulnerable to broken bones from seemingly minor injuries, (2) they may continue to use a fractured limb, (3) people with dementia may not tell you they are in pain or may forget they have fallen. A bruise may not be in evidence for several days. Even minor head injuries can cause bleeding within the skull; this must be treated promptly to avoid further brain damage.

Check the person routinely for cuts, bruises, and blisters that may be caused by accidents, falls, pacing, or uncomfortable clothing. Feet and mouth are frequently overlooked sites of pain. Changes in behavior may be your only clue to an injury.

PRESSURE SORES

Pressure sores (decubitus ulcers) develop when a person sits or lies down for prolonged periods. They can be caused by tight clothing, swelling, or inadequate nutrition. Older people's skin may be quite vulnerable to pressure sores. Pressure sores begin as red areas and can develop into open sores. They are more common over bony areas: heels, hips, shoulders, shoulder blades, spine, elbows, knees, buttocks, and ankles. Fragile skin can easily be torn and bruised, even in routine washing. You must watch for red spots or bruises, especially over hips, tailbone, heels, and elbows. If any reddening appears, make sure the person does not lie on that spot. Continue to turn her so other sores do not form. Contact your doctor or visiting nurse. Prompt attention can prevent a minor bruise from progressing to something more serious.

Encourage the person to change position: ask her to change the TV channel, go for a walk, set the table. Ask her to come into the kitchen to see if the cake is baking correctly or to come to the window to see something.

Pressure sores are always a risk in people who are no longer able to move or are bed- or chairbound. Develop a schedule in which you move the patient from one side to the other or change her position every two hours.

If the person does not change position enough, you can protect vulnerable areas. Medical supply firms sell "floatation" cushions that the person can sit or lie on. If the person is hospitalized, save the foam mattress from the hospital. There are air cushions, water cushions, gel pads, foam pads, and combinations of these. Select one that has soft, washable covers and shields against spills and odors. Stores also sell heel and elbow pads (these are made of a synthetic sheepskinlike material) that protect these bony areas. Use these *in addition* to frequent turning.

DEHYDRATION

Even people who can walk and appear to be able to care for themselves may become dehydrated. Because we assume that they are caring for themselves we may not watch for the signs of dehydration. Watch for this problem especially in people who have vomiting, diarrhea, or diabetes, or are taking diuretics (water pills) or heart medication. Symptoms include: thirst or refusal to drink; fever; flushing; rapid pulse; a dry, pale lining of the mouth or a dried, inelastic skin; dizziness or lightheadedness; and confusion or hallucinations.

The amount of fluid a person needs varies with the individual and with the season. People need more fluids during the summer months. If you are uncertain whether the person is getting enough fluid, ask your doctor how much the patient should be drinking.

PNEUMONIA

Pneumonia is an infection of the lungs caused by bacteria or viruses. It is a frequent complication of dementia, but may be difficult to diagnose because symptoms such as fever or cough may be absent. Delirium may be the earliest symptom, so pneumonia should be suspected when a person with dementia worsens suddenly. People who choke frequently or who are bedbound are particularly vulnerable to pneumonia.

CONSTIPATION

When a person is forgetful, she may not be able to remember when she last moved her bowels and she may not realize the cause of the discomfort that comes from constipation. Some people move their bowels less frequently than other people; however, they should have a bowel movement every two or three days.

Constipation can cause discomfort or pain, which can cause a worsening of the person's confusion. Constipation can lead to a bowel impaction, in which the bowel becomes partially or completely blocked and the body is unable to rid itself of wastes. You should consult a doctor or nurse if you suspect this. (A person can have diarrhea accompanying a partial impaction.)

Many factors contribute to the development of constipation. One important factor is that most Americans eat a diet high in refined, easy-to-prepare foods and low in fiber-containing foods that encourage bowel activity. Often when a person has a dementing illness or her dentures fit poorly or her teeth hurt, she makes further changes in her diet that aggravate the problem of constipation. The muscles of the bowel that move wastes along are believed to be less active as we age, and when we are less physically active, our bowel is even less active. Some drugs and some diet supplements (given to people who are not eating) tend to increase constipation. Ask the pharmacist whether the drugs the person is taking can cause constipation.

If a person has a dementing illness, you cannot assume that she is able to keep track of when she last moved her bowels even if she seems to be only mildly impaired or if she tells you she is taking care of herself. If a confused person is living alone, she may have stopped eating things that take preparation skills and may be eating too much cake, cookies, and other low-fiber, highly refined foods. It may be impossible to find out how regularly her bowels move. If you suspect that she may be getting constipated, you will need to keep track for her. Do this as quietly and unobtrusively as possible, so that you do not inadvertently make her feel that you are "taking over."

Most people are private about their bodily functions and a confused person can react angrily to your seeming invasion of her privacy. Also, keeping track of someone else's bowel movements is distasteful to many of us, and we tend to avoid doing it. These two feelings can conspire to cause a potentially serious problem to be overlooked.

When a demented person appears to be in pain or has a headache, do not overlook constipation as a possible cause. Bloating or "gas" also signals problems. In the midst of providing care for a seriously impaired person, it is easy to forget to keep track of bowel movements. If you think the person may be constipated, you may want to talk this over with the doctor. He can quickly determine whether the person's bowels are working properly, and, if they are not, he can help manage the problem.

Regular or frequent use of laxatives is not recommended. Instead, increase the amount of fiber and water in the diet, and help the person get more exercise (perhaps a daily walk). Most people should drink at least eight glasses of water or juice every day. Increase the amounts of vegetables (try putting them out as nibbles), fruits (including prunes and apples, as more nibbles or on cereal), whole-grain cereals (bran, whole-grain bread, whole-grain breakfast cereal), and salads, beans, and nuts she eats. Granola and other whole-grain cereals make a good snack.

Ask your doctor whether you should add more fiber by giving psyllium preparations (sold under various brand names, such as Metamucil). Do not use any such product without medical supervision.

MEDICATIONS

Medications are a two-edged sword. They may play a vital part in helping the patient to sleep, in controlling her agitation, or in the treatment of other conditions. At the same time, people suffering from a dementing illness (and older people in general) are susceptible to overmedication and to reactions from combinations of drugs. This includes over-the-counter drugs, unguents, creams, and suppositories. A sudden increase in agitation, a slow stooped walk, falling, drowsiness, incontinence, apathy, sleepiness, increased confusion, leaning, stiffness, or mouth or hand movements may be a side effect of medication and should be called to the doctor's attention. Physicians cannot always eliminate all the side effects of the medication and at the same time get the needed results. You and your physician must work together to achieve the best possible balance. Many people will need behavior-controlling medications to help them through some phases of their illness. However, because these can cause serious side effects, including more confusion, they must be used cautiously. Behavior-controlling drugs are best used when they are targeted to specific symptoms such as sleeplessness, hallucinations, suspicions, and severe irritability. They do not work well for controlling aimless wandering or restlessness. Whenever the physician raises the dosage of a behavior-modifying drug, ask yourself if there are any nondrug changes you can make that might also help. (See pp. 26–28.) Perhaps if you had more time to yourself, you could tolerate more restlessness on her part. Could you respond more calmly to her behavior or divert her before problems develop? Ask whether the drug can be given so that it has its strongest effect at the person's worst time of day.

Your pharmacist is highly trained in the effects and interactions of drugs. Some pharmacists now have special training in geriatric pharmacology. Much of the responsibility for medications, however, will fall to you. Here are some ways you can help.

Be sure that all of the physicians involved in the person's care know about all of the medications she is taking. Some combinations of drugs can make the person's confusion worse. You may want to take all the patient's prescription drugs and over-the-counter medications to your pharmacist and ask him to make up a card listing of all of them. Ask the pharmacist if any of these medications should be listed on the patient's identification bracelet. (Also see the Medic Alert information in Appendix 3.) Whenever the physician prescribes a new drug, ask him to review all the medications to see whether any can be discontinued. This will help reduce drug interactions. Ask him to start the new drug in as low a dose as possible, and to increase the dose later if necessary. People with brain injuries like dementia often develop side effects at low or regular adult doses. Ask whether this drug stays in the body the shortest time and whether another, similar drug would have fewer side effects.

Ask what side effects to watch for. Side effects can appear even three weeks or a month after the person began taking the drug. By then, you and the doctor may not attribute new symptoms to the medication. Ask if there are any possible side effects that you should report to your doctor immediately.

Some drugs must be taken before meals, some after. Some have a cumulative effect (that is, they gradually build up their effectiveness) in the body, some don't. Older people and people with a dementing illness are especially sensitive to incorrect dosages, so it is imperative that you see that the patient gets her medications in the amounts and at the times the doctor specifies. If a medication makes the person drowsy, ask if it can be given at bedtime when it will help her sleep and not be given in the morning when she should be active.

Find out what you should do if you miss a dose or accidentally give a double dose. Your pharmacist can give you information about side effects and medication interactions.

Some patients do not understand why you want them to take a medication and may have a catastrophic reaction. Avoid arguing about it. Next time, tell the person one step at a time what is happening: "This is your pill. Dr. Brown gave it to you. Put it in your mouth. Drink some water. Good." If the person becomes upset, try again later to give her the medicine. Some people will take pills more easily if you routinely put each dose in a cup or envelope instead of handing the person the whole bottle.

Patients may fail or refuse to swallow pills. They may carry the pill around in their mouth and spit it out later. You may find the pills much later on the floor. Getting the person to drink something with the medication helps. If this continues to be a problem, ask the doctor if the medication is available in another form. Pills or a liquid may be easier to get down than capsules. Sometimes the pills can be crushed and mixed into food (applesauce works well). If you are not sure whether the person actually took her pill, find out from the doctor or the pharmacist what you should do. If pills are going on the floor, be sure that children or pets don't find them.

Never assume that a forgetful person is able to manage her own medications. If you must leave the person alone, put out one dose for her and take the bottle away with you. Even people with mild memory impairments and normal people can forget whether they have taken their pills.

When you are tired or upset, you may forget the person's pills. Drug stores and health food stores sell plastic containers with compartments labeled "Monday," "Tuesday," "Wednesday," etc. You can tell at a glance whether today's pills have been taken. (This device is helpful for *you*: do not trust the patient to be able to use it.) You can ask the pharmacist for easy-to-open pill bottles if the childproof ones are difficult for you to open. However, the childproof caps may keep the confused person from taking pills she should not have.

Store medications where the confused person cannot reach them.

This section has been written to meet the needs of families caring for someone at home. In a nursing home, there are fewer reasons for using powerful, and sometimes dangerous, behavior-modifying drugs.

DENTAL PROBLEMS

It is important that the person receive regular dental check-ups. Painful cavities, abscesses, and sores in her mouth may be hard for you to find, and she may not be able to tell you about them. She may refuse to let you look in her mouth. Even mildly forgetful people may neglect their teeth or dentures and develop oral infections because oral problems can increase confusion or worsen behavior. The person's teeth must be pain-free and dentures must fit well. Poor teeth or ill-fitting dentures can lead to poor nutrition, which can significantly add to the person's problems. If the person is in a nursing home, be sure that arrangements are made for continued dental care.

People with dementia tend to lose dentures and partial plates. Ask the dentist to consider alternatives that cannot be removed and lost. Because people with dementia have a shortened life expectancy, treatments that last for many years may be less important than ease of management (for example, a fixed crown versus a removable bridge).

Many people resist going to the dentist. Look for a dentist who understands these patients and who works slowly and gently. Some dentists say they rarely have problems with confused patients. If the dentist recommends a general anesthetic to care for teeth, carefully weigh the need for the care against the risks of the anesthetic.

VISION PROBLEMS

Sometimes it appears that the person cannot see well or is going blind. She may bump into things, pick her feet up very high over low curbs, be unable to pick up her food on her fork, or become confused or lost in dim light. One of several things may be happening. She may have a problem with her eyes such as farsightedness or cataracts. Have her checked by an ophthalmologist. A correctable vision problem should be corrected, if possible, so that her impaired brain can get the best possible information from her eyes. If she is both not seeing well and not thinking well, she will be even less able to make sense out of her environment and will function more poorly. Do not let a physician dismiss her vision problems because she is "senile." Even if he cannot help, he should explain to you what the problem is.

Brain-impaired people may be less able to distinguish between similar color intensities. Thus, light blue, light green, and light yellow may look similar. A white handrail on a white wall may be hard to see. It may be hard for some people to tell where a light green wall joins a blue green carpet. This may cause the person to stumble into walls.

Some people have difficulty with depth perception. Prints and patterns may be confusing. A black and white bathroom floor can look as if it is full of holes. It may be difficult to know whether one is close enough to a chair to sit down. It may be hard to tell how high a step or curb is. It can be difficult to see where to step on stairs. Glare from a window tends to obliterate the detail of objects near it. The older eye may adjust more slowly to sudden changes from bright light to darkness or vice versa.

When the brain is not working well the person will be less able to compensate for these vision problems, but you can help her. She needs to see as well as possible so that she can function at her best level. Paint a handrail dark if the wall is light. Paint baseboards dark if the walls and floor covering are light. The dark line will help the person see the change from floor to wall. Cover the bathroom with washable carpeting that is secured so that it does not slip. Delineate the edges and bottom of the bathtub with colorful strips of waterproof tape. Paint stair risers and treads contrasting colors. The contrast will help.

Increase the light in rooms in the daytime and evening and leave night lights on at night. Install lights in dark closets. Cover chairs in bright, contrasting colors without patterns. Put a towel or spread over the chair if you don't want to recover it. Leave chairs in their familiar places.

People with dementing illnesses can also lose the ability to *know* what they see. In this instance the eyes work all right but the brain is no longer correctly using what the eyes tell it. For example, the person may bump into furniture, not because she has a vision problem but because her brain is not working properly. What seem like vision problems may be part of the dementia. This condition is called agnosia and is discussed in Chapter 8. When problems are caused by agnosia, the ophthalmologist will not be able to help. In fact, it may be difficult for him to test the vision of a person with thinking or language impairments. Obviously, when this is the problem it will do no good to tell the person to watch where she is going. She will need increasing care to protect her from injuries she cannot avoid, and you may need to check her frequently for cuts and bruises.

If the person is laying her glasses down and forgetting them, it often helps to have her wear them on a chain. Keep her old glasses, or buy her a spare pair in case she loses her glasses. Carry her prescription and your own with you if you go out of town. With a prescription, you can replace lost or broken glasses with less trouble and expense.

If the person wears contact lenses, you may need to replace them with glasses before she reaches the point where she is unable to manage contact lenses. If she continues to wear lenses, you must watch for irritations of the eye and be sure she cares for her lenses properly.

HEARING PROBLEMS

Failing to hear properly deprives the confused brain of information needed to make sense of the environment, and hearing loss can cause or worsen suspiciousness or withdrawal (see Chapter 8). It is important to correct any hearing loss if possible. A physician can determine the cause of the hearing loss and help you select an appropriate hearing aid. As with vision problems, it can be difficult for you to separate problems in thinking from problems in hearing. People with Alzheimer's disease develop problems understanding or comprehending what is said to them (see p. 35). An audiologist and your physician should be able to distinguish between this and the type of hearing loss that can be corrected.

Since the ill person cannot learn easily, she may not be able to adjust to her hearing aid. Hearing aids amplify background noises. This can be upsetting to the wearer. You may want to purchase a hearing aid with the agreement that you can return it if it does not work out.

If the person uses a hearing aid, you must be responsible for it and must check regularly to see that the batteries are working.

In addition to correcting the loss with a hearing aid, here are some things you can do:

1. Reduce background noises, such as noise from appliances, the television, or several people talking at once. It is difficult for the impaired person to distinguish between these and what she wants to hear.
2. Lower the pitch of your voice; high-frequency sounds are harder to hear.
3. Give the person clues to where sounds are coming from. It can be hard to locate and identify sounds, and this may confuse the person. Remind her, "That is the sound of the garbage truck."
4. Use several kinds of clues at one time: point, speak, and gently guide the person, for example.

VISITING THE DOCTOR

Visits to the doctor or dentist can turn into an ordeal for you and the patient. Here are some ways to make them easier.

The forgetful person may not be able to understand where she is going or why. This, combined with the bustle of getting ready to go, may precipitate a catastrophic reaction. Look for ways to simplify things for her.

Some people do better if they know in advance that they are going to the doctor. Others do better if you avoid an argument by not bringing up the doctor visit until you are almost there. Instead of saying, "We have to get up early today. Hurry with your breakfast because today is your visit to Dr. Brown, and he has to change your medicine," just get the person up with no comment, serve her breakfast, and help her into her coat. When you are almost there, say, "We are seeing Dr. Brown today."

Rather than get in an argument, ignore or downplay objections. If the person says, "I am not going to the doctor," instead of saying, "You have to go to the doctor," try changing the subject and saying something like "We will get an ice cream while we are downtown."

Plan your trip in advance. Know where you are going, where you will park, how long it will take, and whether there are stairs or elevators. Allow enough time without rushing, but not so much time that you will be early and have a longer wait. Ask for an appointment at the person's best time of day. Take someone with you to help while you drive.

Talk to the receptionist or nurse. She may be able to tell you whether you have a long wait. If the office is crowded and noisy, she may be able to arrange for you to wait in a quieter place. Take along some snacks, a package of instant soup (the receptionist can get you hot water), or some activity the person enjoys doing. If the receptionist knows that you have a long wait, you may be able to take a short walk if you check in frequently with her. Never leave a forgetful person alone in the waiting room. The strange place may upset her or she may wander away.

The doctor may prescribe a sedative for the patient if other methods fail. Usually, however, your being calm and matter-of-fact and giving the person simple information and reassurance are all that is needed.

IF THE ILL PERSON MUST ENTER THE HOSPITAL

People with dementia often become ill with other conditions and need to be hospitalized. This can be a trying time for you and the confused person. The illness that caused the hospitalization may also cause a temporary decline in the person's cognitive function. The unfamiliar environment, the confusion of a busy hospital, and new treatments may precipitate a decline in function as well. It is not unusual for people with dementia to become agitated, scream, or strike out in such circumstances. Additional behavior-controlling medication may be necessary, but it can also further impair thinking or worsen behavior. The person may gradually return to normal after the hospitalization.

There are some things you can do to make hospitalization easier, but recognize that you cannot completely prevent problems. *It is important that you yourself not become exhausted.*

Talk to the doctor in advance of the person's admission about how the dementing illness may complicate the hospitalization. Ask if the treatment can be done on an outpatient basis. This may be difficult, but it shortens the time the confused person must be in a strange setting. If you do this, arrange for home nursing for the first few days after the treatment.

At admission, talk to the nursing staff. Let them know that the person has a dementia. Urge them to tell the person, as frequently as possible, where she is and to be calm and reassuring with her. Write out things the nurses need to know and ask that your notes be put in the chart. Mention things that will help them cope with her, such as nicknames, family whom she might ask about, things she will need to have done for her (like filling out the menu and opening milk cartons), and how toileting is managed.

Hospitals are often short-staffed and nurses often work under pressure. They may not be able to spend as much time with the confused person as they would like. They may not be trained to work with dementia patients.

It is usually comforting for the person to have someone she knows to be with her as much as possible and to accompany her to tests and treatments. A family member can help with meals, see that the person gets enough fluid, and reassure her about what is going on. Some hospitals will let family members stay overnight with confused patients. *But*, sometimes a family member's own anxiety and nervousness upset the patient or get in the way of the staff. Calmness—or nervousness—is contagious. The confused person will be influenced by your feelings. You may want to ask someone else to spend time with the person to give you a break. If you cannot go with the person for tests, explain to the staff how important it is to comfort and reassure her.

We recommend you consider hiring a sitter to stay with the person full-time or to be with the person when you or other family members cannot. If possible, arrange a schedule for children, family, or understanding close friends to be with the person.

Familiar clothing, a familiar blanket, and large photos of family members help reassure the person. Some families write a letter to the person that nurses can use to reassure her when she is anxious. It might read like this:

Dear Mom: You are in the hospital because you broke your hip. You will be coming back home to our house soon. Ted or I will come to see you every night right after you have your supper. The nurses know you have trouble remembering things and they will help you. I love you. Your daughter, Ann.

If the person must be restrained, ask that the restraint be as mild as possible. For example, mittens can be used to keep the person from pulling out tubes. This is usually less frightening than tying her hands.

Do not be alarmed if the person's confusion worsens in the hospital. In most cases the person's level of impairment will return to what it was before the hospitalization.

SEIZURES, FITS, OR CONVULSIONS

The majority of people with dementing illnesses do not develop seizures. Because they are so uncommon, you are not likely to have to face this problem. However, seizures can be frightening for you if you are not prepared to deal with them. Various diseases can cause seizures. Therefore, if the person does have a seizure it may not be related to the dementia.

There are several types of seizure. In a generalized tonic-clonic seizure (the kind we usually associate with a fit or seizure), the person becomes rigid, falls, and loses consciousness. Her breathing can become irregular or even stop briefly. Then her muscles will begin to jerk and she may clench her teeth tightly. After some seconds the jerking will stop and the person will slowly regain consciousness. She may be confused, sleepy, or have a headache. She may have difficulty talking.

Other types of seizure are less dramatic. For example, just a hand or arm may move in a repetitive manner.

A single seizure is not life-threatening. Most important, remain calm. Do not try to restrain the person. Try to protect her from falling or banging her head on something hard. If she is on the floor, move things out of the way. If she is seated you may be able to ease her to the floor or quickly push a sofa cushion under her to soften her fall if she should fall out of the chair.

Do not try to move her or to stop the seizure. Stay with her and let the seizure run its course. Do not try to hold her tongue and do not try to put a spoon in her mouth. Never force her mouth open after her teeth are clenched; you may damage her teeth and gums. Loosen clothing if you can. For example, unfasten a belt, a necktie, or buttons at the neckline.

When the jerking has ceased, be sure the person is breathing correctly. If she has more saliva than usual, turn her head gently to the side and wipe out her mouth. Let her sleep or rest if she wishes. She may be confused or irritable or even combative after the seizure. She may know something is wrong, but she will not remember the seizure. Be calm, gentle, and reassuring. Avoid restraining her, restricting her, or insisting on what she should do.

Take a few minutes after the seizure to relax and collect yourself.

If the person has a partial seizure nothing need be done. If the person wanders about, follow her and try to prevent her from hurting herself. When this type of seizure ends she may be temporarily confused, irritable, or have trouble talking. You may be able to identify the warning signals that a seizure is starting, such as specific repetitive movements. If so, you can make sure the person is in a safe place (out of traffic, away from stairs or stoves, etc.).

Your doctor can be helpful with seizures. He should be called the first time the person has any type of seizure, so that he can check her and determine the cause of the seizure. Stay with the person until the seizure is over and you have had a chance to collect yourself. Then call the doctor. He can prescribe medication to minimize the likelihood of further seizures.

If the patient is being treated for seizures, the doctor should be called if the person has many seizures over a short period of time, if the symptoms do not go away after several hours, or if you suspect that the person has hit her head or injured herself in some other way.

Seizures are frightening and unpleasant to watch, but they are usually not life-threatening nor are they indications of danger to others or of insanity. They can become less frightening for you as you learn how to respond to them. Find a nurse or experienced family member with whom you can discuss your distress and who can knowledgeably reassure you.

JERKING MOVEMENTS (MYOCLONUS)

Patients with Alzheimer's disease occasionally develop quick, single jerking movements of their arms, legs, or body. These are called myoclonic jerks. They are not seizures; seizures are repeated movements of the same muscles, while myoclonic jerks are single thrusts of an arm or of the head.

Myoclonic jerks are not a cause for alarm. They do not progress to seizures. The only danger they may present is inadvertent hitting of something and possible accidental injury. At present there are no good treatments for the myoclonus associated with Alzheimer's disease. Drugs can be tried, but these usually have significant side effects and offer little improvement.

THE DEATH OF THE IMPAIRED PERSON

Whenever you have the responsibility for an ill or elderly person, you face the possibility of that person's death. You may have questions you are reluctant to bring up with the doctor. Often, thinking about such things in advance will help relieve your mind and can make things easier if you have to face a crisis.

The Cause of Death

In the final stages of a progressive dementing illness, so much of the nervous system is failing that the rest of the body is profoundly affected. The person will die of the dementing illness. The *immediate* cause of death is often a complicating condition such as pneumonia, dehydration, infection, or malnutrition, but the *actual* cause of death is the dementing illness. In the past, death certificates often listed only the immediate cause of death. This has made it difficult for epidemiologists to determine accurately how prevalent dementing illnesses are. Reporting practices are changing as physicians become more knowledgeable about dementia.

Some people will die from stroke, heart attack, cancer, or other causes even though they also have Alzheimer's disease. These deaths can come at any time, so some people will be ambulatory and fairly functional up until their death.

Dying at Home

Families sometimes worry that the ill or elderly person will die at home, perhaps in her sleep, and that they will find her. Because of this a caregiver may be afraid to sleep soundly or may get up to check on the sick person several times a night.

One daughter said, "I don't know what I would do. What if one of the children found her?"

Perhaps you have heard of someone who found a husband or wife dead, and you wonder how you would handle this. Most families find it reassuring to plan in advance what they will do first, second, third.

- When the person dies, you can dial 911 or the local emergency number. Emergency personnel or paramedics usually will arrive promptly. Paramedics may routinely begin resuscitation efforts. If you do not want this to happen, you may not want to call them.
- You can select a funeral director or mortician in advance. When death occurs, you have only to call him.
- You might call your clergyman or physician. Discuss with them in advance whether they can respond to an emergency call late at night.
- Some people want a little time to say goodbye; others do not. If you do, the thing to do first might be to sit a little while with the person or cry, and then call someone.

Some families value the peacefulness and privacy that death at home allows, but families often worry about what dying looks like and about what to do. If you want the person to be able to die at home, a home care nurse can show you what care is needed and give you guidance on how to conserve your own energy. Also, there are books available on this. Hospice programs enable people to die either at home or in special facilities that offer comfort without aggressive interventions. In the past, few of them served people with dementia, but now some are taking dementia patients. Some can give you information about terminal care at home.

Dying in the Hospital or Nursing Home

Some families are comforted to know that professionals are in charge at this time, and so they choose a nursing home or hospital. Bedside care of a totally dependent person is hard work and is emotionally draining. Do not feel bad if this is not for you. You may be better able to give loving reassurance if someone else is providing the physical care.

Whatever choice you make is the right one for you; but whatever the setting, it is important to do some advance planning. Families have told us that unless you plan in advance, you may have little control over what takes place and things may be done very differently from the way you and your family member would have wished. Most of these problems revolve around how much and what kinds of life-sustaining interventions should be used.

When Should Treatment End?

When a person has a chronic, terminal illness, the person's family faces the question of whether it would be better to allow life to end or to prolong suffering. This is a difficult question, one that doctors, judges, and clergy struggle with, as do seriously ill people and their families. Each of us must make the decision based on our own background, beliefs, and experiences.

There are no "better" or "worse" choices, as long as the person receives gentle care and is kept comfortable. We describe some of the options, to help you select the kind of care that will be right for you and your family member. Some families want to be sure that everything possible has been done; others have felt hassled or upset by medical interventions they did not want.

Occasionally a physician, a social worker, or a nursing home has strong opinions about life support and resuscitation and will follow those opinions regardless of your wishes. Some act out of fear of lawsuits and some continue a practice because it is "the way we have always done it." Ask your physician and the nursing home what steps they will take. Will they routinely transfer the patient to a hospital? Will they insert tubes or give life-sustaining drugs? What procedures, if any, do they consider "routine" and carry out without your explicit consent? Will they discourage your presence in the patient's room? If an ambulance is summoned, will the paramedics automatically try to resuscitate the person? Will the hospital automatically try resuscitation? Are they open and responsive to your questions, or do they avoid your questions or dogmatically state positions?

You might ask a clergyman or a friend to help you make the necessary phone calls to ask these questions. If there is a local hospice organization, they may be able to tell you what the usual practices in your community are.

If you are not comfortable with the procedures in your hospital or nursing home, write out instructions for the care you want the person to receive. Request that these instructions be placed in the person's chart at the nursing home and hospital. Make one copy for the person's doctor and one copy for the nursing home to send with the patient to the hospital, and sign each copy. Ask the doctor and the nursing home directly if they will honor these instructions. Go with the person to the hospital if possible.

Occasionally, a family will feel so strongly opposed to the care available in a hospital or nursing home that they transfer the person to another nursing home or take her home to die.

What Kind of Care Can Be Given at the End of Life?

When a person has a chronic, terminal illness, the person's family must often make decisions about when to allow treatment and when to accept the declining course of the disease. There are few right or wrong answers, and there are many things that are not understood about the last stages of life. The questions that families often face include whether to use tubes to feed a person who has stopped eating and whether to treat concurrent illnesses with antibiotics or surgery. (You may have faced similar issues earlier in the illness, such as whether to restrain an ambulatory person who might fall; see p. 98.)

As you make these decisions, be cautious about accepting dogmatic opinions from "experts." Like the rest of us, professionals can easily confuse personal values with fact in this emotion-laden area.

When you consider questions about life-support interventions for terminally ill people, such as feeding tubes, oxygen, treating illnesses such as pneumonia with antibiotics, or surgery for acute problems, recognize that many things are not known about these difficult issues, and we sometimes understand even less about the effects of life-supporting interventions on patients with dementia. It is difficult to know whether an abrupt decline is part of the dementing illness or whether, if treated, the person might continue comfortably for some time. It is just as difficult to determine when a person with dementia is "terminally ill" or to predict when a person with late-stage dementia will die. These uncertainties add to the family's burden. Neither you nor the doctors may be able to say whether an intervention will help or will be distressing to a patient close to death.

We often do not know how the ill person experiences treatments— whether the severely impaired person is frightened by feeding tubes, bathing and turning, or restraints; whether lack of food or fluids is painful. We do not know if a patient who tries to pull out tubes does so because they are frightening or uncomfortable. It is risky to generalize about patients with dementia from what we know about patients who are dying from other illnesses.

The dementing illnesses are gradually progressive, and you may have to make these painful decisions several times in the course of the illness. Each decision must be made separately. For example, when pneumonia causes an ambulatory and apparently content person to stop eating, you may decide to use tube feeding. Later when she is severely impaired, you might decide not to use tube feeding if she stops eating.

Pain medication can be given even when a decision has been made not to use antibiotics, forced feeding, or other physical treatments; but pain medications often carry risks—they can impair a person's ability to breathe, for example. Nevertheless, you may decide that the benefit of pain relief outweighs the risk. Explicitly discuss this with the patient's physician and nurses.

Decisions will be easier if you weigh the ethical issues *after* you have obtained the best medical information available.

Mrs. Allen's children argued among themselves over whether it was against their religion not to give her food through a tube. She tried to pull out the tube and seemed frightened. When the doctor told them that even with the tube she would live only a few days, it was much easier to decide not to use tube feeding but to give her spoonfuls of ice cream from time to time to moisten her mouth.

Ask your physician how likely it is that the person will return to some previous level (that of a week ago or a month ago, for instance). Is it likely that the person's death will be delayed by hours, days, or months by the proposed intervention? What are the available alternatives? Are there any other interventions that might be less distressing? (See p. 71.)

Who makes the decision? Sometimes the patient has left a written statement about her wishes for life-prolonging care. Other people have told their families how they wish to be cared for or have made statements such as "I never want to be kept alive the way Mabel was."

If possible, you should arrive at an agreement with the rest of the family on the kind of care to give. Usually, providers must honor the patient's previous statement of wishes or the request of the person with legal responsibility for the person's care. Providers are often reluctant to give palliative care when the family members are in disagreement.

It can be difficult for family members to discuss these painful issues. Some people may refuse to talk about them; others may get angry. Some feel that it is wrong to "plan" for a death. However, talking things over often relieves feelings of anxiety and dread as death approaches and, as we have said, unless plans are made, the family may have little control over the last days of the person's life.

You might show this section to your family members and ask your physician, social worker, or clergyman to help coordinate a family discussion. Suggest that family members not bring up old disagreements but focus on this issue.

The death of the ill person, even after so long an illness, may be painful, and the practical tasks surrounding death are distasteful to many of us. Still, arranging a gentle and dignified death is one way you can give love and care to the ill person, and it will allow you to grieve in the way that is right for you without intrusions from strangers.

7

PROBLEMS OF BEHAVIOR

THE THINGS PEOPLE WITH DEMENTIA DO—their behaviors—can be the most distressing part of their illness. Chapter 3 discusses some of the common problems, including irritability, anger, and agitation. It also discusses why people act as they do: *Dementia damages the brain, so the person cannot make sense out of what he sees and hears.* This confusion may make the person frightened and anxious. This is why he sometimes insists on "going home," why he lashes out in anger at you or resists care. Most of these behaviors are not under his control, and he usually is trying as hard as he can.

Here are some general guidelines for managing difficult behaviors. Ask yourself if this behavior could result in someone—you or the confused person—being hurt. Or is the behavior making life intolerable for others (yourself, other residents, or staff) even though it is not dangerous?

If the behavior is potentially harmful, then you probably need to find a way to stop it, even if you must use a medication that has side effects. If it is not dangerous you should strongly consider letting it continue. This may be easier to tolerate if you get away from the person once in a while.

THE SIX *R'*S OF BEHAVIOR MANAGEMENT

Some families tell us that the ill person does some things that create serious problems. Do not assume that you will face all or even most of the problems listed in this chapter. But if you do face problems, one of the first places to seek help is the Alzheimer's Association support group in your area. It was from families that we learned many of the things we suggest in this book. Most Alzheimer's Association chapters publish newsletters. You can subscribe to several. They contain excellent ideas.

One husband does not call these "problems." He calls each difficulty a "challenge." This helps him approach it with a positive outlook. You will find that you solve problems better when you are not exhausted: find some time for yourself. Behaviors have different causes in different people and different solutions will work in different households. Some families have found these six *R*'s helpful in thinking through a problem.

Restrict. The first thing we often try is to get the person to stop whatever he is doing. This is especially important when the person might harm himself or someone else. But trying to make the person stop may upset him more.

Reassess. Ask yourself: Might a physical illness or drug reaction be causing the problem? Might the person be having difficulty seeing or hearing? Is something upsetting him? Could the annoying person or object be removed? Might a different approach upset the person less?

Reconsider. Ask yourself how things must seem from the patient's point of view. People with dementia are often unaware of the extent of their impairment. When you try to bathe or dress someone who does not understand that he needs help, he may get upset. The person's anxiety is understandable when things are going on that he can't make sense of.

Rechannel. Look for a way that the behavior can continue in a safe and nondestructive way. The behavior may be important to the person in some way that we cannot understand. One man who had been a mechanic continued to take things apart around the house, but he could not get them back together. His wife had an old automobile carburetor steam cleaned and gave it to him. He was able to enjoy taking it apart for several months, and he left the household appliances alone.

Reassure. When a person has been upset, fearful, or angry, take time to reassure him that things are all right and that you still care for him. While the person may not remember the reassurance, he may retain the feeling of having been reassured and cared for. Putting your arm around the person or hugging him is a way of reassuring him.

Take time to reassure yourself as well. You are doing the best you can with a demanding and difficult job. Give yourself a pat on the back for surviving one more challenge. If possible, find some time away from the person to regain your energy.

Review. Afterward, think over what happened and how you managed it. You may face this problem again. What can you learn from this experience that will help you next time? What led up to this behavior? How did you respond to it? What did you do right? What might you try next time?

CONCEALING MEMORY LOSS

People with a deteriorating dementing disease can become skillful at hiding their declining abilities and forgetfulness. This is understandable; no one wants to admit that he is getting "senile."

This tendency to hide limitations can be distressing for families. The person living with someone suffering from a dementing illness may know that the person is impaired yet get no support or understanding from others who cannot see the problem. Friends may say that "he looks and sounds perfectly all right. I don't see anything wrong, and I don't see why he cannot remember to call me." Family members may not be able to differentiate between real memory loss and plain contrariness.

When a person has been living alone, family, neighbors, and friends may be unaware for a long time that anything is wrong. When the person does not know that he has any memory problems, he may manage for years until a crisis occurs. Families are often shocked and distressed by the extent of the problem when they finally learn of it.

You may wonder what the person is still able to do for himself and what needs to be done for him. If he is still employed, has responsibility for his own money, or is driving, he may not realize or may be unwilling to admit that he can no longer manage these tasks as well as he once could. Some people recognize that their memory is slipping. Different people cope with this in different ways. While some people don't want to admit that anything is wrong, others find relief and comfort in talking about what is happening to them. Listen to their thoughts, feelings, and fears. This can be comforting and can give you a chance to correct misconceptions.

Others may successfully conceal their impairment by keeping lists. They may use conversational devices, such as saying "Of course I know that" to cover their forgetfulness. Some people get angry and blame others when they forget things. Some people stop participating in activities that they have always enjoyed.

A frequent characteristic of the dementing illnesses is that personality and social skills appear nearly intact while memory and the ability to learn are being lost. This condition enables a person to conceal his illness for a long time. One can talk with such a person about routine matters and fail to recognize that his memory or thinking is impaired. Psychological testing or an occupational therapy evaluation can be helpful in such situations because the evaluation will give you a realistic measure of how much you can expect from the impaired individual and what things the person can still do. Because dementing illnesses can be so deceiving, even to people close to the person, the assessment these professionals can give is most important to you in helping you and your family plan realistically. These professionals may also talk over their findings with the impaired person and show him ways he can remain as independent as possible.

WANDERING

Wandering is a common and frequently serious problem that deserves thoughtful consideration. Wandering behavior can make it difficult to manage a person at home. It can make it impossible for day care centers or nursing homes to care for a person. The impaired person is endangered when he wanders into busy streets or into strange neighborhoods. When a confused person becomes disoriented and lost, he may feel frightened. Because some people do not understand dementia, strangers who try to help the individual may think he is drunk or insane. When wandering occurs at night it can deprive the family of needed rest. However, it can often be stopped or at least reduced.

Since it appears that there are different kinds of wandering and different reasons why brain-impaired people wander, identifying the cause of the behavior may help you plan a strategy to manage it.

Reasons Why People Wander

Wandering may result from getting lost. Sometimes a person sets out on an errand, such as going to the store, makes a wrong turn, becomes disoriented, and gets completely lost trying to find his way back. Or he may go shopping with you, lose sight of you, and get lost trying to find you.

Wandering often increases when a person moves to a new home, begins a day care program, or for some other reason is in a new environment.

Some people wander around intermittently for no apparent reason. Some wandering behavior appears aimless and can go on for hours. It appears different from the wandering associated with being lost or with being in a new place. Some people develop an agitated, determined pacing. When this continues it gets on everyone's nerves. It can be dangerous when the person is determined to get away. This seemingly incomprehensible pacing may be associated with the damage to the brain. Occasionally, continuous pacing and wandering can cause the person's feet to swell.

Some people wander at night. This can be dangerous for the impaired person and exhausting for you.

Many of us can sympathize with the confused person's experience of becoming disoriented. We may have lost our car at a parking lot or gotten "turned around" in a strange place. For a few minutes we feel unnerved until we get hold of ourselves and work out a logical way to find out where we are. The person with a memory impairment is more likely to panic, is less able to "get hold of himself," and may feel that he must keep his disorientation a secret.

When wandering is made worse by a move to a new home or by some other change in the environment, it may be because it is difficult for a confused, memory-impaired person to learn his way around in a new setting. He may not be able to understand that he has moved and may be determined to go "home." The stress of such a change may impair his remaining abilities, which makes it harder for him to learn his way around.

Aimless wandering may be the person's way of saying, "I *feel* lost. I am searching for the things I feel I have lost." Sometimes wandering behavior is the person's way of trying to communicate feelings.

> *Mr. Griffith was a vigorous man of sixty who kept leaving the day care center. The police would pick him up several miles away hiking down the highway. Mr. Griffith always explained that he was going to Florida. Florida represented home, friends, security, and family to Mr. Griffith.*

Wandering may be the person's way of expressing restlessness, boredom, or the need for exercise. It may help to fill the need of an active person to be "doing something." It may signal a need to use the toilet.

A constant or agitated pacing or a determination to get away may be difficult to manage. Sometimes this is a catastrophic reaction. Something may be upsetting the person. He may not be able to make sense out of his surroundings or may be misinterpreting what he sees or hears. Sometimes this agitated wandering appears to be a direct result of the brain damage. It is hard to know exactly what is happening to the brain, but we do know that brain function can be seriously and extensively disrupted. Remind yourself that this is not a behavior that the person can control.

Night wandering can also have various causes, from simple disorientation to a seemingly incomprehensible part of the brain injury (see p. 22).

The Management of Wandering

The management of wandering behavior depends on the cause of the wandering. If the person is getting lost and if you are sure he can still read and follow instructions, a pocket card may help him. Write *simple* instructions on a card he can carry in his pocket and refer to if he is lost. You might put at the top of the card the written reminder "stay calm and don't walk away." You might write on the card "call home" and put the telephone number, or write "ask a clerk to show you to the men's wear department and stay there. I will come for you." You may need different cards for different trips. This will make it possible for a mildly confused person to help himself.

It is essential that you get the person a bracelet with his name and your phone number on it, and the statement "memory impaired." A bracelet that is securely fastened (so the patient cannot take it off) and too small to slip off is probably safer than a necklace. This information will help anyone who finds the person if he gets lost. You can have an inexpensive bracelet engraved in a store that engraves mugs, key rings, etc. Have a "memory impaired" bracelet made *now* if there is any possibility that the person will wander or get lost. This is so important that some clinics require that their patients have such identification. A lost, confused person will be afraid and upset, and this can cause him to resist help. He may be ignored or assumed to be crazy by the people around him. Under stress he may function more poorly than he usually does.

You can purchase bracelets with medical information on them from pharmacies. You may want the person to wear one, especially if he has a heart condition or some other serious health problem. You can order a Medic Alert bracelet reading *"Alzheimer's/memory impaired."* These bracelets also have a telephone number that can be called for further information about the person. Medic Alert maintains a trust fund to help low-income families pay for bracelets. Several similar products are also available. (See Appendix 3 for further information.)

Some forgetful people will carry a card in their pocket or wallet which gives their name, address, and phone number. Others will lose it or throw it away. However, ID cards are worth trying.

To reduce increased wandering when the person moves to a new environment, you may want to plan in advance of the move to make it as easy as possible for the impaired person. When a person is still able to understand and participate in what is going on around him, it may help to introduce him gradually to his new situation. If he is moving to a new home, involve him in planning the move (see p. 249) and visit often in the new setting before he moves. When a person's impairment makes it impossible for him to understand what is happening, it may be easier not to introduce him gradually but simply to make the move as quietly and with as little fuss as possible. Each person is unique. Try to balance his need to participate in decision making with his ability to understand. If you have a choice, make a move early in the illness; it will probably be easier for the person to adjust then and learn his way around.

If you are considering a day care center, we urge you to do so early in the illness. (See Chapter 10.) Day care centers and nursing homes have found that people adjust best when (1) they do not stay long the first few visits, (2) the caregiver stays with them the first few times, and (3) someone from the program visits them at home before the transition. Leaving a confused person alone to adjust or asking the family not to visit at first may add to the person's panic.

When a confused person finds himself in a new place, he may feel that he is lost, that you cannot find him, or that he is not supposed to be where he is. Reassure the disoriented person often about where he is and why he is there. "You have come to live with me, Father. Here is your room with your things in it," or "You are at the day care center. You will go home at 3:00."

When we give this advice, families sometimes tell us, "It doesn't work!" It doesn't work in the sense that the person may continue to insist that he doesn't live there and keep trying to wander away. This is because he is memory impaired and does not remember what you told him. He still needs to be gently and frequently reassured about his whereabouts. It takes time and patience to get him to accept the move and gradually come to feel secure. He also needs this frequent reassurance that you know where he is. A gentle reassurance and your understanding of his confusion help reduce his fear and the number of catastrophic reactions he has. Our experience with people who are hospitalized for their dementia is that, even with difficult people, frequent gentle reassurance about where they are sometimes helps them become comfortable (and easier to manage). However, this may take several weeks.

A move often upsets a person with a dementing illness, causing him to wander more or making his behavior worse for a period of time. It is helpful to know that this is usually a temporary crisis.

Because changes may make the person's behavior or wandering worse, it is important to consider changes carefully. You may decide that a vacation or an extended visit is not worth upsetting the confused person.

When the wandering seems to be aimless, some professionals suspect that exercise helps to reduce this restlessness. Try taking the person for a long, vigorous walk each day. You may have to continue an activity plan for several weeks before you see whether it is making a difference.

When wandering seems to be the person's way of saying, "I *feel* lost" or "I am searching for the things I feel I have lost," you can help by surrounding the person with familiar things, for example, pictures of his family. Make him feel welcome by talking with him or by taking time to have a cup of tea with him.

An agitated pacing or determined efforts to wander away are sometimes caused by frequent or almost constant catastrophic reactions. Ask yourself what may be happening that is precipitating catastrophic reactions (see p. 29). Does this behavior happen at about the same time each day? Does it happen each time the person is asked to do a certain thing (like take a bath)? Review the way people around the confused person are responding to his wandering. Does their response increase his restlessness and wandering? If you must restrain a person or go after him, try to distract him rather than directly confronting him. Tell him you will walk with him. Then lead him around in a big circle. Usually he will accompany you back into the house. Talking calmly can reassure him and prevent a catastrophic reaction that will change aimless wandering into a determination to get away. Wandering can often be reduced by creating an environment that calms the person.

When Mrs. Dollinger came into the hospital, she had been making constant, determined efforts to leave the nursing home. In the hospital, which was also a strange place, the nurses had much less difficulty with her.

In both places Mrs. Dollinger felt lost. She knew this was not where she lived and she wanted to go home. Also, she was lonely; she wanted to go back to her job, where her fogged mind remembered friends and a sense of belonging. So she wandered toward the door. The overworked nursing staff at the nursing home would yell loudly to her "Come back here." After a few days, one of the other residents in the home began to "help." "Mrs. Dollinger escaped again!" she would shout. The noise confused Mrs. Dollinger, who doubled her efforts to get out. This brought a nurse on the run; Mrs. Dollinger would panic and run away as fast as she could, straight onto a busy street. When an attendant caught her arm and held her, Mrs. Dollinger bit him. This happened several times, exhausting the staff and precipitating almost constant catastrophic reactions. The family was told that Mrs. Dollinger was unmanageable.

In the hospital Mrs. Dollinger headed for the door almost at once. A nurse approached her quietly and suggested they have a cup of tea together (distraction rather than confrontation). Mrs. Dollinger never stopped wandering to the door, but her vigorous effort to escape and assaultive behavior did stop.

If you think the person is wandering because he is restless, try giving him some active task like dusting or stacking books. Adult day care provides both things to do and companionship and therefore can be beneficial for those who wander.

Medication may reduce the patient's restlessness. However, some drugs can induce restlessness as a side effect. Medications must be closely supervised by a physician. Occasionally, the judicious use of major tranquilizers, under close medical supervision, can lessen wandering significantly. *They should be used only after all nondrug interventions have been tried.*

If incessant wandering causes the person's feet to swell, try sitting down with him and helping him to put his feet up. He may sit still as long as you sit with him. Other measures (see p. 125) may be necessary if you cannot get him off his feet. Be sure to check with the doctor about swelling or injured feet. The discomfort can make the person's behavior worse.

Changing the environment to protect the person is an important part of coping with wandering. One family found that the confused person would not go outside if he did not have his shoes on. Taking his shoes away and giving him slippers kept him inside.

It is often helpful to install locks that are difficult to operate or that are unfamiliar to the confused person, so that he cannot go outside unsupervised. Sometimes inexpensive devices such as a spring-operated latch are sufficient because the impaired person cannot learn the new task of opening them. A confused person is less likely to look for a lock at the bottom of the door. Make sure you can operate the locks quickly in case of a fire. There is an inexpensive plastic gadget available in hardware stores called a childproof door knob. It slips over the existing door knob. You can still open the door, but the confused person cannot figure out how to operate it.

Check other means of exit as well as doors. Confused people may climb out second story windows. Secure locks protect you as well as ensure the person's safety. The police department can advise you about inexpensive ways to secure your windows and patio doors.

If the person does go outside, be alert to hazards in the neighborhood, such as busy streets, swimming pools, or dogs. The person may no longer possess the *judgment* to protect himself from these things. You may want to take a walk through the neighborhood in which the person lives and look around thoughtfully for things that are dangerous for a person who no longer has the ability to assess his surroundings appropriately. At the same time, you may want to alert people in the neighborhood to the problem, reassuring them that the person is not crazy or dangerous but just disoriented.

The person himself can be his own worst hazard. When he looks healthy and acts reasonable, people tend to forget that he may have lost the judgment that would keep him from stepping over the side of a swimming pool or in front of a car.

Other people are also an environmental hazard to the confused person who wanders. In addition to those who don't understand are the cruel and vicious who seek out the elderly and the frail in order to harass, torment, or rob them. Unfortunately, there seem to be enough such people, even in the "nicest" neighborhoods, for you to recognize this hazard and protect the confused person from them.

There are physical devices to restrain a person in a chair or bed. The decision to use a restraint should be made jointly between you and the health care professional who knows the person best, and these should be used *only after all other possibilities have been tried*. (We are addressing here the use of restraints at home. The use of restraints in a nursing home involves other issues and will be discussed in Chapter 16.) The most familiar restraint is the Posey restraint. A patient can turn, shift position, or roll to the side in a Posey. Poseys can be rented from a medical supply house. It is very important that a Posey be properly applied; a nurse should show you how to use it.

A Gerichair is like a recliner with a tray on it that prevents the person from getting up. It will elevate a person's feet. A person can eat, sleep, or watch television in a Gerichair. These can also be rented or purchased.

Nurses occasionally find that a restraint, especially at night, provides the person with a firm reassurance that he must stay where he is. However, restraints further agitate some people.

Either a chair or a Posey restraint may help to keep a person still and safe long enough for you to take a bath or fix supper. Using restraints or a chair gives the person's feet a chance to recover.

Very agitated people can hurt themselves fighting against the bed while in restraints or may tip over a chair in which they are restrained. People cannot be left unsupervised for long periods in either Poseys or Gerichairs. *Never* leave a person alone in the house while he is restrained, because of the possibility of a fire. You should be able to release any restraining device quickly in case of emergency.

People with dementing illnesses can be difficult to manage, and wandering can be a serious problem. The responses vary with each person. One confused woman was only looking for the bathroom when she wandered away. A sign solved the problem. Another man got a screwdriver and took the door off its hinges when he found that he could not operate the lock.

You may reach a point when the wandering behavior is more than you can manage or when a person cannot be kept safely in a home setting. If this time comes, you will have done all you can and will need to plan realistically for institutional care for the person. Many places will not accept a patient who is agitated, combative, or a wanderer. See Chapter 16 for a discussion of placement issues.

SLEEP DISTURBANCES AND NIGHT WANDERING

Many people with dementing illnesses are restless at night. They may wake to go to the bathroom and become confused and disoriented in the dark. They may wander around the house, get dressed, try to cook, or even go outside. They may "see things" or "hear things" that are not there. Few things are more distressing than having your much-needed sleep disrupted night after night. Fortunately, there are ways to reduce this behavior.

Older people seem to need less sleep than younger people. People with dementing illnesses may not be getting enough exercise to make them tired at night, or they may be dozing during the day. Often it seems that the internal "clock" within the brain is damaged by the dementing illness. Some nighttime behavior problems may be in response to dreams that the impaired person cannot separate from reality.

If the person is napping during the day he will be less tired at night. Try to keep him occupied, active, and awake in the daytime. If he is getting tranquilizing drugs to control his behavior, these may be making him drowsy during the day. Discuss with the doctor the possibility of giving most of the tranquilizer in the evening instead of spreading the dose throughout the day. This may provide the behavior control without making the person sleepy during the day. If he must sleep during the day, try to get some rest yourself at the same time.

Often people with dementing illnesses are not very active and don't get much exercise. It may be helpful to plan a regular activity program—a long walk, for example—in the late afternoon. This may make the person tired enough to sleep better at night. A car ride makes some people sleepy. Day care centers are one of the best ways to keep a person active during the day.

See that the person has used the bathroom before going to sleep.

Older people may not see as well in the dark and this may add to their confusion. As our eyes age, it becomes more difficult to distinguish dim shapes in poor light. The confused person may misinterpret what he sees, so he thinks he sees people or thinks he is in some other place. This can cause catastrophic reactions. Leave a night light on in the bedroom and bathroom. Night lights in other rooms may also help the person orient himself at night. Reflector tape around the bathroom door may help. Try renting a commode that can sit right beside the bed.

Many of us have had the experience of waking from a sound sleep and momentarily not knowing where we are. This may be magnified for the confused person. Your quiet reassurance may be all that is needed.

Be sure the sleeping arrangements are comfortable: the room is neither too warm nor too cool, and the bedding is comfortable. Quilts are less likely to tangle than blankets and sheets. Bedrails help some people remember they are in bed. Other people get upset and try to climb over them, which is dangerous. You may want to rent bedrails and see if they help. Bedrails are available for most beds.

If the confused person gets up in the night, speak softly and quietly to him. When you are awakened suddenly in the night, you may respond irritably and speak crossly. This may precipitate a catastrophic reaction in the impaired person, which will get everybody up in the middle of the night. Often all that is needed is to remind the person gently that it is still nighttime and that he should go back to bed. A person will often go back to sleep after he has used the bathroom or had a cup of warm milk. Encourage him to go back to bed and sit with him quietly while he drinks his milk. A radio playing softly will quiet some people. Try using night-darkening shades and quietly remind the disoriented person that it is dark and the shades are drawn, therefore it is time to stay in bed.

Sometimes a person who will not sleep in bed will sleep in a lounge chair or on a sofa. If the person gets up in the night and gets dressed, he may sit back down again and fall asleep in his clothes if you don't interfere. It may be better to accept this than to be up part of the night arguing about it.

If the person does wander at night, you must examine your house for safety hazards. Arrange the bedroom so the person can move around safely. Lock the window. Can he turn on the stove or start a fire while you are sleeping? Can he unlock and walk out the outside doors? Can he, while trying to get to the bathroom, fall down the stairs? A gate across the stairs may be essential in houses where a disoriented person sleeps.

Finally, if these measures fail, sedative-hypnotics are helpful. However, you cannot simply give the person a sleeping pill and solve the problem. Sedatives affect the chemistry of the brain, which is complex and sensitive. Your doctor faces a series of difficult, interacting problems when he begins to prescribe sedatives.

Older people, including the well elderly, are more subject to side effects from drugs than are younger people. Side effects of sedatives are numerous and some are serious. Brain-injured people are more sensitive to drugs than well people. Older people are more likely to be taking other drugs that can interact with a sedative or to have other illnesses that can be aggravated by a sedative.

Sedating the person may make him sleep in the daytime instead of at night or it may have a hangover effect that worsens his cognitive functioning during the day. It can make him more confused, more vulnerable to falls, or incontinent. Paradoxically, it may even worsen sleep. Each person is different; what works for one may not work for another.

The effect of the sedative may change—for many reasons—after it has been used for a while. Your doctor may have to try first one drug and then another, carefully adjusting the dosage and the time at which it is given. Drugs may not make the person sleep all night. Therefore, it is important that you do all you can to help the person sleep with other methods. This does not mean that we discourage the use of sedatives; they are a very useful tool, but only one of several tools that can be used to manage a difficult problem. When the person is living at home, the doctor may prescribe sleeping medication for him so that you can get some rest. However, this should not be done in a nursing home where adequate, caring staff can use other interventions.

WORSENING IN THE EVENING

People with dementing illnesses often seem to have more behavior problems in the evening. We do not know what causes this. It may be that the person cannot see clearly in dim light and misinterprets what he sees, causing catastrophic reactions. Leaving lights on often helps. Telling the person where he is and what is happening may help.

A whole day of trying to cope with confusing perceptions of the environment may be tiring, so a person's tolerance for stress is lower at the end of the day. You are also more tired and may subtly communicate your fatigue to the confused person, causing catastrophic reactions.

Plan the person's day so that fewer things are expected of him in the evening. A bath (which is often difficult), for example, might be scheduled for morning or midafternoon if this works better.

Sometimes there are more things going on at once in the house in the evening. This may overstimulate the already confused and tired person. For example, are you turning on the TV? Are more people in the house in the evening? Are you busy fixing supper? Are children coming in? Being tired may make it harder for him to understand what is going on and may cause him to have catastrophic reactions.

If possible, try to reduce the number of things going on around the person at his worst times of day or try to confine the family activity to an area away from the impaired person. It is also important to try to plan your day so that you are reasonably rested and not too pressed for time at the times of day that you observe are worst for the confused person. For example, if he gets most upset while you are getting supper, try to plan meals that are quick and easy, that are left over from lunch, or that you can prepare in advance. Eat the larger meal at midday.

Sometimes the trouble is that the person wants your constant attention and becomes more demanding when you are busy with other things. Perhaps you can occupy the person with a simple chore close to you while you work, or get someone else in the family to spend some time with him.

You may want to talk to the doctor about changing the schedule for giving medications if other methods don't help change this pattern.

Periods of restlessness or sleeplessness may be an unavoidable part of the brain injury. Reassure yourself that the person is not doing this deliberately, even though it may seem like he acts up at the times of day that are hardest for you.

LOSING, HOARDING, OR HIDING THINGS

Most people with dementing illnesses put things down and forget where they put them. Others hide or collect things and forget where they hid them. Either way, the result is the same; just when you need them most, the person's dentures or your car keys have vanished and cannot be found.

First, remember that you probably cannot ask the impaired person where he put them. He will not remember, and you may precipitate a catastrophic reaction by asking him.

There are several things you can do to reduce this problem. A neat house makes it easier to locate misplaced items. It is almost impossible to find something hidden in a cluttered closet or drawer. Limit the number of hiding places by locking some closets or rooms.

Take away valuable items such as rings or silver so they cannot be hidden and lost. Do not keep a significant amount of cash around the house. Make small, easily lost items larger and/or more visible—for example, put a large attachment on your key ring. Have a spare set of necessary items such as keys, eyeglasses, and hearing aid batteries if at all possible.

Get in the habit of checking the contents of waste baskets before you empty them. Check under mattresses, under sofa cushions, in waste baskets, in shoes, and in everyone's bureau drawers for lost items. Ask yourself where the confused person used to put things for security. Where did he hide Christmas gifts or money? These are good places to look for lost dentures.

Some people hoard or save food, dirty clothes, or other possessions. (See p. 67.) Some people hoard things because they have always collected things. Others seem to need to "hold on" to something or to "keep things safe." If this happens occasionally, it is best to ignore it. If possible, when you clean up, leave a little of the person's "stash." He may feel less need to add to the collection than he would if he found his supply wiped out.

One daughter said, "I solved my problem when I decided that it was all right to keep the silver in a laundry hamper. Now I look for it there instead of carrying it back to the dining room several times a day."

RUMMAGING IN DRAWERS AND CLOSETS

Some people rummage through dresser drawers or take everything out of closets. This makes a mess for you to clean up. It can be particularly upsetting when they rummage through other people's things. You may have to put a hard-to-work latch on some drawers and closets. You may need to put a lock on one drawer and put dangerous or valuable things in it, or you may need to move such things to a safer place. If there are young people in the household, they especially will need a private and unmolested place. It may help to fill a top dresser drawer or a box on top of the dresser with interesting things for the person to sort through. Select items that will interest the person: small tools and machine parts will appeal to one person while sewing supplies would interest another.

INAPPROPRIATE SEXUAL BEHAVIOR

Sometimes confused people take off their clothes or wander out into the living room or down the street undressed. For example,

One teenage boy came home to find his father sitting on the back porch reading the newspaper. He was naked except for his hat.

Occasionally, confused people will expose themselves in public. Sometimes very confused people will fondle their genitals. Or they will fidget in such a way that their fidgeting reminds others of sexual behaviors, which is upsetting.

One man repeatedly undid his belt buckle and unzipped his trousers.

A woman kept fidgeting with the buttons of her blouse.

Sometimes brain damage will cause a person to demand sexual activities frequently or inappropriately. But much more common than actual inappropriate sexual behavior is the myth that "senile" people will develop inappropriate sexual behaviors.

One wife who brought her husband to the hospital for care confessed that she had no problems managing him but that she had been told that, as he got worse, he would go into his "second childhood" and start exposing himself to little girls.

There is *no* basis to this myth. Inappropriate sexual behaviors in people with dementing illnesses are uncommon. In a study of our patients we found no instances of such behavior.

Accidental self-exposure and aimless masturbation do sometimes happen. Confused people may wander out in public undressed or partially dressed simply because they have forgotten where they are, how to dress, or the importance of being dressed. They may undo their clothes or lift up a skirt because they need to urinate and have forgotten where the bathroom is. They may undress because they want to go to bed or because a garment is uncomfortable. Urinary tract infections, itching, or discomfort may lead to handling the genital area. Check with your doctor.

Don't overreact to this. Just lead the person calmly back to his room or to the bathroom. If you find the person undressed, calmly bring him a robe and matter-of-factly help him put it on. The man who sat on the porch undressed had taken off his clothes because it was hot. He was unable to recognize that he was outside, was in sight of other people, and was not in the privacy of his home. Most confused people will never exhibit even this kind of behavior because their lifelong habits of modesty may remain.

Undressing or fidgeting with clothing can often be stopped by changing the kind of clothing the person wears. For example, use pants that pull on instead of pants with a fly in them. Use blouses that slip on or zip up the back instead of buttoning in front.

In our culture we have strong negative feelings about masturbation, and such actions are upsetting to most families. Remember, this behavior, when it occurs, is a part of the brain damage. The person is only doing what feels good. He has forgotten his social manners. This does not mean that the person will develop other offensive sexual behaviors. If this occurs, try not to act upset, because it may precipitate a catastrophic reaction. Gently lead the person to a private place. Try distracting him by giving him something else to do. If a person's fidgeting is suggestive or embarrassing, also try giving him something else to do or something else to fidget with.

We know of no case in which a person with a dementing illness has exposed himself to a child, and we do not wish to contribute to the myths about "dirty old men" by focusing on such behavior. However, should such an incident occur, react matter-of-factly and without creating any more fuss than is absolutely necessary. Your reaction may have much more impact on the child than the actual incident had. Remove the person quietly and explain to the child, "He forgets where he is."

We have observed that some people with dementing illnesses have a diminished sex drive, and some have more interest in sex than they did previously. If a person develops increased sexuality, remember that, however distressing this is, it is a factor of the brain injury. It is not a factor of personality or a reflection on you or your marriage. (See p. 22.)

Occasionally a father may make inappropriate advances to his daughter.

This is not incestuous behavior. While this can be terribly upsetting for everyone, it usually only means that he is disoriented. Probably he has mistaken his daughter for his wife. Daughters often look much as their mothers did when the mother was a young wife. The confused person may remember that time much more clearly than the present. Such gestures indicate that he does remember his wife and their marriage. Gently redirect him when this happens and try not to be too distressed.

Don't hesitate to discuss upsetting sexual behavior with the doctor, a counselor, or even other families. They can help you understand and cope with it. The person you choose should be knowledgeable about dementia and comfortable discussing sexual matters. He may make specific suggestions to reduce the behavior. Also see Chapter 12, "Sexuality," and Chapter 16, "Sexual Issues in Nursing Homes."

REPEATING THE QUESTION

Many families find that confused people ask the same question over and over and that this is extremely irritating. In part, this may be a symptom of the fear and insecurity of a person who can no longer make sense out of his surroundings. The person may not remember things for even brief periods, so he may have no recollection of having asked you before or of your answer.

> *One husband was particularly upset when his wife asked every night, "Who are you? What are you doing in my bed?" He stopped trying to explain to her and began simply ignoring the question. He would turn his head away slightly or turn his back on her and pretend she had not said anything. Eventually she stopped asking.*

This will work with some people but it will upset others, who will get angry because you did not answer them. Use what works for you.

Sometimes, instead of answering the question again, it is helpful reassure the person that everything is fine and that you will take care of things. Sometimes the person is worried about something else, which he is unable to express. If you can correctly guess what this is and reassure him, he may relax. For example,

> *Mr. Rockwell's mother kept asking, "When is my mother coming for me?" When Mr. Rockwell told her that her mother had been dead for many years, she would either get upset or ask the question again in a few minutes. Mr. Rockwell realized that the question really expressed her feelings that she was lost, and he began saying, "I will take care of you." This obviously calmed his mother.*

Mr. Rockwell might also try saying, "Tell me about your mother," or "Do you remember when your mother took us to the play?"

REPETITIOUS ACTIONS

An occasional and distressing behavior that may occur in people with a brain disease is the tendency to repeat the same action over and over.

Mrs. Weber's mother-in-law folded the laundry over and over. Mrs. Weber was glad the older woman was occupied, but this same activity upset her husband. He would shout, "Mother, you have already folded that towel five times."

Mrs. Andrews had trouble with baths. She would wash just one side of her face. "Wash the other side," her daughter would say, but she kept on washing the same spot.

Mr. Barnes paces around and around the kitchen in the same pattern, like a bear in a cage.

It seems as if the damaged mind has a tendency to "get stuck" on one activity and has difficulty "shifting gears" to a new activity. When this happens, gently suggest that the person do a specific new task, but try not to pressure him or sound upset, because you can easily precipitate a catastrophic reaction.

In the case of Mrs. Weber's mother-in-law, ignoring the problem worked well. As Mr. Weber came to accept his mother's illness, the behavior ceased to bother him.

Mrs. Andrews's daughter found out that gently patting her mother's cheek where she wanted her to wash next would get her out of the repetitious pattern. In this example, a stroke had lessened her mother's awareness of one side of her body. Touch is a very good way to get a message to the brain when words fail. Touch the arm you want a person to put in a sleeve; touch the place you want the person to wash next; touch a hand with a spoon to get a person to pick it up.

Mr. Barnes's wife found ways to distract him from pacing by giving him something to do. "Here, Joe, hold this," she would say, and hand him a spoon. "Now hold this," and she would take the spoon and give him a potholder. "Helping" would enable him to stop pacing. It kept him busy and perhaps also made him feel needed.

DISTRACTIBILITY

People with dementia may "get stuck" or be too easily distracted. The person may look elsewhere or grab at other things while you are trying to get his clothes on; he may eat the food on someone else's plate; he may walk off while you are talking to him. Part of our brain filters out things we do not want to pay attention to—this is how you "tune out" unimportant noises, for example. When the dementing illness damages this ability, the person may be equally attracted to everything that is happening, no matter how unimportant it may be.

If you can identify the things that distract him—people, animals, and sudden noises are common distractions—and reduce them, he may be better able to focus on one activity, such as dressing. Put his plate a little farther from the other plates; have fewer visitors at once; visit in a calm, quiet area. If he is distracted by the television or radio, turn it off. Plan eating and other activities in an area where other people are not moving about and talking.

CLINGING OR PERSISTENTLY FOLLOWING YOU AROUND

Families tell us that forgetful people sometimes follow them from room to room, becoming fretful if the caregiver disappears into the bathroom or basement, or that they constantly interrupt whenever the caregiver tries to rest or get a job done. This can be distressing. Few things can irritate more than being followed around all the time.

This behavior can be understood when we consider how strange the world must seem to a person who constantly forgets. The trusted caregiver becomes the only security in a world of confusion. When one cannot depend on himself to remember the necessary things in life, one form of security is to stick close to someone who does know.

The memory-impaired person cannot remember that if you go in the bathroom, you will be right back out. To his mind, with his confused sense of time, it may seem as if you have vanished. Childproof door knobs on the bathroom door may help give you a few minutes of privacy. Sometimes, setting a timer and saying, "I will be back when the timer goes off" will help. One husband got himself a set of headphones so he could listen to music while his wife continued to talk. (Then he got her a set because he discovered that she enjoyed the music.)

It is most important that you try not to let annoying behaviors such as these wear you down. You must find other people who will help with the person so you can get away and do the things that relax you—go visiting or shopping, take a nap, or enjoy an uninterrupted bath.

Using medication to stop behaviors like this is often unsuccessful and the side effects can be disabling. Unless the behavior places the person with dementia or someone else in danger, medication should be used only after other attempted solutions have failed.

Find simple tasks that the person can do, even if they are things that you could do better or things that are repetitive. Winding a ball of yarn, dusting, or stacking magazines may make a person feel useful and will keep him occupied while you do your work.

Mrs. Hunter's mother-in-law, who has a dementing illness, followed Mrs. Hunter around the house never letting her out of her sight and always criticizing. Mrs. Hunter hit upon the idea of having her mother-in-law fold the wash. Since Mrs. Hunter has a large family, she has a lot of wash. The older woman folds, unfolds, and refolds (not very neatly) and feels like a useful part of the household.

Is it being unkind to give a person made-up tasks to keep her occupied? Mrs. Hunter doesn't think so. The confused woman needs to feel that she is contributing to the family and she needs to be active.

COMPLAINTS AND INSULTS

Sometimes people with dementing illnesses repeatedly complain, despite your kindest efforts. The confused person may say things like "You are cruel to me," "I want to go home," "You stole my things," or "I don't like you." When you are doing all that you can to help, you may feel hurt or angry when the confused person says such things. When he looks and sounds well or when such criticism comes from someone you have looked up to, your first response may be to take the criticism personally. You can quickly get into a painful and pointless argument, which may cause him to have a catastrophic reaction and perhaps even scream, cry, and throw things at you, leaving you exhausted and upset.

If this happens, step back and think through what is happening. Even though the person looks well, he actually has an injury to his brain. Having to be cared for, feeling lost, and losing possessions and independence may seem to the confused person like cruel experiences. "You are cruel to me" may really mean "life is cruel to me." Because the person cannot accurately sort out the reality around him, he may misinterpret your efforts to help as stealing from him. He may not be able to accept, understand, or remember the facts of his increasing impairment, his financial situation, the past relationship he had with you, and all of the other things you are aware of. For example, he knows only that his things are gone and you are there. Therefore, he feels that you must have stolen his things.

A family member contributed the following interpretations of the things her husband often said. Of course, we cannot know what a brain-impaired person feels or means, but this wife has found loving ways to interpret and accept the painful things her husband says.

He says: "I want to go home."
He means: "I want to go back to the condition of life, the quality of life, when everything seemed to have a purpose and I was useful, when I could see the products of my hands, and when I was without the fear of small things."

He says: "I don't want to die."
He means: "I am sick, although I feel no pain. Nobody realizes just how sick I am. I feel this way all of the time, so I must be going to die. I am afraid of dying."

He says: "I have no money."
He means: "I used to carry a wallet with some money in it. It is not in my back pants pocket now. I am angry because I cannot find it. There is something at the store that I want to buy. I'll have to look some more."

He says: "Where is everyone?"
He means: "I see people around me but I don't know who they are. These unfamiliar faces do not belong to my family. Where is my mother? Why has she left me?"

In coping with remarks such as these, avoid contradicting the person or arguing with him; those responses may lead to a catastrophic reaction. Try not to say, "I didn't steal your things," "You *are* home," "I gave you some money." Try not to reason with the person. Saying "Your mother died thirty years ago" will only confuse and upset him more.

Some families find it helpful to ignore many of these complaints or to use distractions. Some families respond sympathetically to the feeling they think is being expressed: "Yes, dear, I know you feel lost," "Life does seem cruel," "I know you want to go home."

Of course, you may get angry sometimes, especially when you have heard the same unfair complaint over and over. To do so is human. Probably the confused person will quickly forget the incident.

Sometimes the impaired person loses the ability to be tactful. He may say, "I don't like John," and you may know he never did like this person. This can be upsetting. It helps for those involved to understand that the person is unable to be tactful, that while he may be being honest he is not being purposefully unkind.

Perhaps you can cope with these remarks, but what about other people? Sometimes people with dementing illnesses make inappropriate or insulting remarks to other people. These can range from naïve directness, such as telling the pastor's wife she has a run in her stocking, to insults, such as shouting at the neighbor who brings dinner, "Get out of my house, you're trying to poison us."

Confused people may tell casual friends or strangers stories such as "My daughter keeps me locked in my room." When you take a confused person to visit, he may put on his coat and say, "Let's go home. This place stinks."

Each brain-impaired person is different. Some will retain their social skills. In others a tendency toward bluntness may emerge as open rudeness. Some are fearful and suspicious, leading them to make accusations. Catastrophic reactions account for some of this behavior. The confused person often misjudges who the person is that he is speaking to or he misjudges the situation.

A secretary was talking with a confused man while the doctor talked to his wife. He was obviously trying to make polite conversation, but he had lost the subtlety he once had. "How old are you?" he asked, "You look pretty old." When she answered another question, "No, I'm not married," he said, "I guess no one would have you."

People chuckle at this sort of behavior in a small child because everyone understands that a child has not yet learned good manners. It will be helpful to you if most of the people around you understand that the person has a dementing illness that affects his memory of good manners. Most people are now aware of Alzheimer's disease. They should recognize that these behaviors are the result of specific diseases and that, while such behavior is sad, it is not deliberate.

To those people who see you and the confused person often, such as neighbors, friends, church members, and perhaps familiar store clerks, you may want to give a brief explanation of the person's illness. When you make this explanation, you should reassure people that this illness does not make the person dangerous and that the person is not crazy. Some caregivers have cards printed up which say something like, "Please pardon my family member who has Alzheimer's disease. Although she looks well, this disease has destroyed her memory." You may want to add a few lines about the disease and how to get more information about Alzheimer's disease.

Should a confused person create a scene in a public place, perhaps due to a catastrophic reaction, remove him gently. It may be best to say nothing. While this can be embarrassing, you do not necessarily owe strangers any explanation.

Distraction is a good way to get a confused person out of what might become an embarrassing situation. For example, if he is asking personal questions, change the subject. When a person is telling others that you are keeping him prisoner or not feeding him, try distracting him. Avoid denying directly, as this can turn into an argument with the confused person. If these are people you know, you may want to explain to them later. If they are strangers, ask yourself whether or not it really matters what strangers think.

Sometimes there is a gossip or insensitive person in a community who may build upon the inappropriate remarks of a person with a dementing illness. It is important that you not be upset by such gossip. Usually other people have an accurate estimate of the truth of such gossip.

TAKING THINGS

Confused people may pick up things in stores and not pay for them or may accuse the sales clerk of stealing their money. One wife reported that her husband was stealing and butchering the neighbors' chickens. He did not realize that they were not his own and was proud to be helping with dinner.

If a person is taking things in stores, he may be doing so because he has forgotten to pay for them or because he does not realize that he is in a store. Several families have found that giving the person things to hold or asking him to push the shopping cart, so that his hands are occupied, will stop the problem. Before you leave the store, check to see if he has anything in his pockets. You may want to dress him in something that has no pockets the next time you go shopping.

If the person continues to do this, you might ask your doctor for a brief letter explaining that the person has Alzheimer's disease and sometimes forgets that he has put things in his pockets. If the person does take something and you discover it later or if he is caught by store personnel, you can show them this letter.

The wife of the man who took chickens had her clergyman explain things to the neighbors and then arranged to replace any chickens that turned up on her dinner table.

FORGETTING TELEPHONE CALLS

Forgetful people who can still talk clearly often continue to answer the telephone or to make calls. However, they may not remember to write down telephone messages. This can upset friends, confuse people, and cause you considerable inconvenience and embarrassment.

Inexpensive telephone call recorders (sold at electronics stores) will record all telephone conversations. (See p. 93.) Attaching the device to an extension phone the impaired person does not often use may be wise. With this taped record of calls, you can call people back, explain the situation, and respond to their call.

One husband writes, "I found out from the tape that she called the dentist five times about her appointment. Since I knew about it I called them and told them how to manage that."

In some areas, the telephone company offers a call-forwarding service, which will transfer calls that come to your home to another telephone number. You may want to check with the telephone company to find out under what circumstances it is legal to tape-record calls.

DEMANDS

Mr. Cooper refused to stop living alone, even though it was clear to his family that he could not manage. Instead, he called his daughter at least once a day with real emergencies that sent her dashing across town to help out. His daughter felt angry and manipulated. She was neglecting her own family, and she was exhausted. She felt that her father had always been a self-centered, demanding person, and that his current behavior was deliberately selfish.

Mrs. Dietz lived with her daughter. The two women had never gotten along well and now Mrs. Dietz had Alzheimer's disease. She was wearing her daughter out with demands: "Get me a cigarette," "Fix me some coffee." The daughter could not tell her mother to do these things herself because she started fires.

Sometimes people with dementing illnesses can be demanding and appear to be self-centered. This is especially hard to accept when the person does not appear to be significantly impaired. If you feel that this is happening, try to step back and objectively evaluate the situation. Is this behavior deliberate or is it a symptom of the disease? The two can look very much alike, especially if the person had a way of making people feel manipulated before he developed a dementing brain disease. However, what is often happening with an impaired person is *not* something he can control. Manipulative behavior really requires the ability to plan, which the person with a dementing illness is losing. What you experience are old styles of relating to others which are no longer really deliberate. An evaluation can be helpful because it tells you objectively how much of such behavior is something the person can remember to do or not to do.

Some demanding behavior reflects the impaired person's feelings of loneliness, fright, or loss. For example, when a person has lost his ability to comprehend the passage of time and to remember things, being left alone for a short time can make him feel that he has been abandoned and he may accuse you of deserting him. Realizing that this behavior reflects such feelings can help you not to feel so angry and can help you respond to the *real* problem (for example, that he feels abandoned) instead of responding to what seems to you like selfishness or manipulation.

Sometimes you can devise ways for the confused person to continue to feel a sense of control over his life and mastery over his circumstances which are not so demanding of you.

> *Mr. Cooper's daughter was able to find an "apartment" for her father in a sheltered housing building where meals, social services, and housekeeping were provided. This reduced the number of emergencies but enabled Mr. Cooper to continue to feel independent.*

> *A medical evaluation confirmed for Mrs. Dietz's daughter that her mother could not remember her previous requests for a cigarette for even five minutes. With the help of the physician, she was able to deal with her mother's addiction to cigarettes and coffee.*

Families often ask whether they should "spoil" the person by meeting his demands or whether they should try to "teach" him to behave differently. The best course may be neither of these. Since he cannot control his behavior, you are not "spoiling" him, but it may be impossible for you to meet endless demands. And since the impaired person has limited ability, if any, to learn, you cannot teach him and scolding may precipitate catastrophic reactions.

If the person demands that you do things you think he can do, be sure that he really can do these things. He may be overwhelmed by the tasks. Simplifying them may make him willing to do them. Sometimes, being very specific and direct with the person helps. Saying "I am coming to see you Wednesday" is more helpful than getting into an argument over why you don't visit more often. Say, "I will get you a cigarette when the timer goes off. Do not ask me for one until the timer goes off." Ignore further demands until then.

You may have to set limits on what you realistically can do. But before you set limits, you need to know the extent of the impaired person's disability and you need to know what other resources you can mobilize to replace what you cannot do. You may need to enlist the help of an outside person—a nurse or social worker who understands the disease—to help you work out a plan that provides good care for the sick person without leaving you exhausted or trapped.(See Chapter 10.)

When demands make you feel angry and frustrated, try to find an outlet for your anger which does not involve the impaired person. Your anger can precipitate catastrophic reactions, which may make him even more recalcitrant.

STUBBORNNESS AND UNCOOPERATIVENESS

"Whatever I want him to do, he won't do it," said one daughter-in-law. Said another, "Whenever it's time to dress Dad, he says he has already changed his clothes. He won't go to the doctor, and whatever I serve for dinner he won't eat."

Families often suspect that a stubborn and uncooperative person with dementia is deliberately trying to frustrate them. It is hard to know whether a person who has always been stubborn is now more so or whether the stubbornness is really because of the dementia. Some people are more uncooperative than others by nature. However, this kind of behavior is usually at least partly caused by the illness.

If a person cannot remember when he last took a bath, he may be insulted when he is told to bathe. This is understandable.

The person may not understand what he is being asked to do (go to the doctor, help set the table), and so he refuses. Uncooperativeness may seem a safer course than risking making a fool of one's self. Sometimes a statement such as "I hate this food" really means "I am miserable."

Be sure that requests are understood. "Can you smell our supper cooking? See the roast? It will be delicious. Sit here and I will give you some."

Focusing on a pleasant experience sometimes helps: "As soon as we leave Dr. Brown's office, we'll celebrate with a big ice cream cone."

If strategies like this do not work (and sometimes nothing does), consider that the negative attitudes are often a part of the illness rather than a personal attack. The person may be too confused to *intend* to insult your cooking. Take the path of least difficulty. Avoid arguments and accept whatever compromise will work.

WHEN THE SICK PERSON INSULTS THE SITTER

When a family is able to arrange for someone to stay with the impaired person, he may fire the sitter or housekeeper. He may get angry or suspicious, insult her, not let her in, or accuse her of stealing. This can make it seem impossible for you to get out of the house, or mean that the impaired person can no longer live in his own home. Often you can find ways to solve the problem.

As with many other problems, this situation may arise out of the impaired person's inability to make sense out of his surroundings or to remember explanations. All he may recognize is that a stranger is in the house. Sometimes the presence of a "babysitter" means a further loss of his independence, which he may realize and react to.

Make sure the sitter knows that it is you, not the confused person, who has the authority to hire and fire. This means that you must trust the sitter absolutely. If possible, find a sitter the person already knows or introduce the person to the sitter gradually. The first time or two, have the sitter come while you remain at home. Eventually the person may become accustomed to the idea that the sitter belongs there. This will also give you an opportunity to teach the sitter how you manage certain situations and to evaluate how well the sitter relates to the confused person.

Be sure the sitter understands the nature of a dementing illness and knows how behaviors such as catastrophic reactions are handled. (Hiring a sitter is discussed in Chapter 10.) Try to find sitters who are adept at engaging the person's trust and who are clever about managing the person without triggering a catastrophic reaction. Just as there are some people who are naturally good with children and others who are not, there are some people who are intuitively adept with confused people. However, they are often hard to find. If the person will not accept one sitter, try another. Ask yourself if your reluctance to use a sitter is part of the problem.

Be sure the sitter can reach you, another family member, or the doctor in the event of a problem.

Often the confused person will adjust to the presence of a sitter if both you and the sitter can weather the initial stormy period.

Introduce the sitter as a friend "who wants to visit with you" and not as a sitter. If the person is suspicious of the sitter, his doctor may be able to reduce the suspiciousness with medication or can write a signed note to the impaired person reminding him to stay with the visitor.

In all events, consider your own health. Even if a sitter does upset the person with dementia, it is essential that you get out from time to time if you are to continue to be able to give care. (See Chapter 10.)

USING MEDICATION TO MANAGE BEHAVIOR

This chapter has listed many ways to control problem behaviors. You may hear different things about using medications to control problem behaviors. Some people say medication should never be used, while others may see medication as the only solution. Medications are most effective when targeted to specific symptoms. They are usually not helpful when they are given for generalized or annoying symptoms. Since all of these medications have potentially harmful side effects, non-drug interventions should be tried first unless the behavior is potentially dangerous to the patient or others or unless a condition for which there is a specific treatment, like depression, is causing the problem.

8

PROBLEMS OF MOOD

DEPRESSION

PEOPLE WITH MEMORY PROBLEMS may also be sad, low, or depressed. When a person has memory problems and is depressed it is important that a careful diagnosis be made and the depression treated. The memory problems may not be caused by Alzheimer's disease and may get better when the depression improves, or the person may have both Alzheimer's disease and a depression that will respond to treatment.

When a person with an incurable disease is depressed, it can seem logical that she is depressed about the chronic illness. But not all people with Alzheimer's disease or other chronic illnesses are depressed. Some seem not to be aware of their problems. A certain amount of discouragement about one's condition is natural and understandable, but a deep despondency or a continuing depression is neither natural nor necessary. Fortunately, this kind of depression responds well to treatment, so the person can feel better whether or not she also has an irreversible dementing illness.

Researchers are trying to understand why we get depressed, but the total answer is not yet in. We obviously feel sad or low when something bad happens to us. But this does not completely explain the phenomenon of depression. For example, researchers are linking some depressions to changes in the brain. It is important that a physician assess the nature of each depression and determine whether it is a response to a situation or a deeper despondency, and then treat the depression appropriately. Indications of a deeper despondency include weight loss, a change in sleep patterns, feelings that one has done something bad and deserves to be punished, or a preoccupation with health problems.

It may be impossible for a depressed person to "snap out of it" by herself. Telling her to do so may only increase her feelings of frustration and discouragement. For some people, trying to cheer them makes them feel that they are not understood.

You can encourage a depressed or discouraged person to continue to be around other people. If she has memory problems, be sure that the activities she tries are things she can still do successfully and are of some use, so that she can feel good about herself for doing them. Help her avoid tasks that are too complicated. Even small failures can make her feel more discouraged about herself. Have her set the table for you. If she doesn't have that much energy, have her set just one place. If that task is too complicated, have her set out just the plates.

If groups of people upset her, encourage her not to withdraw completely but instead to talk with one familiar person at a time. Ask one friend to visit. Urge the friend to talk to the depressed person, to meet her eyes and involve her.

When a person is feeling discouraged, it may be helpful for her to talk over her concerns with a knowledgeable counselor, clergyman, physician, psychiatrist, or psychologist. This is possible only when she can still communicate well and remember some things. This person must understand dementia and adjust the treatment accordingly.

COMPLAINTS ABOUT HEALTH

If the person often complains about health problems, it is important to take these complaints seriously and have a doctor determine whether there is a physical basis for the complaints. (Remember that chronic complainers can get sick. It is easy to overlook real illnesses when a person often focuses on things with no physical basis.) When you and the doctor are sure that there is no physical illness present, he can treat the depression that is the underlying cause of the problem. Never let a physician dismiss a person as "just a hypochondriac." People who focus on health problems are really unhappy and need appropriate care.

SUICIDE

When a person is depressed, demoralized, or discouraged, there is always a possibility that she will harm herself. While it may be difficult for a person with Alzheimer's disease to plan a suicide, you do need to be alert to the possibility that she will injure herself. If the person has access to a knife, a gun, power tools, solvents, medications, or car keys, she may use them to kill or maim herself. Statements about suicide should always be taken seriously. Notify your physician.

ALCOHOL OR DRUG ABUSE

Depressed people may use alcohol, tranquilizers, or other drugs to try to blot out the feelings of sadness. This can compound the problem. In a person with a dementing illness it can also further reduce her ability to function. You need to be especially alert to this possibility in a person who is living alone or who has used medications or alcohol in the past.

People who are heavy drinkers and who also develop a dementing illness can be difficult for their families to manage. The person may be more sensitive to small amounts of alcohol that a well person, so even one drink or one beer can significantly reduce her ability to function. These people often do not eat properly, causing nutritional problems that further impair them. They may also act nasty, stubborn, or hostile.

It helps to recognize that the brain impairment may make it impossible for the person to control her drinking or her other behaviors, and that you may have to provide this control for her. This will include taking steps to end her supply of alcohol. Do so quietly but firmly. Try not to feel that her unpleasant behavior is aimed at you personally. Avoid saying things that put the blame for the situation on anybody. Do what needs to be done, but try to find ways for the person to retain her self-esteem and dignity. There should be no liquor in the house unless it is locked away. One family was able to arrange with the local liquor store to stop selling to the patient.

You may need help from a counselor or physician to manage the behavior of a person with a memory problem who also abuses alcohol or drugs.

APATHY AND LISTLESSNESS

Sometimes people with brain diseases become apathetic and listless. They just sit and don't want to do anything. Such people may be easier to care for than people who are upset, but it is important not to overlook them.

As with depression, we are not sure why some people with dementia become apathetic and listless. It is probably due to the effects of the disease on specific areas of the brain. It is important to keep people with dementia as active as possible. People need to move around and to use their minds and bodies as much as possible.

Withdrawing may be a person's way of coping when things get too complicated; if you insist on her participation she may have a catastrophic reaction. Try to reinvolve her at a level at which she can feel comfortable, can succeed, and can feel useful. Ask her to do a simple task, take her for a walk and point out interesting things, play some music, or go for a car ride.

It often seems that getting the body moving helps cheer a person up. Once a person gets started doing something, she may begin to feel less apathetic. Perhaps she can peel only one potato today. Tomorrow she may feel like doing two. Perhaps she can spade the garden. Even if she spades for only a few minutes, it may have helped for her to get moving. If she stops a task after a few minutes, instead of urging her to go on, focus your attention on what she has accomplished and compliment her on that.

Occasionally, when you try to get a person active, she may become upset or agitated. If this happens, you will need to weigh the importance of her being active against her being upset.

REMEMBERING FEELINGS

People with dementia may remember their feelings longer than they remember the situation that caused the feelings. Mrs. Bishop stayed angry with her daughter for days, but she forgot that there was a good reason why her daughter had acted as she did.

Likewise, some people constantly restate the same suspicious ideas. Their families understandably wonder why they can't remember other things as well. Our brain probably processes and stores the memory of feelings in a different way than it does memories of facts. For reasons we don't understand, emotional memories seem to be less vulnerable to the devastations of the dementing illness. This can have a good side, since people often remember good feelings longer than the facts surrounding them.

One woman insisted that she had been dancing at the day care center, although she was confined to a wheelchair. She meant that she had had a good time there. One man always stayed happy for hours after a visit from his grandchildren even though he forgot the visit itself soon after they had left.

ANGER AND IRRITABILITY

Sometimes people with dementing illnesses become angry. They may lash out at you as you try to help them. They may slam things around, hit you, refuse to be cared for, throw food, yell, or make accusations. This can be upsetting for you and may cause problems in the household. It can seem as if all this hostility is aimed at you, despite your best efforts to take care of the person, and you may be afraid that the person will hurt herself or someone else when she lashes out in anger. This is certainly a real concern. However, our experience has been that it actually occurs rarely and can usually be controlled.

Angry or violent behavior is usually a catastrophic reaction and should be handled as you would any other catastrophic reaction. (See Chapter 3.) Respond calmly; do not respond with anger. Remove the person from the situation or remove the upsetting stimulus. Look for the event that precipitated the reaction so that you can prevent or minimize a recurrence.

Try not to interpret anger in the same way as you would if it came from a well person. Anger from a confused person is often exaggerated or misdirected. The person may not really be angry at you at all. The anger is probably the result of misunderstanding what is happening. For example,

Mr. Jones adored his small grandson. One day the grandchild tripped and fell and began to cry. Mr. Jones grabbed a knife, began to yell, and would allow no one near the child.

Mr. Jones had misinterpreted the cause of the child's crying and overreacted. He thought someone was attacking the child. Fortunately, the child's mother understood what was happening. "I will help you protect the baby," she said to Mr. Jones. She gave Mr. Jones a job to do: "Here, you hold the door for me." Then she was able to pick up and quiet the child.

Forgetfulness is an advantage, since the person may quickly forget the episode. Often you can distract a person who is behaving this way by suggesting something you know she likes.

Mrs. Williams's mother-in-law often got angry and nasty when Mrs. Williams tried to prepare supper. Mr. Williams began distracting his mother by spending that time each day visiting with just her in another part of the house.

Once in a while a person experiencing a catastrophic reaction will hit someone who is trying to help her. Respond to this as you would to a catastrophic reaction. When at all possible, do not restrain her. If this occurs frequently, you may need to ask the doctor to help you review what is upsetting the person and if necessary to consider prescribing medication.

ANXIETY, NERVOUSNESS, AND RESTLESSNESS

People with dementing illnesses may become worried, anxious, agitated, and upset. They may pace or fidget. Their constant restlessness can get on your nerves. The person may not be able to tell you why she is upset. Or she may give you an unreasonable explanation for her anxiety. For example,

Mrs. Berger was obviously upset over something, but whenever her husband tried to find out what it was, she would say that her mother was coming to get her. Telling her that her mother had been dead for years only caused her to cry.

Some anxiety and nervousness may be caused by the changes within the brain. Other nervousness may come from real feelings of loss or tension. The real feelings that result from not knowing where one is, what one is expected to do, and where one's familiar possessions are can lead to almost constant feelings of anxiety. Some people sense that they often do things wrong and they become anxious about "messing up." Longing for a familiar environment ("I want to go home") or worrying about people from the past ("Where are my children?") can create anxiety. Reassurance, affection, and distraction may be all you can offer. Medication only occasionally helps relieve these feelings and should be tried only if other options have failed and if the anxiety is severe.

Even severely ill people remain sensitive to the moods of the people around them. If there is tension in the household, no matter how well you try to conceal it, the person may respond to it. For example, Mrs. Powell argued with her son over something minor, and just when that was solved, her confused mother began to cry because she "felt like something dreadful was going to happen." Her feeling was a real response to the mood in the house, but because she was cognitively impaired, her interpretation of the cause of the feeling was incorrect.

The person may be sad and worried over losing some specific item, like her watch. Reassuring her that you have the watch may not seem to help. Again, she has an accurate *feeling* (something is lost: her memory is lost, time is lost, many things are lost), but the *explanation* of the feeling is inaccurate. Respond with affection and reassurance to her feeling, which is real, and avoid trying to convince her that what she expresses is unreasonable.

Trying to get the person to explain what is troubling her or arguing with her ("there is no reason to get upset") may only make her more upset. For example,

Every afternoon at 2:00, Mrs. Novak began to pace and wring her hands at the day care center. She told the staff that she was going to miss the train to Baltimore. Telling her she was not going to Baltimore only upset her more. The staff realized that she was probably worried about going home, and they reassured her that they would see that she got home safely. This always calmed her down. (They had responded appropriately to her feelings.)

Not all anxiety and nervousness may go away so easily. Sometimes these feelings are inexplicable. Offering the person comfort and reassurance and trying to simplify her environment may be all that you can do to counteract the effects of her brain disease.

When people with dementing illnesses pace, fiddle with things, resist care, shove the furniture around, run away from home or from the day care center, or turn on the stove and all the water faucets, they may make others around them nervous. Their restless, irritable behavior is hard for families to manage without help.

Agitation may be a part of depression, anger, or anxiety. It may be restlessness or boredom, a symptom of pain, caused by medications, or an inexplicable part of the dementing illness. Respond calmly and gently; try to simplify what is going on around the person, and avoid "overloading her mental circuits." Your calmness and gentleness will communicate to her.

You may find it helpful to give the person who is mildly restless something to fiddle with. Some people will play with worry beads or with pennies in their pockets. Giving the person something constructive to do with her energy, such as walking to the mailbox to get the mail, may help. If the person is drinking caffeinated beverages (coffee, cola, tea), switching to noncaffeinated drinks might help.

One woman was restless much of the time. She paced, fidgeted, and wandered. Her husband stopped telling her to sit down and instead began handing her a deck of cards, saying, "Here, Helen, play some solitaire." He took advantage of her lifelong enjoyment of this card game, even though she no longer played it correctly.

Sometimes this behavior is the result of frequent or almost continuous catastrophic reactions. Try to find ways to reduce the confusion, extra stimulation, noise, and change around the confused person. (Read the sections on catastrophic reactions and on wandering.) Medications may help very agitated or restless people.

FALSE IDEAS, SUSPICIOUSNESS, PARANOIA, AND HALLUCINATIONS

Forgetful people may become unreasonably suspicious. They may suspect or accuse others of stealing their money, their possessions, and even things nobody would take, like an old toothbrush. They may hoard or hide things. They may shout for help or call the police. An impaired person may begin accusing her spouse of infidelity.

People with a dementing illness may develop unshakable ideas that things have been stolen from them or that people are going to harm them. Carried to an extreme, these ideas can make the person fearful and resistant to all attempts at care and help. Occasionally they develop distressing and strange ideas that they seem to remember and insist upon. They may insist that this is not where they live, that people who are dead are alive and are coming for them, or that someone who lives in the house is a stranger and perhaps dangerous. Occasionally a person will insist that her husband is not her husband—he is someone who looks like her husband, but is an impostor.

A person with a dementing illness may hear, see, feel, or smell things that are not there. Such hallucinations may terrify her (if she sees a strange man in the bedroom) or amuse her (if she sees a puppy on the bed).

These behaviors are upsetting for families because they are strange and frightening and because we associate them with insanity. They may never happen to your family member, but you should be aware of them in case you have to respond to such an experience. When they occur in the presence of a dementing illness, they are usually the result of the brain injury or a superimposed delirium (see pp. 96, 288) and are not symptoms of other mental illness.

Misinterpretation

Sometimes these problems are due to the person's misinterpretation of what she sees and hears. If she sees poorly in the dark, she may misinterpret the moving curtains as a strange man. If she hears poorly, she may suspect conversations to be people talking about her. If she loses her shoes, she may misinterpret the loss as a theft.

Is the person seeing accurately in the dark or is she hearing as well as she should? The cognitively impaired person must be seeing and hearing as well as possible because she may not realize her sensory limitations. Be sure her glasses and/or hearing aid are working well. If the room is dimly lit, see if improving the lighting helps. If the room is noisy or if sounds are muted, the person may need help identifying sounds.(See "Hearing Problems" in Chapter 6.) Closing the curtains may help if she is seeing someone outside at night.

If you think the person is misinterpreting things, you may be able to help by explaining what she sees or hears. Say, for example, "That movement is the curtains" or "That tapping noise is the bush outside your window."

This is different from directly disagreeing with her, which may cause her to have a catastrophic reaction. Avoid saying, "There is no man in the bedroom" or "Nobody is trying to sneak in. Now go to sleep."

If the person does not hear well, it may help to include her in the conversation by addressing her directly rather than talking about her.

Look directly at her. Some people read lips enough to supplement their hearing. You might say, "Dad, John says the weather has been terrible lately," or "Dad, John says the new grandchild is sitting up now." Never talk about someone in the third person, as if she weren't there, no matter how "out of it" you think she is. This is dehumanizing, and can understandably make a person angry. Ask other people not to do it.

Sometimes the impaired person's brain incorrectly interprets what her senses see or hear correctly. This is often what happens when a person becomes unrealistically suspicious. Sometimes you can help by giving the confused person accurate information or writing down reminders. You may have to repeat the same information frequently, since the person will tend to forget quickly what you say.

Failure to Recognize People or Things (Agnosia)

People with dementing illnesses may lose the ability to recognize things or people, not because they have forgotten them or because their eyes are not working but because the brain is not able to put together information properly. This is called *agnosia*, from Latin words meaning "to not know." It can be a baffling symptom. For example,

> *Mrs. Kravitz said to her husband, "Who are you? What are you doing in my house?"*

This is not a problem of memory. Mrs. Kravitz had not forgotten her husband; in fact, she remembered him quite well, but her brain could not figure out who he was from what her eyes saw.

> *Mr. Clark insisted that this was not his house, although he had lived there many years.*

He had not forgotten his home, but, because his brain was not working right, the place did not look familiar.

You can help by giving the person other information. It may help to say "I guess it doesn't look familiar, but this is your house." Hearing your voice may help her remember who you are. Help her focus on one familiar detail. "Here is your chair. Sit in it. It *feels* familiar."

"You Are Not My Husband"

Occasionally a person with a dementing illness will insist that her spouse is not her spouse or that her home is not her real home. She may insist that it looks just like her real house, but someone has taken the real one away and replaced it with a fake one. We do not understand exactly what is happening but we do know that this distressing symptom is a part of the brain damage.

Reassure the person, "I am your husband," but avoid arguing. Although this may seem heartbreaking, it is important for you to reassure yourself that it is not a rejection of you (the person *does* remember you.) It is just an inexplicable confusion of the damaged brain.

"My Mother Is Coming for Me"

Someone with a dementing illness may forget that a person she once knew has died. She may say, "My mother is coming for me," or she may say that she has been visiting with her grandmother. Perhaps her memory of the person is stronger than her memory of the death. Perhaps in her mind the past has become the present.

Instead of either contradicting her or playing along with her, try responding to her general feelings of loss, if you feel that this is what she is expressing.

Telling the confused person outright that her mother has been dead for years may upset her terribly. Her constant focus on these memories probably means that they are important to her. Ask her to tell you about her mother, look through a photo album from those years, or retell some old family stories. This responds to her feelings without hurting her again and again.

Sometimes people feel that this idea is "spooky" or that the impaired person is "seeing the dead." It is much more likely to be just another symptom like forgetfulness, wandering, or catastrophic reactions.

Perhaps you will decide that this issue is not worth the argument.

Suspiciousness

If a person is suspicious or "paranoid," one must consider the possibility that her suspicions are founded on fact. Sometimes when a person is known to be unusually suspicious, real causes for her suspiciousness are overlooked. In fact, she might be being victimized, robbed, or harassed. However, some people with dementing illnesses do develop a suspiciousness that is inappropriate to the real situation.

Paranoia and suspiciousness are not really difficult to understand. We are all suspicious; it is necessary to our survival. The innate naïveté of the child is carefully replaced by a healthy suspicion. We are taught to be suspicious of strangers who offer us candy, door-to-door salespeople, and people with "shifty" eyes. Some of us were also taught as children to be suspicious of people of other races or religions. Some people have always been suspicious, others always trusting. A dementing illness may exaggerate these personality traits.

Ms. Henderson returns to her office to find her purse missing. Two other purses have disappeared this week. She suspects that the new file clerk has stolen it.

As Mr. Starr comes out of a restaurant at night, three teenagers approach him and ask for change for the telephone. His heart pounds. He suspects that they plan to mug him.

Mrs. Bellotti called her friend three times to meet for lunch and each time the friend refused, giving the excuse that she had extra work. Mrs. Bellotti worries that her friend is avoiding her.

Situations like these occur frequently. One difference between the response of a well person and that of a brain-impaired person is that the latter's ability to reason may become overwhelmed by the emotions the suspiciousness raises or her inability to make sense out of her world.

Ms. Henderson searched for her purse and eventually remembered that she had left it in the cafeteria, where she found it being held for her at the cash register.

The confused person lacks the ability to remember. Therefore, she will never find her purse and will continue to suspect the file clerk, as Ms. Henderson would have if she had not been able to remember where it was.

Knowing that he is in a lighted, well-traveled area, Mr. Starr suppresses his panic and hands over twenty-five cents to the three teenagers. They thank him and run to the phone.

The confused person lacks the ability to assess her situation realistically and to control her panic. She often overreacts. Therefore, she might have screamed, the boys would have run, the police would have been called, etc.

Mrs. Bellotti discussed her concerns with a mutual friend and learned that her friend had been sick and had gotten behind in her work and was eating lunch at her desk.

The confused person lacks the ability to test out her suspicions against the opinions of others and then to evaluate them.

The person with the dementing illness who becomes "paranoid" has not gone crazy. She lives in a world in which each moment is starting over with no memory of the moments that went before, in which things disappear, explanations are forgotten, and conversations make no sense. In such a world it is easy to see how healthy suspiciousness can get out of hand. For example, the person with a dementing illness forgets that you carefully explained that you have hired a housekeeper. Lacking the information she needs to assess accurately what is going on, she makes exactly the same assumption we would if we found a strange person in the house—that the person is a thief.

The first step in coping with excessive suspiciousness is to understand that this is not behavior the person can control. Second, it only makes things worse to confront the person or to argue about the truthfulness of the complaint. Avoid saying, "I told you twenty times, I put your things in the attic. Nobody stole them." Perhaps you can make a list of where things are: "Love seat given to cousin Mary. Cedar chest in Ann's attic."

When she says, "You stole my dentures," don't say, "Nobody stole your teeth, you lost them again." Instead say, "I'll help you find them." Locating the lost article will often solve the problem. Articles that are mislaid seem stolen to the person who cannot remember where she put them and who cannot reason that nobody would want her dentures.

One son securely fastened a key to the bulletin board (so his mother could not remove and hide it). Every time she accused him of stealing her furniture, he replied gently, "All your things are locked in the attic. Here is your key to the attic where they all are."

Sometimes you can distract a person from her focus on suspiciousness. Look for the lost articles; try going for a ride or getting her involved in a task. Sometimes you can look for the real cause of her complaints and respond with sympathy and reassurance to her feelings of loss and confusion.

When many of a person's possessions must be disposed of so she can move into someone's home or a nursing home, she may insist that they have been stolen. When you have assumed control over a person's finances, she may accuse you of stealing from her. Repeated explanations or lists sometimes help. Often they do not, because the person cannot make sense of the explanation or will forget it. Such accusations can be discouraging when you are doing the best you can for someone. These accusations are often, at least in part, an expression of the person's overwhelming feelings of loss, confusion, and distress. They are not really harmful to anyone, except that they are distressing for you. When you understand that they occur because of the brain damage, you will be less upset by them.

Few things make us more angry than being falsely accused. Consequently, the impaired person's accusations can alienate sitters, other family members, neighbors, and friends, causing you to lose needed sources of friendship and help. Make it clear to people that you do not suspect them of anything and explain to them that accusatory behavior results from the confused person's inability to assess reality accurately. Your trust in them must be obvious and strong enough to override the accusations made by the impaired person. Sometimes it is helpful to share with others written materials such as this book, which explain how the brain impairment affects behavior. Part of the problem is that the confused person may look and sound reasonable. She may not look and sound as if this behavior were beyond her control, and, because dementing illnesses are often poorly understood, people may not realize what is happening.

Some suspiciousness goes beyond this explanation; it cannot be explained by the forgetfulness and loss of the ability to correctly assess reality. Such suspiciousness may be caused by the disease process itself. Low doses of medication may help. Treatment not only makes life easier for you but also relieves the ill person of the anxiety and fear that arise from her suspicions.

Hiding Things

In a world that is confusing and in which things inexplicably disappear, it is understandable that a person would put things of importance in a safe place. The difference between being well and being impaired is that the impaired person forgets where that safe place is more often than the well person. Hiding behaviors often accompany suspiciousness, but because they cause so many problems of their own, we have discussed them separately in Chapter 7.

Delusions and Hallucinations

Delusions are untrue ideas unshakably held by one person. They may be suspicious in nature ("The mafia are after me," or "You have stolen my money") or self-blaming ("I am a bad person," or "I am rotting inside and spreading a terrible disease"). The nature of the delusion can help doctors diagnose the person's problem. Self-blaming ideas, for example, are often seen in people who are severely depressed. However, when delusions occur in a person who is known to have a brain impairment from strokes, Alzheimer's disease, or other conditions, the delusion is believed to arise out of the injury to brain tissue. It can be frustrating to have a person seem able to remember a false idea and unable to remember real information.

Sometimes delusions appear to come from misinterpreting reality. Sometimes they are tied to the person's past experiences. (A note of caution: not all odd things people say are delusions.)

Hallucinations are sensory experiences that are real to the person having them but that others do not experience. Hearing voices or seeing things are most common, although occasionally people feel, smell, or taste things also.

Mrs. Singer sometimes saw a dog asleep in her bed. She would call her daughter to "come and get the dog out of my bed."

Mr. Davis saw tiny little men on the floor. They distracted him, and often he sat watching them instead of taking part in activities at the senior center.

Mrs. Eckman heard burglars outside her window trying to break in and discussing how they would hurt her. She called the police several times and earned herself the reputation of a "nut."

Mr. Vaughan tasted poison in all his food. He refused to eat and lost so much weight that he had to be hospitalized.

Hallucinations are a symptom, like a fever or sore throat, which can arise from many causes. Certain drugs can induce hallucinations in otherwise well people. Several disease processes can produce hallucinations. As with a fever or sore throat, the first step is to identify the cause of the hallucination. In an elderly person hallucinations are not necessarily an indication of a dementing illness. They may result from several causes, many of which are treatable. Delirium is one example. If hallucinations or delusions appear in a person who has previously been functioning well, they are probably not associated with dementia. Do not let a doctor dismiss this symptom. The examples we have given are not all examples of people in whom the hallucination is a symptom of dementia.

When hallucinations do develop as an inexplicable part of the dementing illness, your doctor can help. Often these symptoms respond to medications that make the patient more comfortable and life easier for you.

When delusions or hallucinations occur, react calmly so that you do not further upset the confused person. Although this is not an emergency situation, you will want to check with the doctor as soon as is convenient. Reassure the person that you are taking care of things and that you will see that things are all right.

Avoid denying the person's experience or directly confronting her or arguing with her. This will only further upset her. Remember, the experience is real for her. At the same time you should not play along with a delusion or a hallucination. You don't have to agree or disagree; just listen or give a noncommittal answer. You can say "I don't hear the voices you hear, but it must be frightening for you." This is not the same as agreeing with the person. Sometimes you can distract the person so that she forgets her hallucination. Say, "Let's go in the kitchen and have a cup of warm milk." When she returns to her bedroom, she may no longer see a dog in her bed and you will have avoided an upsetting confrontation.

It is often comforting to touch the person physically, as long as she does not misinterpret your touch as an effort to restrain her. Say, "I know you are so upset. Would it help if I held your hand (or gave you a hug)?"

HAVING NOTHING TO DO

As they progress, dementing illnesses greatly limit the things the confused person can do. It becomes impossible to remember the past or to anticipate the future. The confused person cannot plan ahead or organize a simple activity like taking a shower. Many impaired people cannot follow the action on television. While you or the nursing home staff are getting chores done, the ill person may have nothing to do but sit with vacant time and empty thoughts.

Restlessness, wandering, trying to go "home," repetitive motions, asking the same question over and over, scratching, masturbating, and many other behaviors begin as an effort to fill this emptiness. But for you the hours are full. We do not think that a family caregiver, with all the burdens he or she faces, should be expected to take on the additional responsibility of planning recreation. We do think activity is important and urge the use of a day center, other family, friends, or paid help, if possible.

Whenever you or someone else initiates an activity for a person with dementia, you must walk a fine line between providing meaningful activity and overstressing the person. Move at the confused person's pace. Never let an activity become a test of her abilities; arrange things so that she will succeed. Having fun should be more important than doing something correctly. Stop when the person becomes restless or irritable.

9

SPECIAL ARRANGEMENTS IF YOU BECOME ILL

ANYONE CAN BECOME ILL or suffer an accident. If you are tired and under stress from caring for a chronically ill person, your risk of illness or accident *increases*. The spouse of a person with a dementing illness, herself no longer young, is at risk of developing other illnesses.

What happens to the confused, forgetful person if you, the caregiver, are injured or become ill? It is important that you have a plan ready. Perhaps you will never need to put your plan into effect, but because dementia disables a person in such a way that he cannot act in his best interests, you must make advance plans that protect you and the impaired person.

You need a physician who is familiar with your health to whom you can turn if you become ill, and who is available quickly in a crisis. In addition, you need to plan in advance for several kinds of possible problems: the sudden, severe problems that would arise if you had a heart attack or stroke or fell and broke a bone; the less sudden problems that would arise if you had a long illness, hospitalization, or surgery; and the problems that would arise if you got the flu or were at home, sick, for a few days.

Mrs. Brady suddenly began having chest pains and knew she should lie quietly. She told her confused husband to go get their neighbor but he kept pulling at her arm and shouting. When she finally was able to telephone for help, he refused to let the ambulance attendants in the house.

Even an impaired person who appears to function well may, when he is upset, become unable to do things he usually can do. Should you suddenly become ill and unable to summon help yourself, the upset and confused person may not be able to summon help for you. He may misinterpret what is happening and impede efforts to get help.

There are several possible ways you can plan to summon help. If your area has an emergency telephone number (such as 911), try to teach the person to call for help. Post the number over the phone. Or post the number of a relative who lives nearby and who will respond to a confused telephone call. Some telephone companies offer an automatic dialing service. With this device the telephone will automatically dial a prerecorded number of your choice if you or the confused person is able to dial one or two digits. You can paint this digit red with fingernail polish so that it is easily identified.

At least one company manufactures a "panic button" that you can carry with you. It is about the size of a pocket calculator. If you press the button on it, it will activate the automatic dial described above and send a prerecorded message. Such equipment may seem expensive, but in some situations it could be life saving.

Many areas have programs for senior citizens in which someone will call once a day to see if you are all right. This may mean a long delay in getting help, but it is better than nothing.

Be sure that the person who would respond in a crisis has a key to your house. The upset, confused person may refuse to let anyone in.

If you must go into the hospital or if you are at home sick, you will want to plan carefully in advance for the care of the confused person. Changes are upsetting for them, and it is helpful to minimize changes as much as possible. The substitute caregiver should be someone the person knows and someone who knows your routines for managing him. See Chapter 10 for possible sources of temporary help. Be sure that the names and phone numbers of your doctor, the patient's doctor, the pharmacist, your lawyer, and close family members are written down where the person helping out in an emergency can find them.

Some families have made up a "cope notebook" in which they have jotted down the things another person would need to know, for example, "Dr. Brown (555–8787). John gets a pink pill one hour before lunch. He will take it best with orange juice. The stove won't work unless you turn on the switch that is hidden behind the toaster. John starts to wander around suppertime. You need to watch him then."

IN THE EVENT OF YOUR DEATH

When someone close to you has a dementing illness, you have a special responsibility to provide for him if you should die. Probably your plans will never have to be put into action, but they must, for the sake of the sick person, be made.

When a family member is unable to take care of himself, it is important that you have a will that provides for his care. Find a lawyer whom you trust, and have him draw up a will and any other necessary legal papers. Every state has a law that determines how property will be divided among your heirs if you do not make a will or if your will is not valid. However, this may not be the way you wanted your estate to be distributed. In addition to the usual matters of disposing of property to one's heirs, the following questions must be addressed, and appropriate arrangements made. (See Chapter 15.)

What arrangements have been made for your funeral, and who will carry these out? You can select a funeral director in advance and specify, in writing, what kind of funeral you will have and how much it will cost. Far from being macabre, this is a considerate and responsible act that ensures that things will be done as you wish and that saves your distraught family from having to do this in the midst of their grief. Funerals can be expensive, and advance plans make it possible for you to see that your money is spent as you wish.

What immediate arrangements have been made for care of the person with a dementing illness, and who will be responsible for seeing that they are carried out? Someone must be available immediately who will be kind and caring.

Do the people who will be caring for the person with a dementing illness know his diagnosis and his doctor, and do they know as much as possible of what you know about how to make him comfortable?

What financial provisions have been made for the person with a dementing illness, and who will administer them? If he cannot manage his own affairs, someone must be available with the authority to care for him. You will want to select a person whom you trust to do this rather than leave such an important decision to a court or judge. When such decisions are made by a court, they involve long delays and considerable expense.

Sometimes a husband or wife cares for years for a spouse with a dementing illness and does not want to burden sons or daughters with the knowledge of this illness.

Said a daughter, "I had no idea anything was wrong with Mom because Dad covered for her so well. Then he had a heart attack and we found her like this. Now I have the shock of his death and her illness all at one time. It would have been so much easier if he had told us about it long ago. And we didn't know anything about dementia. We had to find out all the things he had already learned, and at such a difficult time for us."

All members of the family need to know what is wrong with the impaired person and what plans have been made. An experience like this is one example of the disservice of "protecting" other members of the family.

You should have a succinct summary of your assets available for the person who will take over. This should include information on the location of wills, deeds, stocks, cemetery lot deeds, and information about the care of the confused person.

10

GETTING OUTSIDE HELP

THROUGHOUT THIS BOOK we have emphasized the importance of finding time for yourself away from the responsibilities of caring for the impaired person. You may also need other kinds of help: someone to see that a person who is alone during the day gets her meals; someone to help give the person a bath; someone to watch the person while you shop, rest, or take a break; someone to help with the housework; or someone with whom you can talk things over.

You may want someone to stay with the ill person part of the day, or a place where the person can stay for several days while you take a vacation or get medical care. At some point you may need to find a place where the ill person can spend time away from you and where she can make friends of her own. Such outside help is called *respite*, because it gives you a break from caregiving. This chapter will describe the kinds of services that may be available. The second part of the chapter will discuss some of the problems you may encounter.

HELP FROM FRIENDS AND NEIGHBORS

Usually, caregivers who feel that they have the support of others manage the burdens of care more successfully. It is important that you not feel alone with your burden. Most people first turn to family members, friends, or neighbors for support and help. Often people will offer to help; at other times you may have to ask them for help.

Family members sometimes disagree or don't help out, or you may hesitate to ask others for the help you need. In Chapter 11 we discuss some ways to handle family disagreement and to ask for help.

Others are often willing to help. Sometimes a neighbor will look in on the confused person, the druggist will keep track of prescriptions for you, the minister, priest, or rabbi will listen when you are discouraged, a friend will sit with the person in an emergency, and so forth. As you plan, you should consider these resources, because they are important to you.

How much help should you accept or ask for from friends and neighbors? Most people like to help, yet making too many demands on them may eventually cause them to pull away.

When you turn to friends and neighbors for help, there are several things you can do to help them feel comfortable helping you. Some people are uncomfortable around those who are visibly upset. You may not want to express all of your distress to such people. Close friends may be more willing to share some of the emotional burden with you than people who do not know you well.

Although most people have heard of Alzheimer's disease, many need more information to understand why the person acts as she does. Explain that the behaviors are the result of the damage to the brain, that they are not deliberate or dangerous.

People may be reluctant to "sit with" or visit with the person because they do not know what to do and feel uncomfortable. You can help by suggesting specific things that the visitor might do with the person. For example, mention that going for a walk might be more fun than a conversation or that reminiscing about old times will be fun for both of them. Tell the visitor what you do when the ill person gets irritable or restless.

Some chapters of the Alzheimer's Association will train family members or friends to be special visitors. Such visitors bring pleasure to the confused person as well as giving you time away from caring.

When you ask people to help you, give them enough advance notice, if possible, so they can plan the time to help you. Remember to thank them and avoid criticizing what they have done.

Look for things others can do that they will not consider inconvenient. For example, neighbors may not mind "looking in" since they live close by, while more distant friends might resent being asked to make a long drive.

GETTING INFORMATION AND LOCATING OTHER SERVICES

At some point, most families look for outside help in obtaining information, making decisions, and planning for long-term care of their afflicted family member. Most families also need some time for themselves away from caregiving. Many families find the help they need and manage effectively without extensive professional assistance. However, the burdens of caring for a person with dementia are enormous, and many people have difficulty finding the services that might make caregiving easier.

KINDS OF SERVICES

People with dementia and their families may need several kinds of services. Most are available for a fee; few are available without charge.

Not all people who have dementing illnesses are elderly. However, there are additional resources for patients sixty or older. Most local offices on aging have a list of free or reduced-fee programs for people over sixty or over sixty-five. The American Association of Retired Persons (AARP) is also a good source of information about such resources.

Some programs offer services such as dental care, discounted dentures, less expensive eyeglasses, legal counseling, social work help, referral services, and free tax assistance to people over sixty, their spouses, and handicapped people. Some programs provide prescription medications or medical appliances at reduced cost. Some provide transportation.

There are a few programs that repair older people's homes at reduced rates. You may be able to use such a program to install wheelchair ramps, locks, grab bars, and other safety devices.

In some areas, programs such as Meals-on-Wheels will bring a daily hot meal to people who cannot get out. These meals are often delivered by friendly, dedicated volunteers who will also check to see how a person living alone is doing, but they provide limited help for a person who is becoming confused and are not a substitute for supervision.

Expanded nutrition programs offer a hot lunch and a recreation program in a sheltered group setting for several hours each weekday. They usually do not provide medical care, give medicines, or accept wandering, disruptive, or incontinent people. They are often staffed by lay or paraprofessional people. Mildly or moderately confused individuals may enjoy the group setting.

Nutrition programs are funded through the Older Americans Act and serve people over sixty and their spouses. You can find them by calling your local commission on aging. Some hot lunch programs are intended for the well elderly and an impaired person would not fit in. Other programs under the same or similar funding offer services to the "frail" elderly. You may be able to attend with your spouse if you wish. *Such programs do not provide adequate supervision for a person living alone.*

Mr. Williams was confused and often became restless. His wife arranged for a senior volunteer to visit and play checkers with him. He loved checkers and the volunteer understood and did not mind that Mr. Williams often forgot the rules. The volunteer became his "checkers pal" and made it possible for Mr. Williams to have a friendship and an enjoyable activity at the same time that it gave Mrs. Williams a break.

There are many other programs; we have referred to some of them in other parts of this book. You should find out what is available in your area even if you don't feel you need the service now. See Chapter 15 for a discussion of financial resources.

Having Someone Come into Your Home

Many families arrange for someone to come into their home to help with the ill person's care. A *homemaker* will help you with tasks such as housework, cooking, laundry, or shopping. A *home health aide* or a *personal care aide* will help the ill person dress, bathe, eat, and use the bathroom. Families of people with dementia most commonly turn to a *paid companion* or *sitter*. Sitters provide supervision and may help the person with meals. Some will give the person a bath. Some have had special training to provide the ill person with socialization and meaningful activities.

Visiting nurse and home health agencies send professionals—nurses, social workers, and other therapists—into homes to provide evaluation and care. A nurse, for example, may monitor the patient's status, change a catheter, and give injections. A speech therapist can help a stroke patient regain language skills, while a physical therapist may exercise the patient. Because a nurse is expensive and because Medicare will pay for this care only under strict guidelines, most families use a nurse only when the person has an acute illness that is difficult to manage at home. Hospice nurses may be available to teach you how to care for a dying person at home.

Home care is the first choice for many families. It is helpful when the person is ill or cannot get out of the house. However, home care provides supervision and personal care, but is less often able to offer socialization and meaningful activities.

Adult Day Care

Adult day care offers several hours a day of structured recreation in a group setting. Lunch and activities such as exercise, crafts, discussion, and music are offered. Programs may be open from one to five days a week; a few offer weekend or evening care.

Many day care programs accept both people with a range of physical impairments and people with dementia, but a growing number specialize in the care of people with dementia. Those that do may take people with severe impairments and may offer more activities designed for people with dementia. However, many programs that mix persons with dementia and those with other conditions provide good care to both groups. The skill of the staff and the philosophy of the program are most important in determining its quality.

Adult day care is one of the most important resources for families. It provides urgently needed respite for the caregiver and *it often benefits the person with dementia*. For most of us, the pressures of family life can be relieved by getting away sometimes to be with friends or to be alone. The person with dementia does not have this opportunity. She must be with her caregiver day after day, but her impairment does not take away her need to have her own friends and time apart. The burden of this enforced togetherness may be difficult for the impaired person as well as for the caregiver.

People with dementia experience failures and reminders of their inadequacies at every turn. But even when they cannot feed or dress themselves, they often retain their ability to enjoy music, laughter, friends, and the pleasures of doing some simple activity. People with dementia may make friends with other impaired people at the center, even when they are so impaired that they may not be able to tell you about their friend. Day care staffs observe that participants regain a sense of humor, appear more relaxed, and enjoy the activities. Good day care programs find ways for people to succeed at little things and thereby feel better about themselves. Day care programs fill empty time with activities the person can do well. Some programs do not offer much stimulation or socialization for the impaired person, but they remain a valuable source of time away for you.

Some programs offer both day care and in-home care. They are flexible so that you can shift from one to the other as your needs change.

Day care programs sometimes will not take clients with severe behavior problems. They may not take those who are incontinent or those who cannot walk independently, although some dementia-specific programs accept these very impaired individuals.

A major barrier to day care is transportation. Transporting people to and from day care is time consuming and expensive. Some programs pick people up, some contract with local transportation or taxi services, and some require that you transport the person. Be sure that the person will be given enough supervision while en route to the program.

In the United States, many families turn to day care or home care as a last resort when nursing home care is what they really need. The confused person's ability to adjust to and benefit from the respite care program is usually greater if you seek respite care early, when the person still has some mental capacity to adjust to and enjoy the new program. Your continued ability to care also depends on getting relief for yourself early.

Day Hospitals

Day hospitals differ from day care in that they offer diagnosis, medical care, and occupational and physical therapy. They are staffed by nurses, social workers, physicians, and other professionals. Geriatric day hospitals are uncommon in this country and funding sources for day hospitals sometimes restrict admission to patients with rehabilitative potential. Other countries report that the day hospital is an ideal setting in which to sort out and treat interacting physical and behavioral problems in a person with dementia. The time a person is allowed to stay in the day hospital is usually limited to the period of evaluation and treatment.

Short-Stay Residential Care

In short-stay respite settings, the confused person lives in a nursing home, boarding home, foster home, or other setting for a short period—a weekend, a week, or a few weeks—while the caregiver takes a vacation, gets needed medical care, or just rests. Although short-stay respite is common in other countries and valued by families there, it is still quite rare in this country. The concept of short-stay respite care may be unfamiliar to you, but you should consider trying it. Caregivers who use it are enthusiastic about it.

There is little funding available for short-stay care and regulations discourage nursing homes from offering this service. Some caregivers are reluctant to use short-stay respite; they fear that once they give up the burden of care, even temporarily, they will be unable to shoulder it again. There must be a clear understanding between the provider and the family about the duration of the stay. As with all respite programs, short-stay care is more effective when families use it *before* they reach the breaking point.

You may negotiate for this service yourself with a foster home or boarding home, or with an individual who will take in one or two clients. Since there is little governmental oversight of such care, you must make sure that the provider understands how to care for your family member and is a kind and gentle person. New surroundings may stress people with dementia, so short-stay respite programs will need enough skilled staff to give individual attention to their guests.

PLANNING IN ADVANCE FOR HOME CARE OR DAY CARE

Once you have found a good respite program, there are a few things you must do to make visits go smoothly. Be sure that the provider understands the nature of the dementing illness and knows how to handle problem behaviors. Write out special information for the provider: how much help will the person need in the bathroom or with meals? What does she like for lunch? What cues does she give that she is getting irritable, and how do you respond? What special needs does she have?

Be sure the care provider knows how to reach you, another family member, or the doctor. Be sure that the provider knows from you that only you have the authority to hire and fire.

If the sick person has complicating health problems, such as a heart or respiratory condition, a tendency to choke or fall, or seizures, you must carefully consider the skills of the person with whom you leave her.

WHEN THE CONFUSED PERSON REJECTS THE CARE

Families often say, "I know my husband. He would never go to day care (or accept a home visitor)." Impaired people often surprise everyone by enjoying day care or a home visitor. Avoid asking the person if she would like to go to day care. She is likely to answer No, because she does not understand what you are suggesting. Some people continue to say they don't want to go even when they are clearly enjoying themselves. This usually means that they do not understand or do not remember their enjoyment. Continue to cheerfully take the person to day care.

When a family is able to arrange for someone to stay at home with the impaired person, the ill person may fire the sitter or housekeeper, may get angry or suspicious, insult her, not let her in, or accuse her of stealing. Confused people may refuse to go to day care or put up such a fuss getting ready that the caregiver gives up.

To the person with dementia, the new person in the house may seem like an intruder. The person entering day care may feel lost or abandoned. What the person says may reflect these *feelings* more than fact.

Be prepared for a period of adjustment. People with dementia adjust to change slowly: it may take a month for a person with dementia to accept a new program. When you are already exhausted, arguments over respite care may seem overwhelming. You may feel guilty about forcing the person to do this so that you can get a break. Make a commitment to yourself to give the program a good trial. Often the confused person will accept the new plan if you can weather the initial storm.

What you say will make a difference. Refer to the respite plan as an adult activity the person will like. Present the home care provider as a friend who has come to visit. Find things the person with dementia likes to do that the two can do together: take a walk, groom the dog, play a game of checkers (even if not by the rules), or make brownies. Call day care anything the person will accept, for example, "the club." Often mildly impaired people prefer to "volunteer" at the center. Most day care programs will support this. "Helping" people who are more impaired allows the person to feel successful while reducing the pressure on her to perform.

Write the confused person a note—say why she is there (or why the home care provider is there), when you will return, and that she is to stay there and wait for you. Sign the note and give it to her or to the provider. If this does not work, have your doctor write and sign such a note. The provider can read it with her each time she becomes restless.

Some families make a short videotape of the care of the confused person. This is particularly helpful when the provider will be assisting in personal care such as dressing or eating. You can show the order in which you do things, like which arm goes in which sleeve first. You might leave written instructions as well.

Day care and home care providers have found that people adjust better when

1. the first visits by the in-home provider or to day care are short enough that the confused person does not get tired in the strange situation.
2. the primary caregiver stays with the confused person the first few times an in-home visitor is used. This may help the confused person begin to feel that she knows this visitor. Although many day care programs ask caregivers to stay with the person the first time or two, a few prefer that they not remain. For most people the presence of the caregiver is reassuring, a few do better on their own away from the caregiver's tension and uncertainty.
3. someone from the day care program visits the person at home before her first visit to day care.

Remember, for the confused person each visit is like starting over. However, most people gradually begin to accept the new routine. More frequent visits to day care or from the home care provider may help the person experience a sense of continuity.

Some caregivers find that the hassle of getting the person ready is so great that day care is not worth it. Perhaps you can arrange for a friend or neighbor to come in to help with this chore. Allow plenty of time; feeling rushed will upset the confused person even more.

Occasionally a person in day care will come home and say to her husband, "My husband is at the center." Of course, this is distressing for the caregiving spouse. The person usually does not mean "husband." Perhaps she is trying to say "friend" but could not find the word. Perhaps "husband" is the closest word she can find to mean companion. It does not imply a romance and it should not affect the marital relationship.

Sometimes the confused person will say, "She hit me" or "They wouldn't give me anything to eat" or "The fat one took my purse." Avoid taking such remarks too seriously. People with dementia can misperceive, misremember, or express themselves inaccurately. Perhaps she can't remember having lunch. Ask the staff what took place.

You may ask the person, "What did you do today?" and she may reply, "Nothing." "Well, did you have a good time?" "No." Answers like this may indicate that she can't remember what went on. Don't embarrass her by continuing to ask. Ask a staff member what she enjoyed today.

If the person says she does not want to go to day care (or have the home care provider), you do not have to take this literally. She may mean that she does not understand what you are suggesting. She may not remember earlier visits at all. Avoid getting into arguments. Reassure her that this is something she can handle, that you will come back for her, and that the people there are nice and will help her.

A few people cannot adjust to home care or day care. Try several different providers. Some people have a way with people with dementia. Ask yourself whether your attitude is affecting her adjustment (see below). If you cannot use a respite program now, try again in a few weeks or months. Often changes in the person's condition will make it easier for her to accept someone later.

YOUR OWN FEELINGS ABOUT GETTING RESPITE FOR YOURSELF

It is not unusual for a family to be discouraged by their first visit to a day care center.

Mr. Wilson said, "I went to see the day care center. The hospital told me this was an excellent center. But I can't put Alice in there. Those people are old and sick. One of them was dragging a shopping bag around and mumbling. One was drooling. Some of them were sleeping in these chairs with a tray across them."

The sight of other disabled or elderly people can be distressing. Our perception of the person we live with is colored by our memory of how she used to be. You may feel that such a program does not offer the individual care that you can give at home or you may feel that no one else can manage the person.

Some families are reluctant to bring a stranger into their home. You may not like strangers in your home or you may worry about whether they are honest. You may not want anyone to see your house in a mess. And many people feel, "My family and I are private people. We take care of our own. We just aren't the kind of people who use public help."

Like you, American families provide almost all of the care of the frail elderly. Seventy-five to eighty-five percent of all care comes from family members. Dementing illnesses cause particularly devastating burdens for family members. Because it is a disease of the mind, you are faced with the grief of losing companionship and communication, with the tasks of dressing, feeding, and toileting the person, and with difficult behavior. These diseases last many years, and caregivers usually cannot leave the ill person for even a few minutes. Many caregivers are doing little more than surviving—just barely hanging on.

If you become ill, as many caregivers do, others will have to assume responsibility for the person you care for. Good care means caring for yourself too. If you are tired and depressed, you may snap at the confused person. She will usually sense your distress and may respond (she can't help it) by whining or wandering or arguing even more. Many caregivers end up using medicine to control these behaviors. This may make the ill person more confused. Ask yourself: Am I rushing her? snapping at her? slapping her?

The best prescriptions we know are to talk with other families and to get some time away from the ill person. Arranging a little time for yourself and coming back a little rested and in better humor can allow you to continue caring.

If the people in day care seem more impaired than your family member, it is likely she will feel comfortable where her difficulties will not be noticed and where she can be the helper. If you have checked references, it is likely that the person coming into your home is honest. Home care workers say they rarely notice how messy the house is. Talk with other families: often they too were reluctant but will tell you that the time apart helps the confused person as well as themselves. Caregivers have told us that knowing that a professional provider is also having difficulty with the person makes them feel better about their own efforts to manage.

Even if the respite situation is not perfect—if the home sitter watches soap operas or the participants in day care seem to just sit a lot of the time—you may want to continue with it. Your continued strength and your ability to keep providing care may depend on your getting regular breaks from caregiving.

Some in-home providers urge that you leave the house while they provide care. This is because they think carers need the time away. It is tempting to stay and talk with the respite worker or help with the confused person, but you may manage better in the long run if you get away, even if all you do is take a walk or visit with a neighbor. If you stay at home, go into another room, away from the patient.

LOCATING RESOURCES

Most towns and cities have no central information source that can tell you what services are offered or how to get them. Even information and referral services often do not have a complete and current list of resources. Therefore, you will need to be persistent and may need to contact several individuals or agencies. The process of locating resources can be long and tedious. If you are providing most of the supervision and care of an impaired person, you may feel too overwhelmed to do this. It may be difficult to make telephone calls in the presence of the confused person. If you are overwhelmed, ask another family member or a close friend to take on the job of locating outside help. If you are not the person with daily responsibility for care, offer to help the caregiver locate outside services.

Before you begin, think about what kinds of help would be right for you and the confused person:

- Do you need help with financial planning?
- Do you need more information about the disease or about diagnosis?
- Should you try day care or a sitter at home?
- If you use day care, will you need transportation for the confused person?
- Do you need help for specific tasks, such as giving baths?
- Do you want to get out one night a week? Or do you need to get out during the day when you can drive?
- Do you need someone to talk to?
- What kind of help will the confused person need? (If she becomes

agitated, wanders, or is incontinent, be sure that the provider can manage this.)
• Does she need help walking or does she need bed care?

Write down your questions before you begin making calls. Keep notes of your conversations. Write down the names of the people you talk to. If you call back later for additional information, this record will be helpful. If the person you speak to does not have the answers to your questions, ask to speak to someone who does. If a person brushes you off, ask to speak to someone else.

Begin by calling the local chapter of the Alzheimer's Association. They will be listed in the telephone directory. Some chapters are small, volunteer-run programs and others have paid, professional staff, but most will be able to tell you about good programs in your area that accept people with dementia. A concerned person—often a family member—will listen to your needs and make suggestions. This organization usually will be able to tell you about programs that serve people with dementia. They usually do not make formal evaluations of the quality of programs but usually they can tell you what other families have thought of the service.

Also call the local office on aging. The name of this state and federally funded organization varies, but you can usually find it under the government listings in the telephone book or in the yellow pages under "senior citizens" or "older adults." Some of these agencies have professionals who will help you locate resources. Some have special programs for people with dementia, including in-home sitters or day care. Some will provide transportation to day care. Some fund limited amounts of day care or in-home care. Not all offices on aging will be helpful. Some are not knowledgeable about dementia or do not have an effective referral system. They may know little about the quality of the services they refer people to.

Adult day care staffs often know what other services are available. It is worth calling them even if you don't want adult day care. If there is a regional Alzheimer's center or resource center near you, their staff members usually know what resources are available for people with dementia. Occasionally a community health center, a community mental health center, a geriatric assessment program, or a nursing home can refer you to resources. They often have information and referral services. Some will be helpful; others will not. Agencies may not know about local services. In a few places each of these agencies provides outstanding day care or in-home care to people with dementia, but in other areas, they do not serve people with dementia or their families.

You may not find what you need; unfortunately, the resources families of people with dementia need are often not available. Don't blame yourself if you can't find the resources you need. Some agencies have a waiting list, or they will take only certain kinds of people, while other agencies may be too expensive. Inadequate resources and services are major problems that can be changed only through public recognition of the dementing diseases and the needs of families.

Perhaps you will want to accept what resources are available, even if they are not ideal, since you may find that obtaining even some help is better than trying to cope alone.

Occasionally families are able to exchange services. Plans can be simple or elaborate; basically, two or three families agree to take turns sitting. You may sit with two confused people in your home for one afternoon a week. Then the next week someone else will sit, while you get an afternoon out. This works best when the impaired people are not agitated and do not wander. They will enjoy the contact with others. The "rules" of exchange services should be clearly spelled out.

An organization of families might want to train one or two people in the management of people with a dementing illness. Such a person would have a full-time job dividing her time among several families.

The person who helps you may be a family member, friend, neighbor, or church member. The Alzheimer's Association will often train people so that they feel more secure in helping care for the confused person while you have some time away. Some families locate a respite care worker by advertising or through word of mouth. Older people who need work but lack formal skills are a good source of help. Also consider college students. Some students are gentle and kind and have had experience with their own grandparents.

PAYING FOR CARE

Fees for day care and in-home care vary, often depending on the sources of governmental or private funding the program has access to. There is no national resource for assisting middle-class families with the costs of day care or in-home care. Although home nursing is usually the most expensive kind of care, if the person needs nursing treatment for specific conditions (usually not associated with the dementia) or if periodic nursing reassessment is needed for an unstable condition, Medicare may pay for part of the cost of the nurse and may also pay for a home health aide.

Medicare regulations change with changes in federal policy and can be confusing to interpret. Ask the social worker or service agency to help you find out whether their services to you are reimbursable. It may be worthwhile to request that a decision be reviewed by Medicare. In general, except for a few demonstration projects, Medicare rarely pays for respite for people with dementia.

Home nursing and home health aides can also be hired from nursing agencies. If you use an agency, be sure you know whether they will replace a person if she does not show up and how much training or experience the person has had in caring for people with dementia.

Home health aides and companions that you locate and contract with yourself are usually less expensive than agency staff, but you can spend considerable time locating them and some are unpredictable. Some people advertise for help in local newspapers, where nurse aides advertise their availability. Families suggest you ask a home aide who is working with someone you know: she may have friends who are looking for work.

If you hire someone, recognize that it is unreasonable to ask a person to both clean the house and watch an ill person. Realistically, a domestic helper probably cannot look after a confused person and clean the house. It is challenging for *you* to do both and often impossible for someone unfamiliar with your house and with the impaired person. You may have to settle for a sitter and a house that is not very well kept. Discuss fees, hours, and exact responsibilities before you hire. Fees may be surprisingly high, particularly in metropolitan areas.

In some states Medicaid pays for home care and day care for a few low-income people, but eligibility is limited; and even this is not available in many areas. Some states have limited funds to pay for in-home or day care through the office on aging. Federal and state governments and some foundations are funding respite care demonstration programs, but these will serve only a few people for limited periods of time.

Some programs provide trained volunteers as in-home or day care workers. These programs work well, but there are costs: for supervisory and training personnel, transportation, and insurance. A fee may be charged to cover these costs.

A few Alzheimer's Association chapters have funds to assist families who need home care or day care. Some programs have sliding fee scales and some have financial aid available.

All these resources are extremely limited, however. Most families can expect to pay at least part of the cost of care. Many families fear the enormous costs of nursing home care. While they hope never to need such care, they feel they must conserve their resources rather than spend money on respite. For a full discussion of paying for nursing home care, see Chapter 16. However, since Medicaid pays for nursing home care only after the person has exhausted her own resources, the family may decide to expend part of the ill person's (*not the spouse's*) resources on respite care, keeping detailed records to prove that the money was spent on her care. Keep back sufficient funds to pay privately for the first few months of nursing home care (to ensure access to a nursing home). When this money is spent, you can apply for Medicaid funds. Because Medicaid rules change frequently, vary from state to state, and are extraordinarily complex, you must evaluate the ill person's resources carefully and consult someone knowledgeable about Medicaid law in your state before taking this step.

SHOULD RESPITE PROGRAMS MIX PEOPLE WHO HAVE DIFFERENT PROBLEMS?

You may have heard that respite programs that specialize in the care of people with dementia are supposed to be better than programs that mix people with different kinds of health problems. Families sometimes worry about what might happen if a frail, elderly person with Alzheimer's disease is in the same program with a younger, strong person who has had a head injury or similar trauma.

Programs that serve a group of people whose needs and levels of functioning are similar can more easily provide specialized programing that meets their needs. However, many programs have successfully mixed people who are confused with people who have head traumas or physical disabilities. In some areas there are not enough people with dementia who have similar needs to make a specialized program cost-effective. Diagnosis does not describe a person's needs and level of function well: the care of an active younger individual with Alzheimer's disease may be more like that of a head trauma patient than like the care of a frail, anxious person with Alzheimer's disease. Anger, grief, and exhaustion are common to most families, regardless of diagnosis. Staff skill is more important than diagnosis in most cases.

It is best to judge a program on how well it provides individual care and how well you think your family member will fit in with the group. A confused person can take great satisfaction from pushing a wheelchair or in handing a dish of cookies to a physically impaired person. On the other hand, a program that offers a lot of discussion groups, reading, and watching films is focusing on activities that will leave out most people with dementia. If you are concerned that your family member will not fit in or is too frail, discuss your concerns with the program director. Some programs are flexible and try to match activities to a person's current abilities. A trial period in the program is often the best idea. People with dementia often surprise us by how well they can fit in.

DETERMINING THE QUALITY OF SERVICES

Since the confused person may not be able to tell you about the care she receives, you must know about the quality of care the program provides. *Many of the agencies that refer you will not have reliable information about the quality of services they refer you to.* This is true even of governmental agencies, which may never have visited the program. To prevent discrimination, some referral programs are required to recommend all programs equally, without regard to the quality of the program. Hospital social workers are often under pressure from the hospital to place people quickly.

Many people assume that some governmental agency is responsible for safeguarding the quality of programs such as adult day care and in-home care. In fact, the federal government has almost no control over such programs. Some states have standards and enforce them; others have no standards, have minimal standards, or do not enforce the standards they have. Existing standards may not take into account the special limitations of people with dementia (for example, that they need more supervision or that they cannot respond to fire alarms).

Never assume that, because you were given the name of a service by an authority, it is a good-quality program, there are standards it must meet, or it has been recently inspected.

In most of the programs we have seen, providers work because they love the job, and they give good care. However, there is an occasional bad apple. Checking on the quality of a service is up to you. Always ask if the program is licensed and by what agency, and whether it meets existing voluntary or required standards.

At a minimum, a day care center or a person coming into your home should be bonded. Workers should be supervised by a professional (usually a nurse or social worker) and should be trained in the safe care of elderly people and in the special care of people with dementia. Ask the providing agency whether your state certifies this level of worker and whether this person is certified. Ask questions, check references, and monitor the care given, particularly in the beginning. In a day center, ask about meal preparation, supervision of wandering, fire emergency plans, and the kinds of activities provided.

People with dementia often misunderstand or misinterpret things. As a result, they may report neglect or poor care that did not really happen. Carefully investigate complaints such as "They didn't give me any lunch" or "She is spying on us."

When her mother was sick, Mary had a woman stay with her in their home. On one occasion Mary's children accidentally left their tape recorder running and when Mary came home and replayed it, she realized the aide had watched soap operas all afternoon instead of spending time with her mother.

It can be difficult to know how well another person is caring for your family member. Carers are almost always honest and caring, and it is important that you have some respite time. Do not avoid getting help because you worry about the quality of care. At the same time, be alert to potential problems.

RESEARCH AND DEMONSTRATION PROGRAMS

The federal government, a few state governments, and some universities have established Alzheimer's Research Centers and Alzheimer's disease clinics. The federal centers carry out research into potential treatments, prevention, or possible cures (see Chapter 18.) Others focus on diagnosis, medical care, and educational services to families. Some centers are closely allied with Alzheimer's Association chapters. Some provide information about respite only to families they serve; others provide information to anyone who requests it. Such centers are a great resource to the families near them.

Federal and state governments and private foundations have begun funding demonstration respite care programs. The object of these programs is to test specific ideas about day care or home care. These demonstration programs are not intended to meet the total community need for respite care; they can serve only a few patients and families. They are trial balloons whose findings will ultimately benefit all families. However, even if you do not participate directly in such a program, these centers may be a valuable source of information about other community resources.

TABLE 1. DEFINITIONS OF CARE SERVICES FOR PERSONS WITH DEMENTIA

Adult day care: A program of medical and social services, including socialization, activities, and supervision, provided in an outpatient setting.

Case management: Client assessment, identification and coordination of community resources, and follow-up monitoring of client adjustment and service provision.

Chore services: Household repairs, yard work, and errands.

Congregate meals: Meals provided in a group setting for people who may benefit both from the nutritionally sound meal and from social, educational, and recreational services provided at the setting.

Dental services: Care of the teeth, and diagnosis and treatment of dental problems.

Home-delivered meals: Meals delivered to the home for individuals who are unable to shop or cook for themselves.

Home health aide services: Assistance with health-related tasks, such as medications, exercises, and personal care.

Homemaker services: Household services, such as cooking, cleaning, laundry, and shopping, and escort service to accompany patients to medical appointments and elsewhere.

Hospice services: Medical, nursing, and social services to provide support and alleviate suffering for dying persons and their families.

Information and referral: Provision of written or verbal information about community agencies, services, and funding sources.

Legal services: Assistance with legal matters, such as advance directives, guardianship, power of attorney, and transfer of assets.

Mental health services: Psychosocial assessment and individual and group counseling to address psychological and emotional problems of patients and families.

Occupational therapy: Treatment to improve functional abilities; provided by an occupational therapist.

Paid companion/sitter: An individual who comes to the home to provide supervision, personal care, and socialization during the absence of the primary caregiver.

Patient assessment: Evaluation of the individual's physical, mental, and emotional status, behavior, and social supports.

Personal care: Assistance with basic self-care activities such as bathing, dressing, getting out of bed, eating, and using the bathroom.

Personal emergency response systems: Telephone-based systems to alert others that an individual who is alone is experiencing an emergency and needs assistance.

Physical therapy: Rehabilitative treatment provided by a physical therapist.

Physician services: Diagnosis and ongoing medical care, including prescribing medications and treating intercurrent illness.

Protective services: Social and law enforcement services to prevent, eliminate, or remedy the effects of physical and emotional abuse or neglect.

Recreational services: Physical exercise, art and music therapy, parties, celebrations, and other social and recreational activities.

Respite care: Short-term, in- or out-patient services intended to provide temporary relief for the primary caregiver.

Skilled nursing: Medically oriented care provided by a licensed nurse, including monitoring acute and unstable medical conditions; assessing care needs; supervising medications, tube and intravenous feeding, and personal care services; and treating bedsores and other conditions.

Speech therapy: Treatment to improve or restore speech; provided by a speech therapist.

Supervision: Monitoring an individual's whereabouts to ensure his or her safety.

Telephone reassurance: Regular telephone calls to individuals who are isolated and often homebound.

Transportation: Transporting people to medical appointments, community facilities, and elsewhere.

Source: Office of Technology Assessment, 1987.

11

YOU AND THE IMPAIRED PERSON AS PARTS OF A FAMILY

CHAPTERS 2–10 have discussed how to get help for the sick person and ways to care for him. However, you and your family are important also. A chronic dementing illness places a heavy burden on the whole family: it may mean a lot of work or financial sacrifices; it may mean accepting the reality that someone you love will never be the same again; it continues on and on; it may mean that responsibilities and relationships within the family will change; it may mean disagreements within the family; it may mean that you feel overwhelmed, discouraged, isolated, angry, or depressed. You and the person with a dementing illness, as well as the other people close to him, all interact as part of a family system. This system can be severely stressed by a dementing illness. It is helpful to consider the changes that may occur in families that are faced with a chronic illness and to identify the feelings you may experience. Sometimes just knowing that what is happening to you has happened to others can make life easier. Often, recognizing what is happening suggests ways to improve things.

It is important to know that almost all families do care for their elderly and sick as long as possible. It is simply not true that most Americans abandon their elderly or "dump" them into nursing homes. Studies have shown that, although many older people do not live with their children, they are closely involved with or cared for by them. Families usually do all they can, often at great personal sacrifice, to care for ill elderly members before seeking help. Of course, there are families who do not care for ill family members. There are some who, because of illness or other problems, are unable to care for their elderly; there are a few who do not wish to; there are some elderly people who have no family to help them. But in the majority of cases, families are struggling to do the best they can for their ill elderly.

Most family members discover a closeness and cooperation as they work together to care for someone with a dementing illness. Sometimes, however, the pressures of caring for an ill person create conflicts in families or cause old disagreements to flare up. For example,

Mr. Higgins said, "We can't agree on what to do. I want to keep Mother at home. My sister wants her in a nursing home. We don't even agree on what is wrong."

Mrs. Tate said, "My brother doesn't call and he refuses even to talk about it. I have to take care of Mother alone."

In addition, the burden of caring for a person with a dementing illness can be exhausting and distressing for you.

Mrs. Fried said, "I get so depressed. I cry. Then I lie awake at night and worry. I feel so helpless."

Watching someone close to you decline can be a painful experience. This chapter discusses some of the problems that arise in families, and Chapter 12 will discuss some of the feelings you may have.

It is important to remember that not all of your experiences will be unhappy ones. Many people feel a sense of pride in learning to cope with difficult situations. Many family members rediscover one another as they work together to care for an ill person. As you help a forgetful person enjoy the world around him, you may experience a renewed delight in sharing little things—playing with a puppy or enjoying flowers. You may discover a new faith in yourself, in others, or in God. Most dementing illnesses progress slowly, so you and your family member can look forward to many good years.

Mrs. Morales said, "Although it has been hard, it's been good for me in a lot of ways. It's given me confidence to know that I can manage things my husband always took care of, and in some ways my children and I have grown closer as he has gotten sick."

Since this book is designed to help you with problems when they do occur, most of what we discuss are unhappy feelings and problems. We know that this is a one-sided view that reflects only part of what life is like for you.

The feelings and problems you and your family experience interact and affect one another. However, for simplicity, we have organized them into separate topics: changes in roles within the family, finding ways to cope with changes in roles and the family conflict that can arise, your own feelings, and finding ways to care for yourself.

CHANGES IN ROLES

Roles, responsibilities, and expectations within the family change when one person becomes ill. For example,

A wife said, "The worst part is doing the checkbook. We have been married thirty-five years and now I have to learn to do the checkbook."

A husband said, "I feel like a fool washing ladies' underwear in the laundromat."

A son said, "My father has always been the head of the household. How can I tell him he can't drive?"

A daughter said, "Why can't my brother help out and take his turn keeping Mother?"

Roles are different from responsibilities, and it is helpful to recognize what roles mean to you and to others in the family. Responsibilities are the jobs each person has in the family. Roles include who you are, how you are seen, and what is expected of you. By "role" we mean a person's place in his family (for example, head of the household, mother, or "the person everyone turns to"). Roles are established over many years and are not always easy to define. Tasks often symbolize our roles. In the examples above, family members describe both having to learn new tasks (doing the wash or balancing the checkbook) and changes in roles (money manager, homemaker, head of the household).

Learning a new responsibility, such as keeping the checkbook or washing clothes, can be difficult when you are also faced with the many day-to-day needs of the confused person, yourself, and your family. However, changes in roles are often more difficult to accept or adjust to. Understanding that each person's responsibilities change and that roles and expectations of others change also will help you to understand the personal feelings and problems that may arise in families. It is helpful to remember that you have coped with changes in roles at other times in your life and that this experience will help you adjust to new responsibilities.

There are many relationships in which role changes occur as the person's dementia worsens. Here are four examples.

1. *The relationships between a husband and wife change when one of them becomes ill.* Some of these changes may be sad and painful; others can be enriching experiences.

John and Mary Douglas had been married forty-one years when John got sick. John has always been the head of the household: he supported the family, paid the bills, made most of the big decisions. Mary saw herself as a person who always leaned on her husband. When he got sick, she realized that she did not know how much money they had, what insurance they had, or even how to balance a checkbook. Bills were going unpaid, yet when she asked John about it, he yelled at her.

For their anniversary Mary fixed a small turkey and planned a quiet time together when they could forget what was happening. When she put the electric carving knife in front of John he threw it down and shouted at her that the knife did not work and she had ruined the turkey. Trying to keep the peace, Mary took the knife, and then realized that she had no idea how to carve a turkey. Mary cried and John stormed. Neither of them felt like eating supper that night.

Having to carve a turkey seemed like the last straw for Mary. She realized that John could no longer do this, nor could he manage their finances, but she suddenly felt overwhelmed and lost. Throughout their marriage Mary had looked to John to solve problems. Now she had to learn to do the things he had always done at the same time that she had to face his illness.

Learning new skills and responsibilities involves energy and effort and means work added to what you already have to do. You may not want to take on new tasks. Few husbands want to learn to do the wash, and more than one has had a load of shrunken sweaters and pale pink jockey shorts before he finds out that he can't wash red sweaters with white underwear. A spouse who has never managed the checkbook may feel that he doesn't have the ability to manage money and may be afraid of making errors.

In addition to having to do the job itself, the realization that you must take this job away from your spouse may symbolize all of the sad changes that have taken place. For Mary, her carving the turkey symbolized John's loss of status as head of the family.

A spouse may gradually realize that she is alone with her problem—she has lost the partner with whom she shared things. Mary could no longer see herself as leaning on her husband. She suddenly found herself, at sixty, on her own and forced to be independent with no one to help her. No wonder she felt overwhelmed by the task. But at the same time, learning new skills gradually gave Mary a sense of accomplishment. She said, "I was surprised at myself, really, that I could handle things. Even though I felt so upset, it was good for me to learn that I could manage so well."

Sometimes problems seem insurmountable because they involve both changes in roles and the need for you to learn new tasks. Having to learn new skills when you are upset and tired can be difficult. As well as recognizing the distress that may be caused by changing roles, you may need some practical suggestions for getting started with new responsibilities.

If you must take over the housework, often you can do it gradually and learn as you go. But you can save yourself the frustration of burned suppers and ruined laundry by getting the advice of experts. The county extension office usually has excellent information on shopping, meal preparation, laundry, budgeting, and home maintenance. You can also get advice from homemakers or a visiting nurse. You may even find useful brochures or recipes in the supermarket.

Mrs. Stearns says, "I know my husband can't manage his money any more, but it seems like it is taking away the last of his manhood to take away the checkbook. I know I have to, but I just can't seem to do it."

Having to take this symbol of independence away from someone you love can be difficult. It can be worse when you are not accustomed to managing money.

If you have never balanced a checkbook or paid the bills you may find it hard to learn this new responsibility. Actually, managing household finances is not difficult, even for people who dislike math. Most banks have staff who will advise you, without charge. They also will show you how to balance a checkbook. There are books in the library on this subject. The fact that you must take over this role, rather than the task itself, sometimes is what makes it hard to do.

The bank or a lawyer can also help you draw up a list of your or the confused person's assets and debts. Sometimes a person has been private about financial affairs, has told no one, and now cannot remember them. Chapter 15 lists some of the potential resources you should look for.

If you can't drive or do not like to drive and must take over the driving responsibilities, look for a driver education course designed for adults. Inquire through the police or the American Association of Retired Persons for driver's education courses and defensive driving programs for older adults. Life will be much easier if you are comfortable behind the wheel.

2. *The relationship of a parent with a dementing illness and his adult children often has to change.* The changes that occur when an adult child must assume the responsibility and care of a parent are sometimes called "role reversal." Perhaps this is better described as a shift in roles and responsibilities, in which the adult son or daughter gradually assumes increasing responsibility for a parent while the roles of the parent change accordingly. These changes can be difficult. You, the adult son or daughter, may feel sadness and grief at the losses you see in someone you love and look up to. You may feel guilty about "taking over."

"I can't tell my mother she shouldn't live alone any more," Mrs. Russo says. "I know I have to, but every time I try to talk to her she manages to make me feel like a small child who has been bad."

To varying degrees many of us as adults still feel that our parents are parents and that we, the children, are less assured, capable, and "grown up." In some families the parents seem to maintain this kind of relationship with their adult children past the time when adult sons and daughters usually come to feel mature in their own right.

Not everyone has had a good relationship with his parents. If a parent has not been able to let his grown children feel grown up, a lot of unhappiness and conflict may develop. Then as the parent develops a dementing illness he can seem to be demanding and manipulative of you. You may find yourself feeling trapped. You may feel used, angry, and guilty at the same time.

What seems demanding to you may feel different to the impaired person. He may be feeling that with "just a little help" he can hold on to his independence, perhaps continue to live alone. As he senses his decline, this may seem the only way he can respond to his losses.

Adult children often feel embarrassed by the tasks of physically caring for a parent—for example, giving their mother a bath or changing their father's underwear. Look for ways to help your parent retain his dignity at the same time that you give needed care.

3. *The sick person must adjust to his changing roles in the family.* This often means giving up some of his independence, responsibility, or leadership, which can be difficult for anyone. (See Chapter 4.) He may become discouraged or depressed as he realizes his abilities are waning. He may be unable to change or to recognize his decline.

The roles a person has held within the family in the past, and the kind of person he is, will influence the new roles he assumes as he becomes ill. You can help him to maintain his position as an important member of the family even when he can no longer do the tasks he once did. Consult him, talk to him, listen to him (even if what he says seems confused). Let him know by these actions that he is still respected.

4. *As the roles of the sick person change, the expectations of each member of the family for the others change.* Your relationships and expectations of members of the family are based on family roles that have been established for years. Changes often lead to conflicts, misunderstandings, and times when people's expectations of each other do not agree. At the same time, adjusting to changes and facing problems can bring families closer together, even when they have not been close for years.

UNDERSTANDING FAMILY CONFLICTS

Mrs. Eaton says, "My brother doesn't have anything to do with Mom now—and he was always her favorite. He won't even come to see her. All the burden is on my sister and me. Because my sister's marriage is shaky, I hate to leave Mom with her for long. So I end up taking care of Mom pretty much alone."

Mr. Cooke says, "My son wants me to put my wife in a nursing home. He doesn't understand that, after thirty years of marriage, I can't just put her in a nursing home." His son says, "Dad isn't being realistic. He can't manage Mother in that big two-story house. She's going to fall one of these days. And Dad has a heart condition that he refuses to discuss."

Mr. Vane says, "My brother says if I kept her more active, she would get better. He says I should answer her back when she gets nasty, but that only makes things worse. He doesn't live with her. He just stays in his own apartment and criticizes."

Division of Responsibility

The responsibility of caring for an impaired person often is not evenly shared by the family. Like Mrs. Eaton, you may find that you are carrying most of the burden of taking care of the person who has a dementing illness. There are many reasons why it is difficult to divide responsibility evenly. Some members of the family may live far away, may be in poor health, may be financially unable to help, or may have problems with their children or marriage.

Sometimes families accept stereotypes about who should help without really considering what is best. One such stereotype is that daughters (and daughters-in-law) are "supposed" to take care of the sick. But the daughter or daughter-in-law may already be heavily burdened and not able to take on this task. Perhaps she has young children, or a full-time job. Perhaps she is a single parent.

Long-established roles, responsibilities, and mutual expectations within the family, even when we are unaware of them, can play an important part in determining who has what responsibility for the impaired person. For example,

"My mother raised me; now I must take care of her."

"She was a good wife, and she would have done the same for me."

"I married him late in life. What responsibility is mine and what responsibility is his children's?"

"He was always hard on me, deserted my mother when I was ten, and he's willed all his money to some organization. How much do I owe him?"

Sometimes expectations are not logical and may not be based on the most practical or fair way to arrange things. Sometimes there have been long-established disagreements, resentments, or conflicts in the family which are aggravated by the crisis of an illness.

Sometimes family members fail to help as much as they might because it is difficult for them to accept the reality of the impaired person's illness. Sometimes a person just can't bear to face this illness. It is painful, as you know, to watch a loved one decline. Sometimes family members who do not have the burden of daily care stay away because seeing the decline makes them feel sad. However, others in the family may view this as deserting the declining person.

Sometimes one family member assumes most of the burden of care. He may not tell other members of the family how bad things are. He may not want to burden them or he may not really want their help.

Mr. Newman says, "I hesitate to call on my sons. They are willing to help, but they have their own careers and families."

Mrs. King says, "I don't like to call on my daughter. She always tells me what she thinks I am doing wrong."

Often you and other members of the family have strong and differing ideas of how things should be done. Sometimes this happens because not all family members understand what is wrong with the person who has a dementing illness, or why he acts as he does, or what can be expected in the future.

Family members who do not share the day-to-day experience of living with a person suffering from a dementing illness may not know what it is really like, and may be critical or unsympathetic. It is hard for people on the outside to realize how wearing the daily burden of constant care can be. Often, too, people don't realize how you are feeling unless you tell them.

Occasionally a family member will oppose your efforts to get outside help. If this happens, insist that the family member help take care of the ill person so that you can get some rest. If the family member lives out of town, ask him to attend a support group in his community or to volunteer some time in a program for people with dementia so that he will better understand what you are facing. Ultimately, the family must accept that the person who provides most of the care should make the final decisions to use day care, in-home care, or a nursing home. Fewer misunderstandings develop when everyone is kept informed about what resources are available and what they will cost.

YOUR MARRIAGE

When the ill person is your parent or in-law, it is important to consider the effect of his illness on your marriage. Maintaining a good marriage is often not easy, and caring for a person with a dementing illness can make it much more difficult. It may mean more financial burdens and less time to talk, to go out, and to make love. It may entail being involved with your in-laws, having more things to disagree over, often being tired, or short-changing the children. It can mean having to include a difficult, disagreeable, seemingly demanding, and sick person in your lives.

A dementing illness can be painful to watch. It is understandable that a person may look at his impaired in-law and wonder if his spouse will become like that, and if he will have to go through this again.

A son or daughter can easily find himself or herself torn between the needs of an impaired parent, the expectations of brothers and sisters (or the other parent), and the needs and demands of a spouse and children. It's easy to take out frustrations or fatigue on those we love and trust most—our spouse and our children.

The spouse of an ill parent may also add problems. He or she may be upset, critical, or ill, or he may even desert his ill partner. Such problems can add to the tension in your marriage, and, if at all possible, should be discussed with everyone involved. It is sometimes easier if a son initiates a solution with his own family or a daughter with her own relatives.

A good relationship can survive for a while in the face of stress and trouble, but we believe it is important that the husband and wife find time and energy for each other—to talk, to get away, and to enjoy their relationship in the ways that they always have.

COPING WITH ROLE CHANGES AND
FAMILY CONFLICT

When the family does not agree, or when most of the burden is on one person, it adds to the problems you face. The burden of caring for a chronically ill person is often too much for one individual. It is important that you have others to help—to give you "time out" from constant care, to give you encouragement and support, to help with the work, and to share the financial responsibility.

If you are getting criticism or not enough help from your family, it is usually not a good idea to let your resentment smolder. It may be up to you to take the initiative to change things in your family. When families are in disagreement or when long-established conflicts get in the way, this may be difficult to do.

How do you handle the often complex, painful role changes that are set in motion by a chronic, dementing illness? First, recognize these as aspects of family relationships. Just knowing that roles in families are complex, often unrecognized or unacknowledged, and that changes can be painful will help you feel less panicked and overwhelmed. Recognize that certain tasks may be symbolic of important roles in the family and that it is the shift of role, rather than the specific issue, which may be painful.

Find out all you can about the disease. What family members believe to be true about this illness affects how much help they provide for a person and affects whether there will be disagreements about caring for the impaired person. Family members who live out of town can attend Alzheimer's Association meetings in their community.

Think about the differences between the responsibilities or tasks that an impaired person may have to give up and the roles that he may be able to retain. For example, although John's illness means he can no longer carve a turkey or make many decisions, his *role* as Mary's loved and respected husband can remain.

Know what the impaired person is still able to do and what is too difficult for him. Of course, one wants a person to remain as self-reliant as possible, but expectations that exceed his abilities can make him upset and miserable. (Sometimes such expectations of how well he can function come from others, sometimes they come from the impaired person himself.) If he cannot do a task independently, try to simplify the job so that he can still do part of it.

Recognize that role changes are not one-time things, but are ongoing processes. As the illness progresses, you may have to continue to take on new responsibilities. Each time you will probably reexperience some of the feelings of sadness and of being overwhelmed by your job. This is a part of the grief process in a chronic disease.

Talk over your situation with other families. This is one of the advantages of family support groups. You may find it comforting to learn that other families have struggled with similar changes. Laugh at yourself a little. When you have just burned supper or hacked up a turkey, try to see the humor in the situation. Often when families of people with dementing illnesses get together they share both tears and laughter over such experiences.

Look for ways to help each other. When a wife has most of the responsibility of daily care for an impaired parent, she may badly need her husband's help with such untraditional jobs as the housework or sitting with the parent while she goes out. She will certainly need his love and encouragement and may need his help with the rest of the family.

You may reach a point where the extent and demands of your job as caregiver are exhausting you. You need to be able to recognize this and to make other arrangements when that time comes. Your responsibilities as decision maker may eventually include making the decision to give up your role as primary caregiver.

A Family Conference

We feel that a family conference is one of the most effective ways to help families cope. Have a family meeting, with help from a counselor or the physician if needed, to talk over problems and to make plans. Together you can make definite decisions about how much help or money each person will contribute.

There are ground rules for a family conference which you might suggest at the beginning: everyone comes (including children who will be affected by the decision), each person has his say uninterrupted, and everyone listens to what the others have to say (even if they don't agree).

If family members disagree about what is wrong with the confused, forgetful person or about how to manage his care, it may be helpful to give other members of the family this book and other written materials about the specific disease, or to ask the doctor to talk with them. It is surprising how often this reduces the tensions between family members.

Here are some questions to ask of each other when you get together. What are the problems? Who is doing what now? What needs to be done, and who can do it? How can you help each other? What will these changes mean for each of you? Some of the practical questions that may need to be discussed are: Who will be responsible for daily care? Does this mean giving up privacy? not having friends over? not being able to afford a vacation? Does this mean that parents will expect their children to act more grown up because the parents will be busy with the sick person? Who will make the decision to put a parent in a nursing home? Who will be responsible for the sick person's money?

If a well spouse of the impaired person is to move into a son or daughter's home with the impaired person, what will this person's roles in the family be? Will she have responsibility for the grandchildren? Will there be two people using the kitchen? An expanded family can be enriching but it also can create tensions. Anticipating and discussing areas of disagreement in advance can make things easier.

It is also important to talk about several other practical areas in which family relationships can get into trouble. It can seem insensitive even to think about matters of money or inheritance when a loved one is sick, but financial concerns are important, and questions about who will get the inheritance are real—if often hidden—factors in determining responsibility for a family member. They can be the underlying cause of much bitterness. Money matters need to be brought out in the open. Ask yourself the following questions.

1. Does everyone know what money and inheritance there is? It is surprising how often one son is thinking, "Dad has that stock he bought twenty years ago, he owns his house, and he has his social security. He ought to be quite comfortable." The other son, who is taking care of his father, knows "the house needs a new roof and a new furnace, that old mining stock is worthless, and he gets barely enough to live on from social security. I have to dip into my own pocket to pay for his medicine."

2. Is there a will? Does someone know or suspect that he has been shortchanged in the will? Do some members of the family feel that others are greedy for inherited money, property, or personal possessions? This is not unusual and it can best be handled when it is openly faced. Hidden resentments often smolder and can emerge as conflicts over the daily care of the person.

3. How much does it cost to care for the sick person, and who is paying these bills? When a family cares for a person at home, there are many "hidden" costs to consider: special foods, medication, special door latches, a sitter, transportation, another bed and a dresser on the ground floor, grab bars for the bathroom, perhaps the cost of a spouse's not working in order to care for the confused person.

4. Does everyone know what it costs to care for a person with a dementing illness in a nursing home, and does everyone know who is legally responsible for those costs? (We discuss nursing home costs in Chapter 16.) Sometimes when a daughter says, "Mother must put Dad in a nursing home," she does not realize that doing so may have serious financial consequences.

5. Do some members of the family feel that money has been unequally distributed in the past? For example,

"Dad put my brother through college and gave him the down payment on his house. Yet now my brother won't take him, so I get the work— and the cost—of taking care of him."

Families sometimes say, "There is no way you'll get my family together to talk about things like that. My brother won't even discuss it on the phone. And if we did get together it would just be a big fight." If you feel that your family is like this, you may be discouraged. Although you need your family's help, you may feel trapped because you feel that your family will not help. It is not unusual for families to need the help of an outside person—a counselor, minister, or social worker—to help work out their problems and to help them arrive at equitable arrangements. (See p. 225.)

One of the advantages of seeking the assistance of a counselor is that he can listen objectively and help the family keep the discussion on the problems you face and not drift aside into old arguments. Your doctor, a social worker, or a counselor may be able to intervene on your behalf and convince everyone involved of the need for a family to discuss issues of concern to them all. Sometimes a family attorney can help. If you seek the help of an attorney, select one who is genuinely interested in helping resolve conflict rather than helping you get into litigation against your own family. If a family is having difficulty and you ask a third party to help you, the first topic of conversation may be to agree that the third party will not take sides with any one person.

You need your family. Now is an excellent time to put aside old conflicts for the sake of the impaired person. Perhaps if your family cannot resolve all your disagreements, you can, in a discussion, find one or two things upon which you agree. This will encourage everyone and the next discussion may be easier.

WHEN YOU LIVE OUT OF TOWN

"My father takes care of my mother. They live about a thousand miles from here and it's hard for me to get back home often. I don't think Dad tells me how bad things really are. It's just terribly hard to be so far away: You feel so guilty and helpless."

"I'm just the daughter-in-law, so I can't say much. They haven't gotten a good diagnosis. They keep going to this old family doctor. I worry that there is something else wrong with her. But every time I make a suggestion, they pretend they didn't hear it."

Not living in the same community as the confused person and the person who provides daily care creates special problems. Long-distance family members care just as much as those close to home and they often feel frustrated and helpless. They worry that they do not know what is really happening, that the caregiver has not gotten the best diagnosis, or that the caregiver should do things differently. They may feel guilty that they cannot be nearby at a time when their family needs them.

In the beginning it can be more difficult to accept the severity of a person's limitations if you see the person infrequently. Later, the shock of seeing how a person has declined can be heartbreaking.

Your support of the person who provides the daily care is probably the single most important contribution you can make to the ill family member. The dementing illnesses usually last for several years. You need to build family cooperation for the long haul. If the person who provides daily care rejects your suggestions at first, she may accept them later.

Consider having the ill person spend several weeks with you or stay with the ill person, to give the usual caregiver a break. Moving an ill person to another home can be upsetting, but, especially early in a dementing illness, it might serve as a "vacation" for the ill person as well as the caregiver.

WHEN YOU ARE NOT THE PRIMARY CAREGIVER, WHAT CAN YOU DO TO HELP?

American families do not abandon their elderly members, nor do they abandon each other. Despite differences, families usually resolve their disagreements enough to pull together for the long haul.

There are many things family members can do. One caregiver may need a telephone call every day; another may need a sitter so he can go out one night a week; one may need someone who can run over on short notice when things get difficult; another may just need a shoulder to cry on.

Stay in close touch. Maintain open lines of communication with the caregiver. This will help you sense when the caregiver needs more help. Caregivers manage better and experience less stress when they feel well supported by their family. It is not solely how much help caregivers receive, but also how well supported they feel that helps them cope better.

Avoid criticizing. Criticism usually does not lead to constructive change. None of us likes to be criticized. Many of us tend to ignore criticism. If you must say something, be sure your criticism is valid. If you do not live close, are you sure you completely understand the problem?

Recognize that the primary caregiver must make the final decisions. Although you can offer help and advice, the person who provides care day in and day out must be the one to decide things like whether she can use outside help and whether she can continue to provide care.

Take on the job of finding help. Caregivers are often so overwhelmed that they cannot seek a sitter or day care program, better medical care, supportive equipment, or help for themselves. Just finding respite can require many telephone calls. Take on this job and be gentle and supportive as you persuade your relative to use respite.

Be informed. You can help most if you understand both the disease and what the caregiver in your family is going through. There are excellent books describing the dementing illnesses and books by caregivers. Attend family support group meetings in your community. You may meet other long-distance family members, and you can learn from primary caregivers what *their* long-distance relatives did that helped most. Avoid the temptation to ignore the problem. These diseases are so devastating that the whole family must pull together.

Call the ill person's physician and others who have evaluated him. If they are willing, ask direct questions (see Chapter 2). If you have concerns about the diagnosis, adequacy of the assessment, or likely course of the disease, ask the professionals who know the person.

Take on tasks the confused person used to do. Balance the checkbook, take the car to the mechanic, bring over a home-cooked meal.

Give the caregiver time off. Care for your relative for a weekend, a week, or a few days so that the primary caregiver can get away. Many Alzheimer's Association chapters will teach you the basics of caregiving before you undertake this. Not only will it be valuable for the caregiver to get away, but this will bring you and the caregiver closer together. Do things that are therapeutic and fun for the ill person: take walks, go out to dinner, play with the cat together, or go window shopping.

Obtain help if you cannot provide it yourself. In many communities you can obtain sitter care and adult day care. You can also pay someone to do the shopping, get the car fixed, or track down resources.

CAREGIVING AND YOUR JOB

Many caregivers are juggling the care of a person with dementia and a full- or part-time job. The double demands of caring and holding down a job can be overwhelming. Some caregivers must take time off from work each time there is a problem with the ill person. Sometimes, when there is no other choice, caregivers must leave the confused person alone even if this is really not safe. Even caregivers who use a good adult day care program or a reliable sitter face extra demands and problems. For example, when the person with dementia is awake and active at night, the caregiver loses sleep.

If you are thinking about leaving your job to provide full-time care, consider the options carefully. Many caregivers have found that they were more stressed and more depressed after giving up a job. Full-time caregiving may mean that you must put up with the person's annoying behavior all the time, and may mean that you will be more isolated and trapped than when you could get out of the house and go to work. Leaving your job usually means a significant loss of income. It may mean putting your career on hold and not staying current in your profession. Returning to work after several years of caregiving can be difficult. Will there be a vacancy? Will you have lost seniority or benefits?

Before you make a decision to leave, discuss your options with your employer. Can you arrange more flexible hours? Can you share the job? Is a paid or unpaid leave of absence possible? Some loving daughters and sons find that a good nursing home is a wiser choice for both themselves and their ill parent.

YOUR CHILDREN

Having children at home can create special problems. They, too, have a relationship with the sick person, and they have complex feelings—which they may not express—about his illness and roles in the family. Parents often worry about the effect that being around a person with a dementing illness will have on children. It is hard to know what to tell a child about a parent's or grandparent's "odd" behavior. Sometimes parents worry that children will learn undesirable behavior from people with dementing illnesses.

Children are usually aware of what is going on. They are excellent observers and, even when things are carefully concealed from them, often sense that something is wrong. Fortunately, children are marvelously resilient. Even small children can benefit from an honest explanation of what is happening to the person with a dementing illness—in language they can understand. This helps them not to be frightened. Reassure children that this illness is not "catching," like chicken pox, and that neither they nor their parents are likely to get it. Tell the child directly that nothing he did "caused" this illness. Sometimes children secretly feel to blame for the things that happen in their family.

One father put a pile of dried beans on the table. He took little pieces of the pile away as he gave his young son the following explanation of his grandfather's illness: "Grandpop has a sickness that makes him act like he does. It isn't catching. None of us is going to get like Grandpop. It's like having a broken leg, only little pieces of Grandpop's brain are broken. He won't get any better. This little piece of Grandpop's brain is broken, so he can't remember what you just told him; this little piece is broken, so he forgets how to use his silverware at the table; this little piece is broken, so he gets mad real easy. But this part, which is for loving, Grandpop still has left."

It is usually best to involve children actively in what is happening in the family and even to find ways in which they can help. Small children frequently relate well to impaired, confused people, and can establish special and loving relationships with them. Try to create an atmosphere in which the child can ask you questions and express his feelings openly. Remember that children also feel sadness and grief, but they may be able to enjoy the childlike ways of an impaired person without feeling at all sad. The more comfortable you feel in your understanding of this illness, the more easily you will be able to explain it to your child.

Children may need help knowing what to tell playmates who tease them about a "funny" parent or grandparent.

It is unlikely that children will mimic the undesirable behaviors of a person with a dementing illness for long if you don't make a big deal out of this should it happen and if the child is getting enough love and attention. Clearly explain (probably several times) to the child that his parent or grandparent has a disease and cannot help what he does but that the child can, and is expected to, control his behavior.

Young people may be frightened by unexplained, strange behavior. Sometimes they worry that something they did or might do will make the person worse. It is important to talk about these concerns and to reassure the young person.

One family with children ranging from ten to sixteen shared with us the following thoughts based on their own experience:

- Don't assume that you know what a youngster is thinking.
- Children, even small children, also feel pity, sadness, and sympathy.
- If we had it to do over again, we would talk more with the children.
- The effects of this illness linger long after the confused person has gone to a nursing home. Get together with the children afterward and continue to discuss things.
- Make an effort to involve all of the children equally in the person's care. Children can find it hard to be depended on or they can feel left out. Sharing in care gives them a sense of responsibility.
- The parent closest to the sick person needs to be aware of the children and the effect of her grief and distress on them. Sometimes parents can be so overwhelmed by their own troubles that they forget the children. Their behavior can be as hard on the children as the illness itself.

Perhaps the biggest problem when there are children at home is that the parent's time and energies are divided between the ill person and the children—with never enough for both. In order to cope with this double load you will need every bit of help available—the help of the rest of the family, the resources of the community, and time—for you to replenish your own emotional and physical energies. You may find yourself torn between neglecting the children and neglecting a "childish" or demanding person with a dementing illness.

As the person's condition worsens, so may your dilemma. The declining person may need more and more care, and may be so disruptive that children cannot feel comfortable at home. You may not have the physical or emotional energy to meet the needs of children or adolescents and the sick person. Children growing up in such a situation may suffer as a result of the person's illness.

You may make the painful decision to place the sick person in a nursing home in order to create a better home environment for the children. If you face such a decision, you and your children need to discuss what is to be done, talking over what your alternatives will mean to each member of the family. "We will have less money for movies, but we wouldn't have Dad shouting all night." "We would move and have to change schools, but I could bring friends home."

The support of your doctor, clergy, or a counselor is helpful at such times. Families often find it easier to make decisions when they know they are not alone.

Teenagers

Adolescents may be embarrassed by "odd" behavior, reluctant to bring friends home, resentful of the demands made on you by the confused person, or hurt by the confused person's failure to remember them. Adolescents can also be extraordinarily compassionate, supportive, responsible, and altruistic. They often have an unspoiled sense of humanitarianism and kindness which is refreshing and helpful. Certainly they will have mixed feelings. Like you, they may experience the grief of seeing someone they love change drastically at the same time that they may feel resentful or embarrassed. Mixed feelings lead to mixed actions that are often puzzling to other family members. Adolescent years can be hard for young people, whether there are problems at home or not. However, many adults, looking back, recognize that sharing in family problems helped them to become mature adults.

Be sure your adolescent understands the nature of the disease and what is happening. Be honest with him about what is going on. Explanations, given gently, help a lot. Children seldom benefit from attempts to shelter them. Involve the adolescent in the family discussions, groups, and conferences with health professionals, so that he, too, understands what is happening.

Take time away from the sick person, when you are not exhausted or cross, to maintain a good relationship with your adolescent and to listen to his interests. Remember that he has a life apart from this illness and this situation. Try to find space for his teenage friends apart from the impaired person.

Remember that you may be less patient or more emotional because of all you are dealing with. Again, breaks for you may help you be more patient with your children.

When a grandparent moves into your home, it is important that both he and your children know who sets the rules and who disciplines the children. When the grandparent is forgetful, it is important that your children know *from you* what is expected of them to avoid conflicts like, "Grandmother says I can't date" or "Granddad says I have to turn off the TV."

When the ill person has adolescent children, these young people are losing a parent at a critical time in their own lives. At the same time, they must cope with the illness and its never-ending problems. They can also feel that they are losing the remaining parent if that person is distracted by grief and fully occupied by caregiving.

In this situation you face almost insurmountable burdens. You must arrange for enough help to maintain your own mental and physical health and to continue to assist your children. Since adolescents often are more comfortable with an outsider than a parent, ask a relative, teacher, or church member to assume the role of "special friend." A few Alzheimer's Association chapters offer support groups for young people. Also read Chapter 14.

12

HOW CARING FOR AN IMPAIRED PERSON AFFECTS YOU

FAMILY MEMBERS TELL US that they experience many feelings as they care for a person with a chronic, dementing illness. They feel sad, discouraged, and alone. They feel angry, guilty, or hopeful. They feel tired or depressed. In the face of the reality of a chronic illness, emotional distress is appropriate and understandable. Sometimes families of people with dementing illnesses find themselves overwhelmed by their feelings.

Human feelings are complex and they vary from person to person. In this chapter we have tried to avoid oversimplifying feelings or offering simplistic solutions. Our goal is to remind you that it is not unusual to experience many feelings.

EMOTIONAL REACTIONS

People have different ways of handling their emotions. Some people experience each feeling intensely; others do not. Sometimes people think that certain feelings are unacceptable—that they should not have certain feelings or that, if they do, no one could possibly understand them. Sometimes they feel alone with their feelings.

Sometimes people have mixed feelings. One might both love and dislike the same person, or want to keep a family member at home and put her in a nursing home, all at the same time. Having mixed feelings might not seem logical but it is common. Often people do not realize that they have mixed feelings.

Sometimes people are afraid of strong emotions, perhaps because such feelings are uncomfortable, perhaps because they are afraid they might do something rash, or perhaps because they are concerned about how others will view them. These and other responses to our feelings are not unusual. In fact, most of us will have similar responses at one time or another.

We do not believe there is a "right" way to handle emotions. We think that recognizing how you feel and having some understanding of why you feel the way you do are important, because your feelings affect your judgment. Unrecognized or unacknowledged feelings can influence the decisions a person makes in ways that he does not understand or recognize. You can acknowledge and recognize your feelings—to yourself and to others—but you have a choice of when, where, and whether to express your feelings or to act on them.

People sometimes worry that not expressing feelings causes "stress-related" diseases. Suppose you know that you are often angry with the behavior of a person with a dementing illness, but you decide not to yell at her because it only makes her behavior worse. Will you develop ulcers, or migraines, or hypertension? Researchers disagree about the relationship between expressing feelings and diseases. However, at present, the causes of conditions such as ulcers, migraines, and hypertension are unknown. It has not been our observation that these conditions are more common among families who care for people with dementing illnesses. We do believe that as families recognize that the irritating behaviors of a confused person are symptoms of her disease, they feel less frustrated and angry and they can care better for the confused person.

As you read this section, remember that each person and each family is different. You may not have these feelings. We discuss them to help those family members who do feel angry or discouraged, tired or sad, etc. Rather than read all this material, you may want to refer to it when you feel a particular section will help you.

Anger

It is understandable that you feel frustrated and angry: angry that this has happened to you, angry that you have to be the caregiver, angry with others who don't seem to be helping out, angry with the sick person for her irritating behavior, angry that you are trapped in this situation.

Some people with dementing illnesses develop behaviors that are extremely irritating and that can seem impossible to live with. You will understandably get angry and may sometimes react by yelling or arguing.

Mrs. Palombo felt that she must not get angry with her husband. They had had a good marriage and she knew that he could not help himself now that he was ill. She says, "We went to dinner at my daughter-in-law's house. I have never felt comfortable with my daughter-in-law, anyway, and I don't think she understands about Joe. As soon as we got in the door Joe looked around and said, 'Let's go home.' I tried to explain to him that we were staying for dinner and all he would say is, 'I've never liked it here. Let's go home.'

"We sat down to dinner and everyone was tense. Joe wouldn't talk to anyone and he wouldn't take his hat off. As soon as dinner was over he wanted to go home. My daughter-in-law went into the kitchen and shut the door and started banging the dishes. My son made me go into the den with him and all the time Joe was hollering, 'Let's get out of here before she poisons us.'

"My son says I'm letting Dad ruin my life, that there is no reason for Dad to act that way, that it isn't sickness, it's that he's gotten spiteful in his old age. He says I have to do something.

"So we got in the car to go home and all the way home Joe hollered at me about my driving, which he always does. As soon as we got home he started asking me what time it was. I said, 'Joe, please be quiet. Go watch television.' And he said, 'Why don't you ever talk to me?' Then I started yelling at him and I yelled and yelled."

Episodes like this can wear out even the most patient person. It seems as if they always start when we are most tired.

The things that are most irritating sometimes seem like little things—but little things mount up, day after day.

Mrs. Jackson says, "I had never gotten along with my mother that well, and since she's come to live with us, it's been terrible. In the middle of the night she gets up and starts packing.

"I get up and tell her, 'It's the middle of the night, Mother,' and I try to explain to her that she lives here now; but I'm thinking, if I don't get my sleep I won't be any good at work tomorrow.

"She says she has to go home, and I say she lives here, and every night a fight starts at two o'clock in the morning."

Sometimes a person with a dementing illness can do some things very well and appear unwilling to do other, seemingly identical tasks. When you feel that the sick person can do more or is just acting up to "get your goat," it can be infuriating. For example,

Mrs. Graham says, "She can load the dishwasher and set the table just fine at my sister's house but at my house she either refuses to do it or she makes a terrible mess. Now I know it's because I work and she knows I come home tired."

Often the person who has most of the responsibility for the care of a sick person feels that other members of the family don't help out enough, are critical, or don't come to visit. A lot of anger can build up around these feelings.

You may be irritated with doctors and other professionals at times. Sometimes your anger toward them is justified; at other times you may know that they are doing the best they can, yet you are still angry with them.

People with a religious faith may question how God could allow this to happen to them. They may feel that it is a terrible sin to be angry with God or they may fear that they have lost their faith. Such feelings may deprive them of the strength and reassurance faith offers at just the time when they need it most. To struggle with such questions is part of the experience of faith.

Said a minister, "I wonder how God could do this to me. I haven't been perfect, but I've done the best I could. And I love my wife. But then I think I have no right to question God. For me that is the hardest part. I think I must be a very weak person to question God."

Never let a person make you feel guilty for your anger with God. There are many thoughtful and meaningful writings discussing such things as feeling angry with God or questioning how God could allow such a thing as this. Two of the books listed in Appendix 1 eloquently describe how others have struggled with these questions. Reading these and talking honestly with your minister, priest, or rabbi can be comforting.

Remember, it is only human to be angry when faced with the burdens and losses a dementing illness often brings.

Expressing your anger to the sick person often makes her behavior worse. Her illness may make it impossible for her to respond to your anger in a rational way. You may find that it improves her behavior when you find other ways to manage both your frustrations and the problems themselves.

The first step in dealing with anger is to know what you can reasonably expect from a person with a dementing illness, and what is happening to the brain to cause irritating behavior. If you are not sure whether the person can stop acting the ways she does, find out from your doctor or other health professional. For example,

An occupational therapist discovered that Mrs. Graham's sister had an old dishwasher that her mother had operated before she got sick. Mrs. Graham had a new dishwasher that her mother could not learn to use because her brain impairment made it impossible for her to learn even simple new skills.

It may be possible to change the person's irritating behavior by changing the environment or the daily routine. However, just knowing that unpleasant behavior is the result of the disease and that the person cannot control what she is doing can be reassuring.

It is often helpful to think about the difference between being angry with the person's *behavior* and being angry with the *person herself*. She is ill and often cannot stop her behavior. Certainly, the behavior can be infuriating, but it is not aimed at your personally. A dementing illness might make it impossible for a person to be deliberately offensive because she has lost the ability to take purposeful action. Mrs. Palombo's husband was not deliberately insulting his family. His behavior was the result of his illness.

It often helps to know that other families and professional caregivers have the same problems.

Says Mrs. Kurtz, "I didn't want to put my husband in day care, but I did it. It helped me so much to find out that his constant questions made trained professionals angry too. It wasn't just me."

Many families find that discussing their experiences with other families helps them to feel less frustrated and upset.

Sometimes it is helpful to find other outlets for your frustrations: talking to someone about it, cleaning closets, or chopping wood—whatever ways you have used in the past to cope with your frustrations. A vigorous exercise program, a long walk, or taking a few minutes to relax totally may be helpful for you.

Embarrassment

Sometimes the behavior of a person with a dementing illness is embarrassing, and strangers often do not understand what is happening.

Said one husband, "Going through the grocery store, she keeps taking things down off the shelves like a toddler, and people stare."

Said a daughter, "Every time we try to give Mother a bath she opens the window and shouts for help. What are we to tell the neighbors?"

Such experiences *are* embarrassing, although much of your embarrassment may fade as you share your experiences with other families. In support groups families often find they can laugh over things like this.

Explaining to neighbors usually helps gain their understanding. You might give them copies of information pamphlets about these diseases. Your neighbors may well know someone else with one of these diseases who needs treatment. Despite the growing awareness of Alzheimer's disease, many misconceptions remain. By explaining to your neighbors the illness and the behaviors that it causes, you are helping to disseminate knowledge.

Occasionally, some insensitive person will ask a rude question, such as "Why does he act like that?" or "Whatever is wrong with her?" Sometimes a simple response, such as "Whyever would you ask?" is best.

One courageous husband says, "I still take my wife out to dinner. I don't like to cook and she likes to go out. I ignore other people's glances. This is something we always enjoyed doing together, and we still do."

Some families prefer to keep their problems "in the family." This may work best for some people, but friends and neighbors usually know a problem exists and can be more helpful and supportive if you've told them what the problem is. The dementing illnesses are so overwhelming that it is almost impossible to manage alone. There should be no stigma associated with having a dementia.

Helplessness

It is not uncommon for family members to feel helpless, weak, or demoralized in the face of a chronic dementing illness. These feelings are often made worse when you cannot find doctors or other professionals who seem to understand dementing illnesses. We have found that families and the people with dementing illnesses have many resources within themselves with which they can overcome feelings of helplessness. Although you cannot cure the disease, you are far from helpless. There are many ways to improve life for both the forgetful person and your family. Here are some places to start:

- Things often seem worse when you look at everything at once. Instead, focus on changing small things that you can change.
- Take one day at a time.
- Be informed about the disease. Read and talk about ways others manage.
- Talk with families who face similar problems.
- Get involved in exchanging information, supporting research, and reaching others.
- Discuss your feelings with the doctor, social worker, psychologist, or clergyman.

Guilt

It is quite common for family members to feel guilty: for the way they behaved toward the person in the past, for being embarrassed by the person's odd behavior, for losing their temper with the person, for wishing they did not have the responsibility of care, for considering placing the person in a nursing home, or for many other reasons, some trivial, some critical. For example,

"My mother's illness ruined my marriage and I can't forgive her for it."

"I lost my temper with Dick and slapped him. Yet I know he is sick and can't help himself."

You may feel guilty about spending time with your friends away from the person you love, especially when the person is your spouse and you have been accustomed to doing most things together.

You may feel vaguely guilty without knowing why. Sometimes people feel that the person with a dementing illness *makes* them feel guilty. "Promise me you will never put me in a nursing home," or "You wouldn't treat me that way if you loved me" is something the confused person may say that can make you feel guilty.

You may feel guilty about things you must do that take independence away from the person. Stopping a person from driving or from living alone is a difficult action for a family member to take. Caring for a person with dementia often makes people feel guilty because it forces them to make decisions for someone who was previously fully able to make decisions for herself.

Sometimes we feel guilty when a person close to us, whom we have always disliked, develops a dementing disease:

"I've never liked my mother and now she has this terrible disease. If only I had been closer to her when I could."

Families sometimes ask if something they did or failed to do caused the illness. Sometimes the caretaking person feels responsible when the person gets worse. You may feel that if only you had taken more time with her or kept her more active she would not have gotten worse. You may feel that surgery or a hospitalization "caused" this condition.

The trouble with feelings of guilt is that, when they are not recognized for what they are, they can keep you from making clear-headed decisions about the future and doing what is right for the sick person and the rest of the family. When such feelings are recognized, they are not surprising or hard to manage.

The first step is to admit that feelings of guilt *are* a problem. They become a problem when they affect your decisions. If you are being influenced by guilt feelings, you must make a decision. Are you going to go around in a circle with one foot caught in the trap of guilt, or are you going to say "What is done is done" and go on from there? There is no way to remedy the fact that you never liked your mother or that you slapped a sick person, for example. However, guilt feelings tend to keep us looking for ways to remedy the past instead of letting us accept it. Make decisions and plans based on what is best now. For example,

Mrs. Dempsey had never liked her mother. As soon as she could she had moved away from home and called her mother only on special occasions. When her mother developed a dementing illness, she brought her mother to live with her. The confused woman disrupted the family, kept everyone up at night, upset the children, and left Mrs. Dempsey exhausted. When the doctor recommended that her mother enter a nursing home, Mrs. Dempsey only became more upset. She could not bring herself to put her mother in a nursing home even though this clearly would be better for everyone.

When the feelings of guilt in such a relationship are not acknowledged, they can destructively affect how you act. Perhaps being faced with a chronic illness is a good time to be honest with yourself about not liking someone. You can then choose whether to give a person care and respect without being influenced by not liking her. We have little control over whom we like or love; some people are not very likeable. But we do have control over how we act toward them. When Mrs. Dempsey was able to face the fact that she did not like her mother and that she felt guilty about that, she was able to go ahead and arrange for her mother to get good nursing home care.

When the person with a dementing illness says things like "Promise you won't put me in a nursing home," it is helpful to remember that sometimes the person with a dementing illness *cannot* make responsible decisions and that you must make the decisions, acting not on the basis of guilt but on the basis of your responsibility.

Not all feelings of guilt are over major issues or keep you from making good decisions. Sometimes you may feel guilty about little things—being cross with the confused person or snapping at her when you are tired. Saying "I'm sorry" often clears the air and makes you both feel better. Often the confused person, because she is forgetful, will have forgotten the incident long before you have.

If you worry that you have caused this illness or made it worse, it is helpful to learn all you can about the disease and to talk over the person's illness with her doctor.

In general, Alzheimer's disease is a progressive illness. Neither you nor your physician can prevent this progression. It may not be possible to stop or reverse a multi-infarct dementia either. Keeping a person active will not stop the progress of such a disease, but it can help the person use her remaining abilities.

A person's condition may first become apparent after an illness or hospitalization, but often, upon close examination, the beginning stages of the illness occurred months or years earlier. At present, earlier identification of Alzheimer's disease does not help to slow or reverse its progression.

If you don't feel right about doing things for yourself and by yourself, remind yourself that it is important for the confused person's well-being that your life have meaning and fulfillment outside of caring for her. Rest and the companionship of friends will do much to keep you going.

When guilt feelings are keeping you from making clear-headed decisions, you may find it helpful to talk the whole thing out with an understanding counselor, a minister, or other families so that you can go on more easily. Learning that most people do similar things helps to put little nagging guilt feelings in their proper perspective. If, after doing the best you can, you still feel immobilized by guilt, this may be a symptom of depression. We discuss depression in caregivers and what to do about it later in this chapter.

Laughter, Love, and Joy

A dementing illness does not suddenly end a person's capacity to experience love or joy, nor does it end her ability to laugh. And, although your life may often seem filled with fatigue, frustration, or grief, your capacity for these emotions is not gone either. Happiness may seem out of place in the face of trouble, but in fact it crops up unexpectedly. The words of a song written by Sister Miriam Therese Winter of the Medical Mission Sisters reflect this:

> *I saw raindrops on my window*
> *Joy is like the rain.*
> *Laughter runs across my pain,*
> *slips away and comes again.*
> *Joy is like the rain.*

Laughter might be called a gift to help us keep our sanity in the face of trouble. There is no reason to feel bad about laughing at the mistakes a confused person makes. She may share the laughter even if she is not sure what is funny.

Fortunately love is not dependent upon intellectual abilities. Focus on the ways you and others still share expressions of affection with the impaired person.

Grief

As the person's illness progresses and the person changes, you may experience the loss of a companion and a relationship that was important to you. You may grieve for the "way she used to be." You may find yourself feeling sad or discouraged. Sometimes little things may make you feel sad or can start you crying. You may feel that tearfulness or sadness is welling up inside you. Often such feelings come and go, so that you alternate between feeling sad and feeling hopeful. Feelings of sadness are often mixed with feelings of depression or fatigue. Such feelings are a normal part of grieving.

We usually think of grief as an emotional experience that follows a death. However, grief is a natural emotional response to loss and so is a normal experience for people who love a person with a chronic illness.

Grief associated with a death may be overwhelming in the beginning, and gradually lessen. Grief associated with a chronic illness seems to go on and on. Your feelings may shift back and forth between hope that the person will get better and anger and sadness over an irreversible condition. Just when you think you have adjusted, the person may change and you will go through the grieving experience over again. Whether it is the grief that follows a death or that which comes with being with a person with a dementing illness, grief is a feeling associated with losing those qualities of a person who was important to you.

Families often say that their own sadness at losing a loved one is made worse because they must watch the suffering of the person as her illness progresses.

Says Mrs. Owens, "Sometimes I wish he would die so it would be over. It seems as if he is dying a bit at a time, day after day. When something new happens I think I can't stand it. Then I get used to it, and something else happens. And I keep hoping—for a new doctor, a new treatment, maybe a miracle. It seems like I'm on an emotional treadmill going around and around and it's slowly wearing me down."

There are certain changes that come with a chronic dementing illness which seem especially hard to bear. Particular characteristics of the people we love symbolize for us who that person is: "He was always the one who made decisions" or "She was always such a friendly person." When these things change, it may precipitate feelings of sadness, which are sometimes not understood by people less close to the situation. For example, when a person is unable to talk or understand clearly, her family may acutely feel the loss of her companionship.

A husband or wife has lost the spouse he or she used to have but is not a single person. This creates a special set of problems, which we will discuss below, in the section "You as a Spouse Alone."

Another problem is that the grief that follows a death is understood and accepted by society, while the grief that comes with a chronic illness is often misunderstood by friends and neighbors, especially when the ill person looks well. Your loss then is not as visible as it is in a death. "Be grateful you still have your husband," or "Keep a stiff upper lip," people may say.

There are no easy antidotes for grief. Perhaps you will find, as others have, that it is eased somewhat when it is shared with other people who are also living with the unique tragedy of a dementing illness. You may feel that you should keep feelings of sadness and grief to yourself and not burden others with your troubles. However, sharing these feelings can be comforting and can give you the strength you need to continue to care for a declining person.

Depression

Depression is a feeling of sadness and discouragement. It is often difficult to distinguish between depression and grief, or between depression and anger, or depression and worry. Families of the chronically ill often feel sad, depressed, discouraged, or low, day after day, week after week. Sometimes they feel apathetic or listless. Depressed people may also feel anxious, nervous, or irritable. Sometimes they don't have much appetite and have trouble sleeping at night. The experience of being depressed is painful; we feel miserable and wish for relief from our sad feelings.

A chronic dementing illness takes its toll on our emotions and provides a real reason for feeling low. Sometimes counseling helps reduce the depression you experience, but counseling cannot cure the situation that has made you depressed; it can only help you deal with it. Many families find that it helps to share experiences and emotions with other families in support groups. Others find that it helps to get away from the sick person and spend time with hobbies or people they enjoy. When you are unable to get enough rest, your fatigue may make your feelings of discouragement worse. Getting help so that you can rest may cheer you up. Still, the feelings of discouragement and depression may stick with you—understandably.

For a few people depression goes beyond—or is different from—the understandable feelings of discouragement caused by this illness. If any or several of the things listed on pages 225–27 are happening to you or someone else in the family, it is important to find a physician who can help you or can refer you to a counselor. They can help significantly.

Caregivers sometimes use alcohol, tranquilizers, or sleeping pills to keep themselves going. Alcohol or medication may increase your fatigue and depression and sap what little energy you have left. If you find this happening to you, you are not alone: many other caregivers have done the same, but it is important that you *seek help now.* See Chapter 13.

Isolation and Feeling Alone

Sometimes a family member feels that he is facing this alone. "Despair," one wife said to us. "Write about that feeling of being alone with this." You may feel very much alone when the one person with whom you could share things has changed.

This is a miserable feeling. We are all individuals and no one else can truly understand what we are going through. The feeling of being alone is not uncommon when people are facing a dementing illness. Remaining involved with others—your family, your friends, other people with ill relatives—can help you feel less alone. Sharing experiences with them will help you to realize that others have similar feelings of aloneness. While you may feel that you can never replace the relationship you had with the confused person, you will gradually find that friends and family are offering love and support.

Worry

Who doesn't worry? We could fill many pages with things people worry about, but you already know them. They are real worries, serious concerns. Worry combines with depression and fatigue and is a fact of life for families. Each person has his own way of coping with worries: some people seem to shrug off serious problems, others seem to fret interminably over trivia, most of us fall somewhere in between. Most of us have also discovered that the kind of worrying we do when we lie awake at night does not solve the problem, but it does make us tired. Some of this kind of worrying is often inevitable; but if you are doing a lot of it, you may want to take yourself in hand and look for other ways to manage your problems.

A woman who faces some real and terrible possibilities in her life has tried this approach to worry: "I ask myself what is the worst thing that could happen. We could run out of money and lose our home. But I know people wouldn't let us starve or go homeless. It seems like I don't worry as much once I've faced what the worst could be."

Being Hopeful and Being Realistic

As you struggle with the person's dementing disease, you may find yourself sometimes chasing down every possible hope for a cure and other times feeling discouraged and defeated. You may find yourself unable to accept bad news the doctors have given you. Instead, you may seek second, third, and even more medical opinions at great expense to yourself and the sick person. You may find yourself refusing to believe that anything is wrong. You may even find yourself giggling or acting silly when you really don't have anything to laugh about. Such feelings are normal and are usually a part of our mind's efforts to come to terms with something we don't want to have happen.

Sometimes, of course, ignoring the problem can endanger the sick person (for example, if she is driving or living alone when she cannot do so safely). Seeking many medical opinions can be futile, exhausting, and expensive, but sometimes seeking a second opinion may be wise.

This experience of a mixture of hope and discouragement is common to many families. The problem is complicated when professionals give conflicting information about dementing illnesses.

Most families find reasonable peace in a compromise between hope and realism. How do you know what to do?

Know that we may be a long way from a major research breakthrough or we may be close. Miracles do happen, and yet not often.

Ask yourself if you are going from doctor to doctor hoping to hear better news. If your reaction is making things more difficult or even risky for the confused person, you need to rethink what you are doing. If you are ignoring her impairments, is she endangering herself by driving, cooking, or continuing to live alone?

Put the sick person in the care of a physician whom you trust. Make sure that this physician is knowledgeable about dementing illnesses and keeps abreast of current research. Avoid quack "cures."

Keep yourself informed about the progress of legitimate research. Join the Alzheimer's Association and local groups to keep abreast of new knowledge.

MISTREATING THE CONFUSED PERSON

"Sometimes I couldn't stand it. My wife would get to me so, always on me about something, and the same thing over and over. Then I would tie her into her chair and go out for a walk. I felt terrible about it, but I couldn't stand it."

"My mother would scratch at herself in one spot until it bled. The doctor said we had to stop it. I tried everything until one day I guess I snapped: I grabbed her and shook her and I screamed at her. She just looked at me and began to cry."

"I never hit my wife, but I would get so mad at her, it was like I would get spiteful: I would tell her I was going to put her in a nursing home if she didn't behave. It would make her cry. I know she couldn't help what she did and I don't know why I did that."

Caregiving is difficult and frustration is understandable: caregivers endure overwhelming burdens. Perhaps you have found yourself hitting or slapping or screaming at the person you care for. Perhaps you have promised yourself it will never happen again, but somehow it does.

In itself, losing your temper is not terrible; it is a warning that you need help with your burden. Anger is common in caregivers. Yelling at the ill person is also common but should be taken as a warning sign that your frustration is building. However, hitting, shoving, shaking, or tying down a person is a sign that you have lost control and need help. Even if this has happened only once, it is a danger signal. You may need regular time away from the person. You may need someone you can talk to, someone who can help you talk about your frustrations. You may need to turn the tasks of full-time care over to someone else, perhaps a nursing home. If you lose your temper and do things you wish you had not, then you *must* ask for the help you need. To continue in silent isolation *is* mistreating the confused person.

Call the nearest chapter of the Alzheimer's Association. Most of the people who answer telephones or lead support groups in the Alzheimer's Association have heard many such problems—or been through them themselves. Most will understand and they will help you find sitters or other outside help. (See Chapter 13.)

Not everyone has the capability to be a full-time caregiver. If the person who needs care is someone whom you did not like or who mistreated you, you may have mixed feelings about caregiving. Sometimes the most responsible thing you can do is to recognize that someone else should provide the day-to-day physical care.

PHYSICAL REACTIONS

Fatigue

People who care for a person with a dementing illness are often tired simply because they aren't getting enough rest. However, being tired can add to feelings of depression. At the same time, being depressed may make you feel more tired. Always feeling tired is a problem for many people who care for a person with a dementing illness.

Do what you can in little ways to help yourself be less exhausted. For example,

> *Mrs. Levin says, "He gets up in the night and puts his hat on and sits on the sofa. I used to wear myself out trying to get him back to bed. Now I just let him sit there. If he wants to wear his hat with his pajamas, it's O.K. I don't worry about it. I used to think I had to do my windows twice a year and my kitchen floor every week. Now I don't. I have to spend my energy on other things."*

It is important to your health that the ill person sleep at night or at least be safe at night if she is awake. (We discuss this problem in more detail in Chapter 7: "Sleep Disturbances.") If you are regularly up in the night and still caring for the person all day, your body is paying a price in exhaustion, and you will not be able to keep up such a routine indefinitely. We know that you cannot always get enough rest. However, it is important that you recognize your own limits. We have made suggestions throughout this book which will help you find ways to avoid complete exhaustion.

Illness

Illness is a camp follower of depression and fatigue. It often seems that people who are discouraged and tired are sick more frequently than others. And people who aren't feeling well are more tired and discouraged. When someone else is dependent on you for care, your sickness can become a serious problem. Who takes care of the confused person when you have the flu? You, probably. You may feel that you have no choice but to keep on dragging yourself around and hope you don't wear out.

Our bodies and our minds are not separate entities; neither is one the slave of the other. They are both parts that make up a whole person, and that whole person can be made less vulnerable—but not invulnerable—to disease.

Do what you can to reduce fatigue and to get enough rest. Eat a well-balanced diet. Get enough exercise.

Arrange to take a vacation or to have some time away from your duties as caregiver.

Avoid abusing yourself with alcohol, drugs, or overeating. Get an expert—a good physician—to check you routinely for hidden problems, such as high blood pressure or anemia and chronic low-grade infections.

Few of us do all that we can to maintain good health even when we have no other serious problems. When you are caring for a chronically ill person, there is often not enough time, energy, or money to go around, and it is yourself that you most often cut short. However, for your sake, and, very importantly, for the sick person's sake, you must do what you can to maintain your health.

SEXUALITY

It can seem insensitive to think about your own sexuality when there are so many pressing worries—a chronic illness, financial concerns, and so forth. However, people have a lifelong need to be loved and touched, and sexuality is a part of our adulthood. It deserves to be considered. Sometimes sex becomes a problem in a dementing illness, but sometimes it remains one of the good things a couple still enjoys. This section is for those couples for whom it has become a problem. Do not read this *expecting* a problem to develop.

If Your Spouse Is Impaired

Despite the so-called sexual revolution, most people, including many physicians, are uncomfortable talking about sex, especially when it involves older people or handicapped people. This embarrassment, combined with misconceptions about human sexuality, can leave the spouse or companion of a person with a dementing illness alone in silence. Many articles on sex are no help; the subject often cannot be discussed with one's friends; and, if one gets up the courage to ask the doctor, he may quickly change the subject.

At the same time, sexual problems, like many other problems, are often easier to face when they can be acknowledged and talked over with an understanding person.

The spouse of a brain-impaired person may find it impossible to enjoy a sexual relationship when so many other aspects of the relationship have changed so drastically. For many people their sexual relationship can only be good when the whole relationship is good. You may be unable to make love with a person with whom you can no longer enjoy sharing conversation, for example. It may not seem "right" to enjoy sex with a person who has changed so much.

When you are feeling overwhelmed by the tasks of caring for a sick person, when you are tired and depressed, you may be totally uninterested in sex. Sometimes the person with the dementing illness is depressed or moody and loses interest in sex. If this happens early, before the correct diagnosis has been made, it can be misinterpreted as trouble in the relationship.

Sometimes the sexual behavior of a person with a brain disorder may change in ways that are hard for her partner to accept or manage. When the impaired person cannot remember things for more than a few minutes, she may still be able to make love, and want to make love, but will almost immediately forget when it is over, leaving her spouse or partner heartbroken and alone. A few such experiences can make you want to end this aspect of life forever.

Sometimes the person you have cared for all day may say "Who are you? What are you doing in my bed?" Such things can be heartbreaking.

Memory loss can sometimes cause a formerly gentle and considerate person to forget the happy preliminaries to sex. This, too, can be discouraging for the partner.

Occasionally a brain injury or brain disease will cause a person to become sexually demanding. It can be devastating to a spouse when a person who needs so much care in other ways makes frequent demands for sex. This problem is rare, but it is difficult to treat when it does occur. Medication is seldom helpful except to sedate the ill person. If the problem persists, you should think about placement out of the home. When the sexual behavior of a person with a dementing illness changes, this very likely relates to the brain injury or brain damage and is something the person cannot help; it is not a purposeful affront to your relationship.

Often what people miss most is not the act of sexual intercourse but the touching, holding, and affection that exist between two people. Sometimes, for practical reasons, the well spouse chooses to sleep in a separate room. Sometimes a formerly affectionate person will no longer accept affection when she becomes ill.

Mr. Bishop says, "We always used to touch each other in our sleep. Now if I put an arm across her she jerks away."

What can you do about problems of sexuality? Like many of the other problems, there are no easy answers.

It is important that you understand from your spouse's physician the nature of her brain damage and how it affects this and all other aspects of behavior. If you seek help with this problem, be sure the counselor is qualified. Since sexuality is such a sensitive issue, some counselors are not comfortable discussing it or they give inappropriate advice. The counselor should have experience addressing the sexual concerns of handicapped people and should clearly understand the nature of a dementing illness. He should be aware of his own feelings about sexual activity in elderly or handicapped people. There are excellent counselors who have talked about sexuality with many families and who will not be shocked or surprised at what you say. There are also some insensitive people posing as sex counselors whom you will want to avoid.

If Your Impaired Parent Lives with You

So far we have discussed the problems of the spouse of a person with a dementing illness. However, if your ill parent has come to live with you, the sexual aspect of your marriage can be badly disrupted, and this can affect other areas of your relationship. You may be too tired to make love, or you may have stopped going out together in the evening and thus lost the romance that precedes love making. Your confused parent may wander around the house at night, banging things, knocking on your door, or shouting. The least little noise may rouse the parent you tried so hard to get to sleep. Love making can turn into hurried sex when you are too tired to care, or it can cease altogether.

Relationships are enriched by all of the parts of a relationship: talking together, working together, facing trouble together, making love together. A strong relationship can survive having things put aside for a while but not for a long time. It is important that you find the time and energy to sustain a good relationship. Carefully review the discussion in Chapter 13. Make yourself find ways to create the romance and privacy you need at times when neither of you is exhausted.

THE FUTURE

It is important that you plan for the future. The future will bring changes for the person with a dementing illness and many of these changes will be less painful if you are prepared for them.

Some husbands and wives discuss the future while both of them are well. If you can do this, you will feel more comfortable later, when you have to make decisions for your spouse. Helping the forgetful person talk about the future and how she would like her possessions disposed of can help her feel that this is her life and that she has some control over her final years. Other people will not want to think about these things and should not be pressured to do so.

Members of the family may also want to discuss what the future will bring, perhaps talking it over a little at a time. Sometimes, thinking about the future is too painful for some members of the family. If this happens, you may have to plan alone.

Here are some of the things you will want to consider. (We discuss each of these concerns elsewhere in this book.)

- What will the ill person be like as her illness progresses and as she becomes increasingly physically disabled?
- What kind of care will she need?

- How much will you honestly be able to continue to give to this person?
- At what point will your own emotional resources be exhausted?
- What other responsibilities do you have that must be considered?
- Do you have a spouse, children, or a job that also demands your time and energies?
- What effect will this added burden have on your marriage, on growing children, or on your career?
- Where can you turn for help?
- How much help will the rest of the family give you?
- What financial resources are available for this person's care?
- What will be left for you to live on after you have met the expenses of care? It is important to make financial plans for the future even if you and the ill person have only a limited income. The care of a severely ill person can be expensive. (See Chapter 15.)
- What legal provisions have been made for this person's care?
- Will the physical environment make it difficult for you to care for an invalid? (Do you live in a house with stairs that the person will eventually be unable to manage? Do you live in a big house that may be difficult to maintain? Do you live a long way from stores? Do you live in an area where crime is a problem?)

As time passes, you, the caretaker, may change. In some ways you may not be the same person you were before this illness. You may have given up friends and hobbies because of this illness, or you may have changed your philosophy or your ideas in the process of learning to accept this chronic illness. What will your future be like? What should you do to prepare for it?

You as a Spouse Alone

This was a difficult section of this book for us to write. We know that husbands and wives think about their futures but we have no "right" answers to give you. Each person is unique. What is right for one person is not right for another, and only you can make those decisions. However, as you think through these things, there are several factors you will want to consider.

Your status changes. Sometimes a spouse feels that he is neither part of a couple (because they can no longer do many things together, talk together, or rely on each other in the same ways) nor a widower.

Couples sometimes find that friends drift away from them. This is a particularly difficult problem for the well partner. "Couple" friends often drift away simply because the friendship was based on the relationship among four people, which has now changed. Establishing new friendships can be difficult when you can no longer include your spouse and yet you still have the responsibility for her care. You may not want to make new friends alone.

You may face a future without the ill person. Statistics indicate that dementing illnesses shorten the life of the victim. It is probable that she will die before you do or that she will become so ill that she needs nursing home care. It is important that, when the time comes that you are alone, you have friends and interests of your own.

A husband told of trying to write an account of what it is like to live with a person suffering from a dementing illness. He said, "I realized that I was telling the story of my own deterioration. I gave up my job to take care of her, then I had no time for my hobbies, and gradually we stopped seeing our friends."

As the illness progresses and the person needs more and more care, you may find yourself giving up more and more of your own life in order to care for her. Friends do drift away, there is no time for hobbies, and you can find yourself alone with an invalid.

What then happens to you after she has become so ill that she must be placed in a nursing home or after she dies? Will you have "deteriorated"— become isolated, without the interests, lonely, used up? You need your friends and your hobbies through the long illness to give you support and a change of pace from the job of caregiver. You are going to need them very much after you are left alone.

Even though placing a person in a nursing home means that others will provide the day-to-day care and that you will have more free time, you may find that you feel as burdened and distressed after the person's placement as you did before. Place reasonable limits on the amount of time you spend at the nursing home. Be prepared for an adjustment period and make plans to resume interests and contacts with friends. (See Chapter 16.)

The problems of being alone but not single are real. Usually the relationship between husband and wife changes as the dementia progresses. For many caregivers, the relationship continues to have meaning. For some this means a continuing commitment to a changed relationship. For others it means establishing a new relationship with another person.

One husband said, "I will always take care of her but I've started dating again. She is no longer the person I married."

A wife says, "It was a terribly difficult decision. For me, the guilt was the hardest part."

Another husband said, "For me, caring for her, keeping my promise, is most important. It is true that she is not the same, but this too is a part of our marriage. I try to see it as a challenge."

Sometimes it happens that a person falls in love again while he is still caring for his ill spouse. If this happens to you, you face difficult decisions about your own beliefs and values. Perhaps you will want to talk this over with people close to you. Perhaps the "right" decision is the decision that is "right" for you. Family members often find that their children and in-laws are very supportive.

Not all marriages have been happy. When a marriage was so unhappy that a spouse was already considering divorce when the person became ill, the illness can make the decision more difficult. A good counselor can help you sort out your mixed feelings.

In any event, should you be faced with questions about new relationships, divorce, or remarriage, you are not alone. Many others have also faced—and resolved—these dilemmas.

WHEN THE PERSON YOU HAVE CARED FOR DIES

People often have mixed feelings when the person they've been caring for dies. You may feel glad in some ways that the ill person's suffering and your responsibilities are over, but sad at the same time. There is no "right" way to feel after the death of someone with a dementia. Some people have shed their tears long ago and feel mostly relief. Others are overwhelmed by grief.

Talking about your feelings with someone you trust can be helpful. Sometimes, saying things out loud helps clarify your feelings and thoughts. If you find your feelings changing over time, remember that this too is normal.

When much of your time and emotional energy were focused on the person's care, often for many years, you may find yourself at loose ends after the death. You may have lost touch with friends, given up your job or your hobbies. No longer carrying the responsibility you have had for so long may bring feelings of both relief and sadness.

One wife said tearfully, "I don't have to tell anyone how they can reach me when I'm away."

13

CARING FOR YOURSELF

THE SICK PERSON'S well-being depends directly on your well-being. *It is essential that you find ways to care for yourself so that you will not exhaust your own emotional and physical resources.*

When you care for a person who has a dementing illness, you may feel sad, discouraged, frustrated, or trapped. You may be tired or overburdened. While there are many reasons for feeling fatigued, the most common is not getting enough rest. You may put aside your own needs for rest, friends, and time alone in order to care for the sick person. If you have multiple responsibilities—family, job, children—your own needs have probably been greatly shortchanged.

Even if you are not caring for the person full time, you may have little time for yourself. You may be going to the nursing home after work several days a week or spending the weekend providing care so the full-time caregiver can get some rest. Whatever your direct care responsibilities may be, you probably feel anxious, saddened, and frustrated.

Throughout this book we have offered suggestions for ways to modify annoying behaviors. While modifying the person's behavior will help considerably, it is often not possible to eliminate some behaviors and they may continue to get on your nerves. To continue to cope, you will need to get enough rest and sometimes to get away from the ill person.

This book has emphasized that behavior problems are caused by the brain damage: neither you nor the confused person can prevent problems. However, your *mood* can affect the ill person's behavior. When you are rushed, tense, or irritable, the ill person may sense your feelings. He may become more anxious or more irritable, move more slowly, or begin an annoying behavior. When you are rested and feel better, the person may manage better and feel better too.

It is not unusual for family members to feel alone in their struggle with a chronic illness. Friends drift away and one doesn't know about other people with similar problems. It may seem impossible to get out of the house, and life narrows down to a tight circle of lonely misery. Feelings of sadness and grief seem more painful when you also feel alone with your problem.

For all of these reasons you need to take care of yourself. You need enough rest, time away from the sick person, and friends to enjoy, to share your problems with, and to laugh with. You may find that you need additional help to cope with your feelings of discouragement or to sort out the disagreements in the family. You may decide that it will help you to join other families to exchange concerns, to make new friends, and to advocate better resources for people with dementing illnesses.

TAKE TIME OUT

"If only I could get away from Alzheimer's disease," Mrs. Murray said. "If only I could go someplace where I didn't have to think about Alzheimer's disease for a little while."

It is absolutely essential—both for you and for the person with a dementing illness—that you have regular times to get away from twenty-four-hour care of the chronically ill person. You must have some time to rest and to be able to do some things *just for yourself*. This might be sitting down uninterrupted to watch television or it might be sleeping through the night. It might mean going out once a week or taking a vacation. We cannot overemphasize the importance of this. The continued care of a person with a dementing illness can be an exhausting and emotionally draining job. It is quite possible to collapse under the load.

It is important that you have other people to help you, to talk with, and to share your problems. We know that it can be difficult to find ways to care for yourself. You may not have understanding friends, your family may not be willing to help, and it may seem impossible to get time away from the sick person. The confused person may refuse to stay with anyone else, or you may not be able to afford help. Finding ways to meet your own needs often takes effort and ingenuity. However, it is so important that it must be done.

If resources to give you time out are difficult to find, perhaps you can piece together a respite plan. For example,

Mr. Cooke persuaded the day care center to take his wife one day a week by agreeing to teach the staff how to manage her. His son, who lived out of state, agreed to pay for the day care. His neighbor agreed to come over and help get his wife dressed on those mornings.

You may also have to compromise, and accept a plan that is not as good as you would like. The care others give may not be the same as the care you try to give. The confused person may be upset by the changes. Family members may complain about being asked to help. Paying for care may mean financial sacrifices. But be persistent in your search for help, and be willing to piece things together and to make compromises.

Taking time out, away from the care of the confused person, is one of the single most important things that you can do to make it possible for you to continue to care for someone with a dementing illness.

Mrs. Murray said, "We had planned for a long time to go to France when he retired. When I knew he would never be able to go, I went alone. I left him with my son. I was scared to go alone, so I went with a tour group. He would have wanted me to, and when I came back I was rested—ready to face whatever came next."

Give Yourself a Present

Could you use a "lift" once in a while? An occasional self-indulgence is another way to help yourself cope. Some people may buy themselves "presents"—a magazine or a new dress. Listen to a symphony or the ballgame (use earphones), stand outside and watch the sunset, order your favorite restaurant meal as a carry out.

Friends

Friends are often marvelously comforting, supportive, and helpful. The support of good friends will do much to keep you going through the hardest times. Remember that it is important for you to continue to have friends and social contacts. Try not to feel guilty about maintaining or establishing friendships on your own.

Sometimes friends and neighbors find it hard to accept that a person is ill when he *looks* fine. Sometimes, too, people shy away from "mental" illnesses. Many people do not know how to act around a person who is forgetful or whose behavior changes. You may want to explain that this is an organic disease that causes gradual deterioration of the mind. The person cannot help his behavior and he is not "crazy" or "psychotic." There is no evidence that the disease is contagious. It is a disease condition and not the inevitable result of old age.

Even if the person can talk quite reasonably and a casual observer cannot see any sign of mental deterioration, he may still not be remembering names or really following conversations. It is important to explain to friends that forgetfulness is not bad manners but something the person cannot avoid.

It can be painful to tell old friends what is happening, especially those who do not live nearby and have not seen the gradual changes a dementing disease causes. Some families have solved this problem by composing a Christmas letter, lovingly and honestly sharing this illness with distant friends.

Avoid Isolation

What can you do if you find yourself becoming isolated? It takes energy and effort to make new friends at a time when you may be feeling tired and discouraged. But this is so important that you must make the necessary effort. Start by finding one small resource for yourself. Little things will give you the guidance and energy to find others. Call your nearest Alzheimer's Association chapter (see p. 229). Join a support group for families or get one going yourself. Renew ties with your church or synagogue. Your rabbi, priest, or minister can offer you comfort and support. Friendships within the church can develop, and many churches have some resources to provide practical help for you.

As you find time for yourself away from the person you are caring for, use that time to do things with other people: pursue a hobby or attend discussion groups. New friends are most easily made when you are involved in activities you have in common with other people.

We know that it is difficult to find the time or energy to do anything beyond the necessary care of the sick person. Some activities can be put on the "back burner" while you are burdened with care, but they must not be completely discontinued. This is important. When the time comes that you no longer have the care of this person, you will need friends and activities.

"I like to go to the Masonic lodge. I still go once a month. When Alice has to go to a nursing home, I'll probably get more involved—volunteer to run the Christmas drive or something. I still have my friends there."

"I play the violin. I can't play with the quartet anymore, but I keep in touch with them and I still practice a little. When I have more time, there will be a place for me in the community symphony."

You may also become involved in new activities, such as joining a local Alzheimer's organization. Some spouses have deliberately sought out new activities.

"My wife got sick just about the same time I retired. All I was doing was taking care of her. I thought I should get some exercise, so I joined a senior citizens' exercise group. I take my wife to a day care center the day I go to that group."

FIND ADDITIONAL HELP IF YOU NEED IT

Mrs. Scott says, "I worry that I am drinking too much. John and I used to have a cocktail when he got home in the evening. Now, of course, he doesn't drink, but I find I have to have that cocktail and another one at bedtime."

Fatigue, discouragement, anger, grief, despair, guilt, and ambivalence are all normal feelings that may come with caring for a chronically ill person. Such feelings may seem overwhelming and almost constant. The burden you carry can be staggering. Sometimes one's coping skills are overwhelmed and things can drift out of control. You may want to seek professional help if this happens.

Recognize the Warning Signs

Each individual is different and each person has his own ways of responding to problems. A healthy response for one person may be unhealthy for another. Ask yourself the following questions: Do I feel so sad or depressed that I am not functioning as I should? Am I often lying awake at night worrying? Am I losing weight? Do I feel overwhelmed most of the time? Do I feel terribly isolated and alone with my problem? While depression and discouragement are common feelings for families of people with chronic diseases, if you are often lying awake at night worrying, if you are losing weight, or if you usually feel isolated, alone with your problem, or overwhelmed, perhaps you need some help to keep your feelings manageable.

Am I drinking too much? Definitions of alcohol abuse vary widely. The amount of alcohol that is too much for one person may not be too much for another. Ask yourself: Is my drinking interfering with how I function with my family, or my job, or in other ways? If it is, you are drinking too much. Are you ever drinking too much to care properly for the sick person? Are others—your co-workers, for example—having to "cover" for you? Alcoholics Anonymous (listed in the telephone directory) is a good self-help organization. Often the group will help you solve the practical problems like transportation and finding a "sitter" so that you can get to the meetings. Call them, explain your special circumstances, and ask for their assistance.

Am I using pills to get me through each day? Tranquilizers and sleeping pills should be used only under the careful supervision of a physician and only for a short time. Pep pills (amphetamines) should never be used to give you an energy boost. If you are already using tranquilizers, sleeping pills, or pep pills on a regular basis, ask a doctor to help you give them up. Some of these drugs create a drug dependency. Abrupt withdrawal can be life-threatening and must be supervised by a doctor.

Suppose you are abusing alcohol or medications. You have joined the ranks of thousands of other ordinary people. You may have a problem for the first time under the stress of caring for someone with a dementing illness. There is no reason to be ashamed. There *is* a reason to get help *now*.

Am I drinking too much coffee each day? While nowhere near as serious as amphetamine abuse, excessive caffeine use can be hard on your body and can reduce your ability to manage stress. (Caffeine is also found in tea and most soft drinks.)

Am I screaming or crying too much? Am I often losing my temper with the impaired person? Am I hitting him? Do I find myself more angry and frustrated after I talk with my friends or family about these problems? Do I find that I am getting irritated with a lot of people—friends, my family, the doctors, my co-workers—more than just one or two people in my life?

How much screaming or crying is too much? One person may feel that any crying is too much, while another feels that crying is a good way to "get things out of my system." You probably know already if your moods are exceeding what is normal for you.

Anger and frustration are normal responses to caring for a person whose behavior is difficult. However, if your anger begins to spill over into many relationships or if you take your anger out on the sick person, it may be helpful to find ways to manage your frustrations so that they do not drive people away from you or make the impaired person's behavior worse.

Am I thinking about suicide?

Mr. Cameron said, "There was a time when I considered getting a gun, killing my wife, and then killing myself."

The thought of suicide can come when a person is feeling overwhelmed, helpless, and alone. When someone feels that he cannot escape an impossible situation or that he has irrevocably lost the things that make life worth living, he may consider suicide. Suicide may be considered when someone feels that the situation he faces is hopeless, when he feels that there is nothing either he or anyone else can do. The present can seem intolerable, and the future appears bleak, dark, empty, and meaningless.

One family member who attempted suicide said, "Looking back, I don't know why I felt that way. Things have been hard, but I'm glad I didn't die. My perceptions must have been all mixed up."

It is not uncommon for our *perception* of things to be more bleak than the reality. If you are feeling this way, it is important to find another person (a counselor, if possible) whose perception of the situation may be different and with whom you can talk.

Do I feel that I am out of control of my situation or at the end of my rope? Is my body telling me I am under too much stress? Do I often feel panicky, nervous, or frightened? Would it help just to talk the whole thing over with someone who understands? If the answer to some of these questions is yes, it may be that you are carrying too heavy a burden without enough help.

Counseling

It may be that all you need is more time away from a seemingly demanding, difficult person or more help in caring for him. But perhaps you see no way to find more help or more time for yourself. Perhaps you see yourself trapped by your situation. We feel that talking these problems over with a trained person is one good way to help you feel less pressured. You and he can sort out the problems you face a bit at a time. Since he is not as caught up in the problems as you are, he may be able to see workable alternatives you had not thought of. At the same time, you will know that you have a life line in this person that you can turn to if you begin to feel desperate. Family or friends can be of help as well, but if they are too close to the situation they may not be able to see things objectively.

Should you get counseling? Do you need "help"? Most people are not "sick," "crazy," or "neurotic." Most people are healthy individuals who sometimes have trouble coping with real problems. They may feel overwhelmed or discouraged, or find that they are thinking in circles. Such a person may find that talking over feelings and problems helps to clarify them.

We believe that most people most of the time do not need counseling. However, we know that counseling is sometimes a great help to families struggling with a dementing illness. Such help may come from discussion groups, clergy, an objective friend, or a social worker, nurse, psychologist, or physician.

The first step in seeking outside help is often the hardest. One's reasoning sometimes goes around and around in circles.

"I can't get out of the house because I can't get a sitter. He's terrible to anyone in the house but me. I can't afford counseling because I can't get a job because I can't leave the house, and a counselor couldn't help me with that anyway."

This kind of circular thinking is partly the product of your situation and partly the way you, in your discouragement, see the problem. A good counselor can help you objectively separate the problem into more manageable parts, and together you can begin to make changes a little at a time.

Sometimes people feel that it is a sign of their own weakness or inadequacy to go to a counselor. With the burden you carry in coping with a dementing illness, you can use all the help you can get, and this is not a reflection on your strength.

People sometimes avoid counseling because they think that the therapist will delve into their childhood and "analyze" them. Many therapists begin directly by helping you in a matter-of-fact way to cope with "here and now" concerns. Find out in advance what approach the therapist you select prefers. If you decide to seek counseling, the kind of counselor you choose may be influenced by what you can afford, who is available, and who is knowledgeable about dementing illnesses.

Psychiatrists are physicians and they are able to prescribe drugs to treat mental illness. They have a good understanding of physical problems that accompany psychological problems. Psychologists, social workers, psychiatric nurses, clergy, and some other professionals can have excellent therapeutic or counseling skills. If they do, they may be an excellent choice for counseling. You will want to select a person whose services you can afford, who is knowledgeable about dementing illnesses, and with whom you feel comfortable.

You have a responsibility to discuss with the counselor your concerns about your relationship with him. If you are worried about your bill, if you don't like his approach, if you wonder if he is telling your family what you have said, *ask* him.

There are several ways to find a counselor. Ask the Alzheimer's Association chapter. If you have an established relationship with a clergyman or a physician with whom you feel comfortable, ask if he can counsel you or can refer you to someone he feels is a good counselor. If you have friends who have had counseling, ask them if they liked the person they consulted. If there is an active family group in your area, ask if there is someone other members have consulted.

If you cannot find someone through such recommendations, counseling services or referrals are available from the community mental health clinic or from religious-affiliated service agencies like Jewish Family and Children's Society, Associated Catholic Charities, or Pastoral Counseling Services (these agencies usually serve people of all religions). The county medical society can give you the names of local psychiatrists.

Not all counselors are equally good, nor are they all knowledgeable about dementia. Select a counselor as carefully as you would any other service you seek and know what his credentials as a therapist are. If, after a period of time, you do not think the counselor is helping you, discuss this with him and then consider trying a different therapist.

JOINING WITH OTHER FAMILIES: THE ALZHEIMER'S ASSOCIATION

The Alzheimer's Association was founded in 1980 by family members determined to bring the dementing illnesses out of the darkness. It has chapters in many cities and a nationwide network of family support groups. The association is dedicated to high-quality patient and family care. It provides educational material for caregivers and professionals, advocates for research and services at the federal and state levels, and funds research into the cause, prevention, and cure of these diseases. Its Medical and Scientific Advisory Board reviews new research findings. The national office publishes several newsletters. It is a voluntary organization, supported by donations. The association charges for some materials and solicits donations.

The Alzheimer's Association maintains an 800 telephone number (see Appendix 2). Callers are given information about the chapter and support groups nearest them. You can ask for free information about the association and the dementing diseases to be mailed to you. Local offices vary in size and resources: in larger cities, chapters often have several paid staff members; smaller chapters may be run by one or two volunteers out of their homes. Chapters operate telephone "Helplines" and run support groups. Books (including this one) and brochures about the dementing illnesses are available through the chapters. Chapters sponsor speakers and films on a wide range of topics related to dementia. They usually can refer families to physicians, respite services, attorneys, social workers, and nursing homes that other families have found to be knowledgeable about dementia. There is no charge for calling the Helpline or attending a support group.

Most chapters have someone who will listen supportively to your concerns and who has been a caregiver or has worked with caregivers. That person may be available over the telephone or in person. You usually do not need an appointment for a telephone conversation and there is no charge. You can usually reach someone quickly during regular business hours. These people offer understanding and suggestions on how to get help. They are usually not trained professionals; they cannot offer therapy or prescribe medications. However, if you need assistance beyond their expertise, they often can refer you to someone who has worked with other families of people with dementia.

Chapters publish newsletters, and many caregivers subscribe to several. The newsletters are full of information, letters from caregivers, and tips on how to manage. Chapters are a good source of information about current research.

Some support groups are not affiliated with the Alzheimer's Association. They may be sponsored by nursing homes, hospitals, state offices on aging, or family service agencies.

Support Groups

"I did not really want to go to a group, but my mother was driving me crazy and so finally I went. The speaker talked about power of attorney—until then I didn't realize I had to get one to take care of my mother's property. Then over coffee I was talking to three other women. One of them told how her mother was driving her crazy hiding the silverware in the dresser. She said one day she suddenly realized it didn't matter where they kept the silverware. Up until then I thought I was the only one dealing with things like that. I told them about my mother and these other women understood."

"There are usually more women than men in groups, you know. I didn't want to go to a hen party, but there was this other fellow there whose mother-in-law lives with them, and he really understood what I am going through. Going to that support group saved my marriage."

Thousands of family members have had the same experiences: people in support groups *understand*. Many support groups meet once a month, but schedules vary. They usually have a film or speaker, followed by coffee and a social period. They may be led by a professional or by family members.

You may find all sorts of people in support groups: bankers and construction workers, men and women, adult children, spouses, long-distance carers, and professionals who work with people with dementia. There are a few support groups for young children of people with dementia.

The dementing diseases strike people of all groups and all races, and their families are struggling with grief, exhaustion, behavior problems, and limited public services. Families of all races are doing all they can to care for their loved ones. Blacks, Hispanics, Asians, and other minorities who join a mostly white support group find that the problems they struggle with are universal, but many people feel more comfortable sharing with people from a similar background. The Alzheimer's Association or the local agency on aging will have the resources to help you get a group started. However, you must guide them in setting up a support group that meets the special needs of your community—when and where the group meets, how it is structured, the role of the group leader, etc.

Excuses

When we are overwhelmed and tired, we find excuses for not joining a support group. We don't have the energy and we don't feel up to facing a room full of strangers. Here are some answers to those excuses shared by families.

I'm not a group type of person. The families we know say "Go anyway," even if this is the only group you ever attend. These diseases are so terrible and last so long that our usual methods of coping are not sufficient. We all can use suggestions on how to cope. Just hearing that someone else deals with similar problems can renew your energy.

I can't leave my patient. Fatigue can lead to inertia. It is easier just to stay home than to find a sitter or to put up with the objections of the ill person. Ask the association if they can help you find a sitter or ask a friend or relative to stay with the person for a few hours. If the confused person objects, ask the sitter to visit a few times while you are there. Read page 225. You may have to just ignore the sick person's objections.

I can't talk to strangers. The people in support groups have faced similar problems and won't remain strangers long. If you are shy, just listen the first few times.

I can't drive at night. Ask the group leader if someone can pick you up. Although problems like these are real concerns, letting them keep you from getting the support you need indicates your depression and fatigue. There are ways around these problems if you are determined.

Sometimes a particular support group is not right for you. For example, if all the members have their family member at home and yours is in a nursing home, you may feel as if you don't fit in. Many areas have several support groups; visit another group or attend a chapter meeting and ask around for a group that has concerns similar to yours.

Support groups aren't for everyone. Some people do not need the extra support these groups give. Others find it more comfortable to talk individually with a knowledgeable person. Before you decide you don't need to attend a support group, we urge you to try one a few times.

ADVOCACY

Until the late 1970s, when the Alzheimer's disease and related disorders movement began, families were truly alone with their burden. They did not know about each other, there were no networks of chapters and helplines, there were no guide books, few professionals had heard of dementia, and the federal budget for basic science research was only $17 million (fiscal year 1981).

In less than ten years the research budget increased sevenfold. Alzheimer's disease research centers have been established at major universities. The federal government allocated funds for a Medicare respite care demonstration project; published *Losing a Million Minds*, a definitive review of many areas of concern to caregivers and professionals (see Appendix 1), and enacted extensive nursing home reform. For the first time, nursing home residents with dementia were considered to be a separate group of patients with special needs (see Appendix 5). Private foundations initiated research and direct care programs for people with dementia. Many states have established task forces to study state needs for service and many have passed dementia-related legislation.

Perhaps the most meaningful advance is that Alzheimer's disease and similar disorders are now widely recognized. Your friends and relatives have probably heard of them. Many professionals in various health-related fields have attended courses about the dementing illnesses.

However, much remains to be done. There is only enough money to fund about half of the good research projects that seek funding; diagnosis and follow-up care are not available everywhere; the federal- and state-funded respite programs are only a drop in the bucket—most families are still unable to obtain financial assistance for day care or help at home; and in many places the Alzheimer's Association chapters, Helplines, and support groups are understaffed, with most of the work being provided by a few hard-working volunteers. Most nursing home care falls short of what people with dementia need. Although federal law now mandates that nurse aides have some training, most of them will learn little about the daily management of dementia.

Families often tell us that participating in advocacy efforts is a way to fight back against this terrible disease. Perhaps you will want to get involved, too. Here are some ways you might contribute.

- Participate in research projects. (See Chapter 18.)
- Answer telephones or assist with office work.
- Volunteer your skills. Can you balance the books for a small, volunteer-run day care program? Can you fix the plumbing for a struggling caregiver?
- Lead a support group. Often the best group leaders are those who have been caregivers.
- Locate and reach out to other caregivers who need support. If you have ties to minority groups, you might contact others and let them know that they are not alone.
- Participate in fund raising. Even small amounts of money make big differences. There are many skills needed in fund raising and good books on how to do it.
- Teach your local elected officials or agency leaders about dementia. Write your congressional representative or your newspaper.
- Spearhead a movement to establish a day care or home care program in your area. Many of the respite care programs for people with dementia have been created by the families who needed them.
- Work for a local political candidate who supports long-term care services.
- You may recognize a particular need in your community—help for people with dementia who are living alone or help for rural families.

There is much to be done and you can find a job that fits your talents and your available time. Many exciting things are going on; coordinate your efforts with others and learn what other communities are trying so that you do not have to reinvent the wheel. Well-informed caregivers are the grass roots that make the difference.

14

FOR CHILDREN AND TEENAGERS

THIS CHAPTER is written especially for the young people who live with or know a person with a dementing illness. Most young people will be able to read and understand the rest of the book as well.

It is important that you understand what is wrong with the person and why he acts as he does. When you understand why the person does certain things, it is easier not to get mad at him. Also, it is important that you understand that he acts as he does because he is sick, not because he wants to or because of you. The person has a disease that destroys part of the brain. With a larger number of brain cells lost, the brain cannot work as it should. That is why the person forgets names, is clumsy, or can't talk properly. Parts of the brain that knew how to do these things have been damaged.

Sometimes these people get upset over little things. That is because the brain can no longer understand what is going on (even when you explain it to the person). The parts of the brain that make us behave as we should are also damaged, so the person cannot control his actions. He cannot help himself. Sometimes people with dementing illnesses don't look sick or act strange, but they may criticize you or correct you too much. The person may not be able to help this because his illness makes him forget things.

You may worry about what will happen to the person or about whether something you do might make him worse, especially when you are not sure what is happening. Most likely nothing you can do will make the person worse. You can make him temporarily more upset, but this does not make his condition worse.

If you worry about things, ask questions. Read other parts of this book. You may want to go back to it from time to time. Read any other material you can find on these diseases. Ask your parents or the doctor treating the person what you want to know. You will get the best results if you bring the subject up when there are not a lot of other things going on and when the adults are not too tired. However, sometimes adults try to keep bad news from young people.

When you read or talk about these diseases, what you find out may be bad news. The person may not be going to get well. You may react by feeling bad about the whole thing. If there are things you really don't want to know, don't feel that you are expected to ask about them. Many people have mixed feelings—you may feel sorry for the sick person but also angry that he has to live at your house. Your moods may change a lot too. Sometimes you may put the whole thing out of your mind and not even be able to think about it. Most of these reactions are the normal result of facing problems.

Even under the best circumstances, living with an illness like this is hard. Here are some of the things that young people have told us are problems.

"No privacy: Grandma walks into my room whenever she wants."

"Having to be quiet. Not being able to play the stereo. As soon as I come in the door I have to get quiet or Granddad gets excited."

"The way he eats makes me sick."

"I can't bring my friends over because they upset Grandma. Also, I don't want to bring them over because she acts so crazy."

"Having to give up my room."

"Everybody depends on me more. I have to take a lot of responsibility."

"Everybody is so busy with Granddad and so tired, we never do anything fun as a family anymore."

"I'm afraid of what she will do."

"I'm afraid he will die."

"I just feel discouraged all the time."

"My parents get mad at me more than they used to."

You may have some of the same concerns as these. You may be stuck with some problems, like having to be quiet or having to give up your room. Some things are easier to deal with when you understand what is wrong with the person. Some things you can't cope with alone and you may need to get an adult to help you. Sometimes it is helpful to pick out the one thing that bothers you the most and ask your family to help you change that. Often, together you can come up with compromises that will help. For example, you might be able to put a lock on your door or get earphones for your stereo. If you have given up your room, perhaps you and your friends can fix up a place in the basement where you can get away from the sick person.

Some young people tell us that it is not the sick person's behavior that is the worst problem, but how their parents or the sick person's husband or wife acts.

"I don't mind Granddad, but Grandmother moved in too, and she wants me to do everything like she did when she was young."

"It isn't Grandma, it's my mother always fighting with my grand-father."

These may be real problems for you. The grandparent who isn't sick is probably upset about the one who is. Even when a person doesn't get upset he may be feeling sad or unhappy, and this may make that person cross or impatient or hard to live with. Probably the best you can do is to be understanding, since you know that grief and worry are the causes of the trouble. When a grandparent is setting strict standards for you or nagging you, ask your parents how they want you to handle this. If things get too difficult, find an adult who is not tired and upset—perhaps somebody outside your family—whom you can talk it over with.

Most of what we have written has been for young people whose grand-parent is sick, because usually people's children are grown before they develop a dementing illness. However, sometimes this illness strikes one's own parents. If it is your father or mother who is sick, things are probably really hard. We hope this book will help you. However, no book can solve problems that are happening in *your* house with *your* family.

It is important for you and your well parent to talk about what is happening and the problems you are having. In addition, it may be helpful for you, your well parent, and any other children in the family to find someone with whom you can all talk from time to time. If your well parent is unable to seek help, you may have to ask the doctor or your teachers to help you. No one with a parent who has a dementing illness should have to cope by himself.

Belonging to a scout troop or a church youth club or an athletic team or some other group will give you a chance to get away from the troubles at home and to get your mind on having fun with other young people.

Things are not all bad when a person has a dementing illness. Young people often have clever ideas about how to solve problems that the rest of the family may not have thought of. Also, perhaps because not too long ago you were little, you probably have a lot of understanding for the person who is confused. You will probably do a lot of growing up during this time and you may look back on it with pride.

It is important to remember, when you are caught in a situation you cannot control, that you *do* have control over how you react to it. You decide how a bad situation affects your life.

If your grades at school drop or if you are fighting with your parents a lot or "tuning out" most of the time, you need to talk the problem over with someone. Often you can talk things over with your parents, other adult friends, or teachers. Some people are easy to talk to and some are not. Sometimes a counselor is a good person to talk with. If you cannot talk to your parents, your teachers can usually help you find a counselor. Some people feel funny about talking to a counselor. It isn't because there is something "wrong" with you that you get counseling. Here are some of the things that happen with a good counselor or someone else who is a good listener.

- You can find out what's going on.
- You can let off steam.
- You can talk with your parents with the counselor helping so that you don't fight with them.
- You can find out what your parents are thinking.
- You can say all you want about your side.
- You can ask about things that worry you—like whether the sick person will die—in private.

None of these things may solve the problem, but they will make living with the problem easier.

15

FINANCIAL AND LEGAL ISSUES

To DISCUSS IN DETAIL the financial and legal issues that may arise around the care of a person with a dementing illness is beyond the purpose and scope of this book. However, we have outlined some of the key factors for you to consider. You may need to seek professional financial and legal advice.

YOUR FINANCIAL ASSESSMENT

Providing care for the person with a chronic illness can be costly. In addition, an older person may be living on a fixed income and inflation can be expected to continue to eat into that income. It is important that you assess both available financial resources and potentially increasing costs of care, and make plans for the impaired person's financial future. If you are a spouse, your own financial future may well be affected by decisions and plans you make now. Many factors must be considered in assessing your financial future, including the nature of the illness and your individual expectations.

Begin by assessing both the current costs of care and the potential costs as the person becomes more severely impaired and by assessing her available resources. Whether the ill person has little income or is affluent, *it is most important that you plan ahead for her financial future.*

The costs of nursing home care are discussed in Chapter 16. If there is any chance that your family member will need nursing home care, you must read this section and plan ahead. Planning can save you money and anguish.

Potential Expenses

Lost income:
Will the impaired person have to give up her job?

Will someone who would otherwise be employed have to stay at home to care for the person?

Will the impaired person lose retirement or disability benefits?

Will the real purchasing power of a fixed income decline as inflation rises?

Housing costs:

Will you or the impaired person have to move to a home that is without stairs, closer to services, or easier to maintain?

Will you move a parent into your home? This may mean expenses of renovating a room for her.

Will the person enter a life care facility, foster care, or sheltered housing?

Will you have to make modifications to your home (new locks, grab rails, safety devices, wheelchair ramps)?

Medical costs:

Will you need

visiting nurses?

doctors?

medical insurance?

evaluations?

occupational therapists? physical therapists?

medications?

appliances (hospital bed, special chair, wheelchair)?

disposable care supplies (adult diapers, moisture-proof pads, egg crate pads, petroleum jelly, tissues, cotton swabs, etc.)?

Costs of help or respite care:

Will you need

someone to clean?

someone to stay with the person?

someone to help with care?

day care?

Food costs:

Will there be costs of having meals prepared or of eating out?

Transportation costs:

someone to drive if you cannot; taxis

Taxes

Legal fees

Miscellaneous costs:

easy-to-use clothing, ID bracelets, various devices for safety or convenience

Nursing home costs:

In addition to basic costs, you may be charged for adult diapers, laundry, medications, disposable supplies, therapies, and hair care.

Potential Resources

The Impaired Person's Resources

You will want to look first at the sick person's own assets and financial resources. Consider pensions, Social Security, savings accounts, real estate, automobiles, and any other potential sources of income or capital.

Occasionally, an impaired person becomes secretive about her finances. At the end of this chapter we list some of the possible available resources she may have and where to look for the relevant documents.

Resources of the Impaired Person's Spouse, Children, and Other Relatives

Laws regarding the financial rights and responsibilities of family members, particularly when they apply to nursing home care, are complex. Not all social workers, tax accountants, or lawyers understand them. The Alzheimer's Association may be able to refer you to professionals with expertise in this area. In addition, families have feelings of obligation to each other. With obligation come dilemmas:

"Dad put me through college. Now it's my turn."

"I want to help my mother, but I also have a son to put through college. What do I do?"

"I know Mom would be better off if I could get dentures for her, but my husband's job depends on his truck and right now the engine has to be rebuilt. I don't know what to do."

These are difficult questions and families often disagree over how money should be spent. Because there are few public programs to help families, these diseases can be financially devastating, particularly for the well spouse.

Resources from Insurance

Health insurance and major medical insurance may help to pay for home care or needed appliances as well as for hospitalization, physicians' services, and medications. Health insurance policies often contain exclusions that affect payment for dementing or chronic illnesses. You need to know exactly what your insurance covers.

Find out what life insurance policies the person has and whether these can be a resource. Some insurance policies waive the premiums if the insured becomes disabled. This can be a significant savings for her.

With few exceptions, relatives other than a spouse are not legally responsible for the support of an impaired person (see p. 281), but adult children and other relatives often contribute to the purchase of care. The legal responsibility of the spouse is defined in two separate bodies of law: the laws governing Medicaid (which often pays for nursing home care) and the family responsibility laws of each state. Both federal and state laws shape Medicaid. Family responsibility law is completely under state control; thus the law is very different in different states. You will need legal advice before taking any steps to protect your financial assets.

Tax Breaks for the Elderly or for the Care of a Person with a Dementing Illness

The elderly are eligible for various tax breaks. General information about these is in the Internal Revenue Service publication "Tax Benefits for Older Americans."

Tax deductions for the care of a person with a dementing illness can make a significant difference to families. You are entitled to medical deductions for someone who is your dependent. The definition of whom you may claim as your dependent for medical deductions and the tax credit for disabled dependents allow you to claim some people who might not otherwise qualify as your dependents.

If you work and must hire someone to care for your disabled dependent, you may be entitled to a tax credit for part of the cost of the care.

Some nursing home costs that are not covered by Medicare or Medicaid may be deductible. The definitions of what part of nursing home care can be deducted and when it can be deducted are complex, and you may want to review carefully the IRS and tax court definitions of whom you can claim as your dependent and what deductions you can take.

The tax laws are being examined by family organizations and some legislators, who are urging tax relief for families who care for a disabled elderly person. You may want to look into the most recent legislation concerning your individual situation.

If you are uncertain about your rights, a tax consultant may be helpful to you. You do not have to accept as final the information given to you by the IRS staff.

State, Federal, and Private Resources

State, federal, and private funds support a range of resources, such as day care centers, Meals-on-Wheels, food stamps, sheltered housing, mental health clinics, social work services, and recreation centers. The funding source usually defines the population to be served in specific terms (such as only people over sixty-five or only people with income under a certain amount).

Pilot programs are programs funded for a brief period to determine their effectiveness.

Research programs are programs in which participants are studied in specific ways. Such programs sometimes offer excellent free or low-cost services. They usually have specific criteria for eligibility. Most research programs must meet exacting standards to assure that research does not harm the subjects. You will be asked to sign a consent form that explains exactly what research is being done, what risks, if any, are involved, and what benefits are to be expected. You also will be given the option of withdrawing from the study at any time.

WHERE TO LOOK FOR THE FORGETFUL PERSON'S RESOURCES

Sometimes an impaired person forgets what financial resources she has or what debts she owes. People may be private about their finances or disorganized in recording them. Sometimes suspiciousness is a part of the illness and the individual hides what she has. Families may not know what resources a person has that could be used to provide for her care.

A wife said, "I did not know the VA hospital would care for him. I was spending $1,500 a month for a nursing home I didn't like and I never even asked about VA."

Finding out what resources a person has can be difficult, especially when things are in disarray or are hidden.

Debts usually turn up on their own, often in the mail. Most businesses will be understanding if a debt or bill is not paid on time. When you do find a bill, call the company, explain the circumstances, and arrange with them how and when the bill will be paid. If the confused person is losing her mail, you may be able to have it held for you at the post office.

Assets may be harder to find. Review recent mail. Look in the obvious places such as a desk, an office, clothing, and other places where papers are kept. Look under the bed, in shoe boxes, in pockets of clothes, in old purses, in teakettles or other kitchen items, under rugs, and in jewelry boxes. One wife asked the grandchildren to join her in a "treasure hunt." The children thought of obscure places to look. Look for: bank statements, canceled checks, bank books, savings books, passbooks, or checkbooks; keys; address books; insurance policies; receipts; business or legal correspondence; or income tax records for the past four to five years (a spouse filing a joint return or a person possessing a power of attorney or guardianship of property can obtain copies from the Internal Revenue Service. The power of attorney must meet IRS standards or be on their form). These items can be used to piece together a person's resources.

There are many kinds of assets.

Bank accounts. Look for bank books, bank statements, checkbooks, savings books, passbooks, statements of interest paid, joint accounts held with others. Most banks will not release information about accounts, loans, or investments to anyone whose name is not on the account. However, they may give limited information (such as whether there is an account in an individual's name) if you send a letter to the bank from your doctor or lawyer explaining the nature of the person's disability and the reason you need the information. Banks will release information about the amount in an account or about current transactions only to a court-appointed guardian or other properly authorized person. However, often you can piece together what you need to know from papers you can find.

Stock certificates, bonds, certificates of deposit, savings bonds, mutual funds. Look for the actual bonds, notices of payments due, notices of dividends paid, earnings claimed on income tax, regular amounts paid out from a bank account, receipts. Mutual funds are accounts held in the name of the broker; look for canceled checks, correspondence, or receipts from a broker. Look for record of purchases or sale.

Insurance policies (life insurance, disability insurance, health insurance). These are among the most frequently overlooked assets. Life insurance policies and health insurance policies may pay lump sum or other benefits. Look for premium notices, policies, or canceled checks that give you the name of the insurer. Contact them for full information about the policy. Some insurers will release this information upon receipt of a letter from a physician or attorney; others will need proof of your legal right to information.

Safe deposit boxes. Look for a key, bill, or receipt. You will need a court order to be permitted to open the box.

Military benefits. Look for discharge papers, dog tags, old uniforms. Contact the military to determine what benefits are available to the person. Dependents of veterans may be eligible for benefits.

Real estate property (houses, land, businesses, rental property, joint ownership or partial ownership of the above). Look for regular payments into or from a checking account, gains or losses declared on income tax, keys, fire insurance premiums (on houses, barns, businesses, or trailers). The insurance agent may be able to help you. Look for property tax assessments. Ownership of real estate property is a matter of public record; the tax assessor's office may be able to help you locate properties if you have some clues.

Retirement or disability benefits. These are also often overlooked. You must apply for Social Security, SSI (Supplemental Security Income), veterans benefits, or railroad retirement if you are eligible. Spouses and divorced spouses may also be eligible for benefits. Federal and state government employees, union members, clergy, and military personnel may have special benefits. Check into retirement or disability benefits from *all* past employers. Look for an old job résumé, which will list previous jobs. Look for benefit letters.

Collections, gold, jewelry, cash, loose gems, cars, antiques, art, boats, camera equipment, furniture, other negotiable property. In addition to looking for such items, look for valuable items listed on property insurance policies. Some of these items are small enough to be easily hidden. Others may be in plain sight and so familiar as to be overlooked.

Wills. If the individual has made a will, it should list her assets. Wills, if not hidden, are often kept in a safe deposit box, recorded by the court, or kept by one's attorney.

Trust accounts. Look for statements of interest paid.

Personal loans. Look for withdrawals, payments, correspondence, alimony payments (occasionally divorce settlements provide for payment of alimony should the wife become disabled).

Foreign bank accounts. Look for statements of interest paid, bank statements.

Inheritance. Find out whether the impaired person is someone else's heir.

Cemetery plot. Look for evidence of purchase.

LEGAL MATTERS

(Also see Chapter 9.)

The time may come when a person with a dementing illness cannot continue to take legal or financial responsibility for herself. This may mean that she can no longer balance a checkbook or that she has forgotten what financial assets or debts she has. It may mean that she is unable to decide responsibly what to do with property or to give permission for needed medical care.

Often these abilities are not all lost at once. A person who is unable to manage her checkbook may still be able to make a will or accept medical care. However, as her impairment increases, she may gradually reach the point where she cannot make any decisions for herself, and someone else will have to assume legal responsibility for her.

It is important that the person herself or family members make legal arrangements for this loss—*early, before the person becomes unable to make her own decisions*. This is called *competency*. It means that the person knows, at that moment and without prompting, that she is making a will or assigning power of attorney, the names of and her relationship to the people who will receive or manage her property, and the nature and extent of the property.

The most efficient way to prepare for an eventual disability (which could happen to any of us) is for the person to make plans for herself *before* she reaches the time when she cannot do so. Such plans usually include making a will and establishing a power of attorney (see below).

Families sometimes find it difficult to face these things when the person still seems quite able. Sometimes a confused person resists these steps. Unfortunately, waiting until the person cannot participate in decision making may cost the family thousands of dollars later or may result in decisions that no one would have wanted.

We believe that it is important to discuss with a lawyer what plans you should make. He can advise you on how best to protect the confused person and which powers should be transferred, and can see that whatever papers are drawn up are legally valid. However, these laws (particularly those governing the financial responsibility of families) are very complex. Lawyers who have not specialized in this area may not have the best information. Ask the Alzheimer's Association or a disability law center for a referral.

Lawyers specialize in different areas of law (criminal law, corporate law, divorce law, civil law). You have a right to know what you can expect from a lawyer and what his fees are. Misunderstandings can be avoided by discussing with him what he charges and what services you will get for that fee. Find out if he practices this sort of law and is knowledgeable about it.

In addition to making a will, a person who is still able to manage her own affairs (by the above definition) may sign a *power of attorney*, which gives a spouse, child, or other person who has reached legal age authority to manage her property. A power of attorney can give broad authority to the specified person or it can be limited. A limited power of attorney gives the person authority to do only specific things (sell a house or review income tax records, for example).

A power of attorney becomes void if the person who granted it becomes mentally incapacitated. This means that if you have a power of attorney to do your mother's banking, you no longer have that authority when she becomes confused. Thus, a power of attorney is of little use to the family of a person with dementia. Because of this, most states have passed laws creating a *durable power of attorney*. This authorizes someone to act in behalf of the person after she becomes unable to make her own decisions. You can tell which kind you have: a durable power of attorney must state that it can be exercised even if the person becomes disabled.

Since a power of attorney authorizes someone to act in another person's behalf, the person giving such power must be sure that the person selected will, in fact, act in her best interests. Someone who holds a power of attorney is legally responsible to act in the other person's best interests. Once in a while someone abuses this responsibility. The risk of abuse is small in a limited power of attorney but a durable power of attorney transfers greater responsibility and requires greater trust. A person who wants to plan ahead for her eventual disability must consider this decision carefully.

By making a will and granting a durable power of attorney while she is still able to do so, the person who feels her memory may be beginning to fail can be sure that if she gets worse her life will continue the way she intended and her property will be distributed as she wished, rather than in a way imposed by a court or by state law. The person may continue to manage her own affairs or part of them until such time as a designated person must take over. Then the appointed person will usually not need to take further steps before she is legally able to take over the management of the sick person's affairs.

Some people are unwilling to sign a power of attorney, have no one that they trust to do this, or may already be too impaired to do so. If this is so, you will need to take steps that require the help of an attorney. If the person is currently unable to manage her property and affairs effectively because of her disability, a *guardianship of property* procedure (also called a conservatorship) may be necessary. In this procedure, the lawyer must file a petition in court. After a hearing, a judge decides whether the person is legally competent to manage her property or financial affairs. The judge may appoint a legal guardian to act for the person in financial matters only. This guardian must file financial reports periodically with the court.

If a home is owned jointly by a husband and wife, and one of them becomes impaired, the well spouse will need a power of attorney or guardianship of the property in order to sell the home.

Sometimes a disabled person is unable to care for her daily needs and must have medical care or nursing home care. She may refuse to consent to this or may be unable to make such decisions. Often a hospital or nursing home will accept the consent of the next of kin: a husband or wife, or a son or daughter. Some states specify by law that certain close relatives may make medical decisions without a guardianship. Sometimes, however, a petition must be filed in court to request a *guardianship of the person*. The judge may then appoint a guardian of the person, order the needed care, or send the person to a hospital. This procedure is more complex than filing for a guardianship of property.

In practice, both financial and medical decisions are handled informally without a guardianship proceeding. At present, particularly in smaller communities, banks and hospitals may waive the requirement that you have legal authority to make decisions for a family member, particularly if they have known you and the confused person for a long time. If you are not a close relative, or if there are serious disagreements within the family over what should be done, making formal arrangements may save you considerable headache later.

16

NURSING HOMES AND OTHER LIVING ARRANGEMENTS

SOMETIMES A FAMILY IS UNABLE to care for a person with a dementing illness at home, even if relief services are available. A number of other living arrangements may be considered. These include sheltered settings where the confused person may be able to manage alone for a time, settings where a couple may be able to manage more easily together, and settings where the ill person receives complete care. However, suitable facilities are limited, are expensive, and may not provide high-quality care. It may be difficult to find what you want.

If you consider having the impaired person live alone in a sheltered setting, carefully evaluate his ability to do so. (See Chapter 4.) Our experience has been that people with dementia do not manage well unless there are others nearby who can provide extensive assistance and reassurance.

GENERAL RULES FOR EVALUATING A CARE FACILITY

1. Be sure the physical plant is clean and safe (check especially the kitchen and the bathroom).
2. Know what the fees are and what they cover. Ask about extra charges. Get it in writing.
3. Know whether the staff understands dementing illnesses and how they care for people like the potential resident.
4. Determine how much and what kind of supervision, recreation, food, transportation, social support, and medical support is available and whether it meets the confused person's needs.
5. Find out who will be responsible for the person's medications.

6. Review the requirements of licensure, and find out how often inspections are carried out and by whom.
7. Find out what is done in the case of a medical emergency.
8. Find out what fire alarms and evacuation plans exist.
9. Use the "nose test." Strong smells of urine and other odors often indicate substandard care.
10. Know the conditions under which the resident would be asked to leave.
11. Carefully review the fine print of the contract. Ask a lawyer to help if you don't understand it.

Good care facilities of all kinds often have waiting lists. It is wise to look into possible alternatives well in advance of the time you may need them. This will enable you to assess how good a program really is and to get on the waiting list. You can always stop the application process if you wish.

Good care costs money. Costs may be borne by the individual, charitable gifts, or governmental programs. There is rarely enough money from these sources to provide high-quality care for all who need it.

When you are evaluating a facility, remember that other caregivers may do things differently from the way you would do them. You may need to accept the differences. Also, remember that the forgetful, confused person may give you an inaccurate report of what is happening. Nevertheless, you remain responsible for monitoring the quality of care.

MOVING WITH A CONFUSED PERSON

Sometimes a caregiver moves to a residence where she can manage the confused person more easily: an apartment or a retirement home, for example. We have discussed ways to help a confused person accept a move on page 272. If you are contemplating moving, there are several things you will want to consider.

1. What are the financial costs of moving, such as the cost of a new residence, moving costs, closing costs, and capital gains tax on property you sell?
2. Will moving mean less property for you to clean or maintain? Will help, such as meal preparation or house cleaning, be provided for you?
3. Will moving bring you close to doctors, hospitals, shopping centers, recreation areas?
4. What kind of transportation will you need?

5. Will moving put you closer to or farther from friends and family who can help you?

6. Will moving affect your eligibility for special programs or financial assistance? (You may not be eligible for some programs until you have lived in a state for a given period of time.) If you have sold your house, you may be required to spend most of your capital on nursing home care before you are eligible for Medicaid. You are not usually required to sell a house in which you are living to pay for care (see p. 260).

7. Will moving provide a safe environment for the person (no stairs, call bells, a ground-floor bathroom, supervision, lower crime rate)?

8. What will you do if your financial or physical circumstances change?

TYPES OF LIVING ARRANGEMENTS

Retirement villages and *senior citizens' apartments or condominiums* are planned for retired people who can live independently. In a condominium, the resident pays for a mortgage plus a monthly condominium fee for services such as the maintenance of buildings and grounds, recreation facilities, security systems, and transportation to shopping areas. In senior citizens' apartments, the resident pays rent. Retirement villages may be set up as rental units or as condominiums. These forms of housing may have emergency call services and easy access to medical facilities, but they generally do not offer special help for confused or ill people.

Assisted living or *sheltered housing* provides apartments or rooms for people who cannot live independently but who do not need constant supervision. Many sheltered housing units have safety features such as grab bars, wheelchair ramps, and call bells. In addition to providing security systems and transportation, these programs often offer meals, social work assistance, and someone to check on residents regularly. Some have a nurse on the staff or a medical clinic in the buildings. To live in these settings, people with dementing illnesses usually must be able to provide their own personal care and not be disruptive or wander. Sheltered housing is funded under several different programs, but funding is scarce: there are usually long waiting lists. Since assisted living does not provide supervision, it is not suitable for most people with dementia. Some programs will not accept people with dementia. Some may illegally try to exclude people with dementia who could live in assisted living (for example, with a spouse).

Life-care facilities provide, in return for an initial down payment or entrance fee plus a monthly fee, a living arrangement similar to that of a retirement village, but as a person declines he will be moved within the facility to a sheltered or skilled nursing setting. Once an individual or couple is accepted, the facility *may* provide care for the rest of their life even if the residents run out of money. These facilities are often owned by for-profit corporations that invest the initial payment and expect to earn more than the resident's care costs them. While some families have found these to be a good retirement option, others have told us about problems. Before investing in such a facility, investigate it carefully. Once you have put your financial resources into such a program, you have little flexibility to change. Among the questions you need to ask beforehand are these:

1. Will the entrance fee or part of it be returned to the resident's estate if it is not spent on his care? Does the initial investment build equity for the resident?
2. What becomes of the resident's investment if the facility goes bankrupt?
3. Is an additional entrance fee or monthly fee charged if a resident has or develops a dementia?
4. What services and activities are included in the monthly fee? Is participation in community meals or activities required? What if a resident doesn't like the food or the activities?
5. Does the facility have a nursing unit? Do you like the nursing unit? Is there an extra charge for it? Does the nursing unit accept people with dementia? Is the staff trained to care for people with dementia? Is there an extra charge for people with dementia on the nursing unit? Are you satisfied with the quality of care offered? Review the guidelines on page 265.
6. Can people with dementia be asked to leave? If a resident is later found to have had a pre-existing dementia, which you did not know about at the time of admission, can he be asked to leave? Under what other circumstances can a person or couple be asked to leave?
7. How are other medical, dental, and vision needs met? Does the facility have its own physician? Is transportation available to medical providers? How are medical needs met in the nursing unit? Do the physicians who work in the facility have expertise in geriatrics and do they understand the medical needs of people with dementia?

Your state may have regulations governing life care fees, but you must carefully examine the policies and the quality of services before making an investment. Check with the state consumer protection office or the Office of the Attorney General.

In an *adult foster home* the confused person lives, for a fee, with an individual who provides a room and may provide care. Ideally, foster homes care for their guests as members of the family, and provide meals, a room, transportation to the doctor, access to social work assistance, and supervision. Many adult foster homes will not accept people with dementia; those that do may provide nothing more than food and a bed. A few adult foster homes specialize in the care of people with dementia and provide excellent care. There is little regulation of foster care in most states. If you use such a program, you generally assume full responsibility for monitoring the quality of care given. Quality can decline rapidly if the management or staff changes or if the impaired person's condition changes.

Boarding or domiciliary homes (also called homes for the aged or personal care homes) provide less care than nursing homes. They usually provide a room, meals, supervision, and some other assistance. A few specialize in dementia and offer excellent care. Some of the best special care programs in the United States are homes for the aged. Others, however, take advantage of the vulnerable person with dementia and of lax regulations. They call themselves "Alzheimer's facilities," but they provide inadequate or dangerous care.

There are no federal quality-assurance standards for these facilities, and state oversight ranges from good to nonexistent. If you use such a program, you must assume full responsibility for ensuring that good care is provided. Facilities can change ownership and the quality of care can deteriorate abruptly.

Fees vary widely. Neither foster care nor domiciliary care is covered under Medical Assistance or Medicare. Many states supplement the federal Supplemental Security Income (SSI) pension to help pay for housing. Some homes accept Social Security as full or partial payment.

Social workers in hospitals may be under pressure to place patients quickly. You should not rely solely on the hospital social worker's word about the quality and reliability of a facility; she may never have visited the facility. Look carefully at any facility you are referred to.

If you are considering adult foster care or a domiciliary home, use the checklists in this book and those available from the Alzheimer's Association to guide you. If the program claims to provide specialized Alzheimer's care, obtain the booklet "Selecting a Nursing Home with a Dedicated Dementia Care Unit," published by the Alzheimer's Association (see Appendix 2). Ask the Alzheimer's Association chapter near you what they know about the home. If your family member takes medication or has an unstable medical condition, be sure that the facility can care for him. Food quality and quantity, sanitation, fire safety, control of communicable diseases, and cleanliness may or may not be supervised by the state. You must check these things yourself. People with dementia usually cannot recognize a fire alarm or leave the building independently. Is there enough staff, particularly at night, to assist everyone in leaving the building in case of a fire? Ideally a facility should have smoke detectors, fire alarms, fire barrier walls and doors, and a sprinkler system. However, these can be expensive and are not required in many domiciliary and foster care settings. Programs that use such systems usually must charge more.

NURSING HOMES

As the disease progresses, it may become more difficult for you to care for a person at home. Taking care of a person with a dementing illness can be a twenty-four-hour-a-day job and may require the skills of a professionally trained individual. At some point the family may be unable to continue providing all the care that is needed.

Placing your family member in a nursing home can be a difficult decision to make and it often takes time. Families usually try everything else first. However, a time may come in the process of caring for a person with dementia when nursing home placement is the most responsible decision the family can make.

Family members may feel great sadness and grief at having to accept the inevitable decline of their spouse, parent, or sibling. They frequently have mixed feelings about nursing home placement. They may experience a sense of relief that a decision has finally been made and that part of the care will be assumed by others yet feel guilty for wanting someone else to take over these real burdens. Family members may feel angry that there are no other choices available to them.

Many people don't want to place a family member in a nursing home. They feel that they should care for their loved ones at home and many have heard that American families "dump" unwanted old people in institutions. Not all families care lovingly for their elderly members, but statistics clearly show that families are *not* dumping their elderly in nursing homes, that most families do all they can to postpone or prevent nursing home admission, and that they *do not* abandon their elderly members after placement. Instead, most families visit in the nursing home regularly.

We tend to think of the "good old days" as a time when families took care of their elderly at home. In fact, in the past not many people lived long enough for their families to be faced with the burden of caring for a person with a dementing illness. The people who did become old and sick were in their fifties and sixties and the sons and daughters who cared for them were considerably younger than you may be when your parent needs care in his seventies and eighties. Today many children of an ailing parent are themselves in their sixties or seventies.

The term *nursing home* brings negative images to many people's minds, but often nursing homes give good care and are the best alternative for an ill person. Some nursing homes do not give adequate care, and there has been much publicity about them. Not all homes, however, deserve a bad reputation, and this publicity has brought about needed changes that have improved the quality of nursing home care.

It is not unusual for family members to disagree about nursing home plans. Some members of the family may want the impaired person to remain at home while others feel the time has come for him to enter a nursing home. It is helpful if all involved family members discuss the problem together. Misunderstandings and disagreements are often worse when everyone does not have all the facts. Everyone in the family should discuss at least these three topics: the cost of nursing home care and where that money is to come from (see p. 255), the characteristics of the home you select (see p. 265), and the changes that placement will make in each person's life.

Going to live in a nursing home is a major change for the afflicted person. His ability to respond to this change will be influenced by how ill he is. You will want to help him participate in this move and adjust to this change as much as he is able.

Once you have decided to look for nursing home care for someone, you will need to begin a four-step process:

1. Investigate all funding resources.
2. Have the ill person see a physician if he has not seen one recently. (Most homes require a recent medical exam.)
3. Locate a suitable home.
4. Make the placement and adjust to the changes that the placement brings about for both you and the person who has moved to the nursing home.

There is no "right" time to place a family member in a nursing home. A time may come when the caregiver is just worn out. Other demands, children, spouse, or job may make it impossible for anyone in the family to be a full-time caregiver. A common reason for placement is that the patient needs more care than the family can provide. Older adult children and spouses are likely to have health problems of their own. In many households today, both husband and wife work outside the home; it is often financially impossible for a family member to stay at home and care for the confused person. Caregivers often wait too long to place a family member in a nursing home: both you and the ill person may find it easier if you plan for placement before you are exhausted and while he still has the ability to adjust to a new setting.

It is important that you plan ahead, even if you do not need a nursing home now. It takes time to select a good facility. There are serious shortages of nursing home beds for people with dementia. If you find a facility that you feel offers exceptional care, get on the waiting list well in advance. If you delay until you must place the person quickly (for example, following a hospitalization), you may have to take whatever is available, at least in the short term, even if it does not offer the quality of care you want.

Some families accept whatever is available but remain on the waiting list of the home they prefer. They can then decide whether to move the person when there is an opening in the preferred home.

Paying for Care

Nursing home care is expensive. Before you can make a final decision, you need to know how much the care is going to cost, how this cost will be met, and whether meeting the cost will create a financial burden for members of the family.

There is no national governmental program for funding long-term nursing home care. People often must bear the cost of their own care unless they are impoverished. However, nursing home care is so expensive that many patients exhaust their personal resources and become eligible for Medicaid (see below).

There are several ways in which families can pay for nursing home care. Some families, or the impaired person himself, will be able to pay for the full cost of care. The patient may have private insurance that will pay for a portion of the nursing home costs. Many insurance policies, however, contain clauses that exclude people with dementing illnesses from coverage. Long-term care insurance is often expensive and offers limited benefits.

If the person is a veteran, find out from the Veterans Administration to what extent the VA will be a resource for you (see p. 261).

In some cases, Medicare pays for part of the cost of nursing home care for a limited time. However, in planning for nursing home placement, it is important that you not overestimate Medicare benefits. We recommend that you identify and check out all resources, because the patient's own funds and Medicaid are usually the only available sources of payment for nursing homes, and Medicaid has serious limitations.

Medicare

Medicare is designed to cover acute care, not chronic or long-term care. However, for people who are acutely and seriously ill and who need intensive rehabilitation or nursing care, Medicare may provide coverage for up to 150 days. Dementia is usually not considered to warrant this kind of care, but if the person has a coexisting condition, you should inquire whether Medicare will cover rehabilitation or intensive nursing for it. There is no longer a requirement that the person enter the nursing home from a hospital.

A nursing home or the hospital social worker will be able to assist you in determining whether someone is eligible for Medicare benefits and for how long. Only care in Medicare-certified nursing homes will be covered. It may be for less than 150 days, and the patient must pay part of the bill (this is called co-payment).

Medicaid (Medical Assistance)

Medicaid is a federal program that is administered on the state level. In general, a person qualifies for it on the basis of the amount of income and assets (savings, property, etc.) he has and on the basis of medical need. Applications and information can be obtained through the local department of the agency that administers the program. This may be the Department of Social Services, Department of Welfare, or Health Department. Any of these agencies can tell you who in your state administers the program.

Eligibility requirements for the Medical Assistance program include separate determinations of the need for medical care and the financial need. Medicaid is based on a legislative policy that tax money should be spent only for people who could not otherwise afford care and should not be spent to allow individuals to save their own money. Thus, individuals are generally required to spend their own income and assets before Medicaid will pay for their nursing home care.

You may have strong feelings of discomfort about taking what some people call "welfare." In fact, Medicaid pays for at least part of the care for about two-thirds of nursing home residents. Nursing home care is so expensive (more than $25,000 a year in most communities) that many middle-class people use up their own resources quickly and then become eligible for Medicaid. It is important to remember that our taxes pay for these social programs and that when you are eligible for a program, you are entitled by law to receive its benefits. The government intends that this program help families manage the high costs of nursing home care.

If you apply for Medicaid, it is important that you receive fair and equitable consideration. Unfortunately, in the past, some families have been determined to be ineligible when, in fact, they were eligible. Some spouses and other family members have been impoverished by the cost of care because of incorrect interpretations of the law. There are both federal and state laws governing Medicaid, so the eligibility requirements vary

Federal law governing nursing home care and eligibility for Medicaid was extensively revised in the 1987 Omnibus Budget Reconciliation Act (OBRA) and the 1988 Catastrophic Health Act. States are now revising their policies to conform to federal requirements. Some parts of the state and federal law may be tested in the courts. It is not possible to know at the time of this writing how these changes in law and regulation will actually affect you. This text provides the best available information, but we urge you to seek legal counsel and obtain information from the Alzheimer's Association, the National Citizens Coalition for Nursing Home Reform, or the state nursing home ombudsman (often located within the state office on aging) (see Appendix 2).

from state to state. Medicaid law is complex, and state laws and interpretations of policy change frequently.

You may have considerable difficulty getting accurate information about your eligibility. Not all lawyers are knowledgeable about this complex law, and social workers and nursing homes may have erroneous or out-of-date information. It is in the best interest of the state to give you the most conservative interpretation of the law. It is in your best interest to know the most generous interpretation that is allowed. Information can be obtained from the Alzheimer's Association, the National Citizens Coalition for Nursing Home Reform, and other advocacy groups. If the ill person or his spouse has some income or assets, you should consider consulting a lawyer who is experienced in Medicaid law *as soon as you realize that the person has a dementia*. State laws differ and the language of the federal law provides for various exemptions, which are too complex to discuss here. New court decisions will also affect the way states interpret the new law.

Medicaid considers assets (resources such as stock, property, life insurance policies, etc.) separately from income. Certain assets are exempt.

Income: Most of the income of a person who enters a nursing home must be spent on his care. He is allowed to keep a small personal needs allowance. If his income is not sufficient to pay for care, Medicaid will make up the difference. Beginning with the first day of the first full month of institutionalization, Medicaid does not require that any income belonging solely to the spouse who remains in the community be paid to support the institutionalized spouse. A spouse remaining in the community may retain for her own use an amount from the couple's joint income or the institutionalized spouse's income up to 122 percent of the federal poverty level (about $786 a month in 1989). This will rise with the inflation rate.

Assets: Laws governing assets vary from one state to another. Usually the institutionalized spouse may retain $2000 of his own assets. Assets (property) held by the spouse who remains in the community generally will not be considered available for the care of the institutionalized person. When assets are held jointly by a married couple, the spouse remaining in the community is entitled to retain half of the assets, or $12,000. Some states allow the spouse to retain more. In certain limited circumstances, the institutionalized spouse can receive Medicaid even if the spouse remaining in the community does not turn over the excess resources.

Families sometimes consider transferring assets out of the ill person's name and into that of another family member so that these assets will not be considered in determining eligibility for Medicaid. This must be done at least *30 months* before the person applies for Medicaid. (Since Alzheimer's disease is a long-term disease, you may have this chance to plan ahead.) The 30-month rule applies to all assets, including the home. However, it does *not* include transfer of the home to the spouse living in the community (see below) or certain other circumstances.

We recommend that you look into the laws and regulations in your state well before you need Medicaid and make financial arrangements accordingly. Alzheimer's Association chapters often have speakers on this subject, and from time to time have information in their newsletters.

The application for the determination of financial eligibility for Medicaid is usually made by a competent family member for the individual needing nursing home placement. Make an appointment at the agency that processes applications.

A hospital social worker or the social worker at the nursing home you are considering may be able to help you. They will ask you to bring evidence of the patient's financial status. The documents required usually include his Social Security number, proof of income to the individual (Social Security benefit letters, pension benefit letters, etc.), bank account statements, insurance policies, and proof of any transfer of funds. Before going to the application appointment, ask about any other information you may need to bring.

You are entitled to a clear and courteous explanation of your eligibility status. You are also entitled to see the state laws and regulations. In the event that you do not get an explanation you can accept or understand, ask to speak to the supervisor. Each agency has an appeals system available to you as a last resort.

If Medicaid is granted, the actual payments to the nursing home will come from two sources. The first source is the individual patient's income from Social Security, pension plans, or insurance. The second is Medicaid, which pays the remainder of the cost.

Often the cost of nursing home care is borne first by one resource and then by another. For example,

Mrs. Campbell has Alzheimer's disease. She was cared for at home by her husband until she had a series of falls and became unable to walk. Mr. Campbell took her to the hospital, where x-rays showed that she had broken her hip. The family decided that it was time for her to enter a nursing home. During the first 150 days, her care was paid for by Medicare because she needed skilled nursing to help her hip heal. Then Mr. Campbell divided the stock he and his wife jointly owned. He kept half of it and used the rest to pay for her care. When all but $2,000 of her half had been spent on her care, he applied for Medicaid, which paid for her care because she had no other source of income and had exhausted her assets. In addition to his half of the stock, Mr. Campbell retained the family home and car, all of his own pension, and a small inheritance from his father (which belonged solely to him).

Here are some of the questions that families often ask about Medicaid:

1. *Are children or other relatives required to support their family member in a nursing home?* Under federal Medicaid law, spouses and adult children are not legally responsible to use their own income to support family members in nursing homes. However, some states have passed "relative responsibility laws," which require family members to support the person. (These are similar to the laws that cover child support and alimony.) Under certain conditions in some states, relatives can be required to pay support for a person who is under 65 and living in a state mental hospital. Until 1988, spouses in some states were told that they must support the person in the nursing home to be eligible for Medicaid. This is not correct. If you are told this, consult the local Alzheimer's Association or an attorney.

2. *If the spouse remaining in the community has no income, how will she manage?* If the income of the spouse remaining in the community is less than 122 percent of the poverty level, she is eligible to receive part of the institutionalized spouse's income as support. If the institutionalized spouse has no income, the spouse remaining in the community may be eligible for Supplemental Security Income (SSI). This is a federal program for people without Social Security or other retirement income. It will provide some monthly income (in 1989, approximately $360 a month). She may also qualify for food stamps and other social benefits. The total monthly income figure will be revised upward by the government

periodically as the cost of living rises, but it usually remains at or near the poverty level.

3. *Will the ill person have to sell his house to be eligible for Medicaid?* The home is exempt as long as it is occupied by the spouse or a dependent child, even if ownership has not been transferred. The home can be transferred to the spouse living in the community at any time; the 30-month rule does not apply.

4. *Can a family member transfer the impaired person's assets (land, stocks, property) out of his name to make him eligible for Medicaid?* A person's assets must be spent on his care before he can be eligible for Medicaid, except: (1) a home shared by the impaired person and the spouse who remains in the community is exempt; (2) half of a couple's assets, up to certain limits, are considered to belong to the spouse who remains in the community; (3) assets that are transferred into some other person's name (including the spouse who lives in the community) at least 30 months before the person's application for Medicaid are exempt; or (4) under certain other infrequent circumstances.

5. *Should the well spouse divorce the ill spouse who is entering the institution to protect income and assets?* When a couple divorces, the court may be obliged to advocate for the impaired person and may order alimony or the transfer of assets greater than what Medicaid would require. The new law should help the well spouse sufficiently to avoid this painful option.

6. *Should I save the person's funds in case he needs nursing home care later?* Since the law requires that the person's assets be spent on his care before he can become eligible for Medicaid, you may decide to spend those assets on respite care and keep the person at home as long as possible. You may also wish to keep enough assets to pay for the first few months of nursing home care. This may help you find a good home that will accept the person.

To ensure that the spouse remaining in the community retains a fair share of assets, you may decide to split assets before purchasing respite. Do so in such a way that Medicaid will not split them again.

Mary and John had a total of $100,000 in assets (excluding their home). When John became ill, Mary divided their assets in half and retained $50,000 in her name. She retained $12,000 to pay for his first six months in a nursing home. With the remainder of John's half of the money, she purchased respite care and was able to care for him at home. She kept careful accounts of all her expenses, including the respite care, special clothing she bought him, adult diapers, travel to day care, and medications, so that she could demonstrate that she had spent his share of their estate on him.

7. *Can a nursing home refuse to accept a person who will need Medicaid at the time he enters the facility?* In most states, Medicaid pays less than the home would receive from a patient paying privately. This creates a financial incentive for nursing homes to limit the number of people they care for who are on Medicaid. Thus, it may be difficult for a family to find a good nursing home for a person who will enter the facility as a Medicaid recipient. The courts may eventually rule that this is discriminatory. It may help to pay privately the first few months if possible. If you have problems, seek guidance from the Alzheimer's Association; they keep abreast of changing state policies and recent court decisions. A person who will be entering a nursing home on Medicaid from a hospital may be required to accept the first available bed even if it is in an unsuitable nursing home or one so far away that visiting is a hardship for the family.

8. *Can a nursing home discharge a person because he changes from Medicare or private payment to Medicaid?* Federal law states that a nursing facility cannot discharge, transfer, or give different care to a person based on the source of payment. However, as stated above, financial incentives often encourage nursing homes to limit the number of Medicaid patients they care for. Some may achieve this result illegally. If a facility transfers a person to a hospital, another facility, or another section of the facility near the time of that person's change-over to Medicaid, investigate to be sure that the transfer is medically justified.

9. *Can a nursing home require that a patient's family give a donation or agree to pay privately for a certain period of time?* If a facility accepts federal funds (Medicaid or Medicare) for any of its residents, it cannot require a third party to guarantee payment, nor can it require a gift or donation as a condition of admission. We are told that the courts have found such agreements not to be binding even if signed. A few homes are entirely private and do not use federal funds. These homes are not bound by the federal law and may set such requirements.

10. *What about the Veterans Administration?* The VA has its own policies and regulations regarding admission, discharge, and the quality of care. They are not under the federal and state Medicaid or Medicare laws. (Also see p. 280.)

Establishing the Need for Medical Care

Once you have made a decision about how to pay for nursing home care, you can proceed to the next step in the process, the establishment of the medical need for care. If the person has been receiving medical attention, this step will probably be quite simple. Nursing homes require basic medical information about the patient and his treatments; many require a recent physical examination by his physician. Homes also require positive proof that the patient does not have tuberculosis, so the patient may need to have a new chest x-ray. If the person or his family will be paying for his care, this may be all that is necessary.

If the person's care is to be covered by Medicare, he must meet Medicare criteria. These generally require that he need skilled nursing or rehabilitative services. The Medicare office will give you a list of approved treatments. If the person needs a treatment not on the list, you may want to appeal the denial.

If the person's care is to be covered under Medicaid, his need for medical care must be demonstrated. In general, Medicaid requires that the person need nursing care above the level of board and room. Medicaid is less restrictive than Medicare, but standards vary from state to state. Federal Medicaid no longer distinguishes between intermediate and skilled levels of care. After the doctor has examined the patient, he will fill out a form. This form will be sent to a review organization, who will decide whether nursing home care is needed.

The Mental Health Screening Requirement

Federal law (PASARR) requires that everyone (whether paying privately or through Medicaid) who is entering a nursing home that uses federal funds have a mental health screening. This is to ensure that people with mental illness or mental retardation not be inappropriately placed in nursing homes. *People with Alzheimer's disease or related disorders are excluded from this requirement.* The states are implementing this law in different ways. It may not present problems in some states but in others may place onerous burdens on families.

Before the person enters a nursing home, be sure that:

1. the person is given a complete neurological examination;
2. the diagnosis of Alzheimer's disease or a related disorder is listed as the primary diagnosis;
3. if the person is taking medications that affect behavior or mood, the doctor states that they are prescribed to treat *specific symptoms* of the dementia;
4. if the person has a psychiatric diagnosis (like depression), the psychiatric diagnosis is listed as secondary to the dementia.

Some people with dementia are also depressed. Sometimes these individuals do not get good care for their depression in a nursing home. Keeping the person in a different setting or paying privately for psychiatric care may be your only option (see Chapter 8). Depression should not make a person with dementia ineligible for nursing home care. However, when a person has both a dementia and a mental illness, such as depression, you may need expert help to get the person admitted to a nursing home.

Finding a Home or Other Facility

We strongly urge you to anticipate the possible need for nursing home care. Investigate financial issues and select one or more homes that you like. While you may never need nursing home care, the problems of trying to locate a good home quickly are enormous. Many families end up losing money or using homes they do not like because they did not anticipate a need.

The process of finding a facility will differ depending on whether you are planning in advance and whether the person enters the nursing home from home or from a hospital.

If you have some time, ask the local chapter of the Alzheimer's Association if they have a list of homes that families have liked or if they can refer you to members who have used the homes you are considering. They are the source most likely to have good, current information about how a facility manages people with dementia. However, these are lay organizations and usually cannot give you more than personal observations.

A friend, acquaintance, or relative who has or has had a loved one in a home can be a good source of information. Ask people you know who have been in a similar situation what they have learned.

The local library, nursing home ombudsman, or nursing home advocacy group (see Appendix 2) may have information about facilities that have not met state or federal standards. Federal law requires that this information be available to the public. However, this information is not always a good reflection of the home's current status. Your own eyes and ears over several visits will be your best guide. It is difficult to correctly interpret the official reports, and the quality of care can change rapidly—for better or worse— with a change of ownership.

Some Alzheimer's Association chapters or local offices on aging have social workers who can advise you on the application process. If the person is being discharged from a hospital, the hospital social worker can help you. Family service agencies have social workers and in larger cities there are private social workers listed in the yellow pages of the telephone directory.

A social worker can help you establish financial and medical eligibility, provide you with a list of nursing homes in your area, and help you through the eligibility process. A social worker may be able to help with other steps in the total process as well, and may also help you handle the painful feelings you may be having about the placement. Agencies and social workers are often prohibited from recommending some facilities over others. So their recommendations usually do *not* imply a judgment about the quality of a facility.

Hospital social workers are caught between their professional commitment to help you and the pressure on hospitals to discharge people as soon as possible. Be aware that if the person is to move from a hospital to a nursing home, you may be pressured to make decisions rapidly. *Planning ahead helps to protect you from serious problems.*

Nursing homes are listed in the yellow pages of the telephone directory. Good homes may be known to other families in your community, or your doctor may recommend a good home. Some physicians have financial interests in nursing homes, which may bias their recommendations. Always get more than one opinion.

When you have a list of possible homes, call to make an appointment to see the administrator and/or the director of nursing and to visit the home. There are some fundamental questions you might ask on the telephone before you visit. First, you will need to find out if the home has openings or a waiting list. You should go to see the home; if it is a good home, you may wish to place the patient on the waiting list. Second, you will need to find out if the home accepts the funding sources you are planning to use.

When you visit the home, you will need to observe and ask questions. Take a friend or family member or a member of the Alzheimer's Association with you. This person will be less emotionally involved and can help you observe the facility and think through your decision. We recommend visiting more than once if there is time: on the second visit you will notice things you missed on the first. Many families have told us that the things you notice when you first enter a home may not be the things that matter as time goes on. Allow plenty of time to visit, talk to alert residents and the staff, and try to picture how your relative will fit in.

When Art first visited Sunhaven Nursing Home he was favorably impressed. He was struck by the spacious lobby, the long clean corridors with the patients' names on their doors. He observed several staff members all in fresh uniforms and he liked the sunny rooms and well-equipped bathrooms. After visiting his father several times at Sunhaven, Art noticed that no residents used the lobby. He decided that what mattered most was whether the aides were friendly to his father and whether they came and helped him in the bathroom when he needed it. His father had always enjoyed meals and the bland, lukewarm food depressed him. He wished the home had spent more money on a cook and less on the lobby. His father had always liked to stay up late at

*night and to sleep late in the morning, but the facility required that
everyone be in bed by 8:30 P.M. and up by 7:00 A.M.*

When meeting with nursing home administrators, you should feel free
to ask questions about the home's accreditation, about financial procedures,
and whether they meet state standards for the quality of care. Discuss
financial arrangements in detail. Do not take anything for granted. If there
are things you do not understand, don't hesitate to ask. All financial
agreements should be in writing, and you should have a copy of the final
contract. See page 255 about the new laws regarding care and financial
matters.

You may wish to discuss the following areas before signing any papers:

1. Will the patient or resident receive a refund of advance payments if
   he leaves the facility?
2. How does the home protect cash and assets that have been entrusted
   to it? Is a receipt given to you or the patient? Are withdrawals noted
   by signed receipt, so that you can keep track of the account?
3. Are the agreed date of admission and the care to be furnished set
   forth in the written agreement?
4. Under what circumstances can the home discharge a person, and
   how much notice must they give you?
5. If the person's condition changes (either improves or declines), will
   the home move him; and if so will it be to another part of the same
   home?
6. What charges are extra (television, telephone, laundry, personal
   care supplies)?

If the staff is reluctant to answer your questions, this may be an indication of how you will be treated after placement.

We have included a checklist of questions you may want to ask as you
visit homes. These will help you evaluate the quality of care the home
provides. You may want to take this list with you. There are three vital
questions:

1. Does the home have a current license from the state?
2. Does the administrator have a current license from the state?
3. Does the home meet or exceed state fire regulations? Because it is
   difficult to evacuate frail elderly people in case of fire, sprinkler
   systems and fire doors are important.

If the above questions cannot be answered yes, do not use the home.

If Medicare and/or Medicaid is needed, is the home certified to accept
it? (If you will pay from another source initially and then switch to

Medicaid, you need to know that the home is certified for it and will be able to keep the patient.)

A 1987 federal law spells out the rights of nursing home residents. These are listed in Appendix 5. If the home you are considering does not meet these criteria, discuss with staff members why it does not. Consider not using the home. People with dementia cannot exercise all of these rights, but you should be able to exercise them in the patient's behalf.

Visiting

Is the home close enough that you can visit frequently? Is there adequate parking and public transportation? Does the home have long and convenient visiting hours? (When a nursing home restricts visiting hours, one wonders what goes on when no family members are around.) May children visit? Can you spend extra time in the beginning to help the person adjust? (See p. 273.) Will you feel comfortable visiting here? Can you and the resident have privacy?

Meeting Regulations

Was the home cited by state inspectors in the last inspection for failure to meet federal or state standards? (See p. 265 or ask the administrators.) If you are considering a home that has been cited, ask what the failure was and what has been done to correct it. Some violations are quickly remedied; others indicate serious problems. If the staff evades your question, you may not wish to use that facility.

Costs

Do you clearly understand what costs are included in the basic charge? Obtain a list of extra charges, such as laundry, television, radio, medications, hair cuts, incontinence pads, special nursing procedures, behavior management procedures. Ask how residents' personal funds are handled. If the resident enters the hospital or goes home for a few days, what charges are involved?

Cleanliness and Safety

Is the home clean? Look at bathrooms and the food-preparation area.

A facility can be clean and still have a warm, comfortable atmosphere. Highly waxed floors and shiny aluminum create glare, which can confuse people with dementia, and may not be the best indicators of cleanliness.

A strong smell of urine may indicate either poor patient care or poor housekeeping. Occasional odors are difficult to avoid.

Are bathrooms and other areas equipped with grab bars, hand rails, non-skid floors, and other devices for residents' safety?

What provisions are made for the safety of people who wander or become agitated? Can staff members spend individual time with someone who becomes upset? Are doors secure (either locked or equipped with a buzzer to alert the staff that someone has gone out)? Are physically frail residents protected from stronger, more mobile confused people? Is the facility well lit, the furniture sturdy, and the temperature comfortable? Is the home reasonably quiet?

It is difficult to balance independence and maximal function for people with dementia and to ensure their safety. Ask how the home has addressed this. Are their policies acceptable to you? What provisions have been made for fire safety? Will their procedures protect your family member in the event of a fire?

Staff

Ask whether there is enough staff to individually assist your family member or to wait while he slowly does some things for himself. The larger the staff, the higher the cost of care; but some individual assistance should be available. How many people must each aide take care of? Does this seem reasonable, given the severity of patients' impairment? How is the facility staffed on evenings and weekends? How well trained are supervisory nurses? Observe how residents are handled. Are they asking for help and not getting it? Do the nurses seem hurried?

Does the staff seem happy and friendly? Happy personnel indicate a well-run institution. Also, contented staff people are less likely to take out their personal frustrations on the residents. Ask staff members how staff turnover rates compare with those at other local homes. The staffs of good nursing homes recommend this as an excellent clue to the level of staff satisfaction.

Ask what training the nursing staff, including nursing aides, have received. Have nurses, aides, social workers, and activity directors had training in the care of people with dementia? Staff members need to know how to manage catastrophic reactions, suspiciousness, wandering, irritability, etc. If they have not had training, how willing are they to accept information from you on how to manage your family member?

Ask about the extent of professional training the social worker and activity director have had. These two people make a significant contribution to the quality of patient care. Ask to meet with them. Ask them how much of their time is spent with people with dementia.

Care and Services

Federal law now mandates that homes have individual care plans for each patient. Ask to see what things are considered in the care plan. Are you welcome to participate in care planning? Do the activity director and the social worker participate?

What things will the home want to know from you about the patient? In addition to many questions about medical history, financial resources, etc., does the home want to know about the person's likes and dislikes, habits, how you manage behaviors, what abilities the person still has? These things are essential for good care.

How much of the time are people with dementia included in activities? Long hours of inactivity indicate poor dementia care. Do the activities offered seem dignified and adult? Will they interest your family member? Ask to observe activities. Do the residents appear to be interested and content, or are they dozing off or wandering away? Are programs available to keep residents alert and involved within the limits of their abilities?

Is supervised daily exercise provided? Even people who are confined to a wheelchair or bed need exercise, and those who can walk should be doing so. Exercise may reduce the restlessness of people with dementing illnesses.

Are there creative and effective planned social activities? A television room is not enough. Nursing home residents need structured programs, such as music programs, recreation groups, and outings, to keep them as involved in interpersonal activities as they are able to be.

Are physical therapy, speech therapy, and occupational or recreational therapy available to residents who need it?

Do clergy visit regularly and can residents attend religious services?

Do residents wear their own clothes and have a locked, private storage space? Is the privacy of their mail and phone calls respected? Can they have privacy with visitors, and is private space provided for visits from a spouse?

Ask to see the home's written policy on the use of restraints. Look around. Do you see people wearing vests or belts or in furniture they cannot get out of? Gerichairs can be used to make people comfortable or to restrain people. Do you see people in restraints being released, repositioned, and taken to the bathroom? Restraints should not be used unless all other measures to control the person have failed and they are necessary to protect him from harm. Experienced staff members can usually manage wandering and agitation without restraints.

Ask to see the home's written policy on using psychoactive drugs to manage difficult behavior. What do they do before resorting to drugs? What behaviors do they treat with medication? (See page 101.) If your family member will need drugs or restraints to control behavior, mood, or sleep, how frequently will a physician see him to review his status? Ask what strategies the facility will try, to reduce his need for medication and/or restraints.

How will the person's medical care be handled? Will the person's own physician visit him or does the home have a physician who sees all the patients? How frequently will this person see the patient? Will this physician meet with you when you have concerns? Can you meet with him ahead of time? Does he have training in geriatric medicine? People with dementia need close, skilled medical supervision and their medical care requires special skills. In the absence of such a physician, does the home employ specially trained nurses or physician's assistants? How does the home provide ongoing good medical care?

If the person is bedbound or has serious health problems, has the staff had special training in these areas?

Does the home have a consulting psychiatrist who can see the person if he develops serious behavioral problems or becomes depressed? How will the home address these problems?

Does the facility have arrangements for the transfer of acutely ill people to a hospital? Is this hospital satisfactory to the family?

How is incontinence managed? Nursing management, such as individualized scheduled toileting, is preferred over catheters for ambulatory people with dementia. Look around. Do you see more than a very few people who have catheter bags hanging from their wheelchairs or beds?

Ask aides or the ombudsman about reports of decubitus ulcers (pressure sores).

People with dementia are sensitive to the way they are treated. Observe how the staff treats residents. Do they address them as adults or as if they were children? Do they stop and pay attention to residents who approach them? Do they greet people before doing something to them? Do they seem sensitive to needs for privacy and dignity?

The Physical Plant

Is the home pleasant to be in and well lit? Is the staff cheerful, is the furniture comfortable, are residents' personal possessions in sight in their rooms? A nursing home that looks like a hospital is not necessarily a pleasant place in which to live. Pleasant surroundings and a kind, patient staff are important to a confused person. Also, you need to feel comfortable when you come to visit.

Do you think the patient will feel comfortable here? There are "homey" nursing homes that have worn furniture but seem more like home to some people. Other people will feel more comfortable in a newer facility. Is it too noisy and confusing for your family member, or too quiet and boring? Does it allow private time for those who seek it and provide social activities for outgoing people?

Glare, noise, and dim light all add to the difficulties a person with dementia experiences. If these things bother you, chances are they will also create unnecessary stress for a person with dementia.

Policies on Terminal Care

What is the home's policy regarding life-sustaining measures? Ask if state laws require that a statement recording the family's preference be placed in the chart. Although this is a painful subject to think about at the time of the person's admission, it is important that you ask about this. Families, nursing homes, and the home's physician often have different opinions about how to respond at the end of a patient's life. Your wishes may not be carried out unless you state them at the beginning. (See pp. 112–13.)

Meals

Visit at mealtime and ask to eat a meal there. Does the food look appetizing? Are meals adequate? Are individual diets available? Are snacks available?

Is the food wholesome, attractive, and suitable for elderly people? Are people with dementia served in a small, quiet area or in a large, noisy dining room? Do you observe nurse aides helping people who cannot feed themselves? Volunteers may be used to help people at mealtimes.

Are people with swallowing problems closely supervised? Long-term use of nasogastric (NG) tubes or other devices that circumvent voluntary eating are not recommended if good nursing management will enable a person to eat.

Rights

The federal government has mandated a nursing home patients' bill of rights (see Appendix 5). Ask how it is carried out for people with dementia.

Is there a resident council that can take problems and complaints to the administrator? Where can you take complaints? Is the social worker readily available to discuss your concerns? Is there a family council?

Ideally you should be able to respond positively to many of these questions. In reality, high-quality care is hard to find. If the person is difficult to manage or if you must rely on Medicaid funding, you may not be able to find an ideal home. Use these questions as a guide to help you decide which things are most important and which ones you are willing to compromise on.

Nursing Home Programs That Specialize in Dementia Care

Some nursing homes have opened special units for people with dementia (often called Alzheimer's units). If you are considering such a unit, use the booklet "Selecting a Nursing Home with a Dedicated Dementia Unit," published by the Alzheimer's Association. (See Appendix 1.) The booklet describes those characteristics that we believe you should seek in specialized care.

Dementia care units range from those that offer no specialized care to those that provide excellent care that meets the unique needs of a confused person. Here are some of the questions to consider:

Does this program offer care that will be helpful to your family member? Do not assume that it will be better for your family member just because it is called special. Some people do not need special care, and some "special care" facilities are not offering care that really meets the needs of people with dementia.

Does this care cost more? If so, is the difference worth the price? Can you afford it? If your family member will need to change to Medicaid after a few years, will the facility keep him? Increased fees do not necessarily mean better care.

Is the facility close enough that you and others can visit easily? Seeing you frequently may be better for the person than whatever special care is offered.

Are people moved off the unit if their condition declines? If so, is this satisfactory to you? Do you like the unit where they would be transferred? Will they be transferred within the same home?

Ask what changes being in the unit produces in most residents. The amount and type of positive change that excellent dementia care can produce in patients are controversial. No large studies have documented particular benefits, but many programs in the United States and abroad report positive changes in patients' social function and behavior, though not in the relentless progress of the disease itself, after the person has adjusted to the program. Some changes that occur in most but not all residents and indicate good care are: minimal use of behavior-controlling medication, evidence of increased enjoyment of activities, decreased agitation and wandering, weight gain, evidence of pleasure in daily life, better control of continence (through staff assistance), evidence that the person feels that he belongs, increased tendency to sleep through the night without sleeping medications, and little or no screaming. Good programs care for very difficult patients without using any physical restraints. Residents in these programs smile and laugh more easily, appear more alert and responsive, and establish eye contact more often and for a longer part of their illness.

Good care can improve the quality of life of a person living with a dementing disease, but *no program has been shown to change the inevitable course of these tragic diseases.*

If you are able to place your family member in a good care facility, you may observe that he does better than he did at home. Families sometimes have mixed feelings about this: while they are pleased to see their family member doing well, they are sad that they could not bring about this change at home. It is easier for the staff to create a therapeutic program: they can leave the resident at the end of an eight-hour shift and they are not doing the caregiving alone! When the person is doing well in a residential setting and you are free of the other demands of care, you have more time and energy for giving the person the love and sense of family that no one else can give.

Moving to a Nursing Home

Once a nursing home has been found and financial arrangements have been made, the next step is the actual move. It involves many of the things important when an ill person changes residence (see pp. 56–58).

Tell the person where he is going if you think there is any chance he will understand. Take familiar items that he is fond of with him (pictures, mementos, an afghan, a radio). If possible, he should help select these. Even a person who is upset or severely impaired needs to feel that this is his life and he is still important.

You may have to close your ears to the person's accusations if he blames you for this move. If he repeatedly becomes upset when the home is mentioned, it is not helpful, we feel, to keep mentioning it. You may need to go on matter-of-factly with arrangements. Try to avoid dishonest explanations such as "we are going for a ride" or "you are going for a visit." This can make the person's subsequent adjustment in the nursing home more difficult.

In some states the family does not have the legal right to move a person against his will. If the hospital or nursing home raises this issue, consult an attorney. All states have legal provisions for allowing families to make decisions for someone who is not competent to do so.

Many people with dementia will make a better adjustment to the nursing home if the family visits frequently in the early weeks. People vary: some residents need some time on their own before they begin to join in facility activities. If the person continues to be uncomfortable in the home, ask yourself whether your own tension and anxiety are making it more difficult for the resident to relax in the new surroundings. Avoid a facility that asks you to stay away until the person gets used to his surroundings. This only increases his feeling of being lost. You may be exhausted at this point and the person may greet you with accusations or beg you to take him home with you. Remember that these may be the only words he can find to express his understandable anxiety and unhappiness. Offer reassurance and affection and avoid being drawn into arguments. After the first weeks, taper your visiting to fewer hours. Find a schedule that supports the resident while allowing you to regain your own resources.

Some families have written out information about the person for the staff. Does the person take his bath in the morning or at night? Does he go to bed early or late? Who are the people in his life he may ask for? What do certain words or behaviors mean? How do you respond to things he often does? What will comfort him? What will trigger outbursts?

You may not find a nursing home you really like or you may feel that the staff is not giving the patient the kind of care he should receive. However, you may have no alternative but to leave the person in that home. The director of an excellent home suggests that you avoid complaints and do all that you can to establish a friendly relationship with the staff. This may mean a compromise on your part, but may well encourage their cooperation. Offer them information about dementia.

If you are moving the person to the nursing home from a hospital, you may have had little or no time to search for a home and to plan an orderly transition. You may be exhausted by all that had to be done in a few hours or days. If this happens, at least try to go with the person to the home and to have some familiar things waiting there for him.

Adjusting to a New Life

The change to living in a nursing home means major adjustments for the impaired person. Making these adjustments takes time and energy for staff, residents, and family, and it can be a painful process. Remember that the move to a nursing home need not mean the end of family relationships. As time goes on, your relationship with the impaired person may improve. Your relative can continue to be a part of the family even though he has moved into a setting that better meets his needs. There are some practical suggestions for things that you can do to make the adjustment to the new home easier. However, we know that the most difficult part of the adjustment may be the feelings you and your relative have about it.

Visiting

It is important to your family member that you visit. Even if the person does not recognize you or does not seem to want you there, your regular visits help at some level to sustain his awareness that he is valued and is a part of a family. Sometimes people beg to be taken home or cry when you leave. It's tempting to avoid such scenes by visiting less often, but usually the benefits to everyone from the visit far outweigh the upset that comes at the end. Expressing grief and anger at being in a nursing home is understandable.

You may be distressed by the atmosphere of the nursing home or by the other sick people you see there. Family members find it painful to see a loved one so impaired. Because dementing illnesses interfere with communication and comprehension, families can have difficulty thinking of things to do when they visit. In the following section we describe things that families tell us make visiting easier.

You can help your relative orient himself in his new home. While you are visiting, explain again why he is there (for example, say, "You are too sick to stay at home"). Review what the daily routines of the home are; make a schedule for him if he can read it. Help him find the bathroom, dining room, television, and phone. Help him find his things in his closet. Think of a way to identify the door of his room as his. Decorate his room with things that are his.

Tell him exactly when you will visit next and write this down for him so he can use it to remind himself. Some families write a letter to the resident mentioning highlights of the most recent visit and the time of the next. The staff can read the letter with the resident between visits to reassure him that you do come frequently. Try to continue to involve him in family outings. If he is not acutely ill, take him for rides, shopping, home for dinner or overnight, or to church. Even if he resists going back he may eventually come to accept this routine, and he will benefit from the knowledge that he is still part of the family. Select activities that do not overly stress or tire him. Occasionally it continues to be difficult to get the person to return. In this instance it is better to visit him at the home.

Help him to remain a part of special family events such as birthdays and holidays. Even if he is depressed or confused, he usually should still be informed of sad events.

Telephone calls between visits help a forgetful person keep in touch and remind him that he is not forgotten. Don't expect him to be able to remember to call you.

Take an old photograph album, an old dress from the attic, or some other item that may trigger memories of the past and urge the person to talk about things he remembers from long ago. If he always tells you the same story, accept this. It is your listening to him and your presence that communicate that you still care about him.

Talk about the family, neighbors, gossip. Even if the person is not fully aware of the issues, he can enjoy the act of listening and talking. Being together is important to both of you. Confused people may not be interested in some topics, such as current events. If the person seems restless, do not insist on bringing him up to date on information.

Be sympathetic about his complaints. Listening to the things he complains about tells him that you care about him. He may make the same complaint over and over because he forgets that he told you. Listen anyway; it is your empathy he needs. Investigate his complaint thoughtfully, however, before you complain to the staff or act on it. Remember that his perception of things may not be accurate, although there may be an element of truth in his complaint.

Sing old, familiar songs. Don't be surprised if other residents drift by to listen or participate. Music is a wonderful way to share. Nobody will remember if your singing isn't very good. Take along tape recordings of the family or the children.

Make a personal history scrapbook telling the story of the person's life—where he grew up, when he married, his children, his job, hobbies, and so on. Write in large letters. Illustrate it with photographs, clippings, bits of fabric, medals, etc. Making the scrapbook can occupy both of you for several visits. Reviewing it may help him recall his past. Even if he does not remember, he may be reassured that he *has* a past.

Make a personal history box. Put in items that will trigger memories; treasured keepsakes, antique kitchen or farm tools that will be familiar to the person, assorted screws and bolts for a handyman or spools of thread for a seamstress. Look for items with interesting colors, weights, textures, and sizes. The person may enjoy sorting and touching the things in this box. You and the staff can use it to trigger memories. Include a card that gives information about the items: "This is an old-fashioned apple corer like the one Mother used when she made apple butter for her five children," "Dad wore these dancing shoes until he was seventy."

Avoid too much excitement. Your arrival, news, and conversation may overexcite the impaired person and could precipitate a catastrophic reaction.

Do things that show that you are interested in his new home. Walk around it together, read the bulletin board to him, talk to his roommate or other residents and staff. Remind him to smell the flowers and see the birds when you walk around outside.

Help him care for himself. Eat a meal together, do his hair, rub his back, hold hands, help him get some exercise. Bring a treat that you can eat together while you are there. Avoid bringing food the staff must store. If the person has difficulty eating, you may want to come at mealtimes and help feed him. If other confused or upset residents interrupt your visit, you may be able to tell them gently but clearly not to talk with you now. If necessary, ask where there is a more private place for you to visit. Sometimes visits go more smoothly if you include one or two other residents in a simple activity.

If he enjoys it and if it does not precipitate a catastrophic reaction, take along children (one at a time) or a pet (ask the staff in advance). Seeing the people in a home is usually helpful for children. You can prepare the child by talking about the things he might see, such as catheters or intravenous tubes, and explaining that they help such people maintain their bodily functions.

Sometimes a person is so ill that he cannot talk or recognize you or respond to you. It is hard to know what to say to such a person. Try holding hands, rubbing the person's back, or singing. One minister said this about his visits:

"I've grown in these visits. I am so used to doing, doing, doing and there is nothing I can do for these people. I've learned to just sit, to just share being and not to feel I have to do or talk or entertain."

Sharing family life and loving a person who is in an institution and who is in the late stages of a dementing illness are not easy, but perhaps you will find your own meaning in doing so, as this man has.

Your Own Adjustment

You also will have changes in your life when a family member has moved to a nursing home. If the person lived with you, and especially if he is your spouse, the adjustment may be difficult. You may be tired from the efforts of arranging for the placement and, on top of your fatigue, you may feel sad at the changes that have happened. The move to a nursing home may intensify your feelings of grief and loss. At the same time you may wish that you could somehow have kept the person at home, and you may feel guilty that this was not possible. You may have mixed feelings of relief and sorrow, guilt and anger. It *is* a relief not to have to carry the burden of care, to be able to sleep or read uninterrupted. Still, you probably wish things were different and that you could have continued to care for this person yourself.

Families often tell us that in the first few days they feel lost. Without the usual demands of caring for a sick person, they cannot decide what to do with themselves. At first you may not be able to sleep through the night or relax enough to watch television.

The trips to the nursing home may be tiring, especially if the home is some distance from where you live. The visits may be depressing. Sometimes confused people are temporarily worse until they adjust to a new setting, and this can upset you. Sometimes, too, the other people in the home are depressing to see.

Nursing home staff members are geared to provide care for many people and you may not feel that your loved one is getting the individual care that you would like. Other things about the home or the staff may upset you. It's not unusual for family members to feel angry with the nursing home staff from time to time. If you are upset with the home or the staff you have a right to discuss your concerns with them, to be given answers, and not to jeopardize the patient's care or status in the home by doing this. It is against federal law for a facility to discharge a resident because his family raised questions about his care.

If there is a social worker in the home, she may help you work out your concerns. If there is not, discuss your concerns in a calm, matter-of-fact way with the administrator or the director of nursing.

Often things are better after placement, especially when they have been difficult at home. With other people responsible for daily care, you and the patient can relax and enjoy each other. Since you are not always tired, and can get away from the person's irritating behaviors, you may be able to relax and enjoy your relationship for the first time in a long while.

If other family members do not visit, it may be because they find it very hard to face visiting in a nursing home or don't know what to talk about. If someone in your family reacts this way, try to understand that this may be their way of grieving and you may not be able to change them.

Sometimes family members spend many hours at the nursing home, helping with the patient. Only you can decide how much time you should spend visiting. Ask yourself if part of your reason for being there has to do with your loneliness and grief, and might it be better if you spent less time there so the resident can make his adjustment to his new home.

Time does pass, and gradually the acute phase of adjustment also passes. As time goes on you will settle into a routine of visits. It is natural for you gradually to build a life apart from the person who has changed so much.

When Problems Occur in the Nursing Home

Sometimes serious problems about patient care do arise.

Mr. Rosen says, "My father has Alzheimer's disease and we had to put him in a nursing home. He got terribly sick and was transferred to a hospital, where they said his condition was made worse because he was dehydrated. Apparently the home failed to give him enough fluid. I feel like I am guilty of not checking up on this and I feel like I can't send him back to a home that neglects him."

As you know, people with dementing illnesses can be difficult to care for, especially in the late stages of the disease. If Mr. Rosen complains to the nursing home staff, he may only make them angry; if he tries to move his father to another home, he may find there are no other homes that are any better or that will accept a person with Alzheimer's disease or who is receiving Medicaid.

The dilemma you, Mr. Rosen, and many other families face lies not so much with one home but with national policy, value systems, federal training budgets, and so forth. These things are gradually changing through the efforts of organizations such as the Alzheimer's Association and the National Citizens Coalition for Nursing Home Reform.

We hope you will not encounter problems like this. If you do encounter problems, first take time to consider what kind of care you can reasonably expect. You should expect that the person be kept as well as possible, well fed and hydrated, protected from obvious risks, and clean and comfortable. Concurrent illness should be recognized and patients watched for drug reactions and interactions.

However, people with dementia are difficult to care for and sometimes the facility can be "wrong if they do and wrong if they don't." It is often not possible to treat completely every condition or solve every problem. For example, allowing a person to walk independently may be good for his heart, fitness, and self-confidence but may result in a fall. Asking the staff about the risks and benefits of the care they are providing can help you decide what risks you are willing to take.

Staff problems are a frequent cause of inadequacy in care. A facility cannot give the kind of individual care to one person that you could give at home. However, if there are not enough staff members to keep residents clean, comfortable, and fed, and their medical needs monitored, then something is wrong. The National Citizens Coalition for Nursing Home Reform publishes information about laws governing nursing home quality. Reading this material will help you judge what you can expect from a home.

Talk over your concerns honestly but calmly with the administrator, director of nursing, or social worker and offer her the information you have about the care of people with dementia. How do they respond? Do they thank you for talking to them and say they will take care of the problem or do they make excuses or brush you off? If a physician or other professional should be aware of the problem, ask for that person's support in correcting the situations.

Mr. Rosen said, "The doctor at the hospital was so helpful. He called the nursing home and talked to them, explained that people with dementia can easily become dehydrated and should be watched."

If this does not solve the problem, contact the Alzheimer's Association chapter and the local nursing home ombudsman (usually in the office on aging). Both have resources to help you. As a final resort, report the problem to the state nursing home inspector's office. However, problems are often most successfully solved by working informally with the administrator and staff of the home.

The problem may be that the staff needs more information about how to care for people with dementia. The Alzheimer's Association has information about training resources. Encourage all levels of staff, from the nurses and administrator to the aides, to get training.

It is against the law to discharge a person because the family has made a complaint. It is also against the law to mistreat a patient whose family has complained. You must closely monitor the care your family member receives.

Sexual Issues in Nursing Homes

Sometimes confused residents in nursing homes undress themselves in public, masturbate, or make advances to staff members or other residents. The sexual needs and behaviors of residents in nursing homes are a controversial issue. Sexual behavior in a nursing home differs in significant ways from such behavior at home: it no longer is a private matter, but in one way or another has an impact on the staff, other residents, and the families of residents; and it raises the ethical issue of whether a person who is impaired can or should retain the right to make sexual decisions for himself.

While our culture seems to be saturated with talk about sex, it is the sexuality of the young and beautiful that is being discussed. Most of us are uncomfortable considering the sexuality of the old, the unattractive, the handicapped, or those with dementia. Nursing home staff members also often feel uncomfortable.

If the nursing home staff reports inappropriate behavior to you, remember that much of the behavior that at first seems sexual is really behavior of disorientation and confusion. You and the nursing home staff can work together to help the person know where he is, when he can use the toilet, and where he can undress. Often all that is needed is to say, "It isn't time to go to bed yet. We'll put your pajamas on later." Distractions, such as offering a glass of juice, are helpful.

Confused persons may become close friends with another resident, often without a sexual relationship. Friendship is a universal need that does not stop when one has a dementia. Occasionally one hears stories about people getting in bed with other residents in a nursing home. This is not hard to understand when we consider that most of us have shared a bed with someone for many years and have enjoyed the closeness this sharing brings.

The confused person may not realize where he is or whom he is with. He may not realize that he is not in his own bed. He may think that he is with his spouse. Remember that nursing homes can be lonely places where there is not much opportunity for being held and loved. How you respond to such an incident depends on your attitudes and values and on the response of the nursing home.

Some nursing home residents masturbate. The staff usually ignores such behavior, which is usually done in the person's room. If it occurs in public the person should be quietly returned to his room.

Flirting is a common and socially acceptable behavior for men and women. In a nursing home a person may flirt to reinforce old social roles. It makes a person feel younger and more attractive. Tragically, the dementia may cause the person to do this clumsily, making offensive remarks or inappropriate gestures.

When the staff are trained to remind the person matter-of-factly and kindly that this behavior is not acceptable, it seldom remains a problem. Residents can be provided with other opportunities to reexperience their social roles.

THE VETERANS ADMINISTRATION

The Department of Veterans Affairs is obligated to serve people with service-related illnesses first, and other veterans as the space and the availability of services permit. Occasionally a person with dementia will be admitted to a VA long-term care hospital but may be discharged later. A few VA facilities also offer respite or family support services. In some cases the VA will pay for six months of care in a community facility. Policies vary with each Veterans Administration hospital. What is available in one area may not be available in another. Your Congressional representative may be able to help you obtain services through the VA.

STATE MENTAL HOSPITALS

Occasionally a person with a dementing illness exhibits behaviors that are so difficult to manage that no nursing home will accept him. Perhaps the person has hit or harmed other residents. Such a patient may be referred to the geriatric unit of a state mental hospital.

You may have heard that care in state mental hospitals is poor. A few state hospitals deserve their bad reputation. However, some do provide good care, and most are doing the best they can within their limitations.

Find out how your hospital is regarded by local psychiatrists, psychologists, and the Mental Health Association.

Most states have been mandated by the legislature to reduce their mental hospital populations. These hospitals have experienced drastic budget cuts. They may be reluctant to accept new patients. These factors may mean that there is no place for your family member to go. Fortunately, there are things you can do.

Often, severe behavior problems can be reduced with skilled psychiatric intervention. A combination of low doses of medication and a staff trained to work with these people can make a big difference.

Some states have programs designed to help impaired people avoid state hospital placement if possible, by mobilizing other resources to address these people's needs. Such programs may be staffed by psychiatrists, nurses, and social workers. Their staff may be able to evaluate the person's problem, prescribe medication, and train nursing home staff. If such a team is not available in your state, seek the help of your physician, social worker, clergyman, and elected representatives to mobilize the resources needed to help your family member. The Alzheimer's Association may be able to recommend experts who can teach specialized patient care to the nursing home staff. Also, your state nursing home ombudsman can advocate for improved nursing home care, which reduces patients' agitation.

If a nursing home attempts to discharge a person on the grounds that his behavior is evidence of mental illness, be sure that the person has been given a primary diagnosis of Alzheimer's disease or a related disorder and enlist the Alzheimer's Association and your Congressional representative to help you.

State hospitals usually require that families support the person. Their financial restrictions can be severe; find out all that you can.

A few state mental hospitals have opened dementia units where people with severe behavior problems are treated. Some are excellent programs and have had dramatic success in reducing problem behaviors, such as hitting or injuring other patients.

You can continue to visit and be involved with a family member who is in a state hospital.

17

BRAIN DISORDERS AND THE CAUSES OF DEMENTIA

SOMETIMES THE BRAIN does not work as it should. The problem may be called retardation, dyslexia, dementia, or psychosis. It may be caused by an injury to the brain, a genetic condition, chemicals in the environment that damage the brain, interruption of the supply of oxygen to the brain, or many other things. In this chapter we will explain how dementia differs from other problems of the brain and describe some of the most common causes of dementia.

DEMENTIA

Doctors and scientists group the different things that can go wrong with the brain by their symptoms. Just as fever, coughing, vomiting, and dizziness are symptoms of several different diseases, memory loss, confusion, personality change, and problems with speaking are also symptoms of several diseases.

Dementia is the medical term for a group of symptoms. It describes a decline in several areas of intellectual ability sufficiently severe to interfere with daily functioning in a person who is awake and alert (not drowsy, intoxicated, or unable to pay attention). This decline in intellectual functioning means a loss of several kinds of mental processes, which may include mathematical ability, vocabulary, abstract thinking, judgment, speaking, or physical coordination. It may include changes in personality. "Not feeling quite as sharp as you used to" does not mean that one is developing a dementia. The person's ability must decline from what was normal for him. Dementia is different from mental retardation, in which a person has been impaired since infancy.

The symptoms of dementia can be caused by many diseases. Some of these diseases are treatable; some are not. In some, the dementia can be stopped; in some it can be reversed; in others it cannot be changed. Some of these diseases are rare; others are more common, but do not usually cause dementia. Do not assume that a dementia is the inevitable result of having these diseases. A *partial* list of the conditions that can cause dementia follows:

Metabolic disorders
    Thyroid, parathyroid, or adrenal gland dysfunction
    Liver or kidney dysfunction
    Certain vitamin deficiencies, such as vitamin B_{12} deficiency
Structural problems of the brain
    Normal pressure hydrocephalus (abnormal flow of spinal fluid)
    Brain tumors
    Subdural hematoma (bleeding beneath the skull, which results in collections of blood that press on the brain)
    Trauma (injuries to the brain)
    Hypoxia and anoxia (insufficient oxygen)
Infections
    Tuberculosis
    Syphilis
    Fungal, bacterial, and viral infections of the brain, such as meningitis or encephalitis
    Acquired immune-deficiency syndrome (AIDS)
Toxins (poisons)
    Carbon monoxide
    Drugs
    Metal poisoning
    Alcohol (Scientists disagree about whether alcohol can cause dementia.)
Degenerative diseases (causes generally unknown)
    Alzheimer's disease
    Friedreich's ataxia
    Huntington's disease
    Parkinson's disease
    Pick's disease
    Progressive supranuclear palsy
    Wilson's disease
Vascular (blood vessel) disease
    Stroke or multi-infarct disease
    Binswanger's disease

    Autoimmune diseases
      Temporal arteritis
      Lupus erythematosus
    Psychiatric disorders
      Depression
      Schizophrenia
    Multiple sclerosis

Korsakoff's syndrome causes an impairment only in memory and not in other mental functions. It looks like a dementing illness but, because it affects only one area of mental function, it is not a true dementia.

Most research indicates that about 50 percent of the cases of dementia are caused by Alzheimer's disease, 20 percent are caused by multi-infarct disease, and 20 percent are caused by a combination of Alzheimer's disease and multi-infarct disease. About 10 percent of the cases of dementia are caused by one or another of the remaining conditions.

Alzheimer's Disease

Alzheimer's disease was first described by a German physician, Alois Alzheimer, in 1907 and the condition was named for him. The disease Alzheimer originally described occurred in a woman in her fifties and was called *presenile dementia*. Neurologists now agree that the dementia that occurs in the elderly is the same as or similar to the presenile condition. It is usually called senile dementia of the Alzheimer's type (SDAT), dementia of the Alzheimer type (DAT), or Alzheimer's disease (AD).

The symptoms of the disease usually are a gradual, though sometimes imperceptible, decline in many areas of intellectual ability and an accompanying physical decline. Early in the illness only the memory may be noticeably impaired. The person is more than a little forgetful. She may have difficulty learning new skills or difficulty with tasks that require abstract reasoning or calculation, such as math. She may have trouble on the job or may not enjoy reading as much as she used to. Her personality may change or she may become depressed.

Later, impairments in both language and motor abilities are seen. At first the person will be unable to find the right word for things or will use the wrong word, but she will gradually become unable to express herself. She will also have increasing trouble understanding explanations. She may give up reading or stop watching television. She may have increasing difficulty doing tasks that once were easy for her. Her handwriting may change or she may walk with a stoop or shuffle or become clumsy. She may get lost easily, forget that she has turned on the stove, misunderstand what is going on, show poor judgment. She may have changes in her personality or uncharacteristic outbursts of anger. She will be unable to plan responsibly for herself. Families often do not notice the beginnings of language and motor problems, but as the disease progresses all of these symptoms will become apparent.

Late in the illness the person becomes severely impaired, incontinent, and unable to walk or may fall frequently. She may be unable to say more than one or two words, and may recognize no one or only one or two people. She will need nursing care from you or from professionals. She will be physically disabled as well as intellectually impaired.

Alzheimer's disease usually leads to death in about seven to ten years, but it can progress more quickly (three to four years) or more slowly (as much as fifteen years). Occasionally Alzheimer's disease progresses slowly for years and then more rapidly. The relatively stable periods are sometimes called "plateaus." Typically the disease is slowly but relentlessly progressive.

Under a microscope, changes can be seen in the structure of the brain of a person who suffered from Alzheimer's disease. These include abnormally large numbers of structures called neuritic plaques and neurofibrillary tangles (see Chapter 18). This is clearly an injury to the brain itself. A diagnosis of Alzheimer's disease can be made on the basis of the type of symptoms, the way the symptoms progress over time, the absence of any other cause for the condition, and a compatible CAT scan. However, a final diagnosis of Alzheimer's disease rests on the presence of these specific abnormal structures (neuritic plaques and neurofibrillary tangles) in the brain tissue. A brain biopsy is the only way of making this determination. The biopsy is done by removing a piece of skull bone and taking out a small piece of brain tissue. The removal of this small amount of tissue has no effect on mental function. Brain biopsies are not routinely done at present because no treatment for the disease is available even if a diagnosis is made. This may change as research in dementia progresses.

Multi-Infarct or Vascular Dementia

In the past, dementing illnesses of old age were thought to be caused by *hardening of the arteries* of the brain. We now know that this is not the case. In multi-infarct dementia, repeated strokes destroy small areas of the brain. The cumulative effect of this damage leads to a dementia.

Multi-infarct dementias affect several functions, such as memory, coordination, or speech, but the symptoms differ somewhat depending on what areas of the brain are being damaged.

Multi-infarct dementias generally progress in a step-like way. You may be able to look back and recall that the person was worse after a specific time (instead of the gradual, imperceptible decline in Alzheimer's disease). Then she may not seem to get worse for a period, or she may even appear to get a little better. Some multi-infarct dementias progress as time passes; others may not get any worse for years. Some multi-infarct dementias may be stopped by preventing further strokes; in others the progression cannot be stopped.

Sometimes the cause of the repeated strokes can be identified and treated, and further damage prevented. Recent evidence suggests that low doses of aspirin may slow the progression of the disease. Ask your doctor.

Some people may have both Alzheimer's disease and multi-infarct disease.

Depression

Depression is a treatable cause of dementia. In a study of patients seen at the Johns Hopkins Hospital, about one-quarter of those who had symptoms of dementia were depressed. Eighty-two percent of patients with dementia caused by depression got better when the patient received treatment for the depression. Occasionally a physician may not recognize dementia caused by depression. The symptoms of the depression are usually easily recognizable when they cause dementia.

People with Alzheimer's disease or multi-infarct dementia also often have symptoms of depression, such as tearfulness, hopelessness, poor appetite, restlessness, or refusal to do activities previously enjoyed. These people usually have been forgetful and had problems with language and motor skills, which suggests that they have both depression and Alzheimer's disease or multi-infarct dementia.

Whenever a person with a memory problem is depressed, she should be evaluated to determine whether the depression is the cause of her dementia or vice versa. *Her depression should be treated whether or not she has an irreversible dementia.* Do not allow a physician to dismiss depression. However, keep in mind that while the person's depression may improve, her memory problems may not.

Treating a depression even when the person also has an irreversible dementia is important. It often relieves her misery, helps her enjoy life, improves her appetite, and can reduce annoying behaviors.

Binswanger's Disease

Binswanger's disease (sometimes called leukoariosis) is an uncommon vascular (blood vessel–related) dementia. It can be identified on an MRI or CT scan and at autopsy. It is probably caused by sustained high blood pressure. The diagnosis has been made more frequently since MRI scans became available, but experts have not yet developed a standard set of criteria for making the diagnosis and the implications of this diagnosis are being debated. At present, controlling high blood pressure is the only specific treatment available and it is not known whether this slows the progression of the disease.

AIDS

AIDS (acquired immune-deficiency syndrome) first appeared in the late 1970s. We now know that it is caused by a virus: the human immunodeficiency virus (HIV). The virus attacks the immune system, making it unable to fight off other diseases; it is the other diseases that kill the person. This virus can be spread through sexual contact, contact with infected blood, and the use of hypodermic needles previously used by someone infected with the virus.

All blood used for transfusions in the United States is tested for the virus, so transfusions are safe. Those most at risk of contracting the disease are people with multiple sexual partners, intravenous drug users, and children born to infected people. Since young adults are more likely to engage in these behaviors, AIDS usually afflicts young and middle-aged people, although cases are now occurring in elderly people.

AIDS often causes a dementia. We do not know how frequently this happens, but it is suspected that more than half of the people with AIDS may suffer impairment in thinking at some time during their illness. AIDS dementia occurs when HIV infects the brain. There is some evidence that the AIDS virus specifically attacks certain types of brain cells.

Because of their weakened immune system, AIDS patients may also develop parasitic, fungal, bacterial, or other viral infections of the brain. These too can cause dementia and delirium (see p. 288); the medications used to treat these infections can also cause delirium.

Unfortunately, there is not yet any cure for AIDS, although treatments have been developed that appear to slow the growth of the virus. Much of the care AIDS victims need is similar to the care required by victims of other dementias.

A few nursing homes are accepting people with AIDS. Other patients' families may be alarmed if a person with AIDS is near their family member. Unlike colds or flu, AIDS is difficult to transmit. The virus cannot survive outside of certain body fluids, such as blood, so it cannot be transmitted on toilet seats or by casual touching. It is not airborne. If your family member is in a nursing home that accepts AIDS patients, be sure that the staff has been trained to prevent disease transmission, and learn about the disease yourself. Remember that those patients' families are also dealing with dementia, an imminent death, and heartbreak.

OTHER BRAIN DISORDERS

There are several other mental conditions that are not dementias.

Delirium

The term *delirium* describes another set of symptoms that can have various causes. Delirium is often confused with dementia. Like the person with dementia, the delirious patient may be forgetful or disoriented. Unlike a demented person, *the delirious person shows a changed level of consciousness*. She may have a reduced ability to shift attention, focus attention, or sustain attention; sometimes attention is heightened rather than diminished. Other symptoms of delirium may include misinterpretation of reality, false ideas, or hallucinations; incoherent speech; sleepiness in the daytime or wakefulness at night; and increased or decreased physical (motor) activity. Symptoms of delirium often develop over a few hours or days. They tend to vary through the day.

Older people who do not have dementing illnesses may show symptoms—often intermittent—of impaired alertness, confusion, or memory problems. This may be a delirium caused by some other illness or by medication. Such a delirium should be regarded as a symptom, and the causative disease should be identified and treated, if possible.

People who have a dementia are more likely than other people to develop a delirium in addition to the dementia. You may observe a sudden worsening in a person who has other problems such as constipation, the flu, an infection, or even a slight cold. The complications of conditions like prostate cancer, diabetes, heart failure, chronic lung disease, or other serious illnesses also often cause a delirium.

The person with a delirium may become more irritable, seem more confused and drowsy, and be less alert. She may become incontinent, agitated, or fearful. She may become apathetic. You may notice an increase or decrease in activity level, a decreased level of alertness, or an increase or decrease in the amount of movement or motor activity. Visual hallucinations are common in delirium. Such changes are sometimes assumed to be a worsening of the dementia, and the underlying problem then goes untreated. Always consider the possibility of an illness and delirium when you observe a sudden change in behavior. Too much medication, or medication interactions, can also cause a delirium, even weeks after the medication was begun.

Senility, Chronic Organic Brain Syndrome, Acute or Reversible Organic Brain Syndromes

The word *senile* merely means *old*. Thus, *senility* does not describe a disease, and the term is considered by many people to be derogatory or prejudicial.

Chronic organic brain syndrome and *acute or reversible organic brain syndromes* are terms used by some to refer to those dementias that could not be treated (chronic) and to deliriums that respond to treatment (acute), respectively. These terms are no longer used because they are not specific and because they include implications of prognosis. We hope that in time there will be no chronic brain syndromes.

TIA

TIA stands for *transient ischemic attack*. This is a temporary impairment of brain function that is due to an insufficient supply of blood to part of the brain. The person may be unable to speak, or may have slurred speech. She may be weak or paralyzed, dizzy or nauseated. These symptoms usually last only a few minutes or hours, then the person recovers. This is in contrast to a stroke which may have the same symptoms but after which some deficit remains. Very small deficits may not be noticeable. TIAs should be regarded as warnings of stroke and should be reported to your doctor.

Localized Brain Injuries

Damage can happen to the brain or head and temporarily or permanently affect either small or greater parts of the brain. This can be caused by brain tumors, strokes, or head injuries. Unlike dementia, such damage may not be generalized, although it may affect more than one mental function. The symptoms can tell a neurologist just where the damage is. This is called a *focal* (localized) *brain lesion* (injury). When the damage is widespread the symptoms may be those of dementia.

Major *stroke*, which causes such things as sudden paralysis of one side of the body, drooping of one side of the face, or speech problems, is an injury to part of the brain. Strokes can be caused by a blood clot blocking vessels in the brain or by a blood vessel bursting and causing bleeding in the brain. Often the brain cells are injured or impaired by swelling but can recover when the swelling goes down. It may be that other parts of the brain can gradually learn to do the jobs of damaged sections of the brain.

People who have had a stroke may get better. Rehabilitation training is important for people who have had a stroke. The chance of having another stroke can be reduced by good medical management.

Head Injuries

Head injuries can destroy brain tissue directly or by causing bleeding within the brain. Sometimes blood collects between the skull and the brain, forming a pool of blood. This puts pressure on the brain cells and damages them. It is called a *subdural hematoma*. Even mild falls can cause such bleeding.

People with dementing diseases are vulnerable to falls and may not be able to tell you about them. If you suspect that a person has banged her head, she should be seen promptly by a doctor, because treatment can prevent permanent damage. The bleeding beneath the skull may not occur in the same place as the head was hit. Bleeding may be slow, and symptoms may not appear until hours or days after the fall. Bleeding inside the skull may occur on the side opposite the injury.

Anoxia or Hypoxia

When a person suffers a heart attack, the heart may stop pumping blood for a period of time before the person is resuscitated. During that time the brain may not get enough oxygen. This can result in brain damage that looks similar to Alzheimer's disease, except that it does not get progressively worse and usually does not affect language or the ability to carry out physical actions. People with hypoxic brain damage need much the same care as people with Alzheimer's disease or multi-infarct dementia.

─── 18 ───

RESEARCH IN DEMENTIA

WE HAVE REACHED an exciting point in research into dementia. Not long ago, most people assumed that dementia was the natural result of aging, and only a few pioneers were interested in studying it. In the last twenty years that has changed. It is now known that:

1. dementia is not the natural result of aging;
2. dementia is caused by specific, identifiable diseases;
3. diagnosis is important to identify treatable conditions; and
4. a proper evaluation is important in the management of diseases that at present are not curable.

Today an increasing amount of research is focused on the dementing illnesses. With new tools for study we can get a much clearer look at what goes on in the brain. Because of better public understanding, there is a growing demand for solutions.

The federal budget for dementia research increased from $4 million in 1976 to $120 million in 1989. Most of the current research is supported by the National Institute of Neurological Disorders and Stroke (NINDS), the National Institute of Mental Health (NIMH), the National Institute on Aging (NIA), and the Veterans Administration (VA). The NIA has funded Alzheimer's Disease Research Centers, which pull together talented researchers, and much exciting work is taking place in these centers. Some additional research funds are contributed by nongovernmental sources, such as foundations and drug companies. However, many potentially productive research projects go unfunded each year. (In contrast, the National Cancer Institute is funded at about $1.6 billion per year and the National Heart, Lung and Blood Institute at about $1.1 billion per year.)

UNDERSTANDING RESEARCH

The increased public awareness of Alzheimer's disease has been accompanied by a number of announcements of "breakthroughs" and "cures." Some of these are important building blocks in the search for a cure, but each breakthrough, in itself, is but one small step in the direction of a cure.

Understanding the therapeutic implications of the research can challenge scientists and families alike. Here are some things you need to know about research to help you understand what you read.

- Research scientists need to make their findings public, and the public wants to know what researchers are finding. The enthusiasm of the press in publicizing these findings plays an important role in maintaining public support for research funds, yet families are discouraged when the press makes announcements of "breakthroughs" that turn out to be disappointing.
- Science must go down some blind alleys. For a while, something will look like a good lead, and families and scientists will be excited. Then the trail will go cold. This is frustrating, but each time we rule out something, there is one less avenue to investigate. Many clues, like the pieces of a jigsaw puzzle, will eventually fit together to form the answer, but the pieces often do not go where we thought they would.
- Conditions like Alzheimer's disease are different from infectious diseases, such as diphtheria, chicken pox, or polio. Each infectious disease has one cause, an infectious agent, leading to one outcome. So far, no single cause for Alzheimer's disease has been identified. Alzheimer's might be a family of diseases, like cancer. This would explain the variability of the disease from one patient to another and the variety of possible causes. It may take a combination of several triggers for a person to develop the disease. If this turns out to be the case, researchers will have to track down several causes and treatments.
- The study of the brain is unlike the study of any other organ. Scientists can study the structure of other organs under a microscope and often can observe a living organ at work. The brain's function cannot be deduced from its appearance and the chemical messengers that do its work quickly dissipate when the brain dies. Until the development of the PET scan (see p. 301), scientists had no way of observing the

workings of the brain. The brain is extremely complex, it works very quickly, and its many parts interact at multiple levels.

- It is essential that studies eliminate the influence of other factors. Sometimes when a new technique or drug is tried, the patient gets better. Sometimes families who participate in drug studies believe that their family member improved while taking the drug. There are many reasons why this happens, from wishful thinking on the part of clinicians and families to temporarily cheering up the patient or brightening his thinking. This is called the placebo effect and it is quite common. Good studies of drugs are carefully designed to eliminate the possibility that other factors cause improvement.

- Preliminary studies are often done on small groups of people. The small size of the sample increases the chances that extraneous factors confuse the outcome. If you hear of exciting results from a small-group study, remember that these results may or may not be confirmed by tests on a large group or tests done by another researcher.

- The presence of two factors together does not mean that one causes the other. Both A and B might be found in the brains of dementia patients, but this does not mean that A caused B; A and B might both have been caused by an unknown factor, C. It may be years before the relationships among these factors are understood.

- The drugs that may affect the brain of an Alzheimer's victim are likely to cause serious side effects throughout the body. Sometimes research on such drugs must be stopped because their potential damage to other organs outweighs their therapeutic value.

- You may have heard of studies done with laboratory animals. Animal research allows scientists to learn more about how the living brain works and to test drugs that cannot safely be tested on humans. The federal government has laws to assure that animals are treated humanely. Researchers who work with animals take into account the ways in which the animals' reactions are similar to human reactions and the ways in which they are not. Giving large doses of a chemical to an animal with a short life span magnifies the chances of seeing a relationship, if one exists, between the chemical and a disease.

- The Alzheimer's Association releases reports to the chapters on major breakthroughs and on highly publicized claims. These reports are drafted by the association's Medical and Scientific Advisory Board and are intended to provide families with accurate information. If you hear of research you have questions about, your chapter can telephone the Chicago office of the association and usually obtain good information from one of the association's consulting scientists.

Bogus Cures

Some unscrupulous individuals promote "cures" that can be expensive, dangerous, or ineffective, or that unfairly raise hopes. The Alzheimer's Association has a list of some of the fraudulent products and treatments and can advise you about which treatments are generally believed by doctors to be of little or no value. If a treatment makes a claim of benefit or cure which exceeds what the Alzheimer's Disease Research Centers or the Alzheimer's Association says is possible, we urge you to check it out thoroughly before participating.

RESEARCH IN MULTI-INFARCT DEMENTIA AND STROKE

Multiple strokes are the second most common cause of dementia. If ways can be found to prevent these strokes or to improve rehabilitation, many thousands of people would benefit.

Scientists are seeking to determine how hypertension, obesity, diet, smoking, heart disease, and other factors increase a person's vulnerability to stroke or multi-infarct dementia. They are studying the relationship between larger strokes and the multiple strokes that cause dementia. At present, the best way to prevent stroke is to eliminate the risk factors.

Researchers are also studying which areas of the brain are most likely to be damaged and what changes in brain chemistry take place after a stroke. They are looking at how, when, and to what extent rehabilitative training helps a person. They are examining the effectiveness of drugs in preventing stroke, dilating blood vessels, increasing the oxygen supply to the brain, and preventing blood clotting. Some studies are evaluating the effects of surgery to remove atherosclerotic plaque from the arteries that deliver blood to the brain.

Scientists are examining the relationship of stroke, depression, and the dementia that accompanies depression. They have found that it is important to treat depression when it occurs following a stroke.

RESEARCH IN ALZHEIMER'S DISEASE

Structural Changes in the Brain

When Alois Alzheimer looked at tissue taken from the brain of a woman who had the behavioral symptoms of dementia, he saw microscopic changes called neuritic (senile) plaques and neurofibrillary tangles. Similar structures are found in much smaller numbers in the brains of normal older people. Scientists are analyzing the structure and chemistry of these plaques and tangles for clues to their formation and their role in the disease.

Brain Cell Structure

The brain is made of billions of nerve cells, which carry out all the tasks of thinking, remembering, feeling emotion, directing body movement, and many others. Researchers have learned that a small area deep in the brain loses most of its cells when a person has Alzheimer's disease. The cells in this area look a little like trees with many branches reaching into the front and top of the brain. As the disease progresses, these cells gradually lose their branches and finally die. As the branches are lost, the cells gradually stop communicating with other brain cells, causing problems in thinking.

Neurotransmitters

Chemicals in the brain called *neurotransmitters* pass messages from one cell to the next. These neurotransmitters are made, used, and broken down within the brain. There are many different neurotransmitters for different types of cells and probably for different kinds of mental tasks. In some diseases, there is less than the normal amount of certain neurotransmitters. For example, a person with Parkinson's disease has abnormally low amounts of the neurotransmitter dopamine. The drug L-dopa increases the amount of dopamine and alleviates the person's symptoms.

Scientists have found that people with Alzheimer's disease have deficiencies in several neurotransmitters, particularly acetylcholine. Somatostatin, norepinephrine, serotonin, and corticotrophin-releasing factor may also be deficient. If a way could be found to increase the amount of acetylcholine and the other deficient neurotransmitters, the symptoms of Alzheimer's disease might be relieved.

Abnormal Proteins

The cells that make up the human body and the elements inside these cells are made up of proteins. The body takes food, breaks it down into amino acids, and then builds the proteins that it needs. Several lines of research are exploring the possibility that Alzheimer's disease results from abnormalities in some of these proteins.

Amyloid Protein

Abnormal deposits of a protein called amyloid are found in the brains of patients with Alzheimer's disease. Neuritic plaques (see page 294) have amyloid at the center and some patients have deposits of amyloid along blood vessels. The production of this protein is controlled by chromosome 21. It is not known how this protein is involved in the disease process.

Protein Abnormalities within Brain Cells

Brain cells contain other proteins that act like highways, by which chemicals travel within cells. Some patients with Alzheimer's disease appear to have either increased amounts or abnormal forms of these proteins. Among these are tau protein and MAP (microtubule-associated protein). One theory suggests that the systems of people with Alzheimer's disease cannot break down these proteins in the way they should. This might explain why there are accumulations of abnormal proteins in the brains of people who die from Alzheimer's disease.

Nerve Growth Factors

Cells within the brain and spinal cord (as well as nerve cells outside the central nervous system) develop in specific patterns that are directed by chemicals called nerve growth factors. Nerve cells outside the central nervous system (called peripheral nerves) can regrow or regenerate after an injury, but cells within the brain are thought not to have this ability. Scientists are studying whether nerve growth factors might be used to stimulate the replacement or regrowth of damaged nerves in the brains of people with Alzheimer's disease.

Transplants of Brain Tissue

Much excitement has been generated in recent years about the possibility of replacing damaged brain cells by transplanting new cells. Work in animals has shown that certain cells from fetuses or laboratory-grown cell cultures will grow and manufacture neurotransmitters when they are transplanted into animals with brain damage. Cells have been transplanted into the brains of a few people with Parkinson's disease. So far, this has had only limited success. It is not known whether this technique will be applicable for patients with Alzheimer's disease. Because some of the cells for tissue transplants are obtained from tissue taken from human fetuses, this has generated controversy. However, it is most important that research *on animals* be permitted to continue, to determine whether this procedure has any possibility of helping patients with Alzheimer's disease. It may be possible to grow the needed cells in a laboratory.

Drug Studies

Hundreds of drugs have been studied for their effect on Alzheimer's disease. Most of them will quickly be found to be ineffective or to have toxic side effects. A few will make the news because there is some preliminary evidence that they alleviate symptoms.

In the 1980s most of the drug research was focused on ways to increase the amount of the neurotransmitter acetylcholine in the brain. The brain uses chemical raw materials to manufacture acetylcholine within its cells. The acetylcholine then transmits its message to other brain cells. With the message received, these cells break down the used acetylcholine. This gives researchers several possible approaches: to increase the amount of acetylcholine in the brain by giving a medication containing it, to encourage increased manufacture of acetylcholine by brain cells, or to prevent the breakdown of the small amount of acetylcholine the brain is making.

Lecithin and choline, substances occurring in many foods, are known to be used by the body to make acetylcholine. Studies have been done in which lecithin has been given to groups of people with dementia, but the results are disappointing. Families often give people lecithin bought from a health food store, but there is no evidence that this has improved memory, mood, or behavior. More needs to be known about why acetylcholine appears to be in short supply in Alzheimer's disease.

In 1993 the Food and Drug Administration (FDA) approved the first specific medication for the treatment of Alzheimer's disease. This drug, tacrine (brand name Cognex®), has been studied extensively in the U.S. and elsewhere. These studies show that:

1. It is helpful to some people with Alzheimer's disease but a majority do not respond. Twenty percent of those started on the medicine show a noticeable improvement. Another 20 percent show improvement only on tests. There is no evidence, as of yet, that tacrine delays the progression of the disease. Clearly, it is not a cure.
2. Approximately 20 percent of people taking tacrine develop liver inflammation which goes away if the medication is decreased or stopped.
3. People show more improvement when they take the highest dosage. However, this dose causes nausea and vomiting in some individuals. Fortunately, it can be beneficial at less than the maximum dosage.

Metals

Aluminum has been found in larger than expected amounts in the brains of some people with Alzheimer's disease. Other metals, such as manganese, are known to be associated with other forms of dementia. It now seems most likely that the presence of aluminum is a result of whatever is causing the dementia rather than aluminum itself being a cause of dementia. People sometimes wonder if they should stop taking antacids or cooking with aluminum pans or using deodorant (all sources of aluminum). There is no evidence that their use is a cause of dementia. Studies of people who have been exposed to much larger amounts of aluminum indicate that exposure does not lead to dementia. Treatments that promote the elimination of aluminum from the body do not benefit patients with Alzheimer's disease, and some of these treatments have serious side effects.

Viruses

Some tentative research led scientists to suspect that a viral defect could be causing Alzheimer's disease. You may read about Creutzfeld-Jacob disease or Kuru. Both of these rare diseases have been studied because they cause dementia and appear to be transmitted by a viruslike agent.

Prions are living particles even smaller than viruses. It has been suggested that these particles might be a cause of Alzheimer's disease. While this has not been totally disproven, it now seems quite unlikely.

There have been many efforts to determine whether Alzheimer's disease is infectious, that is, whether it can be transmitted. At present there is no evidence to support the hypothesis that Alzheimer's disease is caused by a slow virus, prion, or other infectious organism.

Immunological Defects

The immune system is the body's defense against infection. Studies show that some of the proteins the body uses to fight infection are present in abnormally low levels in patients with Alzheimer's disease.

Sometimes the body's defense system, which is designed to attack outside cells such as disease organisms, goes awry and attacks cells in the body. One theory says this is what is happening in Alzheimer's disease. Numerous studies are being done which approach the problem from this angle.

Other studies are searching for the factor or factors (such as an injury, chemical toxin, or gene) that might set off an immune response. Some scientists hypothesize that if there is a faulty immune reaction, the body would produce antibodies. Their presence would give us a positive tool to diagnose the disease.

Head Trauma

Several studies report that Alzheimer's patients have had head injuries more often during their lives than people the same age who do not have Alzheimer's disease. Supporting this theory is the finding that some boxers develop a dementia similar to Alzheimer's disease and have tangles, but not plaques, in the brain. The condition is called the punch drunk, or *dementia pugilistica*, syndrome. This raises the possibility that subtle brain damage triggered by the head injury eventually leads to a more generalized cell death through immunological or other mechanisms.

One well-designed study has not confirmed the head injury theory. It seems unlikely that head trauma is the cause of Alzheimer's disease in most people.

EPIDEMIOLOGY

Epidemiology is the study of the distribution of diseases in large groups of people. The epidemiology of dementing illnesses may eventually show scientists a link between a dementing illness and something else as yet unknown—for example, a hereditary factor, diet in childhood, or the use of a medicine many years ago. If you have participated in research programs, you may have been asked many questions that don't seem in any way related to your problem, but these give researchers important epidemiologic information.

So far, Alzheimer's disease has been found in all groups of people whose members tend to live long enough to reach late life, when the risk is greater, but it may be less common in Japan than in Europe or North America. Epidemiological research is expensive and can take many years. However, studies now under way in the United States and other countries may yield valuable clues.

DOWN'S SYNDROME

People with Down's syndrome (a form of mental retardation) develop plaques and tangles similar to those in Alzheimer's disease as they reach their forties. They do not all develop the symptoms of Alzheimer's disease, although some do experience a further decline in intellectual function. Because Down's syndrome is known to be caused by an extra chromosome 21 or an extra piece of this chromosome, many scientists have been studying the role this chromosome might play in Alzheimer's disease.

OLD AGE

Living into very old age increases the risks of developing Alzheimer's disease. While an adult's risk of developing Alzheimer's disease is about 1–2 in 100 at age 65, at age 80 his risk is 1 in 5. But the statistics also mean that 4 out of 5 people at age 80 have normal or nearly normal intellectual function.

HEREDITY

Families often worry that this disease is inherited and that they or their children will develop it. We know that an adult's risk of developing Alzheimer's disease at age 65 is about 1–2 in 100, but the odds increase fourfold if a close relative has had the disease—to about 8 in 100. Recently, researchers studying family histories found a few families in which a few members in each generation had the disease. In these rare families the disease is clearly genetic and a family member's risk can be as great as 1 in 2. However, *this is not the case in most families that have one or even more members with the disease.*

If you are worried that you may belong to such a family, consult a genetic counselor at one of the Alzheimer's Disease Research Centers. Simply having more than one family member with the disease is *not* evidence of a familial predisposition to Alzheimer's disease. Some individuals have jumped to the conclusion that they are a high risk and have suffered unnecessary anguish because they did not have good information. If it turns out that you are at risk, you should make financial plans for yourself and your family well in advance.

As of 1994, linkages to 3 different chromosomes have been described. Abnormalities on chromosomes 21 and 14 are associated with the rare forms of Alzheimer's disease that begin in people in their 40s and 50s. The much more common late-life onset form of Alzheimer's disease is associated with a gene on chromosome 19 called APO-E. This gene directs the manufacture of a protein that carries cholesterol in the blood stream. Three normal forms of this gene exist: E_2, E_3, and E_4. People who inherit one or two copies of the E_4 gene have an increased likelihood of developing the disease. Researchers hope that the identification of the mechanisms by which APO-E genes interact with the nervous system will lead to effective treatments and prevention.

Even if an abnormality on a chromosome is eventually found to be a cause, this will not mean that the disease is always or even usually inherited. A genetic factor may mean only that people inherit a *tendency* to be more vulnerable to the disease, not that they will necessarily develop the disease. Additional triggers may still be necessary for the disease to develop.

To put this in perspective: most of us inherit risk factors for some disease—such as heart disease or cancer. We know that for these diseases there are additional precipitants, like diet, smoking, and exercise, over which we have some control. Researchers are seeking the possible precipitants of Alzheimer's disease.

GENDER

Some investigators believe that women are more prone to Alzheimer's disease than men but that men are more prone to multi-infarct dementia. This may be simply because men are more likely to develop vascular disease, while women tend to live longer and the incidence of Alzheimer's disease increases with age. Researchers are looking for clues to whether this is so.

PROMISING CLINICAL AND RESEARCH TOOLS

Neuropsychologists use a combination of questions, simple tasks, and observation to evaluate patients. They can identify the kinds of mental skills a person has lost and those he retains. With this knowledge, clinicians can devise individual plans that help a person use his remaining skills and that place minimal demands on his diminished abilities. Information from a neuropsychological examination helps a family understand why a person cannot do some things but can successfully do similar activities. Neuropsychology can also help to confirm a diagnosis and potentially could identify subtypes of Alzheimer's disease.

The PET (positron emission tomography) scan provides a picture of the brain at work. That is, the image it produces shows which areas of the brain are working hardest during a particular kind of mental activity. Like the CT and MRI scan (p. 15), it requires that the patient lie on an x-ray table. The patient is given a radioactive material that goes through the bloodstream into the brain. (This material is in a small dose and lasts in the body only a few minutes.) Special equipment measures the amount being used in each area of the brain.

The SPECT (single positron emission computerized tomography) scan is similar to the PET scan but is less expensive and may eventually be used in diagnosis.

These two scans provide scientists with information about how the brain is working and thus hold great potential for research. Because they have not been in use very long, not enough is known about the images a normal brain produces. Therefore, we do not yet know what is abnormal in Alzheimer's disease. We do not yet know whether these scans can identify early Alzheimer's disease.

It has long been known that different parts of the brain carry out different mental tasks (physical activity, talking, feeling emotions, etc.) and that still other parts coordinate these mental activities. By identifying what areas of the brain are afflicted most severely, neuropsychological evaluations and scans give researchers information about the disease and give clinicians and families information about how to provide good care.

KEEPING ACTIVE

People often wonder if keeping mentally alert and involved or maintaining physical exercise will prevent a person from developing a dementing illness. As far as is known, neither physical exercise nor keeping mentally active will prevent or alter the course of Alzheimer's disease. Activity will help to maintain general health and improve the quality of life. Some studies that did not differentiate among causes of dementia have produced misleading results about the effect of activity on dementia. Sometimes people seem to develop a dementia after they retire. Upon close examination, however, it usually appears that the early stages of a dementia were developing before the person retired and that this early, unidentified dementia may have been a factor in the person's decision to retire.

Many people wonder if continuing to exercise after Alzheimer's disease develops will slow the progress of the disease or help people remain active longer. While we know of no good scientific evidence to support this, we believe that common sense supports keeping active within realistic limits (see page 72).

THE EFFECT OF ACUTE ILLNESS ON DEMENTIA

Sometimes people appear to develop a dementia after a serious illness, hospitalization, or surgery. Again, as far as is known, these things do not affect or alter the course of Alzheimer's disease. Upon close examination it often is clear that the dementing illness had begun before the person had surgery or developed another disease. The stress of the acute illness and the tendency of people with a dementia to develop a delirium make the person's thinking worse, so his dementia is noticeable for the first time. Then his brain impairment will make it more difficult for him to adjust after the acute illness, making the dementia more apparent.

RESEARCH INTO THE DELIVERY OF SERVICES

Scientists are now focusing on Alzheimer's disease, multi-infarct disease, and stroke. In time we will learn to prevent or treat each disease. But research is not limited to the pursuit of treatments and cures. Also important are studies that tell us how to help the victims of these diseases live comfortable, satisfying lives despite their disease and studies that tell us how to assist the families who care for them. No one knows how long it will take to find a cure, but many experts suspect that it may take some time. Thus, this research is important, to help families and patients now.

We already know how to change the quality of life for some people with dementia: we can make changes that help them to function as well as possible, we can reduce their anxiety and fear, and we can make it possible for them to enjoy things sometimes. Researchers are studying the kinds of living arrangements that are best for those people with dementia who go into nursing homes and are seeking ways to help those who live at home function at their best. This is an exciting and rewarding field. Researchers have observed people who had previously paced, screamed, and struck out become relaxed and begin to participate in enjoyable activities. Even though we cannot cure these diseases, we can treat some symptoms and sometimes reduce suffering.

We know that families need help: day care, home respite, support groups, and other assistance. Researchers are studying how best to reach families, what things families need most, how to encourage families to use respite services, and the most cost-effective ways to provide respite. While it may seem that the answers to these questions are obvious, different kinds of families have different needs and people do not always do what researchers predict they would. Careful study will prevent money wasted on unnecessary services or services families do not know about.

PROTECTIVE FACTORS

Several studies suggest that estrogen, non-steroidal anti-inflammatory drugs (such as aspirin, ibuprofen), and even nicotine might protect against or delay the onset of Alzheimer's disease. This research is in the very early stages and is unlikely to make major contributions to the prevention, treatment, or delay of developing the disease.

Appendix 1. Further Reading

THERE ARE many good books, magazine and news articles, videocassettes, and television shows about dementia and Alzheimer's disease. This list includes only a sampling of the available materials. The National Council on the Aging (see Appendix 2) publishes an annotated bibliography. Professional journals review or list new materials.

The Alzheimer's Association publishes pamphlets and brochures and is developing a bibliography. Some of their brochures are aimed at nurses, police, and others who come in contact with people with dementia. Many chapters also publish materials. You can obtain these through your chapter office or by writing to the national office (see Appendix 2). Ask to see a complete list of the items they publish, because a local chapter may not have all the resources in stock.

FOR LAYPERSONS

Books

Personal Experience

Doernberg, M. *Stolen Mind: The Slow Disappearance of Ray Doernberg*. Chapel Hill, N.C.: Algonquin, 1989. In paperback; a wife's story.

Honel, R. W. *Journey with Grandpa: Our Family's Struggle with Alzheimer's Disease*. Baltimore: Johns Hopkins University Press, 1988. Told by a daughter-in-law; the family included children growing up at home.

Jury, M., and D. Jury. *Gramp: Photographs*. New York: Grossman, 1976. A pictorial account of a family's encounter with dementia. This book uses outdated terms for the illness.

Care

Coons, D., L. Metzlaar, A. Robinson, and B. Spencer. *A Better Life: Helping Family Members, Volunteers, and Staff Improve the Quality of Life of Nursing Home Residents Suffering from Alzheimer's Disease and Related Disorders*. Columbus, Ohio: The Source for Nursing Home Literature, 1986. Chapters 1–5 provide information for families planning nursing home placement and suggestions for effective visiting in a nursing home.

Gwyther, L. P. *Care of Alzheimer's Patients: A Manual for Nursing Home Staff.* ADRDA and AHCA, 1985. Although written for nursing home staff members, this book explains common behaviors.

Robinson, A., B. Spencer, and L. White. *Understanding Difficult Behaviors: Some Practical Suggestions for Coping with Alzheimer's Disease and Related Illnesses.* Ypsilanti, Mich.: Geriatric Education Center of Michigan, Michigan State University, 1988.

General

Aronson, M. K., ed. *Understanding Alzheimer's Disease: What It Is, How to Treat It, How to Cope with It.* New York: Scribners, 1988.

Cohen, D., and C. Eisdorfer. *The Loss of Self: A Family Resource for the Care of Alzheimer's Disease and Related Disorders.* New York: Norton, 1986.

Congress of the United States, Office of Technology Assessment. *Losing a Million Minds: Confronting the Tragedy of Alzheimer's Disease and Other Dementias.* Washington, D.C.: Government Printing Office, 1987. A source book that includes chapters on many issues.

Kushner, H. S. *When Bad Things Happen to Good People.* New York: Schocken, 1981.

Lewis, C. S. *A Grief Observed.* New York: Harper and Row, 1963.

The books by Kushner and Lewis are drawn from the authors' personal losses and place those experiences in the perspectives of their religions.

Reisberg, B. *A Guide to Alzheimer's Disease: For Families, Spouses and Friends.* New York: Free Press, 1983.

For Children

Guthrie, D. *Grandpa Doesn't Know It's Me: A Family Adjusts to Alzheimer's Disease.* New York: Human Sciences Press, 1986.

Magazine and News Articles

Many of the Alzheimer's Association chapters, as well as its national office, publish newsletters. These are valuable sources of information about current research and public policy, and they provide a network for the exchange of information among caregivers. Some chapters charge a small fee for their newsletter.

American Journal of Alzheimer's Care and Research, 470 Post Road, Weston, Mass. 02193. This bimonthly journal is for both family members and professionals.

In Foreign Languages

The first edition of *The 36-Hour Day* is available in the following translations. If you cannot obtain these through your local bookstore or the Alzheimer's Association, write to the publisher listed and ask for the names of foreign-language bookstores in your area that could order the book for you.

Danish: *36 timer i døgnet* (Hans Reitzels Forlag A/S, Nørre Søgade 35, Postboks 1073, DK-1008 Copenhagen, Denmark)

Dutch: *Een dag van 36 uur* (Wetenschappelijke uitgeverij Bunge BV, Postbus 13341, 3507 LH Utrecht, The Netherlands)

German: *Der 36-Stunden Tag* (Hans Huber AG, Medical Publisher and Bookseller, Länggass-Str. 76, Postfach, CH-3000, Berne 9, Switzerland)

Hebrew: *36 Sha'ot Biyemmama* (MELABEV, Geriatric Department, P.O. Box 293, Jerusalem 91002, Israel)

Italian: *Un Giorno di 36 ore* (Il Pensiero Scientifico Editore SRL, via Panama 48, I-00198 Rome, Italy)

Japanese: *Boke ga Okkotara* (The Simul Press, Inc., Kowa Bldg. No. 9, 1–8–10 Akasaka, Minato-Ku, Tokyo 107, Japan)

Norwegian: *Døgnet som aldri tar slutt* (Gyldendal Norsk Forlag, Universitetsgaten 16, P.b. 6860, St. Olavs Plass, Oslo 1, Norway)

Spanish: *Cuando el dia tiene 36 horas* (Editorial Pax-Mexico, Libreria Carlos Cesarman, S.A., Av. Cuauhtemoc No. 1434, Col. Santa Cruz Atoyac, Mexico 13, D.F.)

Swedish: *36-Timmarsdygnet* (Bokforlaget Naturoch Kultur Publishers, P.O. Box 27323, S-102 54 Stockholm, Sweden)

FOR PROFESSIONALS

There is an extensive literature on dementia in publications on medicine, psychiatry, neurology, gerontology, nursing, social work, public policy, long-term care, and other related subjects. Professionals will find the international literature helpful as well. *Losing a Million Minds* (full reference shown above) is an excellent reference resource (up to 1987), as are the books listed below.

Cummings, J. L., and D. F. Benson. *Dementia: A Clinical Approach*. Boston: Butterworth, 1983.

Edelson, J. S., and W. H. Lyons. *Institutional Care of the Mentally Impaired Elderly*. New York: Van Nostrand Reinhold, 1985.

Light, E., and B. D. Lebowitz, eds. *Alzheimer's Disease: Treatment and Family Stress*. Rockville, Md.: National Institute of Mental Health, 1989.

Lishman, W. A. *Organic Psychiatry: The Psychological Consequences of Cerebral Disorder*. Oxford: Blackwell Scientific Publications, 1987.

Mace, N. L., ed. *Dementia Care: Patient, Family, and Community*. Baltimore: Johns Hopkins University Press, 1990. A multidisciplinary book on clinical care.

Volicer, L., K. J. Fabiszewski, Y. L. Rheaume, and K. E. Lasch, eds. *Clinical Management of Alzheimer's Disease*. Rockville, Md.: Aspen Publishers, 1988.

Zgola, J. M. *Doing Things: A Guide to Programing Activities for Persons with*

Alzheimer's Disease and Related Disorders. Baltimore: Johns Hopkins University Press, 1987.

If you are a layperson exploring the professional literature, you can find most journals in university libraries. Begin with the references listed in *Losing a Million Minds* and *Dementia Care* (full references shown above).

Some community libraries have a computer hook-up to nearby university libraries and can obtain copies of articles from them for you. The literature on dementia has grown enormously in the past ten years; if you use a computer search, you will need to make your request narrow and specific.

Appendix 2. Organizations

MANY NATIONAL organizations have local or state chapters throughout the United States. Check your telephone directory.

Administration on Aging, 330 Independence Ave. S.W., Washington, D.C. 20201. This organization can provide the address of the office on aging and nursing home ombudsman nearest you.

Alliance of Information and Referral Systems, P.O. Box 3546, Joliet, Ill. 60434; tel. 815-744-6922

Alzheimer's Association, 70 E. Lake St., Suite 600, Chicago, Ill. 60601; tel. 800-621-0379, in Illinois 800-572-6037. Call or write them to find the chapter nearest you.

Alzheimer's Disease International, staffed through the Alzheimer's Association, 70 E. Lake St., Suite 600, Chicago, Ill. 60601; tel. 312-853-3060. An international organization of associations dedicated to the dementias. They will provide the addresses of member organizations in other countries.

American Association for Geriatric Psychiatry, P.O. Box 376-A, Greenbelt, Md. 20768; tel. 301-220-0952

American Association of Homes for the Aging, 1129 20th St. N.W., Suite 400, Washington, D.C. 20036; tel. 202-296-5960. The association of nonprofit nursing homes.

American Association of Retired Persons (AARP), 1909 K St. N.W., Washington, D.C. 20049; tel. 202-872-4700

American Cancer Society, 1599 Clifton Rd., Atlanta, Ga. 30329; tel. 404-320-3333

American Diabetes Association, P.O. Box 25757, 1660 Duke St., Alexandria, Va. 22313; tel. 703-549-1500

American Geriatrics Society, 770 Lexington Ave., Suite 400, New York, N.Y. 10021; tel. 212-308-1414. A professional association of geriatric physicians.

American Health Care Association, 1201 L St. N.W., Washington, D.C. 20005; tel. 202-842-4444. An association of for-profit and not-for-profit nursing homes; they have several publications.

American Heart Association, 7320 Greenville Ave., Dallas, Tex. 75231; tel. 214-373-6300

American Society on Aging, 833 Market St., Suite 512, San Francisco, Calif. 94103; tel. 415-543-2617. Publishes the journal *Generations*.

Familial Alzheimer's Disease Research Foundation, 8177 S. Harvard, Suite 114, Tulsa, Okla. 74137; tel. 918-493-8476

Family Service America, 11700 W. Lake Park Dr., Milwaukee, Wis. 53224; tel. 414-359-2111

Family Survival Project, 425 Bush St., Suite 500, San Francisco, Calif. 94108; tel. 415-434-3388, in California 800-445-8106. A resource center serving the San Francisco Bay area, for families of brain-damaged adults, including people with dementia. Their publications are available to caregivers and professionals.

Foundation for Hospice and Homecare, 519 C St. N.E., Stanton Park, Washington, D.C. 20002; tel. 202-547-6586

Gerontological Society of America, 1275 K St. N.W., Suite 350, Washington, D.C. 20005; tel. 202-842-1275. A professional organization; publishes *The Gerontologist* and *Journal of Gerontology*.

Gray Panthers, 311 S. Juniper St., Suite 601, Philadelphia, Pa. 19107; tel. 215-545-6555. An advocacy organization for older people.

Help for Incontinent People, P.O. Box 544, Union, S.C. 29379; tel. 803-585-8789. Publishes a resource guide.

Huntington's Disease Society of America, 140 W. 22nd St., 6th Floor, New York, N.Y. 10011; tel. 800-345-4372

National Association for Home Care, 519 C St. N.E., Stanton Park, Washington, D.C. 20002; tel. 202-547-7424

National Association of Private Geriatric Care Managers, P.O. Box 6920, Yorkville Station, New York, N.Y. 10128. For a fee, the agency will coordinate care for an elderly person.

National Association of Social Workers, 7981 Eastern Ave., Silver Spring, Md. 20910; tel. 301-565-0333

National Citizens Coalition for Nursing Home Reform, 1424 16th St. N.W., Suite L2, Washington, D.C. 20036; tel. 202-797-0657. A coalition of organizations concerned with nursing homes; has been an effective advocate for improved nursing home quality.

National Council on the Aging, 600 Maryland Ave. S.W., West Wing, Suite 100, Washington, D.C. 20024; tel. 202-479-1200. Publishes an annotated bibliography; has information about adult day care, in-home care, and other forms of respite.

National Hospice Organization, 1901 N. Moore Dr., Suite 901, Arlington, Va. 22209; tel. 703-243-5900

National Mental Health Association, 1021 Prince St., Alexandria, Va. 22314; tel. 703-684-7722

National Stroke Association, 300 E. Hampden Ave., Suite 240, Englewood, Colo. 80110-2622; tel. 303-762-9922

Older Women's League, 730 11th St. N.W., Suite 300, Washington, D.C. 20001;

tel. 202-783-6686. An advocacy organization addressing many issues of concern to caregiving families.

Veterans Administration (VA), 810 Vermont Ave. N.W., Washington, D.C. 20005; tel. 202-628-3030

FEDERAL INSTITUTES

National Institute on Aging, National Institutes of Health, 7550 Wisconsin Ave., Room 618, Bethesda, Md. 20892; tel. 301-496-5345. Brochures and information about the federally funded dementia centers and other federal initiatives; publishes a free directory of organizations that serve elderly people.

National Institute on Mental Health, Mental Disorders of Aging Branch, Room 11C-03, 5600 Fishers Lane, Rockville, Md. 20857; tel. 301-443-1185.

National Institute of Neurological Disorders and Stroke, Office of Scientific and Health Reports, National Institutes of Health, Building 31, Room 8A-06, Bethesda, Md. 20892; tel. 301-496-5751.

Appendix 3. Where to Buy or Rent Supplies

Incontinence supplies, eating aids, bathroom aids, wheelchairs, geriatric chairs, etc.

Sears, Roebuck and Co.: Ask for their home health care resources catalog; call 800-323-3274.

AARP has a home care catalog. Write them at 3557 Lafayette Rd., Indianapolis, Ind. 46272.

Medical supply houses: Listed in the yellow pages of the telephone directory, these sell and rent a wide selection of equipment, including beds, chairs, egg crate foam, and adaptive devices.

Medicare publishes a list of the supplies and rentals it covers. Medical supply stores can also tell you what will be covered by Medicare.

Adult incontinence wear (diapers)

Adult briefs are sold in most drug stores and grocery stores. If they are not out on the shelves, ask for them. There are many kinds, in different sizes and for different purposes. Discuss with the pharmacist which will be best for your needs.

There are adult diaper services in some areas. Look in the yellow pages of your telephone directory.

The organization Help for Incontinent People (see Appendix 2) publishes useful information and a resource guide.

Bracelets

Information about identification bracelets may be obtained through local pharmacies or by writing to: Medic Alert, Turlock, Calif. 95380; or Health Enterprises, 15 Spruce St., North Attleboro, Mass. 02760.

Miscellaneous health aids

Several catalogs advertise special clothing and home care, safety, security, and activity products for people with dementia and their caregivers. The Alzheimer's

Association (see Appendix 2) maintains a list of those that have come to their attention; write to them for this information.

Neither the Alzheimer's Association nor the authors of this book support or endorse individual products. While some may be useful, others are not. Avoid products that are juvenile. No safety product can substitute for supervision and awareness, and no activity product can replace time lovingly spent in a shared pleasure.

Appendix 4. Locating Your State Office on Aging and State Nursing Home Ombudsman

THE STATE office on aging may have referral information, information about respite resources, and useful pamphlets. In some states the office will have extensive information and can be helpful.

The ombudsman is an advocate for nursing home residents. This person will have information about whether a home is meeting licensure standards and what complaints, if any, have been made against it. The ombudsman may also have literature on how to select a facility. If you have a complaint about a nursing home, start with the ombudsman. In some states the ombudsman's office is located in the state office on aging. The state office on aging is required by law to provide the address and telephone number of the nearest ombudsman.

Below is a list of state offices on aging, their locations, and their telephone numbers. This list is current as of January 5, 1990. If you find that an address or telephone number has been changed, check with the reference department of your public library for the current address and telephone number.

Alabama
Commission on Aging, 136 Catoma St., Second Floor, Montgomery 36130; tel. 205-242-5743

Alaska
Older Alaskans Commission, Department of Administration, Pouch C, Mail Station 0209, Juneau 99811-0209; tel. 907-465-3250

Arizona
Aging and Adult Administration, Department of Economic Security, 1400 W. Washington St., Phoenix 85007; tel. 602-542-4446

Arkansas
Division of Aging and Adult Services, Arkansas Department of Human Services, P.O. Box 1417, Slot 1412, 7th and Main Sts., Little Rock 72201; tel. 501-682-2441

California
Department of Aging, 1600 K St., Sacramento 95814; tel. 916-322-5290

Colorado
Aging and Adult Service, Department of Social Services, 1575 Sherman St., 10th Floor, Denver 80203-1714; tel. 303-866-3851

Connecticut
Department on Aging, 175 Main St., Hartford 06106; tel. 203-566-3238

Delaware
Division on Aging, Department of Health and Social Services, 1901 N. DuPont Highway, New Castle 19720; tel. 302-421-6791

District of Columbia
Office on Aging, 1424 K St. N.W., 2nd Floor, Washington, D.C. 20005; tel. 202-724-5626

Florida
Program Office of Aging and Adult Services, Department of Health and Rehabilitative Services, 1317 Winewood Blvd., Tallahassee 32301; tel. 904-488-8922

Georgia
Office of Aging, 878 Peachtree St. N.E., Room 632, Atlanta 30309; tel. 404-894-5333

Guam
Division of Senior Citizens, Department of Public Health and Social Services, Government of Guam, P.O. Box 2816, Agana 96910

Hawaii
Executive Office on Aging, Office of the Governor, 335 Merchant St., Room 241, Honolulu 96813; tel. 808-548-2593

Idaho
Office on Aging, Statehouse, Room 114, Boise 83720; tel. 208-334-3833

Illinois
Department on Aging, 421 E. Capitol Ave., Springfield 62701; tel. 217-785-2870

Indiana
Division of Aging Services, Department of Human Services, 251 N. Illinois St., P.O. Box 7083, Indianapolis 46207-7083; tel. 317-232-7020

Iowa
Department of Elder Affairs, Jewett Building, Suite 236, 914 Grand Ave., Des Moines 50319; tel. 515-281-5187

Kansas
Department on Aging, Docking State Office Building, 122-S, 915 S.W. Harrison, Topeka 66612-1500; tel. 913-296-4986

Kentucky
Division of Aging Services, Cabinet for Human Resources, CHR Building–6th West, 275 E. Main St., Frankfort 40621; tel. 502-564-6930

Louisiana
Office of Elderly Affairs, 4550 North Blvd., P.O. Box 80374, Baton Rouge 70806; tel. 504-925-1700

Maine
Bureau of Elder and Adult Services, Department of Human Services, State House, Station 11, Augusta 04333; tel. 207-289-2561

Maryland
Office on Aging, State Office Building, 301 W. Preston St., Room 1004, Baltimore 21201; tel. 410-225-1100

Massachusetts
Executive Office of Elder Affairs, 38 Chauncey St., Boston 02111; tel. 617-727-7750

Michigan
Office of Services to the Aging, P.O. Box 30026, Lansing 48909; tel. 517-373-8230

Federated States of Micronesia
Department of Human Resources, Kolonia, Pohnpei FM 96941; tel. 691-320-2733

Minnesota
Board on Aging, Human Services Building, 4th Floor, 444 Lafayette Rd., St. Paul 55155-3843; tel. 612-296-2770

Mississippi
Council on Aging, Division of Aging and Adult Services, 421 W. Pascagoula St., Jackson 39203; tel. 601-949-2070

Missouri
Division on Aging, Department of Social Services, P.O. Box 1337, 2701 W. Main St., Jefferson City 65102; tel. 314-751-3082

Montana
Governor's Office on Aging, State Capitol Building, Capitol Station, Helena 59620; tel. 406-444-3111

Nebraska
Department on Aging, P.O. Box 95044, 301 Centennial Mall South, Lincoln 68509; tel. 402-471-2306

Nevada
Division for Aging Services, Department of Human Resources, 340 N. 11th St., Las Vegas 89101; tel. 702-486-3545

New Hampshire
Division of Elderly and Adult Services, 6 Hazen Dr., Concord 03301-6501; tel. 603-271-4680

New Jersey
Division on Aging, Department of Community Affairs CN807, S. Broad and Front Sts., Trenton 08625-0807; tel. 609-292-4833

New Mexico
State Agency on Aging, 224 E. Palace Ave., 4th Floor, La Villa Rivera Building, Santa Fe 87501; tel. 505-827-7640

New York
Office for the Aging, New York State Plaza, Agency Building 2, Albany 12223; tel. 518-474-4425

North Carolina
Division of Aging, 693 Palmer Dr., Raleigh 27603; tel. 919-733-3983

North Dakota
Aging Services, Department of Human Services, State Capitol Building, Bismarck 58505; tel. 701-224-2577

Northern Mariana Islands
Office of Aging, Department of Community and Cultural Affairs, Civic Center–Susupe, Saipan 96950

Ohio
Department of Aging, 50 W. Broad St., 9th Floor, Columbus 43266-0501; tel. 614-466-5500

Oklahoma
Aging Services Division, Department of Human Services, P.O. Box 25352, Oklahoma City 73125; tel. 405-521-2281

Oregon
Senior Services Division, 313 Public Service Building, Salem 97310; tel. 503-378-4728

Pennsylvania
Department of Aging, 231 State St., Harrisburg 17101-1195; tel. 717-783-1550

Puerto Rico
Gericulture Commission, Department of Social Services, Apartado 11398, Santurce 00910; tel. 809-721-4010

Rhode Island
Department of Elderly Affairs, 160 Pine St., Providence 02903-3708; tel. 401-277-2858

American Samoa
Territorial Administration on Aging, Office of the Governor, Pago Pago 96799; tel. 684-633-1252

South Carolina
Commission on Aging, 400 Arbor Lake Dr., Suite B-500, Columbia 29223; tel. 803-735-0210

South Dakota
Office of Adult Services and Aging, Kneip Building, 700 N. Illinois St., Pierre 57501; tel. 605-773-3656

Tennessee
Commission on Aging, 706 Church St., Suite 201, Nashville 37219-5573; tel. 615-741-2056

Texas
Department on Aging, P.O. Box 12786, Capitol Station, 1949 IH 35, South, Austin 78741-3702; tel. 512-444-2727

Utah
Division of Aging and Adult Services, Department of Social Services, 120 North–200 West, Box 45500, Salt Lake City 84145-0500; tel. 801-538-3910

Vermont
Department of Rehabilitation and Aging, 103 S. Main St., Waterbury 05676; tel. 802-241-2400

Virginia
Department for the Aging, 700 Centre, 10th Floor, 700 E. Franklin St., Richmond 23219-2327; tel. 804-225-2271

Virgin Islands
Senior Citizen Affairs, Department of Human Services, 19 Estate Diamond, Fredericksted, St. Croix 00840; tel. 809-772-4950

Washington
Aging and Adult Services Administration, Department of Social and Health Services, OB-44A, Olympia 98504; tel. 206-586-3768

West Virginia
Commission on Aging, Holly Grove, State Capitol, Charleston 25305; tel. 304-348-3317

Wisconsin
Bureau of Aging, Division of Community Services, 217 S. Hamilton St., Suite 300, Madison 53707; tel. 608-266-2536

Wyoming
Commission on Aging, Hathaway Building, Room 139, Cheyenne 82002-0710; tel. 307-777-7986

Appendix 5. Nursing Home Residents' Rights

IN 1987 a federal law mandated that certain rights be provided to all nursing home residents. If a resident is disabled by dementia, the family can exercise these rights in his behalf.

Several important provisions of the law are outlined below, reprinted, with permission, from *Establishing a Nursing Home Community Council* (Washington, D.C.: American Association of Retired Persons, 1988), pp. 20–23.

Quality of Life

The new law requires each nursing facility to "care for its residents in such a manner and in such an environment as will promote maintenance or enhancement of the quality of life of each resident." This principle places a new emphasis on dignity, choice, and self-determination for nursing home residents.

Providing Services and Activities

The new law requires each nursing facility to "provide services and activities to attain or maintain the highest practicable physical, mental, and psychosocial well-being of each resident in accordance with a written plan of care which . . . is initially prepared, with participation to the extent practicable of the resident or the resident's family or legal representative."

Participation in Facility Administration

The new law emphasizes the importance of "resident and advocate participation" as criteria for good facility administration.

Specific Rights

Under the new law, each nursing facility must "protect and promote the rights of each resident," including:

A.   Rights to Self-determination

Nursing home residents have the right

318

- to choose their personal physician;
- to full information, in advance, and participation in planning and making any changes in their care and treatment;
- to reside and receive services with reasonable accommodation by the facility for individual needs and preferences;
- to voice grievances about care or treatment they do or do not receive without discrimination or reprisal, and to receive a prompt response from the facility;
- to organize and participate in resident groups (and their families have the right to organize family groups) in the facility.

B. Personal and Privacy Rights

Nursing home residents have the right

- to participate in social, religious, and community activities as they choose;
- to privacy in medical treatment, accommodations, personal visits, written and telephone communications, and meetings of resident and family groups; and
- to confidentiality of personal and clinical records.

C. Rights regarding Abuse and Restraints

Nursing home residents have the right

- to be free from physical or mental abuse, corporal punishment, involuntary seclusion, or disciplinary use of restraints;
- to be free of restraints used for the convenience of staff other than the well-being of residents;
- to have restraints used only under a physician's written orders to treat a resident's medical symptoms and ensure his safety and the safety of others;
- to be given psychopharmacologic medication only as ordered by a physician as part of a written plan of care for a specific medical symptom, with annual review for appropriateness by an independent, external expert.

D. Rights to Information

Nursing homes must

- provide residents with the latest inspection results and any plan of correction submitted by the facility;
- notify residents 30 days in advance of any plans to change their room or roommate;
- inform residents of their rights to admission and, upon request, provide a written copy of the rights, including their rights regarding personal funds and their right to file a complaint with the state survey agency;
- inform residents in writing, at admission and throughout their stay, of the services available under the basic rate and of any extra charges for extra services (including, for Medicaid residents, a list of services covered by Medicaid and those for which there is an extra charge); and
- prominently display and provide written and oral information for residents

about how to apply for and use Medicaid benefits and how to receive a refund
for previous private payments that Medicaid will pay for retroactively.

E.   Rights to Visits

The nursing home must

- permit immediate visits by a resident's personal physician and by representatives from the health department and the ombudsman program;
- permit immediate visits by a resident's relatives, with the resident's consent;
- permit visits "subject to reasonable restriction" for others who visit with the
  resident's consent;
- permit reasonable visits by organizations or individuals providing health,
  social, legal, or other services, subject to the resident's consent; and
- permit ombudsmen to review the resident's clinical records if the resident
  grants permission.

F.   Transfer and Discharge Rights

Reasons for transfer: Nursing homes "must permit each resident to remain in the
facility and must not transfer or discharge the resident unless"

- the facility is unable to meet the resident's medical needs;
- the resident's health has improved to such a degree that he no longer needs
  nursing home care;
- the health or safety of other residents is endangered;
- the resident has failed, after reasonable notice, to pay an allowable facility
  charge for an item or service provided upon the resident's request.

Notice to residents and their representatives before transfer:

- Timing—at least 30 days in advance, or as soon as possible if more immediate
  changes in health require more immediate transfer
- Content—reasons for transfer; the resident's right to appeal the transfer; and
  the name, address, and phone number of the ombudsman program and
  protection and advocacy programs for the mentally ill and developmentally
  disabled
- Returning to the facility—the right to request that a resident's bed be held,
  including information about how many days Medicaid will pay for the bed
  to be held and the facility's bed-hold policies, and the right to return to the
  next available bed if Medicaid bed-holding coverage lapses
- Orientation—A facility must prepare and orient residents to ensure safe and
  orderly transfer from the facility.

G.   Protection of Personal Funds

A nursing facility must

- not require residents to deposit their personal funds with the facility;
- if it accepts written responsibility for residents' funds

—keep funds over $50 in an interest-bearing account, separate from the facility account;

—keep other funds available in a separate account or petty cash fund;

—keep a complete and separate accounting of each resident's funds, with a written record of all transactions, available for review by residents and their representatives;

—notify Medicaid residents when their balance comes within $200 of the Medicaid limit and the effect of this on their eligibility;

—upon a resident's death, turn funds over to the resident's trustee;

—purchase a surety bond to secure residents' funds in its keeping; and

—not charge a resident for any item or service covered by Medicaid, specifically including routine personal hygiene items and services.

H.   Protection against Medicaid Discrimination

Nursing homes must

- establish and maintain identical policies and practices regarding transfer, discharge, and the provision of services for all individuals, regardless of source of payment;
- not require residents to waive their rights to Medicaid, and must provide information about how to apply for Medicaid;
- not require a third party to guarantee payment as a condition of admission or continued stay; and
- not "charge, solicit, accept or receive" gifts, money, donations, or "other consideration" as a precondition for continued stay for persons eligible for Medicaid.

Index